# God's Voice *from the* Void

SUNY Series in Judaica:
Hermeneutics, Mysticism, and Religion

Michael Fishbane, Robert Goldenberg,
and Elliot Wolfson, editors

# God's Voice *from the* Void

OLD AND NEW STUDIES IN

BRATSLAV HASIDISM

*Edited by*

## Shaul Magid

State University of New York Press

Published by
State University of New York Press, Albany

For information, address State University of New York Press,
90 State Street, Suite 700, Albany, NY 12207

Production by Dana Foote
Marketing by Michael Campochiaro

**Library of Congress Cataloging-in-Publication Data**

God's voice from the void : old and new studies in Bratslav Hasidism /
edited by Shaul Magid.
p. cm. — (SUNY series in Judaica)
Includes bibliographical references and index.
ISBN 0–7914–5175–5 (alk. paper) — ISBN 0–7914–5176–3 (pbk. : alk.
paper)
1. Bratslav Hasidism. 2. Nahman, of Bratslav, 1772–1811—Teachings.
3. Hasidism. I. Magid, Shaul, 1958–    II. Series.
BM198.52 .G63 2001
296.8'332—dc21
2001054173

10 9 8 7 6 5 4 3 2 1

For Yehuda
(who has made it to the other side)

# CONTENTS

# INTRODUCTION AND ACKNOWLEDGMENTS

Scholarly inquiry on the Hasidic ideology and personal religiosity of Rabbi Nahman ben Simhah of Bratslav (1771–1810) remains essential for understanding the nature of Jewish mysticism as it developed in the late eighteenth and early nineteenth centuries in Eastern Europe. Although Martin Buber's studies in the first part of the twentieth century and Arthur Green's intellectual biography of R. Nahman, *Tormented Master,* introduced this unique religious personality to the English-speaking scholarly world, little else has appeared since and many of the older German and Hebrew studies remain untranslated and, in some cases, unavailable. Although other scholarly articles have appeared in various journals throughout the years, both in Hebrew and in English, I felt it would be of use to the larger academic community to produce a volume dedicated to some interesting new approaches to the study of Bratslav Hasidism and to include translations of some of the classic literature into English, enabling the academic and religious communities to more fully comprehend this seminal figure's contribution to Hasidic thought.

This volume is divided into two parts. Part 1 includes new studies either on the Bratslav tradition or on Rabbi Nahman. Part 2 includes translations of three classic studies on Bratslav Hasidism, published in German, Yiddish, and Hebrew.

Most of the new studies in part 1 take a fresh approach to the study of Hasidism in general and Bratslav Hasidism in particular. Aubrey Glazer's translation and annotation of *Shiur Yedidut,* a poem written by an anonymous Bratslav Hasid and printed at the beginning of many editions of Bratslav literature, serves as the antechamber to this collection. The poem resonates with many of the themes dealt with in the writings of R. Nahman and his disciples. The first chapter maps out *Likkutei MoHaRan*'s diverse and complex hermeneutical theory by suggesting various ways in which the ambiguous term *behinot* is used by R. Nahman to create a "frame of meaning" into which his ideas are developed. Utilizing theories from the general area of hermeneutical theory, this chapter serves as an introduction to the creative and complex world of R. Nahman's discourse. David Roskies presents a provocative thesis that the modern Yiddish story as it developed in Jewish Enlightenment literature draws heavily from R. Nahman's "Tales" *(Sippurei Ma'asiot)*. Roskies argues that the Yiddish writers of the nineteenth century used the "Tales" as a model for their own creative contribution to Jewish literature. Elliot Wolfson, developing his many earlier studies on gender in medieval Kabbala, takes a new look at the issue of gender as it unfolds in R. Nahman's understanding of circumcision. Nathaniel Deutsch offers a new approach to the Hasidic doctrine of the zaddik as androgyny as developed in *Likkutei MoHaRan,* viewing it from the context of contemporary gender theory and literary criticism. Yakov Travis revisits R. Nahman's move from Bratslav to Uman, a central theme in Bratslav Hasidism. Taking issue with Mendel Piekarz's earlier study on this topic, arguing that R. Nahman's move largely had to do with his infatuation with the *Maskilim* and their heretical ideas, Travis rereads some of the Bratslav sources on this issue, without necessarily adopting their conclusions. Martin Kavka offers a critical appraisal of Marc-Alain Ouaknin's recent book entitled *The Burnt Book* that discusses literary theory and Talmud based on his interpretation of the legend of R. Nahman's "Burnt Book" *(Sefer Ha-Nisraf),* a treatise that R. Nahman commanded his disciples to destroy before it could be made public. Kavka analyzes the final chapter of Ouaknin's book that deals specifically with this legend and its implications. Ouaknin then offers a response to Kavka's criticism.

Part 2 is a collection of three seminal articles on Bratslav written in German, Hebrew, and Yiddish. One of these older studies deals with issues that are revisited in part 1. Zeitlin's chapter on R. Nahman as Messiah deals with some of the same material Wolfson and Deutsch analyze in their chapters. Samuel Abba Horodetzky's comparative analysis of Schleiermacher and R. Nahman is important, albeit somewhat dated, in that it attempts to see common threads in the spiritual lives of two important thinkers in Christianity and Judaism in the nineteenth century. Finally, Joesph Weiss's chapter constructs a typology of Hasidism, placing Bratslav on the side of "faith," as opposed to the more intellectual trends of Hasidism, such as Habad.

The preparation of this volume was a long time coming. In some sense it began the instant I left the Bratslav community in Jerusalem many years ago, although many more years passed before the idea began to take form in words. Scholarship is usually about criticism—criticism for the sake of clarity—and in that sense this volume is no different. However, for those of us who have lived with R. Nahman's words for some time, criticism does not adequately express what appears on these pages. It is also a testament to his creativity, some say his genius, while acknowledging the dangerous edge, the narrow bridge one must walk in order to remain on the margins of his larger circle of admirers. Many voices hover over these words, many of whom I'd like to thank, some of whom may feel uncomfortable being mentioned. Thanks to Franci Levine-Grater for her editing and for providing helpful comments to many of the chapters included in this volume. Rabbi Chaim Brovender, whose Friday morning classes in *Likkutei MoHaRan* in the early 1980s will forever be appreciated as will Dovid Din z"l, my teacher in the deepest sense, one who knew R. Nahman like few others. I'm grateful to my old friend, roommate, and study partner *(havruta)*, Baruch Gartner, although we took different exits on the path of Judaism, memories, especially good ones, remain. Thanks to Ben Zion Solomon and his family for bringing R. Nahman to life in their music. You have been a constant source of inspiration. To friends who have been supportive throughout: Aryeh Cohen, Talya Fishman, Pinhas Giller, Gloria Greenfield, Shai Held, Ely Stillman, and Elliot Wolfson. Thanks to Ryan Dulkin for making the index and Hila Ratzabi for her proofreading. Thanks to all my students, (who were also often my teachers) in my Bratslav seminars at Harvard Hillel in 1994, at Rice University in 1996, and at the Jewish Theological Seminary in 1998. Moshe Mykoff, whose friendship transcends all boundaries—spiritual, ideological, and geographic, has been a constant support, critical, loving, and above all, understanding. To Nancy, my life-partner and life-giver, who tolerates my love of R. Nahman even as she lives in a very different intellectual universe. To Chisda and Miriam, for whom R. Nahman's voice is still foreign, may you someday hear it in your own way. Finally, this is for you, Yehuda, a gift of what matters to me—to you, who matters above all.

# PART I
# NEW STUDIES

# Shir Yedidut:
# A Pleasant Song of Companionship

*From our Master, our Teacher and Rabbi as a blessing,*
*in memory of a Righteous and Holy One.*

### Anonymous

*These are the words of our Rabbi, his memory as a blessing, the Pleasant Song that includes many matters in great brevity, for the brevity houses its immensity. A song that speaks wonders about the glory of our Holy Teachings and about the glory of our Rabbi Moses, peace be upon him. Wondrous Teachings of edification and deep arousal to awaken the soul in every one. It speaks of the majesty of the blessed Creator and the wonders of his creatures. It leads in chorus in [our Teacher's] poem to recount the sweet wonders and delights of the time-that-is-coming and his pleasures to all so meritorious. The poem will be aroused in the time-that-is-coming, in opposition to the bitterness of pain and the bluntness of teeth[2] for those displaced and those in a pit of abandonment. It will awaken the sleepers, rustle the slumbrous, fortify the fatigued, as it proclaims a portion of the potential of each being to be worthy of these pleasures [of recitation].[3] Like a ram's horn, it lifts its cry to incline our hearts towards the blessed Creator in unified worship. This then is a taste of the poem's ways. And the Holy Name along with that of his father [Simcha] are inscribed in the beginning of each stanza, in doublets, triplets, and quadruplets.*

(i).
N-Norms[4] of humanity's laws cannot equal our Law
H-Their sages fabricated from their hearts' laws and through human intellect
M-Moses ascended the mount enshrouded in a cloud[5]
N-The Necessary One[6] spoke each time[7] to Moses, so his separation from his wife.[8]

(ii).
N-Contemptible, down-trodden, & swept away[9] are we.
H-From No-thing is His Wisdom found,[10] yet a good portion have we taken from him.[11]
M-A King in Jeshurun and our Law,[12] like two brothers[13] never to be ensnarled.
N-Neither his pristine[14] life-breath *[neshamah]* nor body ever straying one from the other.[15]

(iii).
N-Numerous are their desires *[nafshotam]*, opinions and divergent suppositions.

*3*

**H**-Recently emergent,[16] their works have come forth.
**M**-Their thoughts are not ours, nor are our ways theirs.[17]
**N**-Our desires are one and do not incline to their expansive icons.

(iv).

**N**-O my desire, proud and shrewd,[18] why have you neglected yourself and forgotten the one who nurtured and gave you sweets, clothed you in crimson. And now, O my desire, are you trampled beneath the heels of the flock[19] and its feet of lust, which are thick and corporeal. While you are naked and disclosed,[20] the wine of your meal is now a banquet of tears, becoming.

**H**-Have courage.[21] Be not as the giant elephant, nor as the wandering camel, even with a mouse luring through its trunk, the elephant does nothing to oppose it.[22]
For that mouse is unrelenting[23]—all this is [the elephant's] folly, when unaware of one's strength—not for my desire, so clever and so strong.
**W**-What will you do upon the Day of Reckoning,[24] and what reply would you give your sender awakening you. Disregard time's braying. For your body is weak and emaciated. Time endlessly surges on. Already it may have arrived— the body's day for reckoning.
**N**-Now pierce the heart of stone and shine a sliver of your countenance upon me from above. Bright as sun, magnificent as moon. Do not be muted and silent. Rustle your mellifluous voice in song and praise, opening your mouth to utter your exquisite words before the Holy One, Blessed be He. Your eyes lifted skyward, recalling your primordial love.

(v).

**N**- Rivers, streams, fountains, majestic and tiny seas.
**N**-Wondrous and varied in their colours, tastes, and natures.
**H**-Small and great celestial beasts amidst each one, without number to their kinds.
**M**-In all their limbs, they praise and glorify the Name, Blessed be He.
**M**-Constantly speaking words, their leaders will not deny them.
**N**-Sparkling from their depths, jewels and pearls.
**N**-Hidden lights within their vessels.

(vi).

**N**-Life-breaths hewn from beneath the Glorious Throne
**N**-Forever longing to be joined back to its sources.[25]
**H**-It draws forth anointed high life and compassion from Davidic grace
**H**-Charismatic spirited wind of Edenic drippings are never lost from Her.
**M**-A palatial dwelling and tent of peace for each one marked with a glorious marking.

**M**-Messengers ponder: *What has this deity wrought?*—scurrying,[26] comet-like,[27] with message in hand.

**M**-One whose paths are aberrant[28] is distant and removed from pleasures.[29]

**N**-In famine and disgrace do they remain, as they are flung to and fro in the sling's hollow.[30]

**N**-Return unto the Name and be lost not.

**N**-Enshrouding the Father in eternity, in love we shall receive evil and good.

(vii).

**B**-Birthing the earth and its planets, the lands encircling Her[31]

**B**-Beings, earthen, each one its *langue*,[32] each one its faith.[33]

**N**-New flowers, buds, and to each its fruit.

**N**-Kingdoms falling from all sides.

**N**-Nevertheless, She remains with the constellations encircling Her.

(viii).

**S**-Spirits and demons fluttering to and fro through the air[34]

**S**-Sounds of the heavenly decree now being heard, reigning over the four types of primordial mayhem:[35] the ox, the pit, the field-waster, and the field-burner.

**M**-Each doled their just desserts,[36] messengers as above so below.

**M**-From the holy covenant do they retreat,[37] when Abraham is ordered: *Be circumcised!*

**H**-Striking, as with rods in different forms.

**H**-Sorcerers the magical fellowships subdue them through their conjurations of intended names.

**A**-Holy Law protects us from all impurity.

**A**-Righteous ways spare us from sordid deaths.[38]

(ix).

**N**-We no longer have prophecy.[39]

**H**-We no longer have understanding, the nations' teeth gnashing upon the unique nation.

**M**- They negotiate how to make us lap up acrid anguish

**N**-Until the coming of the Subdued One, shall we suffer.[40]

(x).

**B**-Beloved Son searching impassioned amidst the Father's storehouse.[41]

**N**-With a diadem shall we crown[42] the Beloved One.

(xi).

**S**-Song of messianic times will we sing[43]
**M**-So by index finger[44] shall every devout one point, Monarch, our King!
**H**-Teaching, inscribe it upon the heart of all, lest it be effaced[45]
**A**-Death shall be forever swallowed up,[46] as the incense offering's scent.

(xii).
**N**-Let us bring a wise heart to understand the body's properties, the distances of its joints, and the combination of its limbs.
**H**-The necessity of understanding these features helps us to know the Former of all forms[47]
**M**-He heals tormented masters, the blind, the lame, the leprous, the smitten, the anxious and the pained.
**N**-Let us eat only enough to sustain our appetites, and to diminish our natural desires.[48]

—Translated and annotated by Aubrey L. Glazer


## Notes


*Acknowledgments:* Gratitude to my teachers: Elliot R. Wolfson, for correlating Nahman's theosophy to its lurianic and zoharic kabbalah; Raymond P. Scheindlin, for listening to the poetics within; Shaul Magid, for opening the world of bratzlav hasidism in his seminar.

1. Cf. M. Pierkarz, *Studies in Bratslav Hasidism.* (Jerusalem, 1972), pp. 146–147, 208. Pierkarz ascribes redaction of the *quntros* (notebook) *Shir Yediduth* to R. Yehiel Menachem Mendel of Medvokevka. However, there are at least three other poems of the same title (including the conflation, *SHIR Yediduth* with *SHIR Naim,* thus our rendering, *A Pleasant Song of Companionship*). It is unclear whether the notebook identified by Pierkarz is this poem before us, a collection of poems, or an extended annotation of these poems as printed in contemporary editions. However, regarding the extant poems, one is attributed to R. Nathan, the scribe of Nahman. The role of this poem relative to the text it generally precedes remains unarticulated. I speculate elsewhere (my forthcoming article) that its role is part of a palimpsestic and highly choreographed ritual including the poem's recitation for intentionality *(kavvanah)* before engaging in study and the transmission of *gnosis.* Furthermore, our translation of *SHIR Yediduth* limits the dual denotation of *Shir* (either as a song or poem) as a song implying its ritual performance.

So much of the word play cannot be translated into English, yet this is the task at hand. Further limitations occur with words like *nefesh, ruach,* and *neshama* that have lost their pristine power in English when rendered so often as variations of Soul and Spirit. Thus my decision to recover some of this pristine power in each term: (a) *Nefesh,* biblically understood as the primal appetite, comes to be the resting soul in the World of Completion, which shall be referred to as the "desire" (b) *Ruach* is the spiritual wind in the World of Formation, which shall be referred to as the "Wind of Spirit," and (c) *Neshama* is the pneuma in the World of Creation, which shall be referred to as the "Life-Breath."

2. *Keheyuth shinayim* denotes a "blunting or dulling of the teeth"; its connotation, however, is more often associated with old age and its concomitant frailty. See *Yalkut Lamentations* #996.

3. The exact nature of the ritual taking place is uncertain in all extant sources, both oral and written to date. However, I speculate that the recitation is one component of a more complex ritual, interweaving a theophany of dance (akin to the *Mevlevi Dervishes* whirling round a pole to invoke the presence of their absent master, *Jelaludin Rumi,* or Luria's confraternity encircling the Sabbath table in the ha'qafat of ha'shulkhan). It is a series of choreographed encirclements *(ha'qafot)* to catalyze the self-inscription of every reader into this text. See my forthcoming article in this regard.

4. *Nimus* denotes a *nomos,* i.e. norms of human behavior. These are societal mores based upon experience and enlightenment (as opposed to a divine *nomos).* The poem follows a series of recurrent dichotomies that should be noted at the outset: Human/Divine *nomos,* body/soul, demons/angels, exile/redemption, and so forth.

5. *B. Tal. Sukkah* 5a, wherein Moses' ascent (as is the case with Elijah's) is recounted as not having exceeded a buffer zone of 20 cubits, after which the threshold is crossed into the celestial realm. Moses ascended (Exod. 19:3) to encounter God on the precipice (namely, at the twentieth cubit) of Mount Sinai, since God descends embodied upon the mountain (Exod. 19:20). According to the Haggadah, if ShaDaI envelops Moses in the Cloud of Glory below the tenth handbreadth, then Moses must be stretching to grasp onto the foot of the celestial throne. Compare with Nahmanides' commentary on Exod. 19.

6. In opposition to the Philosophers (Epicureans) who claim that material reality is necessary and not contingent, R. Nahman juxtaposes this philosophical way with the Mosaic prophetic way. In his ascent to the precipice of Being, Moses discovers God, *qua* Ultimate Necessity, which justifies all material existence. Thus, *creatio ex nihilo* demonstrates Divine Omnipotence over all worlds (both created and destroyed), as iterated in *Liqqutei MoHaRaN* 52:1.

7. Compare with the theophany of Exod. 33:11.

8. Regarding Moses' separation from Zippora, his wife, as a Foucaultian technology of self within asceticism as a preparation for prophecy, see Exod. 19:15. See also, *B. Tal. Shabbat* 87a.

9. See *B. Tal. Yebamot* 47a. This *baraita* records the formulaic exhortation

of the court *(beit din)* to Gentiles seeking to convert to Judaism. *"What could you possibly have seen that prompted you to convert? If only you knew that in our time Israel is contemptible, impelled, swept away, preyed upon, with many hardships befalling them."* Compare with the vision of R. Nahman's self-identification as Messiah son of Joseph, who leads the Gentiles to crowding his table, finally breaking it. "Are these messianic times, that gentiles should approach the zaddiqim as in *All the nations shall flow unto him?*" (Isa. 2:2). Cf. *Hayyey MoHaRaN* 1: 6; A. Green, "Messianic Strivings" In *Tormented Master: The Life and Spiritual Quest of Rabbi Nahman of Bratslav* (Vermont, 1992), pp. 190 n. 20. [Henceforth, *Green TM.*]

10. Compare with Job 28:12, as quoted in *B. Tal. Sotah* 21b (wherein the words of the Law are actualized only by the one who abides by this scriptural passage, requiring humility and naïveté). See also, *Liqqutei MoHaRaN* 4:7 that attributes such a realization to Moses. However, it is Job 28:12 that evokes the near impossibility of mere humans, despite themselves, actually recovering divine wisdom. Where can this place be found? This passage allows for a further wordplay, as is prevalent in *Sefer ha-Bahir,* for example, in evoking this nonplace as *Ayin* (*Nothingness* or *Boundlessness*) from which *Hochmah (Wisdom)* is drawn, in accord with its Kabbalistic mapping. However, the present state of loss centers around the presence of the absent teacher. The question whether this teacher is Moses or Nahman recurs enough to be unambiguous, a concealing while revealing. Ultimately, every seeker must see the face of the one who possesses the desired teaching for transmission. Along the path to the Boundless is the face of the *Tzaddik*. See also, *Liqqutei MoHaRaN* 19:2 (s.v. *Aki tzarikh l'zakekh et ha-panim*).

11. Namely, from Moses and his prophecy. The ambivalence between the prophecy of Moses and that of Nahman is part of the poetics at play.

12. Compare with Deut. 33:5.

13. This is the inextricable interrelation of the Prophet Moses (exemplifying the king of Jeshurun) and the spiritual superiority of the Divine Laws. Each one relies on the other and is not to be unraveled.

14. The purity being glorified is corporeal, thus necessarily erotic. This reiterates the ascetic preparations that Moses made in order to engage in continual prophetic revelation. See also n. 8.

15. See *Liqqutei MoHaRaN* 22:5, wherein it is taught that one should be aware and compassionate to the body's needs and tend to them, so that this corporeal vessel is purified to receive the influx and noetic available from the *Life-breath (Neshama)*. Compare with *Liqqutei Tinyana* 83, wherein the preparations for the Messianic age transfer such purificatory rites to prayer. This preparation centers the cosmos; only then is it ready to influence the body's return to its holy, Edenic state of purity.

16. The innovation of *nomos* without connection to a spiritual tradition.

17. Compare with Isa. 55:8, *"and not in our ways are their ways."*

18. Compare Jer. 32:19 with Gen. 3:5 for the serpent symbolizing the seductive nature of Enlightenment or unmitigated knowledge. Also, see *Liqqutei MoHaRaN* 19.

19. Compare with *Song of Songs* 1:8.

20. Compare Ezek. 16:7 *(arom)* to Gen. 3:1 *(arum)*.

21. Strength is not to be drawn by the power of lust.

22. The poet is perhaps referring to a ring or a bit that harnesses the camel under its master's control (see *B. Tal. Shabbat* 91b). The camel strays easily from the path without a harness to repress these wandering lusts. This motif of taking on the task of becoming a cattle-driver over one's cattle (i.e. passions) is illustrated in Nahman's tale of "The Exchanged Children." Kaplan's commentary on this tale remarks that: "In general, driving animals means being in control of them. This indicates that the king's true son was hired by his conscience (the merchant) to take control of his animal passions." Cf. "The Exchanged Children," in Rabbi Nachman's Stories. (tr. A. Kaplan). Breslav Research Institute. (Jerusalem: 1983), p. 244. The poet is also be drawing on a larger oral tradition in folklore that correlates the mouse and the elephant's trunk. Cf. Thompson-Bayls. *Motif & Type Index of Oral Tales of India* (Bloomington: 1966). In vol. 5, entry L314.4, there is an Indian tale regarding an elephant killed by cutting off its trunk that is poked into a cave. In vol. 4 K825.2, there is an Indian-Congo tale regarding an elephant killed by a mouse that runs up the open end of its trunk to its head and therein smears poison over its brain. Fear of such a punishment is further evoked in the *agadah* regarding the nemesis of Titus, who after enjoying wine and a hot bath has a gnat appear in his brain that seven years later when split open resembles a sparrow *(B. Tal. Gittin* 55b–57a; Gen. R. 10:17) This terrifying motif may be utilized to emphasize a fear of castration stemming from uncontrollable desire. (loss of the trunk through poisoning the brain). At the very least, these tales reinforce the paradox of the mammoth animal who cannot defend itself against its most insignificant intruder. Loss of control in the face of such symbolic desire's infiltration into the many corporeal cavities is a key, especially as concerns behavior in conversation and in sexuality. Regarding the mouse as a sign for desire, see note 23. Finally, the nostril signifies the original embodiment of anger/arrogance and the possibility for its rectification through humility, see *Liqqutei MoHaRaN* 22:2, 6 (thanks to Rabbis Morris Shapiro and David Weizmann for suggesting this connection).

23. Both the elephant and the camel represent an antonymic parallel to the control of desire *(nefesh)*. Restoration of these desires to a state of wisdom and fortification is only possible with an equally desirous tendency to be facile and weak. Recall that the camel is already differentiated from other animals as *"unclean*

*for chewing its cud"* (see Lev. 11:4). What the nature of this *"uncleanliness"* is, as rendered in its symbolic connotation, here remains somewhat ambiguous if not obscure. However, the choice of a camel to symbolize the desire's controlled appetite's *(nefesh)* tendency to wander and obstruct spiritual growth is reinforced in *aggadic* lore. *"Ten things adversely affect one's capacity to learn: passing under a camel's bit—all the more so, under the camel itself."* (See *B. Tal. Sanhedrin* 90a, Tos. Sanhedrin 12:10).

Another of the more strange creatures in the natural world is the elephant (see *B. Tal. Berachot* 58b). Inside Noah's ark, the camel is fed straw, while the elephant is fed vine tendrils (see *Genesis Rabbah* 31:11, and Gen. 7:23 Rashi ad loc.). Perhaps the polarity being evoked here is between the ideal of asceticism (eating meagerly and avoiding wine, like the camel) and the temptation of epicureanism (gorging and imbibing wine, like the elephant).

Most relevant as a bridge between these two tendencies within one controlled desire *(nefesh)* is the role of the mouse. Mice are associated with plagues (I Sam. 5:6), specifically in tearing out a culprit's innards. So clever are these mice, that even when the Ashdodians attempt to guard themselves from this plague with copper sitting vessels, the mice penetrate and leap up out of the deep and pull out their innards (see *Midrash Tehilim* 78:11). Mice are rightfully persecuted for their insatiable desire to devour all their eyes can take in (see *B. Tal. Horaoth* 13a, *P. BM* 3:5, 9b). Evident throughout the poem is this earnest struggle to exist as an embodied being while integrating soul-consciousness. It is in weaving webs of perpetual self-inadequacy, according to Moshe Mykoff, that one further obscures the path toward the spiritual fray. The poet is perhaps lamenting this illusion and the nascent power of the desire to really control the urges of the body.

24. This Messianic scenario of the final eschaton, as described in Isa. 10:3 (also compare with II Sam. 24:13, I Chron. 21:12), is portrayed here also as the Life-Breath's final Day of Reckoning. The poem's wording allows for R. Nahman's messianic identity as Messiah son of Joseph to flow into this dialogue with his Life-Breath as a double Day of Reckoning (the nexus of the end of days with the end of his body). Cf. *Green, TM,* pp. 182–220, esp. pp. 190–191. A nexus within this thematic of rupture occurs throughout the poem, in this case within the dichotomies of body/life-breath and exile/redemption.

25. Compare with *Liqqutei MoHaRaN* 22:5.

26. Compare with *Liqqutei MoHaRaN* 6:4 for R. Nahman's recasting of the kabbalistic notion of angels "scurrying to and fro" in front of the Celestial Throne (i.e., *Zohar II: 213b* whose Aramaic locution is *d'ayil nafik).* The sound of their wings beating amid this scurrying as portrayed in Ezekiels's vision (Ezek. 1:14, *"And the celestial creatures ran back and forth, like a lightning flash."*) is interpolated in prayer as pervading all space during the recitation of the doxology.

27. *B. Tal. Berachot* 58b, Rashi s.v. *Kocha d'shavit,* ad loc.

28. The meaning of *abat* is uncertain in its context of Joel 2: 7 (i.e., to lend on pledge or an interchange). Thus, many of the commentators understand it as a band of travelers or a fellowship, closer to *aevat*). In this context as a noun, *abit* most likely denotes a pledge to a fellowship. Compare *orchot* with Ps. 8:9 wherein it is rendered as paths, specifically related to the paths of one's sexual behavior.

29. Compare with Job 1:7, *"And the Lord said to the Opposer: From where have you come? And the Opposer responded, 'From going to and fro on the earth, and from walking back and forth on it.'"*

30. A folkloristic tradition depicts the slingshot as one of the torturous modes by which the wicked ones in Purgatory *(Gehenom)* are flung from one end of the universe to the other. Cf. *Even-Shoshan,* A. s.v. *"Kaf ha-kela"* in *Milon Hadash,* vol. 6 (Kiryat Sefer, 1990), p. 2352.

31. The focus is now shifting toward the world exiled from Her, namely, Israel.

32. The double entendre intrinsic to *lashon* is best rendered by the French loanword into English, *langue,* rather than by the more connotative "tongue." *Langue,* however, allows for the connotative possibilities of both orality and tongue simultaneously.

33. Building on the particular notion of the aforementioned *nomos,* see Deut. 32:8–9.

34. The four legal categories of damages *(avoth ha-nezikin)* are iterated in the *Mishna, Baba Kama* 1:1. These damages then give rise to the primordial categories of mayhem. See the following Kabbalistic renditions in (1) *Zohar II* 172a; (2) *Zohar II* 191a, (3) *Zohar II* 48b, and (4) *Zohar II* 29 a.

35. The zoharic locution is *tavnit ha-shor* (in the form of an ox). Compare with *Zohar II* 191a, wherein the etiology of chaos into order it is recounted how from the dregs of "primordial wine" (see *B. Tal. Berachot* 34b, B. Tal. Sanh. 99a, wherein *"the wine is guarded for the righteous since the six days of creation."*) From this wine, there was cast out a demonic element. This casting out lead to the realization of the first damage, its encroachment upon the holy, and then its descent into the profane. In its descent, it takes the form of an ox *(tavnit ha-shor)* from which the three other types of damage are derived. Further in *Zohar II* 48b, the fourfold face comprising the Chariot in Ezekiel's vision has the ox on the leftmost side. However, it is the face of *Adam* (earthling) which contains all gradations within it, including the form of the ox (which itself contains the fourfold damages). The context is clarified by the next line in the poem, which suggests that both humans and angels are judged according to their desserts. The descent from the supernal to the terrestrial realm is what links angelic responsibility to its human counterpart.

36. Compare with *B. Tal. Hagiga* 16a, wherein evil spirits are compared (in six ways) to heavenly messengers (in three ways) and certain humans (in three

ways). Like heavenly messengers, the evil spirits have wings, can traverse all ends of the universe, and can predict the future. Like earthly humans, the evil spirits can eat and drink, procreate, and die. See Nahmanides' *Commentary to Lev.* 16–19, wherein he exacts the comparison of evil spirits to earthly humans as limited by matter and spirit, but ultimately humans differ by degree in their material composition. The evocation of this comparison in the poem is to iterate a partnership in responsibility, in that both the heavenly messengers and earthly humans are doled their just desserts. Each is thus dependent, to some degree, upon the behavior of the other. Moreover, both supernal and terrestrial actions affect the Godhead.

37. See Gen. 17:13 and then compare with *Zohar II:* 95b, wherein the merit of Abraham's self-circumcision exemplifies the transformation that one undergoes regarding an internalization of the divine (becoming fully self-inscribed within ShaDaI). This inscription serves as protection against the evil spirits that would otherwise attack him *("ma'an d'itgazar kol innun d'lo kadishin itrahkan minei v'lo shlitin bei.")*

38. Compare with Shmuel's statement that righteousness will save you from accidental or unnatural death *("v'tzedakah tazeil mi'mavet v'lo me'meita meshuna ela me'meita atzma."* [*B. Tal. Shabbat* 156b]).

39. Compare with *Liqqutei Tinyana* 8:8. Every spiritual leader is endowed with *ruach ha'nevuah* (the spirit of prophecy) even though canonical prophecy within the Hebrew Bible has come to an end. By virtue of being a spiritual leader, one is *de facto* differentiated from other leaders with this *ruach ahairet* (unique spirit), which is in the category of *ruach ha'nevuah*. Even though this unique spirit is not oracular by nature, it is still on a par with the spirit of prophecy. In continually seeking out a spiritual leader, one repairs and fortifies individual faith by way of this sacred encounter.

40. Referrence is being made to the Messianic vision (Zech. 9:9) of the redeeming king appearing "lowly and riding a donkey" *en route* to Jerusalem.

41. Compare with *Liqqutei Tinyana* 5:15. The prodigal son utterly abandons his Will unto that of his ruler. By choosing to be fully enslaved to his Master's Will, the son qua slave abandons (philosophical) knowledge in order to more fully experience this Will. Only then would the King reveal further compassion upon this slave. The context of this teaching is *tiqqun ha-mohin* (restoration of consciousness) of both the teacher and the student as well as of the rebbe and *hasid*.

42. Compare *Song of Songs* 3:11 with Isa. 52:3. The coronation of Solomon as king is celebrated with his dedication of the Temple. In the former image, the Queen-Mother coronates a diadem upon Solomon within the precincts of the royal court. In the latter image, the Crown of Splendor's coronation in Isa. 52:3, denoting a national redemption of Jerusalem among the nations. Both images suggest a form of *hieros gamos,* between *Yesod/Tzaddiq* (Foundation/Righteous

One) and *Malkhut/Shekhina* (Sovereignty/Presence). For further reflections on the gender transvaluations of this imaginal reality, cf. E. R. Wolfson, "Mystical Fellowship as Constitution of the Divine Face" in *Through a Speculum that Shines* (New Jersey, 1994), pp. 368–377. [Henceforth, *Wolfson, E. R. TSS*].

43. See Ps. 96:1, Rashi ad loc. This song is referring to the future and the time-that-is-coming proves the point "for He who comes to judge the earth." In every place where it is so written, as *"shir hadash"* (new song), it is referring to the future (Redemption)."

44. Compare with *B. Tal. Ta'anit* 31a, wherein this eschatological vision is adumbrated. The devout are pointing with the index finger as they cleave, contemplating the Godhead in *unio mystica*. At this eschatological nexus, the devout will chant *"This is my God, and I will beautify Him."* (see also, *B. Tal. Shabbat* 133b, *B. Tal. Sotah* 30b–31a). However, the word choice describing "the flesh of the finger" may also be a metonymic intercourse (*Zivuga Kaddisha*) between Tzaddiq and Shekhina. Cf. *Wolfson, E. R. TSS,* 368–377.

45. Compare with Isa. 8:16.

46. Compare with Isa. 25:8.

47. Divine embodiment can only be understood from the perspective of human embodiment, and vice versa. Cf. *Wolfson, E. R. TSS,* 3–11; 393–397.

48. In this final moment the presence of this absence is marked in *Hayei MoHaRaN* 126, while the centrality of the third meal as an inspired time for teaching fills *Hayei MoHaRaN* (i.e., 12, 21, 116, 117, 143, 247, 263, 386). The final image reiterates the poem's prevalent themes of separation: of Human from Divine *nomos;* of the body from the soul; of an exiled people from their land, and so forth. The poem culminates its journey with a sacramental meal that takes place to repair this recurrent theme of rupture. Traditionally, within the imaginality of the Lurianic Kabbalah, so much a part of Nahman's teachings, the Sabbath's third meal is a "propitious moment," revealing in its concealment the deepest of messianic realizations. It is no coincidence then that many of R. Nahman's teachings were delivered at such "propitious moments." However, the paradox remains that for the majority of these table fellowships, Nahman was present in his absence from the table, opting rather to occupy an adjacent room of his own. This absent presence echoes further throughout the poem's structural acrostic, awakening return. This return amidst the cracks of existence is a gesture of toward unification within language and its act of naming, to a unification amid disparities of naming through language.

# 1

## Associative Midrash:
### *Reflections on a Hermeneutical Theory in* Likkutei MoHaRan

### *Shaul Magid*

"When I use a word," Humpty Dumpty said in rather a scornful tone, "it means just what I choose it to mean—neither more nor less."
"The question is" asked Alice, "whether you *can* make words mean so many different things."
"The question is" said Humpty Dumpty, "which is to be master—that's all."

—Lewis Carrol, *Alice in Wonderland*

Rabbi Nahman ben Simha of Bratslav (1772–1810) remains one of the most celebrated and controversial masters in the history of Hasidism.[1] His collected homilies, published as *Likkutei MoHaRan* (1805) and *Likkutei MoHaRan Tinyana* (1811) continue to inspire both disciples and scholars alike.[2] In this chapter I will explore two related issues in the study of these homilies. First, the ways in which R. Nahman's homilies retrieve and reconfigure older models of Jewish exegetical and sermonic stratagems, both the classical proemic *(petihta)* literature of late antique midrash and the formalized sermons in the Middle Ages and early modern period. Second, I will engage in a preliminary discussion about his hermeneutical method and the constructive ways in which he reads Scripture, focusing on his use of the term *behina* as a literary trope that serves as the foundation of his project of reconstructing the tradition.

I will make three basic claims in this exploration into the method and style of *Likkutei MoHaRan*. (1) I will argue that R. Nahman shifts the focus of midrashic reading from text to praxis.[3] While the midrashic proem was focused on offering innovative ways to read Scripture, R. Nahman's Hasidic proem offers its readers new devotional methods and precepts, constructing an edifice of Jewish piety built on the foundations of halakha but going beyond it. More than an explanation or defense of the law, R. Nahman offers new ways to live while obeying the law that often includes behavior having no basis in the law itself. This pietistic edifice is constructed through creative midrashic reading integrating the exegetical program of the midrashists and the devotional agenda of the pietists. (2) I will argue that the Bratslav tradition has an unprecedented relationship to its central text, *Likkutei MoHaRan,* whose sanctity reaches the level of Scripture itself. This text is envisioned by disciples as the embodiment of the unique zaddik, the externalization of his lofty soul, and a reflection of his spiritual stature. The fact that no master succeeded R. Nahman becomes more understandable when we see his disciples' unique relationship to his text. Becoming absorbed in *Likkutei MoHaRan* through devotional reading and living by its precepts does not only give the disciple access to the teachings of the zaddik—it gives him/her access to the zaddik himself. (3) I will argue that R. Nahman's intention in his use of *behina* as a metamidrashic literary trope is intended to train his reader to perfect her imagination, the final *tikun* before the advent of the Messianic Age. R. Nahman's associative reading liberates one from the confines and strictures of midrashic and kabbalistic hermeneutics. Through the *torah* of the zaddik, whose imagination is free of blemish and distortion, one can develop one's own imaginative ability and thus participate in the unfolding messianic consciousness.

Given the fact that our knowledge of the Hasidic imagination is almost exclusively derived from published sermons originally delivered orally, no serious study of Hasidic texts can proceed without paying close attention to the ways in which this literature moves from orality to literacy.[4] In the case of *Likkutei MoHaRan,* as opposed to most early Hasidic texts, we stand in good stead. Not only are we privy to a history of its first printing, but we also have an elaborate history of the text's redaction and editing, strengthened by the fact that the first volume was carefully reviewed by R. Nahman himself, who lived to see its publication.[5] This enables us more readily to evaluate the structure of the homilies in *Likkutei MoHaRan* as literary documents rather than focusing solely on the text as a transcription of an oral discourse that may or may not conform to its oral origins.[6] The importance of the text in Bratslav is unique among Hasidic groups.[7] In my view this is an extension of the fact that, even during the waning years of R. Nahman's life, his disciples knew that no master would succeed him. All the contributions in this collection are built on close readings of these complex homilies, either as texts or contexts for wider discussions of R. Nahman's worldview and influence. Here I will consider some hermeneutical themes that arise from close readings of these homilies in light of recent scholarship in the hermeneutics of Midrash and Kabbala.

For the scholarly reader exposed to the world of philosophical hermeneutics and recent studies in hermeneutical theory in Midrash and Kabbala,[8] the homilies contained in *Likkutei MoHaRan* present a good illustration of the highly nonlinear and indeterminate nature of midrashic reading.[9] This phenomenon is accentuated in kabbalistic literature in different ways. The Kabbalist (here I am limiting myself to the theosophical Kabbala of the Zohar and its progeny that most deeply influenced R. Nahman's work)[10] reads Scripture and the rabbinic corpus in what one might call a "liberated midrashic sense."[11] While the theosophic Kabbalist, as a product of rabbinic culture, may think midrashically, his reading of Scripture is unmidrashic in the sense that verses are read through a mystical grid devised of mythical and symbolic constructs not born out of the classic rabbinic enterprise.[12] It may be true that the Kabbalist constructs his myth from images and ideas embedded in Scripture, but these scriptural and rabbinic referents are lifted out of their context to become independent symbols, only to return later as a hypertext used to uncover dimensions of Scripture heretofore concealed. Kabbalistic (and to some degree Hasidic) hermeneutics is thus not inter- but intratextual in that it constructs a mythical hypertext using scriptural models and images that are then used to reveal the inner message of the text, that is, the soul of Torah.[13]

    Kabbalistic myth is not midrashically (i.e., exegetically) determined in any conventional sense.[14] Biblical and rabbinic images, which serve as the foundation of kabbalistic myth, are intermingled with more conventional midrashic motifs in most of theosophical Kabbala.[15] As Moshe Idel has noted, "[t]he symbolic-narrative as well as the static-symbolic and the nonsymbolic types of interpretations allowed the Kabbalists a relatively free choice in his hermeneutical project."[16] That is, the Kabbalist was able to reread the Bible (symbolic-narrative) through the lens of its own myth (static-symbolic and nonsymbolic types), which was constructed with biblical images and characters yet free from the limitations of understanding them via biblical exegesis. Betty Rojtman understands it this way: "The anagogic reading found in Kabbala propounds, in effect, a conventional, systematic deciphering of all of the terms of the Torah, determining for each a specific and precise reference which is lexically codified. This reading presents itself then as radically severed from any context: it is autonomous and invariable, chosen from among what the Kabbala considers the values founding the world."[17] Rojtman goes further than Idel by suggesting that the lexical codification of biblical terms in the Kabbala allows the Kabbalist to freely use these terms without referring back to the biblical narrative. When the Kabbalist turns back toward Scripture and uses these terms to interpret the Torah, they are already stripped of their contextual meaning and serve as independent symbols used to reconstruct the biblical narrative for the Kabbalist's own ends.

    Typical of his time, R. Nahman was nourished from childhood almost exclusively on a diet of rabbinic and kabbalistic literature,[18] thereby developing a way of reading that was highly attuned to the midrashic imagination[19] combined with the symbolic and mythical imagination of the Zohar and Lurianic Kabbala.[20] These tools and methods were then filtered through his intense and passionate psyche, coupled with the Hasidic notion of the zaddik he inherited from his great-grandfather, the Baal Shem Tov, and from his disciples.[21] As is the case with much of Hasidic literature (and much of classical Jewish homiletic literature in general),

R. Nahman's sermons, like classical midrash, are comprised of texts reading texts.[22] Theological speculation is always contextual, emerging via imaginative interpretation rather than via pure philosophical argumentation. Yet, while it may be true that R. Nahman's use of Scripture in *Likkutei MoHaRan* resembles earlier models of classical midrash and Kabbala, these models serve quite a different purpose in his Hasidic imagination.[23]

   Unlike midrash, R. Nahman is not focused on opening the text for purposes of reading (or rereading) Scripture. Unlike classical Kabbala, R. Nahman does not exegetically construct his homilies in order to facilitate a mystical experience, reenact the historical event of Sinai, or convey esoteric knowledge.[24] He is interested in accomplishing at least three basic objectives: (1) to create a textual representation of his own inner life, the life of the zaddik of the generation,[25] disclosing and enveloping his imagination in the garments of midrashic reading and kabbalistic imagery (his is accomplished through the complex hermeneutical scheme of his homilies in *Likkutei MoHaRan*); (2) to transmit his advice regarding the ways of worship, both existentially and practically, in order to enable his disciples to embody his innovative understanding of devotion, enacted within the confines of the halakhic system but not identical to it[26] (this is accomplished in *Sefer Ha-Middot, Kizur Likkutei MoHaRan,*[27] *Likkutei Ezot, Sihot Ha-Ran, Shivhei Ha-Ran,* and other advice literature including R. Nathan Sternherz of Bratslav's multivolume *Likkutei Halakhot*); and (3) to transcend normative modes of Torah discourse by conveying its essential messages in the garments of fable narratives. This third objective serves three distinct functions all of which have messianic implications: (a) to perfect the imaginative faculty as a prerequisite of prophecy and the necessary precursor to the messianic era;[28] (b) to "awaken the masses from slumber," an allusion to the depth of exile where the exiled lose consciousness of their exilic state; and (c) to universalize Torah by transcending its external (rabbinic) framework, i.e., text and exegesis, making way for a return to the institution of prophecy.[29] This is accomplished in his interpretations of the Raba Bar bar Hana agadot in *Likkutei MoHaRan* and later in his thirteen tales. [30]

   *Likkutei MoHaRan* and all subsequent Bratslav literature is intended to extrapolate the *torah* of the zaddik which serves as the authoritative text for R. Nahman's disciples. This point is expressed succinctly by his disciple, R. Nathan Sternharz, in his introduction to *Likkutei MoHaRan* when he says that the vocation of the zaddik is to translate the supernal Torah to the masses. "[To teach] great and lofty things . . . holy and spiritually refined, and to envelop them in many garments and veils *(zimzum)* until they become accessible to all."[31] This assertion is more than a reiteration of the conventional notion of the zaddik as translator of Torah in Beshtean Hasidism. These "lofty things" are not ideas already in the possession of the elite (e.g., Kabbala) that R. Nahman made accessible to the masses. Rather, these "lofty things" are ideas that have never before been revealed;

they are true innovation *(hidush)*, the source of which is the primordial Torah the Zohar calls the Ancient of Days *(Atik Yomin)*.[32] R. Nathan's statement presents R. Nahman as a master modeled after the heroic figure of R. Shimon bar Yohai in the Zohar, the master of esoterica who revealed that which has not yet existed in this world.[33] This affinity to R. Shimon can be seen in the Talmudic passage R. Nathan chooses as the beginning of his introduction to *Likkutei MoHaRan*. "What is 'concealing *Atik*' (Isaiah 23:18)? This refers to one who has concealed that which *Atik Yomin* has concealed. And what are these? The secrets of the Torah." This passage plays a central role in the zoharic treatise, the *Idra Raba*, in that it serves as the source of R. Shimon's activity as the one who reveals secrets.[34] Yet R. Shimon does not claim to be revealing the messianic Torah of *Atik Yomin*, only the intermediate stage that prepares the world for the messianic Torah.[35] R. Nathan's utilization of the talmudic description of the primordial Torah, so central in the Zohar, may very well be intended to present *Likkutei MoHaRan* as the culmination of the zoharic project—revealing the primordial Torah so that it would be accessible to all. Therefore, R. Nathan does not see R. Nahman's homilies as part of any traditional chain of interpretation, Hasidic or otherwise. He sees R. Nahman's teachings as representing "things that stand in the supernal heights," revealing to the world elements of primordial existence precisely by concealing them in the many garments of complex reading.[36] For R. Nahman's disciples, *Likkutei MoHaRan* becomes the new sacred text of Judaism, a lens through which the entire tradition is reread.

It should not be surprising that the post-Nahman Bratslav tradition never produced any text that is not based on *Likkutei MoHaRan*. Almost all post-Nahman literature, even the most recent literature in English for the non-Hasidic and even non-Jewish audience, consists solely of interpretations, extrapolations, and reflections on *Likkutei MoHaRan*. There are few instances in Jewish literature that exhibit such focus on one postrabbinic text. This program has clear messianic dimensions, as does Hasidism in general, built on the foundations of the zoharic notion that revealing the esoteric Torah is a necessary prelude to the messianic era. For the Zohar, however, the text contains its own sanctity, connected but not identical to R. Shimon bar Yohai, its mythical author.

Hasidism gives rise to the centrality of the zaddik as *axis mundi*, shifting focus from the text to the master. Relation and attachment to the zaddik becomes the way in which the Hasid perfects his own soul.[37] In the case of Bratslav Hasidism, whose sole zaddik left the world over 180 years ago, the zaddik as person is embodied in the zaddik as text. The *torah* of the zaddik becomes both the sacred text *and* the way one maintains an attachment to the zaddik, its author. [38] This is not accomplished merely by studying the text, but also by living its precepts, aligning one's entire spiritual life with R. Nahman's devotional advice. In the Bratslav tradition the zaddik is not only a figure to become attached to but to emulate, primarily through studying his words and living his dictates. One could draw the conclusion that, for R. Nahman, the zaddik embodies the "image of God" in the world and devotional life should be focused on emulating the zaddik himself. The problematics of such an assertion (largely but not exclusively in its similarity to Christianity) have been pointed out by anti-Hasidic polemicists for centuries, resulting in the softening of the centrality of the zaddik by later Hasidic masters.[39] However, I would argue that many early Hasidic texts, particularly *Likkutei MoHaRan,* endorse such a position, which should be taken seriously in assessing the radical nature of early Hasidic religiosity.[40]

R. Nahman's originality as a religious figure rests on the radical independence he displays, reflected in his proclamation "I am something that has never before existed in the world."[41] He never wavered from his audacious claim of uniqueness. "The world has not yet tasted any part of me. If they would hear one of my lessons, recited with its appropriate song *(niggun)* and dance, the entire world, including animals and vegetables, would instantly be overcome (*mitbatlin,* lit. nullified) by the great joy and pleasure they would experience."[42] In this chapter I am not interested in his claim of uniqueness as a religious figure, only the ways in which he read and reconfigured the literary tradition through his interpretive scheme. He read by deconstructing biblical and rabbinic passages, reconstructing them by means of loose midrashic and associative connections, resulting in an independent edifice that radically transformed the texts that served as its foundation.[43]

Since the midrashic elements in *Likkutei MoHaRan* are commonplace in Jewish literature, one could argue that, apart from its use of kabbalistic images and categories, R. Nahman's reading is no different than midrash. While this claim may contain some truth, I would argue that R. Nahman breaks away from midrash in two distinct ways. First, by recasting the midrashic proem in a devotional frame. The classical midrashic proem begins by citing two disparate verses and proceeds to tie them together through midrashic interplay. R. Nahman begins many of his homilies by citing one verse and then a devotional precept, tying them together in the body of the homily.[44] The substitution of a behavioral precept for a scriptural verse signifies that R. Nahman wanted his reader to realize the intimate correlation between reading and praxis filtered through the *torah* of the zaddik, resulting in an amalgam of piety and exegesis. The second departure from midrash is his use of the term *behina,* a literary/midrashic trope. As we will see, this term enabled R. Nahman to expand the more formalized midrashic method and thus to broaden the possibilities of imaginative reading.

As just mentioned, then, Hasidic texts (*Likkutei MoHaRan* in particular) are not philosophical nor purely exegetical texts committed to rational method or to the interpretation of Scripture. Like midrash, their claims are exegetically determined and are never rationally substantiated, if we define reason as a universal principle external to any particular tradition or body of texts.[45] However, unlike midrash, Hasidic texts are built upon an extratextual foundation in the form of kabbalistic images and readings of Scripture (both of which are taken to have the authority of Scripture) which are often undefined and almost always unexplained.[46] Moreover, the Hasidic lemma or lesson is intended to convey a very explicit devotional message, constructed via its quasi-midrashic style of reading.

### Is *Likkutei MoHaRan* Poetic Midrash?

In the few studies that have treated the relationship between midrashic and Hasidic literature, the question of the poetic nature of Hasidic discourse has never been addressed. Isaac Heinemann, following Maimonides, defined classical midrash as poetry in *Darkei Ha-Agaddah*.[47] Daniel Boyarin, analyzing Heinemann's claim in *Intertextuality and the Reading of Midrash,* challenged Heinemann's basic assumptions, arguing that they are based on a misrepresentation of what midrash (and literature in general) is about. Paraphrasing Heinemann's claim and then responding to it, Boyarin writes,

> Poetry also creates new discourse out of fragments of quotation, allusion, and transformation of earlier discourses. The explicit claim of poetry is that it creates new discourse; any violations (and preservations) of the "original meaning and context" are legitimated by that authorial claim to be speaking in his/her own voice. . . . Since Adam, then, all discourse is dialogue with the past and all literature is therefore intertextual and double-voiced. . . . Midrash, which is a stipulated post-Adamic literature, represents in this sense only a more open intertextuality than other literatures. Midrash, however, explicitly claims to be a hermeneutic discourse; to be representing in its discourse the discourse of an earlier (and authoritative) text. It is not sufficient, therefore, to compare midrash to poetry; it must also be studied as a species of hermeneutic discourse.[48]

Boyarin's definition of the clear exegetical agenda of classical Midrash disqualifies it as poetry. However, this equivocation (or outright rejection) of Heinemann's claim regarding Midrash may be a support for my claim that *Likkutei MoHaRan* would indeed constitute poetry couched in a proemic (i.e., midrashic) form.[49] According to Boyarin, while midrash creates a "new" discourse out of its reading of Scripture, it never severs itself from Scripture. This is the foundation of its overt hermeneutical agenda.[50] At best midrash teaches us new and even radical ways of reading Scripture, because Scripture remains its ultimate concern, even, or perhaps precisely, when it is reading against the scriptural message. Though midrash rarely claims its message as its own (i.e., it never speaks consciously in its "own voice"), it maintains that its message, as original as it may sound, is embedded in the texts it reads.

Boyarin convincingly argues that Midrash's ardent interest in limiting itself to reading Scripture disqualifies it as poetry. This is not to say that poetry is not engaged in reading the past. But, as Boyarin suggests, poetry must be about more than just reading the past. According to Harold Bloom, for example, reading the past is precisely the backbone of poetry but not its end.[51] Bloom argues that the poet reads her past with anxiety, misreading it in an attempt to carve out her own independent stance, fighting against the "facticity" of the past, which would result in mere repetition, in favor of radically revising the past, which results in "originality."[52] Originality only comes about by "completing the precursor" (not by rejecting it) retaining its terms but meaning them in another sense, by taking them further until they are read against themselves.[53] Strong poetry is a "heretical act," although the poem may never constitute formal heresy in that its break *with* the past is through its reading *of* the past without severing its connection *to* the past. Bloom's depiction of the strong poet, from Milton through Kafka, Freud, and even Gershom Scholem, strongly resembles our knowledge of R. Nahman's personality. For example, originality (strong poetry) necessarily stands on the margins of heresy and thus absorbs the brunt of critique from the center, a phenomenon R. Nahman knew quite well.[54] R. Nahman never tried to dissuade the criticism against him, advising his disciples that such critique was the necessary response to speaking things "that never existed before (i.e., originality)." On this he says, "I do not want the dispute against me to diminish. Every moment that I am challenged I move from one level [of sanctity] to the next. If I knew that where I stand now is where I stood before, I would no longer want to be in the world!"[55] The destiny of such a strong poet is to suffer anxiety on two fronts: first from his own battle against authority, and second from those who seek to conflate originality with heresy, preventing what R. Nahman thought was the necessary revision of Torah to prepare the world for the Messianic Age.[56] This conflation is common in traditional societies who often view innovation as a threat to the maintenance of traditional norms and precepts. R. Nahman understood himself as a *hidush* (a true innovation), one who brought forth new elements of Torah to the world. He understood the dangers of this endeavor and the ways in which it could easily be misconstrued as heretical. He also understood that this vocation would incite contempt from those who could not make the fine distinction between true originality and heresy. As Arthur Green suggests, R. Nahman saw himself as the suffering messiah, in our explanation the strong poet who suffers in that his misreading (originality) is itself misread and deemed heretical.[57]

The anxiety of the original poet is precisely the despair at not having been self-begotten, being confined to a past yet having outgrown it. This anxiety is also a messianic trope, the inspiration and despair that constantly flows beneath the surface of R. Nahman's teaching, emerging in his protestation against the conformity of his antagonists and his resolute stubbornness against seeing himself as part of any tradition. Departing from the midrashic posture presented by Boyarin, R. Nahman did not have a commitment to the texts he read and interpreted, although their sanctity was never questioned. By this I mean that his use of the classical tradition in *Likkutei MoHaRan* was not geared toward offering a reading of Scripture or the rabbinic corpus but rather toward constructing his own vision of Judaism built on the foundation of these sources. His reading of the canon was courageous, one may even say audacious, in that he did not limit himself to classical hermeneutical tools (midrashic or kabbalistic). Never leaving the canon as the sacred foundation of his own religiosity, R. Nahman, through "strong reading," was able to reconfigure the canon to serve his own religious orientation. Marc-Alain Ouaknin understands it this way: "the role of interpretation [for R. Nahman] is clear. It is not a matter of repeating, or paraphrasing the original text, but, literally, of unsticking it, of going 'beyond the verse,' going from the text to one's personal text; by this creative reading, the reader is born. . . ."[58] However, originality never became heresy (as it did, e.g., with Shabbtai Zvi and Nathan of Gaza) because his reading transformed, but never effaced, the practical conclusions of rabbinic reading. A diligent student of the Kabbala, R. Nahman deeply understood the exegetical and doctrinal freedom in Judaism, that is, that heresy was largely behaviorally determined. In a famous passage he says, "One who wants to offer innovative interpretations of *my* Torah *(l'hadash b'Torah)* may freely do so as long as his interpretation does not result in any halakhic change *(din hadash).*"[59] This exegetical freedom is displayed in his use of the term *behina* as an associative literary trope, breaking free of the confines of classical interpretation (and sometimes doctrine) while staying within the borders of traditional Judaism.

Borrowing Harold Bloom's categories in *Ruin the Sacred Truths,* I would argue that R. Nahman intuitively knew the difference between canonical, creative, and heretical writing.[60] The first merely repeats tradition, even as it may recontextualize it. The second, which Bloom calls "strong poetry," revises tradition by misreading it. The third severs the new poem from its mooring to the old, breaking free but also losing its past. In Susan Handelman's words, "Bloom maintains that heresy alters the balance of received doctrine, while revisionism alters the stance through creative correction."[61] I would suggest that the revisionist turns the doctrine away from itself while never allowing its new face to consume the old. The heretic effaces the "received doctrine," uprooting its authority. Aligned with Hasidism in general but going significantly further, R. Nahman's psychologized hermeneutics severed midrashic reading from its exegetical moorings yet stayed within the anxiety-ridden realm of creative reading by revising the tradition through associative midrash, which we will discuss in the next section.

Therefore, *Likkutei MoHaRan* cannot be considered either an exegetical or a classically midrashic text, but an example of "poeticized midrash."

*Likkutei MoHaRan* also comes closer to poetry than classical Midrash in that its revision of, and independence from, the texts it reads comes close to what Bloom calls an "original poem." The sacred Jewish canon includes numerous texts of this sort, such as the Zohar and the Lurianic corpus, both of which revise tradition by reading it "strongly." In their tension *against* and adherence *to* tradition, these texts require the tradition to expand so that they may find a place within that tradition.[62] In my view, *Likkutei MoHaRan* can be included in this category of "original" canonical texts. However, departing from earlier texts of this sort that claim to be the result of spiritual inheritance (i.e., an esoteric tradition) or of prophetic inspiration *(gilluy Eliahu)*, R. Nahman emphatically and audaciously claimed to be speaking in his "own voice," the voice of the zaddik of his generation, whose teaching needs no corroboration nor precedent.[63] One illustration of this radical independence is the fact that *Likkutei MoHaRan* is one of the only Hasidic texts that rarely cites any previous Hasidic master or Jewish classic beyond Scripture, Talmud and Midrash, the Zohar, and Lurianic Kabbala.[64]

My suggestion that *Likkutei MoHaRan* is an example of midrashic poetics would make R. Nahman a kind of midrashic poet.[65] Such a claim is not just the result of the independent nature of his literary oeuvre—it is also drawn from the anguish he suffered about his own work, expressed in the ambivalence about concealing and revealing his discourses, even submitting one whole book to flames.[66] R. Nahman understood his suffering as an integral part of his creativity and his vocation as the unique zaddik of his generation. It has been duly noted that *Likkutei MoHaRan* is an autobiographical text, more so than almost any other product of premodern Jewish literature.[67] Arthur Green's *Tormented Master* exhibits the complexity of R. Nahman's personality as embodying the suffering servant of Isaiah, destined to suffer for the sake of the nation.[68] As is often the case with such individuals, R. Nahman acknowledged that his suffering was the source of his genius as well as the sign of his qualifications for leadership.[69] Describing this phenomenon in a letter to his wife while viewing Cezanne's paintings in Paris, the poet Ranier Maria Rilke wrote:

> Surely all art is the result of one's having been in danger, of having gone through an experience all the way to the end, to where no one can go any further. The further one goes, the more private, the more personal, the more singular an experience becomes, and the thing one is making is, finally, the necessary, irrepressible, and, as nearly as possible, definitive utterance of singularity.[70]

R. Nahman's sermons, both in form and content, display the genius, anxiety, and tension of a complex mind striving only for the "singularity" of the simple path *(emunah peshuta)*, the simplicity that lies beyond (yet does not circumvent) the complexity of the struggle.[71] Each lesson is a journey unto itself, moving deeper into the labyrinth of R. Nahman's rewriting of the classical tradition in his own image, externalizing his image through his reading of the tradition.[72] Such rewriting takes a more radical turn later in his life when he abandons the exegetical mode altogether and enters totally into the realm of fantasy.[73] It is no coincidence that his thirteen tales bury the exegetical enterprise, making it part of the esoteric nature of the tale itself, as his narratological expression becomes the new phase of his exegetical imagination.[74]

## Writing and Audience:
### The Inevitability of Writing and the Sacred Text

The homilies included in both volumes of *Likkutei MoHaRan* have always been read differently by different communities. The more important question regarding the sociology of reading is something that weighed heavily on the minds of many Hasidic masters in their deliberations about allowing their discourses to be written. Many Hasidic writers were ambivalent about writing precisely because they knew they would lose control of their audience.[75] The emphasis on community development through discourse lies at the root of Hasidic preaching, the spoken word being the vehicle for spiritual revival.[76] As Paul Ricoeur argues, writing results in the "universalization of the audience," speaking to a particular community as well as creating a community that may not share the sensibilities of the text being read.[77] "A written work often creates its public. In this way it enlarges the circle of communication and properly initiates new modes of communication . . . the recognition of the work by the audience created by the work is an unpredictable event."[78] It is interesting that the Bratslav community never had the ambivalence about publishing that was common in early Hasidic circles.[79] Although R. Nathan knew that *Likkutei MoHaRan* would be read by a larger audience than the small circles of R. Nahman's disciples, he never wavered in his belief that this text would revolutionize Jewish life. The fear of distortion and/or ridicule by his Hasidic antagonists and by the Jewish Enlightenment *(Haskala)* never seemed to deter him. The ways in which the Bratslav community published and reprinted their master's writings (often at great personal expense and danger) in a Hasidic community that feared publishing, points to the way this text was seen as sacred in its community of readers.[80] The text represented the zaddik himself. Therefore, to widen its audience of readers simply maximized the zaddik's influence on the world. The underlying belief was that the sacrality of the text would ultimately conquer any distortion or critique waged against it.

R. Nahman's personal relationship to writing is quite complex. He knew personally and from tradition the limitations of writing, yet also knew of its usefulness and necessity. The delicate balance between writing and orality was a "narrow bridge" for him, one that he felt only the zaddik knew how to traverse. He teaches that one of the characteristics of the zaddik was to know "what can be written and what cannot be written." In the following lesson, R. Nahman teaches that the unique characteristic of the Jew juxtaposed to the Gentile is the power of orality. Yet the zaddik, who knows how to distinguish between what to write and what cannot be written, is able to write while not writing, so to speak. That is, he is able to write something "unwritable" without destroying its orality—without destroying its Jewish uniqueness.

> Know: there are distinctions between types of *torot.* There is *torah* which is not fit to be verbalized, *torah* that is not fit to write and *torah* that is fit even to write, as it is taught in Tractate Gittin (50b) "Things that are transmitted orally are not permitted to be written." One who knows how to distinguish between these types of *torot* is also able to distinguish between a Jew and a Gentile. If a Jew should stand in the midst of a group of Gentiles, one would be able to recognize the Jew. . . . The essential distinction between Jew and Gentile is the same as the difference between the written and oral Torah, as it is written "because of this the Jews were given the Oral Law." That is, they were given the Oral law because it was anticipated that they would dwell in exile and would relinquish the Written Law to the nations. This law (the Oral Law) should not be written (for the Gentile), because it is oral. The essential distinction and superiority of the Jew over the Gentile is embodied in the Oral Law, which is not fit (or permitted) to be written. Each Jew has a portion of the Oral Law. Therefore the one who knows what can be written and what cannot be written can distinguish between Jew and Gentile as this is their essential difference.[81]

Bracketing R. Nahman's obvious disdain for the Gentile, he is specifically interested here in drawing the parallel analogy between Jew and Gentile and writing and orality based on the historical fact that Christianity is founded on the Written Law (the Old Testament) without the accompanying Oral Law (rabbinic corpus). The unique quality of orality versus the writing is complicated by the ability of the zaddik to "write orally," as only he is the "the one who can distinguish" between what can and cannot be written. Therefore, the zaddik is able to write something that will maintain its oral (authentic) nature. The zaddik, who internalized the distinction between the three types of *torot* (unspoken, spoken, and written), is able to "transgress" the rabbinic dictum against writing and communicate in writing that which can only be preserved orally. The permissibility to write here is different than the pragmatic decision of the rabbis to "write down" the Oral Law as an act of preservation. For R. Nahman the unique zaddik could "write" (or his *torah* could be transcribed) without losing its uniquely Jewish (i.e., oral) quality. This is likely the result of what he determined was his teaching's eternal nature. Only eternality can be reproduced without any loss of meaning. Writing is dangerous as it makes one's oral teaching vulnerable to distortion (perhaps this is the way he viewed Christianity's use of the Written Law). For the unique zaddik, this danger does not apply. Therefore, the Bratslav tradition was fearless in its commitment to publishing R. Nahman's teaching in a world that was ambivalent about liberating the Hasidic message from the confines of the controlled Hasidic community.

Another illustration of R. Nahman's attempt to maximize his text's influence is his directive to publish an abbreviated version of *Likkutei MoHaRan* alongside the full version. For his community of disciples (from his death to the present), the hermeneutical complexity of *Likkutei MoHaran* is merely the backdrop for the message contained therein, the message being the path to righteousness embodied in the "advice" of the zaddik. While the text's complexity mirrors the complexity of its author, R. Nahman wanted his own text and, by extension his personality, to be understood in a more accessible and simplified manner. To achieve this he encouraged R. Nathan to publish an abbreviated version of these homilies to accompany the expanded edition of the first volume of *Likkutei MoHaRan*.[82] This abbreviated version, *Kizur Likkutei MoHaRan* (1811), contained the practical lessons stripped of their exegetical complexity, easily accessible to one not able to access them through close readings of the homilies themselves.[83] These abbreviated lessons subsequently became topically ordered, including additional information, making his message even more accessible. This text was published posthumously by R. Nathan as *Likkutei Ezot* (1842) and then later by R. Nahman of Cheryn as *Likkutei Ezot Ha-M'Shulash* (Warsaw, 1922).[84]

Scholars and disciples alike have often read these homilies in order to unearth the autobiographical nature of R. Nahman's theology. Although any careful reader of these texts will necessarily have to navigate her own interpretive path, little scholarly work has been done on the hermeneutical and structural dimensions of these lessons. I want to turn my attention more directly to the literary style and hermeneutical theory that underlies these complex homilies. I will divide my discussion into three sections. The first part will include an analysis of two very substantive introductions to these sermons, R. Nathan's Introduction to *Likkutei MoHaRan* and R. Nahman of Cheryn's Introduction to *Pe'arparot l'Hokhma*, both written by disciples of the Bratslav tradition. Each offers valuable insights into the nature, purpose, and structure of *Likkutei MoHaRan* as a literary document. Secondly, I will discuss the proemic structure of many of the longer homilies, paying attention to the way in which R. Nahman reconfigures the classical midrashic frame. A loose version of this proemic form serves as a mechanism to accomplish the Hasidic objective of merging spirituality with metahalakhic devotional practice seen through the lens of midrashic/kabbalistic ex-egesis.[85] Finally, I will discuss R. Nahman's use of *behinot,* a literary trope that stands at the center of his exegetical program.

### Three Hermeneutical Moments

I want to suggest that the lengthy homilies in *Likkutei MoHaRan* generally contain three distinct "hermeneutical moments": (1) the deconstructive, (2) the recon-structive, and (3) the metaconstructive. Briefly, the deconstructive moment is the dislodging of biblical and rabbinic (including zoharic) passages from their context, opening them to new possibilities of meaning via intertextual (midrashic) or mythical/symbolic (kabbalistic) modes of reading. The fragmentation and decon-textualization of classical literature creates the building blocks of the Hasidic homily. This is common to midrashic, postmidrashic, and kabbalistic hermeneu-tics. As opposed to classical exegesis *(parshanut),* which attempts to explain the biblical narrative in context, both midrash and Kabbala detach scriptural verses from the narrative only to return to the narrative to offer new insights.[86] There-fore, the first moment in R. Nahman's homilies essentially offers nothing new.

The next moment exhibits two new elements: (1) a devotional and (2) a metamidrashic turn. This second reconstructive moment is the creation of small clusters of ideas, piecing together textual fragments from the decontextualized verses in the first moment. These clusters are almost always presented in a psycho-logical mode, focusing on devotional praxis or practical behavior (i.e., halakha or ritual).[87] The metamidrashic element here is that R. Nahman uses his midrashic reading in the first moment as a building block for his larger homily, instead of turning back to Scripture (classical Midrash) or using these symbols to explicate a kabbalistic myth (zoharic exegesis). These clusters become building blocks for his larger homily.[88]

The final metaconstructive moment is the integration of these smaller clus-ters, constructed in the second moment, into the larger frame of the homily. The "message(s)" of the homily itself emerges by integrating the smaller clusters into the more sweeping narrative. The narrative R. Nahman creates stands indepen-dent of any of its parts. Biblical verses, midrashic inferences, kabbalistic symbols, rituals, pietistic precepts, and Hasidic ideology (e.g., the status of the zaddik) all merge to form a homily usually built on one scriptural verse seen in light of a devotional precept. Each part serves the larger homily and the homily serves to offer innovative insights to each part. The homily is self-standing—it has no relation to any other homily nor any relation to the classical literature that serves as its base. It is the *torah* of the zaddik, pure and simple.

The transition from one hermeneutical moment to the next can be wit-nessed by the speed of the text's movement. One of the first things an attentive reader will notice when studying R. Nahman's lengthy homilies is their erratic pace, exhibited in the sometimes incoherent manner in which the text unfolds. The text moves at two different speeds, the first being an accelerated pace, whereby the text makes quick and unsubstantiated associations moving frenetically from one idea to another. This frenzy of exegetical activity is always followed by a marked decrease in the text's speed, exhibited as the text's own internal review, revisiting old associations and integrating them into the present issue at hand. The initial frenetic speed of the text is largely the result of the use of the *behina* trope, an associative tool enabling complex connections to be made instantaneously, but without substantiation.

The text's own internal review is the mechanism that slows the pace of the text allowing the reader to witness the homily taking shape. R. Nathan suggests that this also enables R. Nahman to weave together different parts of the homily, moving from the first to the second hermeneutical moment.

> Every homily in this book constitutes a great, wondrous and strong edifice. *[Like the Tower of David around your neck], it is built like Talpiot,* (Canticles 4:4) i.e., like a hill *(tel)* that all can turn toward *(ponim bo)*. It includes many rooms, one inside the other, windows and portals, opening from all sides. . . . Each time [R. Nahman] adds more reasons and ideas [to the homily] its depth increases, *like water that covers the sea* (Isaiah 11:9).[89] Every time he moves from one palace to the next, from one room to the next, from one idea to the next . . . one must gaze backward to understand the sweetness and depth of how one thing is born of another and how one thing gives birth to the other. . . . [90]

Repetition is a sign of transition. When the text begins to repeat itself, its associations are usually less frenetic and more substantiated. It has been noted by scholars of oration and sermons that repetition is a common oratory technique that enables the listener to keep track of a complex set of ideas. While this may be true, in *Likkutei MoHaRan,* repetition serves a literary function as well. According to R. Nathan, repetition in *Likkutei MoHaRan* is not merely a homiletic device but a literary technique that serves as a transitional trope from one hermeneutical moment to the next by integrating one piece of the homily into the larger whole.[91]

Both the quickness and the languid pace of the homily play a constructive role, the first serving to connect the smaller clusters one to the other and the second to construct the homily as a whole. The pace of the text may be seen in light of R. Nahman's understanding of the relationship between imagination and reason, each a necessary but insufficient element of human creativity. The first phase, dominated by rapid and unsubstantiated associations, embodies the imaginative faculty, enacted by intuition rather than by reflective reason. The second phase substantiates this intuitive phase with more careful and precise definitions, distinctions, and proofs. R. Nahman often reflects on the need for both faculties to work in tandem, focusing on the need for the intellect to be ancillary to the imagination. In this case, the steadied pace indicative of the second phase of construction (review, reflection, and integration) uses reason, understood by R. Nahman as midrashic reading, to substantiate the imaginative associations made in phase one.

Another analogue might be the relationship between improvisation and melody. Improvisation emerges out of a structured melody, breaking out of its confines by challenging its structure then returning to the melody, enriching its texture.[92] The quickened pace of phase one of this process exhibits the imaginative faculty acting independent of reasoned analysis.[93] This associative method of loose midrashic reading demonstrates an indispensable lack of caution and precision, one might say an improvisational predilection, where formal limits of midrash/Kabbala are challenged by making connections outside of the exegetical or symbolic framework. Phase two of this process is both more reasoned and integrative. Establishing itself through internal review, it slowly feeds the new piece of the homily, constructed via improvisation, into the already existing whole, its original melody.[94] In improvisational music, the return to the melody after an improvisational interlude often results in an expansion of the melody. This is also the case in our homilies, where the integration of new pieces into the larger homily changes the nature and direction of the homily itself.[95] The homily, therefore, is in a constant state of flux, reconstituting itself at every new exegetical turn. It can never be evaluated as long as pieces still remain to be constructed and integrated. This is not to say that each piece only functions within the larger homily. Units within the homily may stand independent of those that precede it and those that follow, even as they inform the larger homily. In fact, much of the later "collection literature" in Bratslav such as Likkutei Ezot draw from these units. From a literary perspective, however, the homily requires the construction and integration of all the pieces before it can be evaluated as a distinct literary document.

There is an unmistakably anti-Maimonidean tone at work here. Whereas Maimonides begins the Guide for the Perplexed with his notion that reason is the "image of God," R. Nahman begins with the notion that the imagination is the "image of God."[96] For example, he reads, Let us make man in our likeness (ki'dmutanu) (Gen. 1:26) as "let us make man endowed with a [perfected] imagination."[97] Whereas Maimonides viewed the perfected human being, that is, the philosopher-prophet, as one who attains the proper balance of intellect and imagination (the latter serving the former),[98] R. Nahman sees the zaddik as one who has overcome the illusion of the intellect by perfecting his imagination.[99] While the Guide of the Perplexed is arguably a book intended to sharpen the reasoning faculty of its reader, Likkutei MoHaRan is clearly intended to perfect its reader's imagination.

In sum, the three hermeneutical moments—the deconstructive, reconstructive, and metaconstructive—serve as the foundation of almost every long homily in *Likkutei MoHaRan*. The transition from one moment to another is usually marked by the speed of the text's exegetical movement and by the ways in which connections are made. The initial phase of R. Nahman's homilies largely reflects classical midrash and Kabbala, deconstructing Scripture by decontextualizing the narrative into distinct verses and phrases to be used to construct the midrashic proem. The reconstructive phase departs from midrash in that it does not turn back to Scripture to reread it, but uses these clusters to construct its own independent narrative distinct from Scripture. The metaconstructive phase contains the homilies unique Hasidic component; it uses Scripture to put forth a new posture of worship. It turns reading into praxis, not by clarifying and instructing obligatory actions (halakha) but by suggesting performative models of devotional behavior. The homily becomes a lesson for living and reading rather than merely a lesson for learning. As opposed to most other early Hasidic literature, *Likkutei MoHaRan* teaches devotion out of a complex hermemeutical program, demanding the reader to enter the zaddik's mind in order to think more imaginatively. Living piously (not just halakhically) and thinking imaginatively (not analytically) is R. Nahman's formula for the messianic age.

## From Speech to Text:
### Constructing the Unconstructed

In an essay on the medieval sermon's of the Amsterdam rabbi R. Shaul Ha-Levi Morteira (ca. 1590–1660), Marc Saperstein maps out various issues and concerns in the scholarly analysis of written versions of oral sermons that are relevant to our discussion of the homilies in *Likkutei MoHaRan*.[100] Sapperstein suggests at least five different criteria essential in determining the sermon's relationship to its oral origins: (1) Was the written sermon (as we have it) a reconstruction or transcription of the oral lecture (by the author or by another) or a reconstruction of notes taken before or after the oral lecture? (2) Were the scriptural and rabbinic references in the written sermon part of the original oral discourse or added when the text was being written for publication? (3) What is the nature of the rhetorical devices that exist in the written version? (4) What conventional and technical patterns does the sermon follow, that is, does it exhibit originality in form or only in content? (5) What did the orator expect from his audience? Some of these criteria can be used to analyze any written document originally delivered orally. In the case of *Likkutei MoHaRan,* some of these questions are dealt with directly by R. Nathan Sternherz in his introduction to *Likkutei MoHaRan.*

R. Nathan's introduction to *Likkutei MoHaRan* is unique among Hasidic introductions for various reasons. First and foremost it was composed by the scribe who brought these homilies from orality to literacy. More than just placing R. Nahman in context or praising his genius, which is often the function of such introductions, R. Nathan speaks openly about the construction of the text itself, both his own work and R. Nahman's editorial contribution.[101] Throughout, R. Nathan stresses the fact that the text intends to be a comprehensive text of Jewish devotion, despite the fact that it is embedded in complex exegetical discourse. Its devotional message is not limited to the performance of specific mitzvot but to behavioral norms and patterns that accompany these mitzvot, including (among other things) the *niggun* (song or chant), the importance of musical instruments, the recitation of psalms, clapping (during prayer), dancing, nonliturgical and informal prayer *(hitbodedut),* the wordless sigh, and the primal scream.[102] R. Nahman is not interested in *ta'amei ha-mitzvot* (reasons for the mitzvot) in any conventional sense, but he is passionately invested in the specific ways in which these mitzvot should be performed.[103] In the tradition of medieval pietism, *Likkutei MoHaRan* is a performative (devotional) rather than an instructive (halakhic) text. Yet, unlike popular pietistic texts such as *Sefer Hasidism, Menorat Ha-Meor,* or *'Orhot Zaddikim,* which often present their directives in a clear and unambiguous fashion, *Likkutei MoHaRan* has a highly complex hermeneutical agenda, its devotional message emerging out of its circuitous exegesis. Therefore, according to R. Nathan, R. Nahman's work is not only useful for those unable to plumb the depths of the halakhic or kabbalistic tradition. It is just as crucial for the elite in that it presents devotional models never before revealed to the world. This is part of what makes it a sacred text built on, but independent of, tradition. As the *torah* of the unique zaddik, it reveals God's will heretofore concealed.

R. Nathan describes the sanctity of this text in at least two distinct ways. First, the text brings into the world the words of the unique zaddik, words "[that] no ear has ever heard . . . secrets that the world needs which were never . . . seen before."[104] Second, and equally as important, R. Nathan claims that his master's text contains the entirety of Torah.

> [This text] includes all the 613 mitzvot and all their branches, including all rabbinic injunctions. It includes the entire written and oral Torah, revealed and esoteric, halakha and Kabbala, even the innermost secrets . . . [R. Nahman] speaks about all of these things many times and in many beautiful, stunning, and innovative ways. All of them are solidified as wondrous directives in achieving closeness to God. [This text] contains every single mitzvah, holy act, and guidance needed for any individual in the world. There is not one dimension [of human behavior] which is not expressed in this holy book.[105]

Heralding this text as a self contained "Torah" is more than hyperbole. "It is said, one could traverse the entire Torah, Prophets, and Writings, including the entire

Oral Law with every lesson and utterance that comes out of R. Nahman's mouth."[106] There is a veneration of the text in Bratslav Hasidism that is unparalleled in Hasidism and perhaps in the history of postmedieval Jewish literature, at least from the appearance of the Zohar onward. In *Hayye MoHaRan*, R. Nathan makes numerous comments about how this book (i.e., *Likkutei MoHaRan*) has a holiness beyond its contents.

> One time he [R. Nahman] was praising his own book. He said it is possible to become a *ba'al teshuvah* merely by reading this book. He stressed to us to print and re-print this book in order to maximize its influence. . . .

> Every person should strive to purchase this book, even if he has to sell his possessions in order to do so. He should even sell the pillow under his head in order to purchase this book. . . .

> One should strive to buy this book, even if it [just] sits on a shelf. His books protect one's house and wealth from potential danger.[107]

The seriousness of this claim is bolstered by what R. Nahman himself determined as his spiritual genealogy, beginning with Moses, Shimon bar Yohai, Isaac Luria, and the Besht.[108] He extends this trajectory even further by suggesting that he achieved the spiritual level of the biblical patriarchs (in Genesis), making his teachings a pre-Sinaitic Torah through the lens of Sinai.[109] "He said, 'My *torah* contains great depths.' That which is written from his mouth should be read with the same precision and care as the Bible itself."[110] The messianic implications of this claim are not far beneath the surface, a fact noticed by any serious reader of *Likkutei MoHaRan*.[111] What I would like to suggest is that such a claim also speaks to the independent nature of the text, not only its author, built on but liberated from its literary predecessors. When one reads the homilies in *Likkutei MoHaRan*, it is crucial to keep in mind R. Nathan's claim that nothing more is needed to achieve closeness to God other than reading this text and enacting its precepts. This underlying claim is an integral part of the text's sacrality.

Another significant literary observation in R. Nathan's introduction, which is developed in the introduction of R. Nahman of Cheryn's commentary to *Likkutei MoHaRan*, *Pearparot l'Hokhma*, is the independent nature of each homily.

> Behold, I will now speak briefly *to all of my brothers and friends* (Psalm 122:8) about the structure of this holy book. . . . See with your eyes and let it gladden your heart—every homily in this book speaks of many specific ideas, pieces of advice, and mitzvot from our holy Torah as well as teaching us how to avoid bad qualities. Each homily speaks of these things in a specific manner unique unto itself in ways which are not replicated in other homilies.[112]

R. Nahman's practice of interpreting one idea in a variety of ways, apparent to any reader of his work, is justified by R. Nathan as having a specific intent, unique to the abilities of this unique zaddik.

> Every idea [in this book] is treated in many different ways, each time in order to show its different valences (lit. to present a different piece of good advice). For example, in lesson # 5 prayer is presented as embodying the power of thunder. Praying in this way enables one to liberate oneself from the crookedness of the heart in order to perform mitzvot joyfully. In lesson # 49 prayer is said to aid in the birth of progeny, which is connected to Sukkah and Erez Israel. In lesson # 44 prayer is seen as that which nullifies haughtiness, distraction, and extraneous thoughts. . . . This is the case for all traits, devotional norms, and holy advice that are included in this book. . . . [The reason is that] our weakened state and the magnitude of our evil inclination requires us to be inspired toward devotion in many different ways. Sometimes a person will be inspired in this way, by means of this homily and sometimes from another homily, all depending upon the individual and his/her stage of development.[113]

Just as the rabbis maintained that the Torah itself has (at least) seventy faces *(panim)*, understood by the Kabbalists as an infinitude of meaning, R. Nathan suggests that devotional norms also have an infinite number of ways they can be understood.[114] In a sense, this challenges the conventional notion of *ta'amei ha-mitzvot* (reasons for the commandments) in that finding a reason or reasons for the mitzvot, either rationally or mystically, implies limitation. Maimonides, for example, argues that each commandment must have a telos for it to be considered divine (*Guide of the Perplexed* III:26). Most Kabbalists also accepted the general principle that mitzvot were directed toward achieving certain ends, be they cosmic or experiential.[115] R. Nathan implies that his master moves outside this teleological circle by speaking about mitzvot in multitudinous ways, each one as true and as valuable as the other. Any devotional precept can inspire many reactions, depending upon the individual's needs and spiritual orientation. Prayer, for example, can mean an infinite number of things, even contradictory things, depending upon how it is presented and then integrated back into the tradition. This observation adds both credence and nuance to R. Nathan's statement that this book contains the entire Torah. He does not mean that the entire Torah is revealed in *Likkutei MoHaRan;* the Torah remains the authoritative text of Israel. What changes is how to enact that authoritative text. R. Nathan claims that *Likkutei MoHaRan* provides a lens through which the entire tradition can be read and, more importantly, lived. This is yet another of its innovative elements and the sources of its sanctity.

Near the conclusion of his introduction, R. Nathan briefly discusses the challenges of creating a text from R. Nahman's oral homilies.

There are numerous homilies in this book that are repeated in an abbreviated and expanded form. This was the way of the master. The homilies he wrote himself included many changes from their original oral presentation. This is because he wrote them with a fluid mind *(rehitat mokho)*. When he would commit these homilies to writing, he would add or subtract things that he said when he delivered the lecture orally. This is not true with the homilies I transcribed. I was always very careful to transcribe exactly what I heard from his holy mouth without any changes. There were some cases in which I had versions of certain homilies and then received R. Nahman's own written version. I found many differences between my version and his. I decided that both were worthy of being printed. I determined that every change that occurred between [his] oral presentation [i.e., my written version] and his written version existed for the intended purpose of innovation.[116]

This statement is a response to numerous literary problems in *Likkutei MoHaRan*, for instance, (1) repetition of homilies in different versions, (2) R. Nahman's terse writing style compared to the lucid style of R. Nathan, and (3) innovation as the motivation of R. Nahman's alterations from oral discourse to written text. The statement itself, however, also raises several issues. For example, how are we to understand R. Nathan's description of R. Nahman's mind as "fluid"? The Hebrew term *rehitat mokho* suggests a quickness of thought, perhaps spontaneity, the product of a mind that could not be bothered with careful methodical thinking, much less writing.[117] The context of this description suggests that R. Nahman could not engage in reflection without innovation. That is, his mind was in a constant state of flux, making any transition from orality to literacy impossible. The result of this was that his own written versions of his oral discourses were very different in style than R. Nathan's "transcriptions" of those same discourses. Somewhat audaciously, R. Nathan argues that his versions were actually *more accurate* accounts of the oral discourse, capturing the oral moment more precisely than R. Nahman's own written versions. His decision to include both versions is based on his assumption that R. Nahman's altered versions exemplified yet another stage in R. Nahman's thinking. However, R. Nathan's versions were not solely his own. We are told that R. Nahman reviewed R. Nathan's drafts and suggested various changes that the disciple incorporated. This would imply that both versions were a step away from their oral origins. R. Nathan's versions captured the essence of the oral discourse, edited for clarity and style. R. Nahman's versions were his own reflections on his oral discourse, sometimes making substantive changes in order to more accurately make his point.

    R. Nathan was a well-trained literary stylist—he knew how to construct a written document out of an oral lecture. Moreover, he had a keen sense of R.

Nahman's own spontaneous mind. Coupled with his own patience, this enabled him to structure R. Nahman's spontaneity without compromising his creativity. When R. Nathan says his versions were "exactly what he heard from his holy mouth" he is probably not referring to the style and structure of the homily but only to its content. The perspicuity and lucidity of these homilies could have easily been the product of R. Nathan and not R. Nahman. R. Nathan knew that pure transcription could not easily result in a coherent, lucid written document. The authenticity of R. Nathan's "transcriptions" lies in R. Nahman's review of the material and his stamp of approval. R. Nahman, however, could not produce the styled writing of his disciple, making the transition from oral lecture to written homily as arduous and despicable task. It is thus very likely that the "internal review" of the homily, that is, that which slows the pace of the text and integrates disparate clusters, is the product of R. Nathan and not part of the original oral discourse. If one would look carefully at the homilies we have from the pen of R. Nahman, one would see that they are much less fluid, less repetitive, and less readable. R. Nathan's homilies in *Likkutei MoHaRan* (which make up the majority of the text) exhibit a similar style to his own *Likkutei Halakhot*.

Another way of translating the term *rehitat mokho* in R. Nathan's introduction is "impatience." This would suggest that R. Nahman could not concentrate on reproducing his oral discourse. For R. Nahman, the act of writing ideas that were previously spoken was a creative process that entailed rewriting, revision, and innovation. For such an impatient mind, the act of writing could only be creative and never merely an act of reproduction. This seems to be the implication behind R. Nathan's choice to include both versions of the identical homily in this collection. R. Nahman's changes were viewed by his disciple as a further elucidation of his original discourse, taking us back to the first part of the introduction where R. Nathan opens with the motif of concealing and revealing the primordial Torah. R. Nahman's impatient mind did not allow him to freeze this process, even when the price was accuracy and precision. Writing was awkward for him, as one can see from his terse and choppy style, precisely because it demanded decisions that he could not bear to make. In sum, a close reading of R. Nathan's introduction yields a picture of *Likkutei MoHaRan* as a text composed by two very different individuals. R. Nahman, whose impatient mind hampered his ability to master the precise and methodical act of writing, and R. Nathan, whose precision was able to take R. Nahman's improvisational spirit and create a literary document that reflected that spirit but harnessed it in the form of literature.

R. Nahman, reviewing the written version, must have agreed with R. Nathan's style, even though writing did not come easily for him. The written text is a product of R. Nahman's mind structured through R. Nathan's pen, without which the text could not adequately communicate the *torah* of the zaddik. "Regarding the writing of this holy book: many lessons he wrote himself, others were

written by disciples, the rest I [R. Nathan] wrote. He [R. Nahman] said that my
writing (lit. language) most accurately captured his intention."[118] This is further
substantiated in the following journal entry of R. Nathan. R. Nathan is speaking
about a series of conversations he had with R. Nahman after the latter's return
from Lemberg to receive medical treatment for his worsening condition.

> After returning from Lemberg, he strongly persuaded me to independently
> write down all of his *torah (hidushim)*. Before he left for Lemberg he would
> write down some of his teachings . . . but afterward he refused to write at
> all. I had a great deal of trouble writing down his *torah* alone, especially the
> lengthy ones he would teach during communal gatherings, such as Rosh
> Ha-Shana, Shabbat Hanukkah, and Shavout. God helped me gather my
> strength to convince him to review with me much of what he taught in
> public. Afterward I would write them alone and bring my drafts to him for
> his approval. . . . [119]

R. Nahman's return from Lemberg in 1807–1808 was momentous for his disciples. Although the definitive reason for his journey was never unearthed, all agree
it included seeking medical advice for his worsening condition of tuberculosis.[120]
His initial impetus to publish his writings started with his return from Erez Israel.
This was accelerated during and after his trip to Lemberg. Upon his return from
Lemberg he refused to write, perhaps realizing that his time was short. Although
his curious unwillingness to write after this trip remains a mystery, it resulted in
increased oral activity. Finding R. Nathan finally released him from the confines of
writing, an activity that never suited him.[121]

The Hasidic Proem:
From Midrash to Praxis

Many medieval and postmedieval homilies are structured along the lines of the
midrashic proem, a dominant literary form in Jewish late Antiquity.[122] Although
this form is not formally taught in institutions of Jewish learning *(yeshivot),* those
trained in rabbinic literature develop an intuitive inclination toward this form
resulting from years of reading, reflecting, and absorbing untold hours of oral
presentations *(drashot).* On the surface, many Hasidic homilies can be seen as
following the general proemic structure of Midrash. However, when looking more
closely at Hasidic literature we see that, for numerous reasons, it is not the best
exemplar of proemic discourse. First, the disciples who collected and subsequently
published the teachings of many of the early Hasidic masters paid little attention
to the literary and textual construction of these teachings.[123] As Zeev Gries has

succinctly put it, "early Hasidism did not consider the book an important tool for the dissemination of hasidic ideas or the construction of a distinctive community ethos; both of these functions were performed primarily by the circulation of oral traditions."[124] The master's personal stature, interpretive skill, and devotional message were far more important for the Hasidic redactor than the literary style of the text itself. Second, much of classical Hasidic texts in the early period were constructed long after the oral discourse on which it was based, often by a redactor who heard oral versions of the Hasidic teaching from others and then wrote them down.[125] In some cases we have earlier written documents, usually in the form of disciple's notebooks, which were collected and used by the editor in the construction of a Hasidic text.[126] In most cases, however, the transition from orality to text was not mediated by any preliminary written document.[127] There is often no original text.

*Likkutei MoHaRan* is unique in this regard for various reasons. First, as indicated in our discussion of R. Nathan's introduction, the text was carefully composed by R. Nathan and then reviewed by R. Nahman. Second, R. Nathan was scrupulous in his construction of the material, using various literary tools to both convey the creative genius of R. Nahman's mind and maximize the accessibility of his message to the widest audience. Third, in light of R. Nahman's emphasis on Torah innovation *(hiddushei torah)* and on R. Nathan's stance that this text *(Likkutei MoHaRan)* is the embodiment of the zaddik (R. Nahman), the text as literary document, in all of its facets, takes on additional significance. The holiness of *Likkutei MoHaRan,* like the holiness of any sacred text, is not subsumed in the message therein but includes the textuality of the text itself, including its literary form and structure and the hidden meanings buried under layers of textual complexity. When we speak of a sacred text in Judaism, the text *is* the message at least as much as the message it contains.[128]

The longer homilies in *Likkutei MoHaRan* utilize the basic proemic structure of classical Midrash with some significant alterations, illustrating the Hasidic emphasis on devotional piety rather than on purely exegetical reading. In the style of midrash, these homilies usually begin with a scriptural verse, known in midrashic parlance as the "close verse" (i.e., a verse relating to the weekly *Torah* portion being interpreted). The midrashic proem then continues with a "distant verse," usually from the later writings, which has no apparent relation to the "close verse." The body of the proem seeks to create a relation or context between these two verses so that we can expand the meaning of the former by rereading it through the lens of the latter.

Most of R. Nahman's longer homilies begin with a scriptural verse or, in some cases, a rabbinic or zoharic dictum.[129] Instead of continuing the proemic program with the "distant verse," R. Nahman usually substitutes a proclamation about divine worship, one that has no apparent relation to the close verse cited.

The body of the lesson unfolds as an elaborate exploration into this dimension of worship through the lens of the classical rabbinic and kabbalistic tradition, often wandering quite far from the initial verse but never abandoning it altogether. This journey gathers other dimensions of Jewish worship and practice, including holidays, mitzvot, and interpretations of biblical stories and rabbinic legends. Even in his most lengthy homilies, R. Nahman never severs his connection from the original "close verse," always returning to it in the summation of the homily. The body of these lessons I will call its "frame of meaning" that is devoted to a more complex and nuanced reading of his initial verse.[130] This alteration of the classical midrashic proem by substituting a devotional precept for a scriptural verse points to a more fundamental question regarding the relationship between the Hasidic proem in *Likkutei MoHaRan* and its midrashic antecedent.

My suggestion here is that Hasidic reading, *Likkutei MoHaRan* being a chief exemplar, is less interested in the text being read per se and more interested in the praxis that can emerge from the act of reading the text. R. Nahman's substitution of devotional advice for the distant verse of the midrashic proem illustrates his attempt to exhibit how reading can disclose new ways of serving God, and serving God (i.e., translating advice gleaned from exegesis) can uncover new ways of reading.[131] In weaving together devotional advice and sacred reading by including the former as part of the midrashic/Hasidic proem, R. Nahman changes the telos of reading "Jewishly." The catalyst for this shift in orientation is the zaddik and emphatically not the *Talmid Hakham* or "Torah Sage." This is because the ability to facilitate a transition from reading to praxis is not merely the product of textual expertise (exemplified in the Torah Sage), but requires a full integration/ embodiment of the textual tradition combined with personal piety. The result is that the interpreter transcends being a reader of the tradition and, in a sense, becomes his text. The authority of the zaddik does not rest on *what* he knows but *how* that knowledge has been absorbed and transformed. The claim is that the zaddik is able to reveal what cannot be learned cognitively through his intimacy with the text, becoming an incarnation of the textual tradition through revealing its secret message. This is different than the kabbalistic idea of decoding the encoded message of the text, a method common in religious esotericism. The zaddik does not teach us something embedded beneath the text's surface—he uses the text to teach us something outside the text. By embodying the text, his *torah* becomes Torah; his teaching becomes God's will.

Disclosing the esoteric meaning of the text may be the goal of certain kabbalistic traditions, but it is not the goal of R. Nahman's reading. For him, the zaddik translates this esoteric wisdom into devotional advice, leading the reader to see study as the vehicle for worship. By reading (exegesis), interpreting (esoteric knowledge), and translating (praxis) the text, the zaddik transforms the text he reads into an expression of himself. By reading the text of the zaddik, the disciple is therefore reading the zaddik. This intimacy between master and disciple is not attained solely as the result of hearing his words or even understanding his message.[132] It is by carefully reading and rereading his text. In my view, this is why R. Nathan was so careful in the construction of *Likkutei MoHaRan*. As stated earlier it was assumed, from the time of R. Nahman's illness, that no other zaddik would replace him. But the text, as an extension of R. Nahman himself, overcame any need for replacement.[133] "R. Nahman said, this entire book is mine/me *(sheli)*. If I did not exist this book would never exist in the world."[134] While the Torah sage may explain the intricacies of the textual tradition through his erudition, the zaddik serves as the translator of the tradition from text to praxis, illustrating how the nonhalakhic aspects of the Torah serve devotional ends and how the halakhic aspects of the Torah are only external constructs for devotional living.[135]

An illustration of the centrality of praxis in *Likkutei MoHaRan* can be seen in another innovation of the Hasidic proem, what I will call its "how-to" units. R. Nahman's homilies are broken up into various units or lemmas, separated by numbered paragraphs in the printed editions. The units have various forms; some are purely interpretive, some repeat and expand a connection rendered in an earlier unit, and some introduce an entirely different set of verses and devotional principles, loosely connected to what immediately preceded it. Almost all of these lengthy homilies contain practical units that usually come after a set of exegetical associations, resulting in a theoretical construct. These how-to units are transitional in nature in that they often serve to mediate between one exegetical frame and another.

Two examples will suffice to show how these how-to units function in the larger context of the lesson. In *Likkutei MoHaRan* I:6, R. Nahman begins his discourse with a verse from Deut. 31:14: *God said to Moses, the day of your death has come near, call Joshua and stand at the tent of meeting* . . . The first unit of this lesson begins with an unusually lengthy "distant devotional message" concerning the need to minimize one's own desire for honor in order to augment the glory of God. The "how-to" unit that supplements this devotional message reads as follows: "One can only merit this [glorification of God's name] through repentance. The fundamental principle of repentance is to hear an embarrassing comment [about oneself] and to remain silent . . ." This short aphorism is then followed by an elaborate combination of kabbalistic word plays and psycho/spiritualistic comments about the nature of the human heart. The heart is seen as the seat of the emotions of anger and revenge, those very emotions that need to be overcome in order to repent. The trope of silence, presented as the fundamental principle of repentance, becomes the dominant theme in this homily. "Silence leads to relinquishing one's appetites," "silence leads to expertise in halakha," "silence leads to the completing of the human form," "silence leads to reaching the celestial throne," and "silence leads to the stature of Moses." Each observation is preceded (or sometimes followed) by an exegetical prelude that connects each theme to silence. One of the more subtle things done here is that R. Nahman takes a halakhic principle, that is, repentance, and severs it from its halakhic moorings. The legal prescriptions for repentance, explicated most comprehensively by Maimonides in his *Mishneh Torah,* play no role in R. Nahman's discussion of devotional repentance in this homily. Repentance here is not about sin, nor is it conditional on sin.[136] Rather, it is the way to minimize one's stature, making room for the divine presence to inhabit the world. This homily is about "how to" repent devotionally, not halakhically.[137] The devotional construct of repentance is used later in the homily to understand the relationship between Moses and Joshua and the transmission of leadership in Deut. 31 (the close verse stated at the outset). Devotional repentance becomes the praxis of humility, the central characteristic of Moses as well as the challenge of the unique messianic zaddik, whose life is continuously challenged by his antagonists.[138]

The second example is from *Likkutei MoHaRan* I:24. The close verse *(pasuk ha-karov)* is Num. 8:2: *Speak to Aaron and say to him, "When you raise up the lamps, let the seven lamps give light at the front of the lampstand."* R. Nahman focuses on Rashi's use of a midrash that comments "the lights went up by themselves (i.e., miraculously, without Aaron's initiative)" (Num. 8:2).[139] The distant devotional fragment speaks about two kinds of human intellection, drawn from Ps. 139:5, *You hedge me before and behind, You lay your hand upon me.*[140] R. Nahman suggests that knowledge can be acquired in two distinct ways: (1) by means of a divine everflow *(shefa eloki)* or (2) by inspiration whereby the heart enables knowledge to "rise by itself" (evoking Rashi's comment to Num. 8:2). The first comes spontaneously while the latter requires both context and background *(hakdamot).* The idea that the heart can only be aroused to seek out God by way of an "unmediated divine consciousness" (the first way) is illustrated by various aspects of Jewish life, including the festival of Sukkot, and the sacred act of betrothal. These are not random deviations from the topic at hand, but are calculated hermeneutical steps, constructing a frame of meaning with arms that can extend and embrace an abundance of Jewish practices and reflection. These "how-to" units are used to show the reader how to take observations about devotion and to put them into practice.

In numerous instances, R. Nahman inserts different versions of these "how-to" units in order to illustrate how his original devotional advice can be embodied.

> Sometimes it happens that this everflow *(shefa eloki)* is concealed. This is the *behina* of pregnancy *(ibur).*[141] At that time, it is wonderful to scream, whether in prayer or study. Concealment as the *behina* of pregnancy can be seen from Deuteronomy 32:18, *You neglected the Rock that begot you,* read in light of Isaiah 37:3, *The babes have reached the birthstool, but the strength to give birth is lacking.* This is like a woman who is exhausted from labor. When she finally reaches the moment of giving birth she screams in 70

voices *(kolot),* that correlate to the 70 words of the Psalm *God will answer you.* Then she is able to give birth. . . . When a person experiences a lack or inability to understand, the scream he performs works like the scream of a woman giving birth . . . the scream is like the scream of the *Shekhina,* as if the *Shekhina* herself is screaming; at that moment understanding (*mohin,* consciousness) is born. This is what is meant by *the voice that awakens the kavanah (intention).* [142]

In this unit the theoretical precept about two distinct ways of human intellection has been transformed into an applied principle of devotional praxis. To argue that this practical application was merely a way of rendering his more theoretical message accessible to the masses is to underestimate the subtlety of R. Nahman's hermeneutical expertise. The practical application of a theoretical construct serves as a central part of his Hasidic proem, facilitating a relationship between reading and praxis that lies at the core of R. Nahman's thinking and constitutes the central contribution of the Hasidic zaddik. If the classical midrashist began with the assumption of the holistic nature of Scripture,[143] R. Nahman begins with the assumption that Scripture is geared toward revealing new ways of serving God, enabling Israel to embody the text through praxis illuminating the zoharic adage that "Israel, Torah, and God are One."[144] As with repentance, most of these "how-to" units are not halakhic but metahalakhic in nature; they deal with the psycho/spiritual way in which devotion is practiced.[145] R. Nahman's Hasidic proem turns midrash into performance, directing his readers to embody the text by seeing the ways in which the text informs their own spiritual struggles.

One can also say that halakha in *Likkutei MoHaRan* is viewed as the performative dimension of the internal psychic exercise of ascent and descent. In *Likkutei MoHaRan* I:6 on repentance, R. Nahman states that repentance requires expertise in halakha in the realms of both study and practice, enabling one to refine the dialectical quality necessary for devotional repentance. But what exactly does he mean by halakhic?

> Now, when a person wants to walk in the ways of repentance, he must be a *baki* (expert) in halakha. This demands that he have expertise in two areas: *baki b'razon* (expertise in running toward) and *baki b'shov* (expertise in return). This is reflected in Zohar 111.292a, "Deserving is one who enters and exists." This corresponds to the verse in Psalms 139:8, *If I ascend to heaven You are there,* referring to 'expertise in running toward'—*If I descend to Hell, here You are* reflects descent, of being, expert in returning.[146]

Even though one may study halakha in order to understand "what to do," in this passage R. Nahman is suggesting "how" the nature of this wisdom, that is, the knowledge of what is permitted and what is forbidden *('issur v' heter)*, enables one to live in a state where God is present by being perpetually destabilized *(razo ve'shov)*. The perception of perpetual motion results in the constant diminishing of self worth for the sake of God's glory. In R. Nahman's mind, the constant movement indicative of the angelic realm prevents the illusion of self importance. The drama of halakhic discourse via its constant intervention into the human psyche as well as one's behavior, provides a model of ascent and decent that R. Nahman holds is the key to humility and thus repentance. This is not because, as is conventionally thought, the halakhic life is obligatory and a fulfillment of divine will, but because such a life propels one's consciousness into a cycle of perceptual motion *(razo ve'shov)*, preventing the sedentary life of the mind that produces false certainty. In this manner the study and application of praxis *(halakha)* is seen through devotional (metahalakhic) lenses, reflecting the psychic state necessary for true worship.

Perfecting the Imagination:
*Behina* as a Literary Trope of Revision
and Reconstruction

One of the more elusive and difficult dimensions of *Likkutei MoHaRan* is its use of term *behina* as a literary trope connecting apparent disparate words, verses, or ideas. The word itself can be defined in various ways, including "realm," "aspect," "dimension," "embodiment," "correlate," "likened to," and "as it is written" *(k'mo shkatuv)*. The term became popularized by R. Moses Cordovero, who used it extensively in his *magnum opus Pardes Rimonim* to define six basic aspects of divine emanation, perhaps best translated as valences, which trace the unfolding of one thing into another. In his attempt to translate this kabbalistic model for his own literary purposes, Harold Bloom likened Cordovero's *behinot* to his own notion of "revisionary ratios."[147] In *Kabbala and Criticism* Bloom attempts to show the ways in which the kabbalistic imagination reflects the poetic mind in that both dwell in an anxiety of reading against the past by reading out of the past. The poet is caught between the past that binds her and the creative impulse that propels her. The past cannot be discarded as it serves as the foundation of the poet's vision of the world but it cannot be repeated as its flaws become too acute to be reproduced. The following is one passage that succinctly summarizes his project.

the configurations or *behinot* [of a sephirah or poem] are precisely tropes, the figurative language that is nearly identical with all poetry. If we vary the analogical identification, and say that each *Sephirah* is a single mind or consciousness, then the *behinot* function as psychic defenses. But trope and defense are held together in the verbal image . . . and every intra-textual image is necessarily what I have called a "revisionary ratio," measuring the relationship between two or more texts. The sequence of Cordovero's revisionary ratios or *behinot* is one that I have found crucially instructive, for in this sequence I believe that Cordovero uncovered the normative structure of images, of tropes and psychic defenses, in many central revisionary texts, including many poems of the last three centuries.[148]

Without digressing too much into Cordovero's use of this term (which is quite different than R. Nahman's), his basic point is to outline kabbalistic notions of Bloom's extentiation that enables something to emerge and achieve attenuated independence while still containing the essence of its source.[149] *Extentiation* is a term used to communicate the delicate nature of emanation whereby one thing brings forth another. This dialectical nature of independence and relation stands at the heart of the kabbalistic notion of creativity. Emanation without independence (repetition) would be futile in that it would not foster creativity. Emanation that results in radical independence (rupture/heresy) would be destructive in that it would require negation as a prerequisite for innovation.[150] Bloom's definition of *behina* as revision, filled with its "anxiety of influence," sheds new light on the kabbalistic tension between the Creator (God) and creativity (cosmos/humanity). According to the basic theosophical idea that each stage of any emanation includes all subsequent stages, Cordovero delineates six basic movements that describe the ways in which something internal to one stage of extentiation is externalized and then liberated from the confines of its predecessor.

Bloom understands these movements *(behinot)* as creative "revisions of the past" that result in a "double priority," a commitment to reading (text) and misreading (creative interpretation/revision).[151] If reading fails to yield independence from the text being read it has no constructive purpose (repetition). If the reading is *too* strong, its own existence becomes conditional on erasing the past (heresy). Bloom's distinction between heresy and revision may be useful here. "Heresy resulted, generally, from a change in emphasis, while revisionism follows received doctrine along to a certain point, and then deviates, insisting that a wrong direction was taken just at that point, and no other."[152] Bloom suggests that the distinction between heresy and originality lies in the difference between emphasis and deviance. A shift in emphasis (e.g., radical messianism) may result in making the precursor subservient to the new agenda, narrowing the trajectory of the tradition. This may be seen (from a Jewish perspective) in early Christian interpretations of the classical prophets, Paul's interpretation of the law, and the messianic theology of Shabbati Zevi. Deviance is less radical in that it adopts the precursor (to a point), expanding its elasticity but never overcoming its basic principles. This is seen as a corrective movement, swerving away from the precursor while taking the precursor with it.[153] Creative reading occurs via revision that balances repetition and effacement. For Cordovero *behina* is the product of internal movement within a particular *sephirotic* cluster as it moves outward. For Bloom this internal movement is a trope for "strong poetry," the model of creative interpretation (originality).

I would suggest that R. Nahman's use of the term *behina* serves as a bridge between Cordovero's theosophical principle and Bloom's literary/interpretive one. R. Nahman overcomes Cordovero's formalistic usage of the term yet falls short of adopting Bloom's purely interpretive scheme. For R. Nahman *behina* is a literary tool of reconstruction rather than interpretation. By this I mean that *behina* is used to construct the revised text of tradition (*Likkutei MoHaRan,* the *torah* of the zaddik) from the deconstructed fragments of tradition that serve as its core, enabling concealed elements of a word or phrase to emerge via their juxtaposition to another idea, all filtered through the vehicle of the refined imagination of the zaddik. Whereas Cordovero used *behina* to explain how the new emerges from the old in the process of extentiation, R. Nahman uses this term as a vehicle for "strong reading" in order to liberate the reader from the exegetical confines of midrash and Kabbala while keeping her within the confines of the normative behavioral tradition.[154] R. Nahman's purpose, as I see it, is to expand the elasticity of the textual tradition in order to absorb the freewheeling nature of the human imagination.[155] He defines his teachings this way:

> My teachings are like a palace containing halls and chambers, exedras and mosaics—all of them beautiful, wondrous, awe-inspiring. And there are staircases upon staircases, each of them novel and terrible. The moment one enters a room and begins to look around, wondering at all the marvels it holds, at that very instant he sees a fantastic passage has opened before him to another room, and so from room to room. . . .[156]

The use of *behinot* opens these doors, doors that only appear at the instant one "looks around" the series of associations and connections made, all of which present possibilities of thinking the tradition anew that were never before possible. Perhaps this is what R. Nahman meant when he said that his *torah* contained lessons ("fantastic passages") heretofore concealed.

This imaginative associative reading also has an erotic dimension: each text submits to its reader's imagination, so the more imaginative/seductive the reader, the more the text opens to being transformed. The three parts of conventional midrashic and kabbalistic reading, text, reader, and laws of exegesis or cosmological doctrines—are overcome, leaving the text alone with the reader's imagination. As opposed to classical midrash, the imagination of the reader is no longer bound to justify her reading by the textual tradition. R. Nahman's use of *behinot* exhibits a kind of "quasi-antinomian reading" whereby the interpreter is liberated from the "laws" of exegetical principles and/or the symbolic doctrines of the Kabbala yet bound to the behavioral norms and doctrines that are derived from these "laws." This results in an anxiety of being caught between adherence to the tradition, both normatively and structurally, and one's own imagination, which demands freedom from these strictures.[157] The anxiety of such a reading is that the *behinot* connections are always built upon some midrashic or kabbalistic observation or inference. The perfected imagination of the zaddik is saturated with the symbols and referents of tradition, yet he cannot be bound by them. While his imagination is bound by the tradition, he is free to work creatively to expand those boundaries. Even as his imagination sometimes challenges these limits, it does so in relation and not external to those boundaries. The zaddik transcends the "law" of reading while remaining under its influence. This, I would argue, is the foundation of R. Nahman's notion of *hiddushei torah* (Torah innovations).

The use of *behinot* as a literary trope is indicative of a vibrant and daring imagination. For R. Nahman the imaginative faculty, which is the foundation of his quasi-antinomian reading, is dangerous and seductive in that it contains the possibility of both illusion and heresy. In order to understand the *torah* of the zaddik, and to subsequently partake of one's own associative reading, one must rectify one's imaginative faculty by means of commitment to the zaddik who serves as the "the master of the imagination [*koah ha'medame*]" similar to the way in which the rabbinic sage functioned as the "master of the law."[158] The zaddik makes his associative imagination the basis of his rewriting of the tradition. This is not meant to confine the reader by dictating doctrine or law but to free her by training her to read the way the zaddik does, yet always within the margins of the zaddik's authoritative voice.

We must remember that R. Nahman assumes his audience is well versed in traditional literature and has a keen sense of how the midrashic mind works. The anxiety of being on "the narrow bridge" between the hallowed past and the uncharted territory of the future also emerges in his homiletic style. He lures his readers into his own creative imaginings by using two different literary techniques, which I will call the "lexicographical" and "ideational/devotional." The first is taken from midrash and classical kabbalistic exegesis, both of which use the words as connectors or signifiers, placing disparate verses together via common words.[159] Traditional readers of *Likkutei MoHaRan* will feel at home with this as it reflects literature they are accustomed to reading. The second is more ambiguous, constituting what Arthur Green calls "associative reading." This type of reading may be called "psychological-translation," that is, translating the world of the text (and its interpretive history) through the imagination of the reader without the aid of traditional exegetical tools.[160]

The lexicographical model, whether midrashic or kabbalistic, uses an external collection of laws (midrashic/exegetical principles) and/or terms (Kabbala) to interpret a particular text. The ideational/devotional model has no external "system" or rules the reader could consult in order to justify the logic of the connections being made. Even though extensive knowledge of the midrashic and kabbalistic tradition will help in understanding the possible basis for these connections, they cannot plumb the depths of R. Nahman's own imaginative reading and will only provide partial answers to his hermeneutical moves. The reader is left to create her own justifications for unexplained associations, using her own imagination (and knowledge of tradition) to construct foundations for R. Nahman's associative jumps.[161] These unexplained associations are not the result of an unfinished or unrefined literary product but are left ambiguous in order to enable the reader to develop her own imaginative world, emulating the text by understanding it and then creating from it. R. Nahman, in defining *hiddushei torah*, illustrates Harold Bloom's notion of misreading as the basis of originality.

> I heard this from one [of his disciples] that he [R. Nahman] implored him to study his Torah very carefully. He said to him, "It would be good if you are able to understand my intentions. However, even if you do not, it is worthwhile to bring forth some new element of Torah [from studying them]. This is a great fixing for extraneous thoughts *(hirhurim)*. Thoughts emerge from the imaginative faculty. Bringing forth new elements of Torah *(hidushei torah)* is the *behina* of imagining one thing into/from another. This rectifies the blemish of Thought which comes into existence through the imagination."[162]

The unfinished text remains opaque unless we emulate the author. Yet even emulating the zaddik does not insure we will understand his intention. For one in pursuit of *hidushei torah* (originality), authorial intention is irrelevant. What matters is to engage in the imaginative process of Torah study in order to purify our imaginations that are filled with extraneous thoughts. Ora Wiskind-Elper puts it this way: "Reb Nahman teaches that innovation is an existential necessity; the very nature of the revealed Written Torah mandates a continually new reading."[163] The reason why R. Nahman constantly warns his readers to "read and reread my book" is that such activity perfects the imagination in order to merit *hidushei torah*. Engaging in this imaginative process also results in emulating the zaddik, whose imaginative faculty has enabled him to transcend conventional forms of Jewish reading.

This points, I believe, to R. Nahman's radical understanding of *hidushei torah* (innovative Torah insights). The term usually refers to the discovery of some original insight through conventional forms of Jewish reading (midrash/Kabbala). For R. Nahman, *hidushei torah* is also a new way of (imaginative) reading, resulting in original insights never before revealed. R. Nahman implies that since the Torah itself is infinite, conventional ways of reading cannot fully unearth its depths. This is because traditional readers are confined by external principles (laws of exegesis) necessary to protect the Torah from distortion. The price paid for such necessary conservatism is limited access to the Torah's depths. These confines were loosened by the Zohar, Luria, and the Besht, yet they, in their own ways, still limited the full expression of the imagination. R. Nahman, who saw himself as the final arbiter of this messianic process of imaginative perfection, perfects this quality in himself and teaches others to do the same by challenging them to understand (or misunderstand) his teaching, which is simultaneously free-form and rooted in the principles of the tradition. The literary trope that brings this new *hidush* into existence is the *behina* or "ideational/devotional connection," which frees the imagination while securing it against nonheretical conclusions.

As a Hasidic master who lived and taught in a highly restrictive society, R. Nahman could easily be construed as ultraconservative in his unrelenting devotion to halakha and adherence to the doctrinal beliefs of traditional Judaism. However, his apparent conservative agenda is, in actuality, quite radical. It is a rewriting of the tradition from the tradition itself, a revision of Torah that may be called "Torah's alterego." This revision cannot be enacted solely by conventional exegetical means (midrash) nor by the extension of a previous revision, that is, the Kabbala. It requires a new "way" of reading to emerge from the recesses of the perfected imagination, incorporating the liberated creativity of the zaddik. The innovative use of *behina* in *Likkutei MoHaRan* serves as the literary tool of such a revision. Its antinomian character is that it stretches preexisting boundaries of Jewish hermeneutics by challenging the elasticity of the sacred canon in three ways. First, new dimensions of divine worship are constructed. The external piety of the Kabbala in the form of custom and ritual and its cosmic justification is extended to include an internal psychological component. Second, the reader attaches herself to the zaddik by entering and emulating his imagination through careful study of the externalized text. Intimacy with the text is likened to intimacy with the psyche of the zaddik. Third, the reader's imaginative faculty is sharpened and purified by emulating the perfected imagination of the zaddik. The text teaches its reader how to read imaginatively.

Perhaps when R. Nahman says "all of my *torah* is *behinot*"[164] he means that his use of *behinot* makes his *torah* possible. That is, revealing that which has never been revealed can only happen by reading "outside" conventional modes of reading. This is what Bloom calls "revision" and R. Nahman calls *hidushei torah* (innovation). For R. Nahman, the logic of midrashic reading must give way to the imagination of associative reading. This requires the rectification of the imaginative faculty, the quality that he claimed to possess and transmit to his readers through his text. It is precisely this quality that he thought, in his more optimistic moments, would yield a redemptive community. "He said, in the future the entire world will be Bratslaver Hasidim, as the midrash states on the verse *I gave you a heart of flesh* (Ezekiel 36:26) do not read 'heart of flesh' *(basar)* but 'heart of gladness' *(bosar).*" The letters for "a heart of gladness [*bosar*]" (LV BSR) are the letters of Bratslav (BRSLV)."[165]

## Notes

1. There is a vast corpus of scholarly literature on R. Nahman and the Bratslav tradition. Three recent studies of note are Arthur Green's *Tormented Master* (Alabama, 1979); Joseph Weiss's *Studies in Bratslav Hasidism* (Jerusalem, 1974); and Mendel Piekarz's *Studies in Bratslav Hasidism* (Jerusalem, 1972). The Breslov Research Institute in Jerusalem has undertaken a large translation project of R. Nahman's collected teachings, *Likkutei MoHaRan,* and publishes a wide variety of popular literature based on his teachings.

2. On the publication of *Likkutei MoHaRan* see Weiss, *Studies,* pp. 251–277.

3. This topic has already been discussed by Zeev Gries. See his *Sifrut ha-Hanhagot* (Jerusalem, 1989), pp. 249–275. Gries focuses primarily on comparing *Likkutei MoHaRan* to the advice literature in the Bratslav tradition. In this study I explore the theoretical underpinning of the ways in which praxis is implemented into R. Nahman's hermeneutical agenda.

4. See Gries, *The Book in Early Hasidism* (Hebrew) (Tel Aviv, 1992), esp. pp. 49–53, 56–59, 64, 65. Cf. Green, "On Translating Hasidic Homilies," *Prooftexts* 3 (1983): 63–72; William Graham, *Beyond the Written Word* (Cambridge, Mass., 1987), pp. 9–44; Walter J. Ong, *Orality and Literacy* (London and New York, 1982), pp. 31–42; Richard Palmer, *Hermeneutics* (Evanston, Ill., 1969), p. 16; and Paul Riceour, *Interpretation Theory* (Fort Worth, Tex., 1976), pp. 25–44. Plato, in the *Phaedrus,* emphasizes the "lost power" that results from writing that which is originally oral. This diminution of power resulting from writing as "imitation" is developed in Jaques Derrida's discussion of Rousseau. See Derrida, *Of Grammatology,* trans. Gayatri Chakravorty Spivak (Baltimore and London, 1974), pp. 95–268. In Hasidism, Gries notes, many Hasidic masters, who understood the performative power of oral expression, often refused to participate in the written transcriptions of their teaching, even as many did not actively prevent the publication of such texts.

5. See *Hayye MoHaRan* (Jerusalem, 1996), "Journey to Lemberg," # 3, *Yemei MoRaNat* (Jerusalem, 1997), I # 26. Cf. Weiss, "The Order of Printing the First Volume of *Likkutei MoHaRan*" (Hebrew) in *Studies,* pp. 251–257.

6. On this see C. Shmeruk, *Sifrut Yiddish b'Polin* (Jerusalem, 1981), pp. 43–63; J. Gartner, "*Seudat Shlishit:* Halakhic Perspectives" (Hebrew) *Sidra* 6 (1990): 5–24; Green, "On Translating Hasidic Homilies," pp. 63–72; and Gries,

"The Hasidic Managing Editor as an Agent of Culture," in *Hasidism Reappraised,* ed. Ada Rapoport-Albert (London, 1997), pp. 141–155.

7. On the lack of emphasis on the "text" in Hasidism, see Gries, *Book in Early Hasidism,* pp. 47–67.

8. Susan Handelman, *Slayers of Moses* (Albany, 1982), esp. pp. 51–82; Daniel Boyarin, *Intertexuality and Midrash* (Bloomington, Ind., 1990); Steven Fraade, *From Tradition to Commentary* (Albany, 1982), Michael Fishbane, *The Garments of Torah* (Bloomington, Ind., 1989), David Stern, *Midrash and Theory* (Evanston, Ill., 1996), and Betty Rojtman *Black Fire on White Fire* (Berkeley, 1998). Cf. the collection of essays in Geoffrey Hartman and Sanford Budick, eds., *Midrash and Literature* (New Haven, 1986).

9. See Fishbane, *Garments of Torah,* pp. 19–32; and Stern, *Midrash and Theory,* pp. 15–38.

10. I would exclude Lurianic Kabbala as its own way of reading Scripture is, in my opinion, a significant departure from the Zohar. On the Zohar, see E. R. Wolfson, "Beautiful Maiden Without Eyes: Peshat and Sod in Zoharic Hermeneutics," in *The Midrashic Imagination,* ed. Fishbane (Albany, 1993), pp. 155–204. In Lurianic Kabbala, see my article "From Theosophy to Midrash: Lurianic Exegesis and the Garden of Eden," *AJS Review* 22:1 (1997): 37–75.

11. On this see Moshe Idel, " PaRDes: Some Reflections on Kabbalistic Hermeneutics" in *Death, Ecstasy, and Other Worldly Journeys,* eds. Fishbane and J. Collins (Albany, N.Y., 1995), pp. 249–268.

12. See Yehuda Liebes, "Myth vs. Symbol in the Zohar and in Lurianic Kabbala," in *Essential Papers in Kabbala,* ed. L. Fine (New York, 1995), pp. 212–242. Cf. Idel, "PaRDes," pp. 252, 253. Joseph Dan argues that this is the case for Jewish mysticism in late antiquity as well.

> They [Hekhalot mystics] did not utilize the midrashic methods in order to glean truth from the ancient texts; instead they claimed that, by using their methodologies, a person may be elevated to the highest realms and that divine truth will be revealed to him in an immediate, colorful and exhilarating experience . . . this is an extreme denial of the most important norms of Rabbinic Judaism, a negation of the Midrash, and an insistence on a better way for the knowledge of God to be revealed to them.

See Dan, "Jewish Mysticism in Late Antiquity: An Introduction," in *idem, Jewish Mysticism: Late Antiquity* (New Jersey, 1998), p. xxii.

13. On intratextuality and interpretation see Harold Bloom, *The Anxiety of Influence* (New York, 1973), pp. 5–7. Cf. Idel, "PaRDes," pp. 257–259; Fishbane, *The Exegetical Imagination* (Cambridge, Mass., 1998), pp. 105–122; Elliot R. Wolfson, "Maiden Without Eyes"; and Magid, "From Theosophy to Midrash," pp. 43–49.

14. See Yehuda Liebes, "*De Natura Dei:* On the Development of the Jewish Myth," in *Studies in Jewish Myth and Jewish Messianism,* trans. Batya Stein (Albany, 1993), pp. 1–64.

15. On myth and Kabbala see Gershom Scholem, "Kabbala and Myth," in *On the Kabbala and Its Symbolism* (New York, 1965), pp. 100–117; Liebes, "Myth vs. Symbol in the Zohar and in Lurianic Kabbala," pp. 212–233; and idem, "The Kabbalistic Myth as Told to Orpheus," ibid., pp. 65–92. For an important study on the way in which Kabbalists use rabbinic myth see E. R. Wolfson, "The Face of Jacob in the Moon: Mystical Transformations of an Aggadic Myth" in *The Seductiveness of Jewish Myth,* ed. S. Daniel Breslaur (Albany, 1997), pp. 235–270.

16. Idel, "PaRDeS," p. 257.

17. On this see Betty Roitman, "Sacred Language and Open Text," in *Midrash and Literature,* pp. 165, 166.

18. It is interesting that although he was the great-grandson of the Baal Shem Tov from his mother's side and the early Hasidic master R. Nahman Horedenka from his father's side he almost never refers to the early Hasidic tradition, even as some early texts were in print during his formative years.

19. See Fishbane, *Garments of Torah,* pp. 33–48; and Marc-Alain Ouaknin, *The Burnt Book* (Princeton, 1986), pp. 261f.

20. Note Yehudah Liebes, "Myth vs. Symbol"; and E. R. Wolfson, "Weeping, Death and Spiritual Ascent in Sixteenth Century Jewish Mysticism" in *Death, Ecstasy and Other Worldly Journeys,* pp. 209–247. Boyarin, *Intertextuality and Midrash,* p. 25 wants to distinguish between poetics and hermeneutics, seeing midrash largely as a product of the latter.

21. Green, *Tormented Master,* pp. 135–181; and idem, "Typologies of Leadership and the Hasidic Zaddik," in *Jewish Spirituality II,* ed. Green (New York, 1989), pp. 127–156 . Cf. Nathanel Deutsch's chapter in this volume.

22. Julia Kristeva, *Semiotike* (Paris, 1969), p. 146, "every text builds itself as a mosaic of quotations, [an] absorption and transformation of another text" cited in Boyarin, *Intertextuality and Midrash,* pp. 22, 135 n. 2. See also idem. p. 14 where he makes a stronger case about the inevitability of intertextuality regarding literature in general. To some degree, this is aligned with Bloom's notion of "misreading" and affinity that Boyarin chooses not to make, although he does equivocate Bloom's statement about "antithetical meaning" on p. 79.

23. Although it is often cited that R. Nahman's teaching was "a commentary to Luria's *Etz Hayyim,*" R. Nahman often spoke against the sustained study of Kabbala. See, for example, *Hayye MoHaRan,* # 521.

24. Fishbane, for example, suggests that the zoharic model of kabbalistic exegesis embodies the notion of "exegetical spirituality" whereby the reader is uplifted through the very act of kabbalistic reading. See Fishbane, *Exegetical Imagination,* pp. 105, 121. Wolfson, also speaking about the Zohar, suggests that

the exegetical narrative of the Zohar, utilizing midrashic and symbolic models of reading the classical tradition, is an attempt to reenact the revelation at Sinai "in a decidedly visual sense." See Wolfson, *Through a Speculum that Shines* (Princeton, 1994), p. 377, "It is through the interpretation of the Torah, in accord with kabbalistic principles, that the mystic participates again in the act of revelation, now understood in a decidedly visual sense." p. 384. "From these passages [Zohar 2.2a, Zohar Hadash 105a] it is clear that mystic contemplation, *interpretive in nature* [italics mine], is a visual sort of comprehension." Cf. idem., "Weeping, Death and Spiritual Ascent in 16th. Century Jewish Mysticism," p. 211.

25. On this see Alyssa Quint's translation of Hillel Zeitlin's chapter in this volume. Cf. Ouaknin, *Burnt Book,* pp. 276–278.

26. All of Bratslav's advice literature was written by disciples except R. Nahman's *Sefer Ha-Middot* (Mahalav, 1811). See Gries, *Sifrut Ha-Hanhagot* (Jerusalem, 1989), pp. 249–275. On the relationship between Kabbala and praxis see Idel, *Kabbala: New Perspectives* (New Haven, 1988), pp. 150–153 and idem, "PaRDeS," p. 263.

27. On R. Nahman's expressed desire to have an abbreviated version of his teachings published, see *Yemei MoHaRaNat* I # 7, p. 14, "In the year 1805 he [R. Nahman] told me to write the practical advice from all of his lessons. I began to write and showed him my first gleaning, which he received with disapproval. Afterward I understood what he intended and I returned and wrote this again. This second version met with his approval and became *Kizur Likkutei MoHaRan.*" Gries argues that this first version that R. Nahman did not approve of was subsequently published after his death by R. Nathan under the title *Likkutei Ezot.* See his *Behavior Literature: Its History and Place in the Life of Beshtean Hasidism* (Hebrew) (Jerusalem, 1990), pp. 232–234. Chaim Kramer sees the history of *Likkutei Ezot* differently. In *Between Fire and Water* (Jerusalem and New York, 1992), p. 358, based on R. Nathan's letters collected in *Alim L'Terufa* (Jerusalem, 1930) and *Yemei MoHaRaNat,* # 107–111, Kramer claims that *Likkutei Ezot* was *written* after R. Nahman's passing.

28. The perfection of the imaginative faculty as a prelude to the messianic era plays a central role in R., Nahman's thinking. See, for example, in *Likkutei MoHaRan* (L.M.), I:25, 2, I:50, 9, II: 5,9. On the messianic underpinnings of the tales see Ora Wiskind-Elper, *Tradition and Fantasy in the Tales of Reb Nahman of Bratslav* (Albany, 1998), pp. 26–33.

29. See, for example, L.M. II:105.

30. Green suggested to me in private conversation that the earlier interpretations of the Raba bar bar Hana aggadot may have been the bridge from R. Nahman's homiletic writings to his thirteen tales.

31. R. Nathan Sternharz, "Introduction to *Likkutei MoHaRan,*" p. 3.

32. In the Zohar and Lurianic Kabbala, the realm of *Atik Yomin* is the divine realm that remains concealed, that which has not yet emanated into the

world. Cf. *Likkutei MoHaRan* I:21, 9, I:60, 6. This redemptive notion of *Atik Yomin,* or *Atika Kadisha* has found expression in many texts influenced by the Zohar and Lurianic tradition. See, for example, Idel, *Messianic Mystics* (New Haven, 1998), p. 194 and the text by R. Kolonymnous Kalman Epstein of Cracow, *Me'or ve Shemesh,* cited and discussed by Idel on pp. 287, 288.

33. See *Hayye MoHaRan,* # 253. There are traditions that claim that the Besht is a unique individual, one who has never existed in the past and will never against exist (until the Messiah). See the introduction to the 1815 Kopys edition of *Shivhei Ha-Besht* (rpt. Tel Aviv, 1961). This introduction is reproduced in the English edition *In Praise of the Baal Shem Tov,* trans. Ban-Amos and Mintz (Bloomington, Ind., 1970), p. 2, "Thus it was that the word of God was given to the Baal Shem Tov. None of the ancients were like him, nor will there be any like him upon the earth." On an analysis of this statement in context see Ada Rapoport-Albert, " Hasidism After 1772: Structural Continuity and Change," in *Hasidism Reappraised,* ed. Rapoport-Albert, p. 80 n. 10.

34. On this see Yehuda Liebes, *Studies in the Zohar* (Albany, 1993), pp. 48, 49. Cf. Zohar III:152a.

35. Zohar III:130b. Cf. Liebes, *Studies in the Zohar,* p. 48, "We find then, that the Torah of *Atik Yomin* has two aspects, one that comes to expression in *Idra Rabba* and another that will be revealed in the future time of the Messiah." In one sense, R. Nahman also viewed himself as a proto-Messiah, becoming more desperate and hopeless about his messianic vocation as his health deteriorated. Yet R. Nathan may have viewed *Likkutei MoHaRan* as the center of R. Nahman's messianic project that contained the totality of the messianic Torah of *Atik* that needs to be disclosed through in-depth study and living according to its precepts.

36. See *Hayye MoHaRan,* "The Greatness of His Torah and Holy Stories," # 353, p. 348.

37. See Green, "The Zaddik as *Axis Mundi* in Later Judaism," *Journal of the American Academy of Religion* 45:3 (1977): 327–347.

38. See Mendel Piekarz, "The Messianic Idea in the Beginning of Hasidism Through the Prism of *Drush* and *Mussar* Literature" (Hebrew) in *The Messianic Idea in Israel: Studies in Honor of the 80ᵗʰ Birthday of Gershom Scholem* (Hebrew) (Jerusalem, 1990) pp. 237–254; and idem. "The Turn in the Messianism in Bratslav Hasidism" (Hebrew) in *Messianism and Eschatology* (Jerusalem, 1994), pp. 325–342. Cf. Green, *Tormented Master,* pp. 182–221.

39. This softening takes place in Polish Hasidism in the nineteenth century, largely through the Przysucha tradition of the "Holy Jew," R. Isaac Jacob Rabinowitz and his disciple R. Simha Bunim of Przysucha. See Aaron Ascoli, *Hasidut B'Polin* (rpt. Jerusalem, 1999), pp. 62–77; and Alan Brill, "Grandeur and Humility in the Writings of R. Simha Bunim of Przysucha," in *Hazon Nahum,* eds. Y. Elamn and J.S. Gurock (New York, 1997), pp. 419–448.

40. It is worth mentioning that Edith Wyschogrod has recently argued that

"sainthood," as an embodied textuality, is an important part of the postmodern turn. See Edith Wyschogrod, *Saints and Postmodernism* (Chicago and London, 1990), esp. pp. 1–30. For a more general discussion see *Sainthood: Its Manifestations in World Religions,* eds. R. Kieckhefer and G.D. Bond (Berkeley and Los Angeles, 1988).

41. See Weiss, "R. Nahman and the Dispute About Him" (Hebrew), in *Studies,* pp. 42–57.

42. *Hayye MoHaRan, #* 340, p. 241. Cf. Micha Ankori, *Heights of Heaven and Depth of Hell* (Hebrew) (Tel Aviv, 1994), pp. 33, 36.

43. Green has noted that R. Nahman's imagination and quick associative mind most resembles the mind of the *Tikkunei Zohar,* whose connections are often looser and less developed than other parts of zoharic literature. Such a conjecture can be substantiated, I believe, by the fact that R. Nahman had a particular inclination for the *Tikkunim.* See *Hayye MoHaRan, #* 359, "He once told us. . . . the world thinks that the Zohar and the Tikkunei Zohar are equal in stature. We understood from his words that there was a significant difference between the holy Zohar and the Tikkunim. Even though the Zohar is very holy [he said], it has no value juxtaposed to the holy secrets of the Tikkunei Zohar."

44. In fact, many of his longer homilies repeat this form throughout, always playing between devotional behavior and scriptural, rabbinic, and zoharic verses.

45. A similar idea was expressed by Emmanuel Levinas in response to a question as to whether he was a "Jewish" philosopher. "I am a Jew, and certainly I have lectures, contacts, and traditions that are specifically Jewish which I do not renounce. But I protest against that formula when one understands by it someone who dares to approach concepts as based solely on traditions and religious texts, without endeavoring to subject them to a philosophical critique." See Francois Poirie, *Emmanuel Levinas—Qui stes-vous?* (La Manufacture, 1987), p. 13 cited in Ze'ev Levy, "Emmanuel Levinas as a Jewish Philosopher," in *Hazon Nahum* (New York, 1997), pp. 580–581. For definitions of "reason" and "rationality" that may be useful for our analysis of R. Nahman's work see Benjamin Ish-Shalom's description of these terms in his study on Rabbi Abraham Isaac Ha-Kohen Kook, *Rav Avraham Itzhak Ha-Cohen Kook: Between Mysticism and Rationalism* (Albany, 1993), pp. 175–180.

46. On the authority of Kabbala as equal to Scripture itself in Hasidic literature see Idel, "PaRDes," p. 263. Cf. idem., *Kabbala: New Perspectives,* pp. 150–153.

47. Isaac Heinemann, *Darkei Aggadah* (Jerusalem, 1970), p. 23.

48. Boyrain, *Intertextuality,* pp. 23, 24.

49. Ibid., p. 6–10.

50. Ibid. p. 24.

51. Bloom, *Anxiety of Influence,* pp. 10f.

52. Bloom defines "facticity" as "a state of being caught up in factuality or contingency which is an inescapable and unalterable context." See Bloom, *Ruin the Sacred Truths: Poetry and Belief From the Bible to the Present* (Cambridge, Mass., 1987), p. 7. What I take Bloom to mean is that "facticity" paralyzes the writer and poet from saying anything that rubs against the accepted sacredness of the text being read. Facticity can only then yield repetition. According to this observation, the sacrality of the text prevents *hidush* (innovation). Originality, on the other hand, demands the writer and poet to break out of the "sacredness" of the text without destroying it. Excess originality results in heresy. Bloom argues elsewhere that originality is the first step toward heresy in that it steps out the sacred in order to take it further.

53. Bloom, *Anxiety of Influence,* pp. 14–16. The revisionist ratios in Bloom's early work are then transposed onto his theory of kabbalistic reading elaborated in his *Kabbala and Criticism* (New York, 1975), esp. pp. 52–71.

54. See, for example, L.M. I:61 much of which responds to the vehement critique against his leadership. Cf. Weiss, *Studies,* pp. 42–57. R. Nahman maintained that the antagonism against him was the necessary result of his uniqueness. See *Hayye MoHaRan,* # 392–402.

55. *Hayye MoHaRan,* # 401. Cf. L.M. I: 161, "Controversy *(makhloket)* elevates one's spirit. . . ."

56. On the necessity of *makhloket* see L.M. I:64, para 4, I: 114, 208, 377, II:13; and Ouaknin, *Burnt Book,* pp. 282–285.

57. See L.M. I:63, 1, II: 75. The suffering servant motif, taken from Isa. 53, appears in Moed Katan 28a and plays a prominent role in the Zohar. See Zohar 1.65a, 2.10b, 53a, 3.71–72. For some other sources see Gries, *Sifrut Ha-Hanhagot,* p. 256 n. 29.

58. Ouaknin, *Burnt Book,* p. 288.

59. *Sihot Ha-Ran* # 267. Cf. L.M. I:281. Ouaknin, *Burnt Book,* calls this passage "A Manifesto for the Right to Subjectivity."

60. Bloom, *Ruin the Sacred Truths,* pp. 4–24; and Susan Handelman, *Slayers of Moses,* pp. 191–193. The nature of R. Nahman's "heretical bent" is part of what was attractive to modern Jewish thinkers, from Hillel Zeitlin to Buber to Green. See Green, *Tormented Master,* pp. 285–336; and Eliezer Schweid, *Jewish Thought in the 20th Century: An Introduction,* trans. Amnon Hadary (Atlanta, Ga.,1992), pp. 326–333.

61. Handelman, *Slayers of Moses,* p. 194.

62. The inclusion of the Zohar and Lurianic Kabbala into the "canon" of Jewish literature did not go uncontested. There was much debate, even until the eighteenth century, as to the status of the Zohar as an authentic and authoritative text. On this see Boaz Huss, "*Sefer Ha-Zohar* as a Canonical, Sacred and Holy Text," in *Journal of Jewish Thought and Philosophy* 7 (1998): 257–307.

63. *Hayye MoHaRan,* # 369.

64. *Likkutei MoHaRan* refers to the Baal Shem Tov four times (L.M. I:113, 133, 207, 225) and R. Dov Baer, the Maggid of Mezritsch, three times (L.M. I:162, II: 58).

65. For another definition of *Likkutei MoHaRan* as "poetics" and R. Nahman as a poet see Ouaknin, *Burnt Book,* p. 295.

66. See L.M. II:32, 1. Cf. Cf. R. Nathan Sternherz, *Yemei MoHaRaNat* I # 26, *The Tzaddik* (English translation of *Hayye MoHaRan)* # 66; Joseph Weiss, "Sefer ha-Nisraf l'R. Nahman of Bratslav" (Hebrew) *Keriat Sefer* 45 253–270; and Weiss, *Studies,* pp. 215–243; Chaim Kramer, *Between Fire and Water,* pp. 134–151; and the illuminating discussion in Ouaknin, *Burnt Book,* pp. 266–273. Cf. Martin Kavka's critique of Ouaknin in this volume.

67. See Micha Ankori, *Heights of Heaven,* pp. 43f. and Weiss, *Studies,* pp. 150–172.

68. This messianic trope of the suffering servant who sacrifices himself for the sake of the nation has a long history in Jewish messianism, particularly in the Zohar and Sabbateanism. See Yehudah Liebes, *Studies in the Zohar* (Albany, 1993), pp. 2–12 and idem., *Studies in Jewish Myth and Messianism,* trans. Batya Stein (Albany, 1993), pp. 93–106. Cf. R. Joseph Al-Ashqau, *Tzafnat Pa'aneah* Ms. Jerusalem 40 154 (Jerusalem, 1989), p. 79 cited and discussed by Idel in *Messianic Mystics* (New Haven, 1998), p. 120. Scholem notes that this trope was used by Solomon Molkho and Shabbatei Tvi, both influenced by the Lurianic tradition. See Scholem, *Sabbatei Tzvi: Mystical Messiah,* trans. R. J. Z Werblowsky (Princeton, 1973), pp. 54, 309.

69. *Likkutei MoHaRan* I:65 and R. Nahman of Cheryn, *Pearparot l'Hokhma,* p. 37c where the suffering of the unique zaddik is necessary to heal the suffering of the world.

70. Maria Ranier Rilke, *Letters on Cezanne* (New York, 1985), p. 4.

71. The notion of "simple faith" in R. Nahman is actually quite complex. At least in one place, it appears that "simple faith" really means faith in the zaddik. See L.M. I:65 and Weiss, *Studies,* pp. 87–95, translated in this volume by Jeremy Kalmanofsky.

72. Handelman suggests that Bloom sees Kabbala as poetic because "it forcefully manipulates, opens, misreads, revises the tradition in accordance with its own catastrophic vision. . . ." See *Slayers of Moses,* p. 189. Bloom adopts Scholem's basic thesis that sixteenth-century Kabbala is a response to the catastrophe of the expulsion from Spain in 1492 and its aftermath of mass conversion to Christianity. Without taking a stand on the veracity of Scholem's position, I would maintain that in the case of R. Nahman, the rereading of the tradition is focused on reflecting his own personal tragedy, the tragedy of the zaddik whose uniqueness results in his rejection.

73. See Green, *Tormented Master,* p. 338; David Roskies, *A Bridge of Longing* (Cambridge, Mass., 1995), pp. 26–33 (reprinted in this volume); and Ora

Wiskind-Elper, *Tradition and Fantasy in the Tales of Reb Nahman of Bratslav*, pp. 41–50. Also note that R. Nahman never stops delivering homilies although he does see his turn toward the tales as a final attempt to convey the message which he felt remained largely misunderstood.

74. See Wiskind-Elper, *Tradition and Fantasy*, pp. 9–22. Wiskind-Elper develops R. Nahman as a poet in her analysis of his thirteen tales. Her comments and observations apply, I believe, to his homiletic work as well.

75. See Gries, *Book in Early Hasidism*, pp. 47–60.

76. The early model of itinerant preacher in Hasidism quickly gave way to Hasidic circles surrounding the master, who would speak to selected audiences throughout the year. This was clearly the case in the Bratslav tradition, especially after R. Nahman's return from Erez Israel. His travels (apart from his trips to Lemberg to receive medical attention) were mostly limited to visiting cells of Bratslav Hasidim in different areas of the Ukraine. On the move for the model of the itinerant preacher to community leader see Ada Rapoport-Albert, "Hasidism After 1772: Structural Continuity and Change," in idem, ed., *Hasidism Reappraised* (London, 1997), esp. pp. 109–119.

77. Paul Ricoeur, *Interpretation and Theory: Discourse and the Surplus of Meaning* (Texas, 1976), pp. 29–44. Cf. William Graham, *Beyond the Written Word* (Cambridge, Mass., 1987), pp. 11–18; and Jack Goody and Ian Watt, "The Consequences of Literacy," in *Comparative Studies in Society and History* 5 (1963): 304–345.

78. Ricoeur, *Internal Theory*, p. 31. Two recent examples of this phenomenon are Wiskind-Elper's *Tradition and Fantasy* and Micha Ankori's *Heights of Heaven and Depths of Hell* (Hebrew) (Tel Aviv, 1994). The former is a literary analysis of R. Nahman's thirteen tales and the latter is a psychological study of R. Nahman's work. It would be interesting to investigate how much the Breslov Research Institute, a Jerusalem-based project dedicated to the dissemination of R. Nahman's works in both Hebrew and English, is motivated by the scholarly studies by nondisciples, who have, in their view, "stolen" R. Nahman's ideas for their own "heretical" purposes. This would be an example of the conflict that results when a text creates its own audience, one that may be ideologically and behaviorally estranged from the "inner-circle" of the Master.

79. Another exception to this is Habad, who were always quite ambitious in publishing the writings of their masters.

80. See Weiss, *Studies*, pp. 266–268. Gries argues that the desire to widen his audience was also at the root of publishing his advice literature. In his attempt to widen his circle of disciples he desired to have abbreviated versions of his teachings made public in order to publicize his miraculous nature. This is the source of the advice literature that have come down to us and the traditions relating to his parapsychological gifts. Gries, *Sifrut Ha-Hanhagot*, p. 243.

81. L.M.II:29.

82. It is not clear whose idea this abbreviated version was. Chaim Kramer claims that R. Nathan began to compile *Kizur Likkutei MoHaRan* in 1805 when R. Nahman instructed him to begin to collect his teachings to be distributed to a small circle of followers. After seeing R. Nathan's work on the abbreviated version he was pleased. See Kramer, *Fire and Water,* p. 100. Yet, on p. 233 Kramer states, "[in 1811] not only did he [R. Nathan] print the second volume of *Likkutei MoHaRan* but also The *Aleph-Bet Book* and his own *Kitzur Likkutei MoHaRan, written on R. Nahman's instructions."* [emphasis mine]

83. See R. Nathan's introduction to *Kizur Likkutei MoHaRan.* For a brief overview of the nature of *Kizur* literature in Jewish texts, see Lawrence Fine, *Safed Spirituality,* which contains a partial translation and annotation of *Kizur Reshit Hokhma* by R. Joseph Poyetto, an abbreviated version of the sixteenth-century pietistic classic *Reshit Hokhma* by R. Elijah da Vidas.

84. *Likkutei Ezot Ha-M'Shulash* is a combination of three collections: (1) *Kizur Likkutei MoHaRan,* (2) *Likkutei Ezot Hadash* (Lemberg, Ukraine, 1864); and (3) *Likkutei Ezot Batra* (Lemberg, Ukraine, 1864). *Likkutei Ezot* has been translated as *Advice* by Avraham Greenbaum (Jerusalem and New York, 1983). A final version of this advice literature was published under the title *Kizur Likkutei MoHaRan Ha-Shalem* (Jerusalem, 1913) which includes all the material from *Kizur Likkutei MoHaRan (Ha-Yashan),* the first *Likkutei Ezot* by R. Nathan Sternharz and *Likkutei Ezot Batra* by R. Nahman Tulchin. For more on the publishing history of these texts see Gries, *Sifrut Ha-Hanhagot,* pp. 234, 235.

85. On this see Scholem, "The Unknowable and the Expression *Kadmut Ha-Sekhel* in Hasidic Literature" (Hebrew), in *Devarim B'Go* (Jerusalem, 1976), pp. 353–360; Idel, *Kabbala: New Perspectives,* pp. 150–153; and idem, *Hasidism: Between Mysticism and Ecstasy* (Albany, 1995), pp. 234–239.

86. This is common in proemic midrashim and in the more exegetical Kabbala such as the main body of the Zohar. Other kabbalistic schools, such as the systematic work of the Kabbalists of Castille and Gerona or the school of Abraham Abulafia and Joseph Ibn Gikitillia, are less likely to use their symbolic "systems" for exegetical purposes.

87. In this sense, *Likkutei MoHaRan* follows the medieval pietistic tradition of *Menorah Ha-Me'or, 'Orhot Zaddikim,* and *Hovot Ha-Levavot.* As opposed to these texts, which are thematic in nature, *Likkutei MoHaRan* exhibits a proemic style closer to classical Midrash.

88. For the most comprehensive study of zoharic exegesis, see Pinhas Giller, *Reading the Zohar* (Oxford and N.Y., 2001).

89. R. Nathan's use of this image is intentional. The entire verse in Isaiah reads, *In all of my sacred mountain, nothing evil or vile shall be done. For the land shall be filled with the consciousness of God (deah 'et YHVH) as water covers the sea.* The sacred mountain, Jerusalem, refers back to the Tower of David. The con-

sciousness of God is translated by *JPS Tanakh* as "devotion to the Lord," which works better with R. Nathan's message here. The sacred mount, that is, Jerusalem, refers both to the messianic age and, in this context, to the one who follows the ways of this book.

90. R. Nathan Sternharz, Introduction to *Likkutei MoHaRan,* p. 5a.

91. See Marc Saperstein, "The Sermon as Art Form: Structure in Morteira's *Giv'at Sha'ul*" *Prooftexts* 3 (1983): 244–245. Sapperstein suggests various rhetorical devices common in oral sermons that may be extraneous to written communication. Although he does not mention repetition directly, this device is common in oral presentations in order to make sure the audience remains with the speaker as he or she moves from one idea to the next.

92. On a discussion of the relationship between melody and harmony that deepens this analogy see Derrida in *Of Grammatology,* pp. 209–215.

93. Green notes that this phase (i.e., the use of *behinot)* almost reaches the limits of "free association." See Green, *Tormented Master,* pp. 286, 287.

94. In line with certain forms of jazz theory, the melody of the text is not given at the outset but is itself constructed via smaller improvisations.

95. When students complain to me about the seemingly irrational nature of R. Nahman's writing, I often tell them to go home and listen closely to John Coltrane in a darkened room concentrating on the melody as Coltrane improvises around it. Many students reported back to me that this exercise helped them in following the complex turns in *Likkutei MoHaRan.*

96. *Guide for the Perplexed* I:1. This distinction may be the underlying principle of R. Nahman's statement that one who studies the *Guide* loses his *zelem elohim* (divine image). It is not only the actual reading of the *Guide* but the *Guide's* very notion of divine image that undercuts, for R. Nahman, the unique (divine) nature of the human being.

97. L.M. II:5, 9, L.M. II:8, 7.

98. See Maimonides, *Mishneh Torah,* "Hilkhot Yesode Ha-Torah," chs. 6, 7. For Maimonides' discussion of the imaginative faculty see *Guide* III: 29, 36, 37, 44.

99. This can be seen most decisively in his thirteen tales, especially in "The Seven Beggars," his last tale completed only months before his death. The villains in most of these tales are those who are convinced that reason is the arbiter of truth.

100. Saperstein, "Sermon as Art Form," pp. 243–261. Cf. idem, *Jewish Preaching: 1200–1800: An Anthology* (New Haven, 1989), pp. 63–78, 89–102.

101. On introductions in Hasidism, see Gries, "Managing Editor" and idem, *The Book in Early Hasidism,* pp. 62–68.

102. See "Introduction to *Likkutei MoHaRan,*" p. 4c. For the recitation of the ten Psalms constituting the *Tikkun Ha-Kelali* see Yehuda Liebes, "*Tikkun Ha-*

*Kelali* of R. Nahman of Bratslav and Its Sabbatean Links," in *Studies in Jewish Myth and Jewish Messianism* (Albany, 1993), pp. 134–136.

103. *Ta'amei Ha-Mitzvot* has a central place in medieval philosophy and in Kabbala. In Kabbala see Jacob Katz, *Halakha and Kabbala* (Hebrew) (Jerusalem, 1984), pp. 9–33; E. R. Wolfson, "Mystical Rationalization of the Commandments in *Sefer Ha-Rimmon*," *Hebrew Union College Annual* 59 (1988): esp. 217–235; and Daniel Matt, "The Mystic and the Mitzvot" in *Jewish Spirituality I,* ed. A. Green (New York, 1986), pp. 367–404. In philosophy see Joseph Stern, *Problems and Parables of Law* (Albany, 1998), esp. pp. 1–15. Discussing Maimonides on *ta'amei ha-mitzvot* Stern (p. 16) suggests two parts to *ta'amei ha-mitzvot,* (1) why was the law commanded and (2) why should an Israelite be motivated to perform such a law. In that case, I would suggest R. Nahman is engaged in part (2) but not part (1).

104. *Sihot Ha-Ran* # 211.

105. Ibid. "This *torah* includes all that each individual who hears it needs to hear . . . [his *torah*] includes all [possible] occurrences in the world. . . . "

106. *Sihot Ha-Ran* # 201.

107. Ibid., # 349, 355.

108. Yet he says, "even if the Baal Shem Tov and the Ari z"l (Luria) were in this world, they would not equal my stature." *Hayye MoHaRan,* # 393. Cf. # 381, "He said, if the Baal Shem Tov were alive and would hear my *torah* it would be new to him, if R. Shimon bar Yohai were alive and would hear my *torah* it would also be new to him!"

109. While the discussion of Torah before Sinai is not unprecedented in Hasidic literature, few others have made such a claim about themselves. See Arthur Green, *Devotion and Commandment* (Cincinnati, 1989), pp. 1–33. Numerous Hasidic texts attempt to portray the Besht as one who reveals things unknown, "since the days of the *Tana'yim* (i.e., early rabbinic sages)." However I am not familiar with many Hasidic texts, however, where the author likens himself to the biblical Patriarchs. For one such case, see R. Yizhak Isik Yehudah Safrin of Komarno, *Nozer Hesed* (Jerusalem, 1982), p.131. Even in the case of Komarno, however, no Hasidic thinker is seen as equal to the Patriarchs, or even higher! In terms of R. Nahman's ambivalent relationship to the prowess of the Besht, one tradition relates that when the young Nahman returned for a visit to the home of his mother Feige, who was living in the house of her grandfather, the Besht, she asked if he had visited the grave of the holy master (the Besht). The teenage Nahman replied, "If my great-grandfather wants me to visit me, he can come to me!"

110. *Hayye MoHaRan,* # 347. Cf. # 362, "Those *torot* that he wrote himself should be read like the Bible."

111. See Green, *Tormented Master,* pp. 116–123, 182–220.

112. R. Nathan's Introduction to *Likkutei MoHaRan,* p. 3a.

113. Ibid., p. 4d.

114. For a kabbalistic example that R. Nahman was surely familiar with see *Shulkhan Arukh Ha-Ari z"l* (Jerusalem, 1984), pp. 93, 94. This text was reprinted many times. The printing closest to R. Nahman, both chronologically and geographically, was the 1788 Lemberg edition, "The soul of one who does not study the Torah according to all four dimensions of interpretation (PaRDS) will transmigrate until which time he completes all these realms. The collective soul of Israel included 600,000 souls [who stood at Sinai]. The Torah is the root of all of these souls. Therefore, there are 600,000 ways of understanding Torah according to each of the 600,000 souls."

115. On this see Wolfson, "Mystical Rationalizations for the Commandments in the Prophetic Kabbala of Abraham Abulafia," in *Perspectives on Jewish Mysticism and Thought,* eds. Alfred L. Ivry, Elliot R. Wolfson, and Allan Arkush (Amsterdam, 1998), pp. 331–380, esp. pp. 331–341.

116. "Introduction to *Likkutei MoHaRan,*" p. 6d. Cf. L.M. I: 61, 2. R. Nahman speaks about writing his *torah* in general, referring to R. Nathan's hand in writing his lessons for posterity. On this R. Nahman of Cheryn writes, "And the truth is that all the power of R. Nathan's pen—came from the spirit of wisdom which R. Nahman gave to him through the "hand of ornament." See *Pearparot l'Hokhma* 61:8. Chaim Kramer describes this lesson, delivered Rosh Ha-Shana 1807, as R. Nahman's last will and testament to his disciples, even though they were unaware of this intention. He had contracted tuberculosis that summer and, even though his condition was stable, he knew this illness would eventually kill him. See Kramer, *Between Fire and Water,* pp. 138–140.

117. See *Hayye MoHaRan,* # 369. R. Nathan relates that R. Nahman complained to him that he had no one to listen to his *torah,* saying "I need someone here so that I can speak *torah* to him." It is interesting that R. Nahman never considered writing as an alternative.

118. *Hayye MoHaRan,* # 379.

119. *Yemei MoHaRaNat,* # 29, pp. 69, 70.

120. See *Hayye MoHaRan,* # 167–184. See Green, pp. 238–247. Green suggests that Lemberg gave R. Nahman his strongest taste of modernity. He returned unhealed with an amplified disdain for medicine (which failed him) and an understanding that he was entering the last phase of his short life. His creativity during the years following his return from Lemberg until his final move to Uman (1810) to die were his most productive. Most of the tales come from that period as well as many of his longer homilies.

121. It should also be noted that he had his famous Burnt Book *(Sefer Ha-Nisraf)* destroyed during this trip, dramatically ending his writing career. The choice to stop writing is not unique to R. Nahman. R. Elijha ben Solomon, the

Gaon of Vilna, made a similar choice at the age of forty. All of his written work was produced before the age of forty, although it was not published until after his death. The reason given by his disciple is similar to what we have found in R. Nahman, "All of his writings were completed before the age of 40. Afterward, everything was written by his disciple(s). His teachings were like a flowing fountain that were almost impossible to contain. . . ." See R. Israel of Skhlov, Introduction to *Pe'at Ha-Shulkhan,* Introduction to *Perush l'Midrash Ruth* (Warsaw, 1865), p. 4a; Joseph Avivi, *Kabbalat Ha-GRA* (Jerusalem, 1991), p. 11.

122. See, for example, Joseph Heinemann, "Petihta'ot b'Midrashei Ha-Agadah-Makoror u Tafkido," in *Fourth World Congress of Jewish Studies* (1965), pp. 43–47; and Peter Schaefer, "Die Petiha—ein Proominum?" *Kairos* 12 (1970): 216–219.

123. See Gries, *Book in Early Hasidism,* pp. 50–56. There are at least three important exceptions to this rule. The first is the entire Habad tradition. Many of the Habad masters wrote themselves and spent a good deal of time on literary structure and form. However, since Habad Hasidism is less homiletic and more systematic, many of the texts do not utilize the proemic midrashic structure and are constructed in more of an essay format. The second exception are masters such as the late nineteenth century masters R. Zaddok Ha-Kohen Rabinowitz and R. Gershon Henokh of Radzin. Both were very prolific, in homilies, lengthy essays and commentaries. The third exception is the twentieth-century master R. Kolonymous Kalman Shapira of Piasczeno who wrote extensively in many areas. His collected homilies, entitled *Derekh Ha-Melekh,* exhibit a precise literary style that integrates both classical and more modern styles of midrashic writing.

124. Gries, "Hasidism as a Managing Editor" pp. 141, 142.

125. Gries, *Early Book in Hasidism,* p. 64–67 and idem, "Hasidism as a Managing Editor," pp. 142–145.

126. This was the case of the Radzin tradition. We have two versions of R. Gershon Henokh of Radzin's commentary to the Pentateuch. The first, entitled *Sod Yesharim 'al Ha-Torah,* was written by the master himself. The second, *Sod Yesharim Tinyana,* was a collection of disciples' notebooks, recording teachings they heard orally. Cf. Gries, *Book in Early Hasidism,* p. 55 on the history of the construction of R. Jacob Joseph of Polnoy's *Toldot Ya'akov Yoseph,* the first Hasidic book printed and his "Hasidism as a Managing Editor" pp. 143–145 on the construction of R. Meshullam Feibush Heller of Zbaraz's *Yosher Divrei Emet* from previous collections of his teachings.

127. Friends in the Breslov community in Jerusalem have told me that the community has numerous pages of R. Nahman's personal handwritten notes used as the basis of certain lengthy homilies. Bratslav literature attests to the fact that R. Nahman often spent many hours preparing for some of these homilies, collecting material and working out some of his ideas in writing. To my knowledge, it is not

clear whether R. Nathan had access to these notes when constructing his written versions of the homilies themselves that appear in *Likkutei MoHaRan*.

128. This is particularly true of the Zohar. See Boaz Huss, "*Sefer Ha-Zohar* as a Canonical, Sacred and Holy Text," pp. 257–307.

129. One noteworthy exception are five homilies each beginning with the first, third, fourth, and fifth chapters of the Zohar's *Sefer Dizniuta*. See L.M. I:19, 20, 21, 22.

130. See Richard Palmer, *Hermeneutics* (Evanston, Ill., 1969), pp. 18,19.

131. The centrality of praxis is made explicit in the Introduction to *Kizur Likkutei MoHaRan*, included in the first edition in 1811, "He [R. Nahman] commanded me to compile this abbreviated version [i.e., *Kizur Likkutei MoHaRan*] because his fundamental intention in all of his writings and wondrous homilies that he revealed to this cherished nation was only in order to facilitate action . . . to teach them the proper way to act in order to achieve eternal life. . . .".

132. R. Nahman strongly emphasized the need to "see the zaddik" deliver his lesson. However, following his death his disciples translate this into hearing someone deliver (teach) one of R. Nahman's lessons. See L.M. I:19, 1.

133. See L.M. I:12a, "When we study the *torah* of zaddikim who have passed, our spirit becomes bound to their spirit, as the rabbis teach (Yebamot 97), "'Their lips quiver in their graves', this occurs by means of the kiss."

134. *Hayye MoHaRan*, # 369. I would suggest reading *sheli* as "me" and not "mine." This has important ramifications. He is saying, among other things, that none of this is "tradition" or gleaned from other sources. This entire book is an innovation *(hidush)*, which has never existed in this world. His unwillingness to be a mouthpiece for his ancestors is quite unusual in traditional societies, where intuiting an earlier opinion is praised with the blessing "Thank God I have intuited the opinions of my ancestors" *(barukh sh'kevanti)*. R. Nahman's position is closer to that of Oscar Wilde, cited in Bloom, *The Anxiety of Influence*, p 6. "While of course I come down from the past, the past is my own . . . I know of no one who has been particularly important to me. My reality-imagination complex is entirely my own even though I see it in others."

135. On Hasidism in general, see Gries, *Sifrut Ha-Hanhagot*, pp. 103–148. Regarding Bratslav in particular see p. 231, "It is important to remember that behavior literature as a literary genre was a age-old way of paraphrasing homilies. Their acceptance in the minds of those who read them became a ritual for guiding daily religious behavior" [my translation].

136. The tension between traditional and pneumatic/spiritualistic ethos is common in Hasidism. See, for example, in Joseph Weiss, "*Via Passiva* in Early Hasidism," in Weiss, *Studies in Eastern European Jewish Mysticism* (Oxford, 1985), pp. 69–83, and Rivka Shatz-Uffenheimer, *Hasidism as Mysticism*, trans. Jonathan Chipman (Princeton, 1993), p. 194.

137. In this sense, R. Nahman's position on repentance is reflected, in different ways, by R. Abraham Isaac Ha-Kohen Kook in his *'Orot Ha-Teshuvah* (Jerusalem, 1970) and by R. Joseph Soloveitchik in his *'Al Ha-Teshuvah,* ed. Pinhas Peli ed. (Jerusalem, 1975). Both Kook and Soloveitchik construct models of repentance that may be based on halakhic principles but go beyond the purely halakhic framework elucidated in Maimonides' *Mishneh Torah.* See Nahum Arieli, "Repentance in the Philosophy of R. Kook," (Hebrew) *Teshuvah ve Shavim* (Jerusalem, 1980) and Pinhas Peli, *Soloveitchik on Repentance* (New York, 1984).

138. The correlation between R. Nahman's own travails and his seemingly obsessive focus on the centrality of dispute *(makhloket)* in many of his lessons was noted and discussed by Weiss and Piekarz.

139. Talmud Shabbat 21a.

140. As is often the case in translating scriptural verses in kabbalistic and Hasidic texts, the *JPS Tanakh* translation does not capture the interpreter's understanding of the verse. This is partially due to the fact that the idiomatic method of translating Scripture is diametrically opposed to mystical translation, which often exhibits a hyperliteralism in the ways words and images in Scripture are used. A study of the hyperliteralist nature of kabbalistic scriptural translation is a desideratum. The *JPS Tanakh* renders this verse, *You have besieged me in frontal onslaught and through the insights that unfold later.* I'd like to thank my friend Talya Fishman for offering this translation in light of R. Nahman's lesson.

141. On *'ibur* in Kabbala see G. Scholem, *On the Mystical Shape of the Godhead,* trans. J. Neugroschel and J. Chipman (New York, 1991), pp. 221–228, 240.

142. L.M. I:21, 7. On the last phrase see Talmud Berakhot 24b and R. Joseph Karo *Shulkhan Arukh,* '*Orah Hayyim* # 62:4 and101. Cf. L.M. II:48.

143. On the holistic nature of Scripture as the centerpiece of the entire talmudic/midrashic project see Saul Lieberman, "Rabbinic Interpretation of Scripture," in his *Hellenism and Jewish Palestine* (rpt. New York, 1994), pp. 47–82.

144. See Zohar 3.73a/b.

145. This is a central theme in Beshtean Hasidism and one of the elements that distinguished Hasidism from their antagonists. This focus on orientation rather than pure obligation sometimes resulted in a loosing of halakhic boundaries, especially regarding the confines of time. See Rivka Shatz-Uffneheimer, *Hasidism as Mysticism,* pp. 111–144, 215–241. Cf. J. Weiss, "Contemplation and Self-Abandonment in the Writings of R. Hayyim Haika of Amdura," in his *Studies in Eastern European Jewish Mysticism,* pp. 142–154.

146. L.M. I:6, 4. Cf. R. Nathan of Bratslav *Likkutei Halakhot,* vol. 1, "Laws on the Blessings over Fruit" 5:19.

147. Harold Bloom, *Kabbala and Criticism* (New York, 1993), pp. 54ff.

148. Ibid., pp. 65–66.

149. The use of the English term *extentiation* is borrowed from Ron Kiener's translation of R. Azriel of Gerona's seminal work *Perush 'al Eser Sephirot* in *The Early Kabbala*, eds. Joseph Dan and Ronald Keiner (New York, 1986), pp. 89–96. The attenuated distinction between source and extentiated product is dealt with by R. Azriel in his distinction between "emanation" and "creation" in the conclusion of the aforementioned text.

150. Bloom develops this distinction between revision and rupture in his comparison of Cordovero's *behinot* and Luria's *zimzum* in *Kabbala and Criticism*, pp. 71–92.

151. Ibid. p. 53.

152. Bloom, *Anxiety of Influence*, p. 29.

153. Ibid. p. 14.

154. See Wiskind-Elper, *Tradition and Fantasy*, p. 63. She calls this a method of "designification" whereby metaphysical ties bind disparate elements of the world. She views this as a second type of designification, the first of which is classical kabbalistic reading.

155. Fixing the imagination was a vital part of R. Nahman's whole project. Late in life R. Nahman openly reversed the conventional notion of the imaginative faculty as lower than the intellect. See L.M. II 5, par. 9. Cf. L.M. II: 8, par. 7 and the discussion in Green, *Tormented Master*, pp. 341–344. Green suggests that R. Nahman's turn to the tales may have been his final attempt to fix the imaginative faculty of Israel before his death. This move may be predicated on his use of the talmudic Rabba bar bar Hanna stories in *Likkutei MoHaRan;* he was then freed from the literary tradition altogether with the tales. The centrality of the imaginative faculty may have also been a source for his adamant antipathy for the entire medieval philosophical tradition, which stressed the intellect as the most elevated part of humanity. See *Hayye MoHaRan*, pp. 384–401, # 407–429.

156. *Shivhei MoHaRan* 16:b, 50, cited in Wiskind-Elper, *Tradition and Fantasy*, p. 11.

157. I would suggest that a similar anxiety flows beneath the surface of R. Soloveitchik's writings, *Halakhic Man* and *Lonely Man of Faith* serving as the two poles of Soloveitchik's worldview. This is substantiated by the fact that Soloveitchik holds that the "image of God" in humanity is creativity, which challenges the norms of an external system while maintaining its structures and doctrines. See, for example, Walter S. Wurzburger, "*Imitatio Dei* in the Philosophy of Rav Joseph B. Soloveitchik," in *Hazon Nahum*, pp. 557–575. Wurzbuerger argues that Soloveitchik adopted the kabbalistic interpretation of *zelem elokim* of R. Hayyim of Volozhin's *Nefesh Ha-Hayyim* as opposed to the rationalist perspective of Maimonides in the *Guide*.

158. L.M. II:5, 9, L.M. II:8, 7; and Green, *Tormented Master,* p. 341.

159. For an analysis of signification as the model of kabbalistic exegesis see Betty Roitman, *Black Fire on White Fire* (Berkeley, 1986), pp. 68–98.

160. For some interesting observations about hermeneutics as translation see Richard Palmer, *Hermeneutics,* pp. 26–28.

161. A good illustration of this is the extensive footnotes in the bilingual editions of *Likkutei MoHaRan* that attempt to flesh out the ambiguous associations using rabbinic and kabbalistic literature. Many of the comments are suggestions, leaving open other possible ways of justifying these associations.

162. L.M. II:105.

163. Wiskind-Elper, *Tradition and Fantasy,* p. 61.

164. L.M. II:105, *Hayye MoHaRan,* # 350.

165. *Hayye MoHaRan,* # 339. The verse in Ezeikel is part of his promise of redemption. "And I will give you a new heart and put a new spirit in you; I will remove the heart of stone from your body and give you a *heart of flesh.* . . . Thus I cause you to follow My laws faithfully and to observe my Rules." R. Nahman saw himself as the one who could prepare Israel for this prophetic promise through his text, both its message and structure.

# 2

## The Master of Prayer
### *Rabbi Nahman of Bratslav*

**David G. Roskies**

The rabbi traveled to the zaddik and he cried: *"Gevald, gevald!*
Help me, oh help me! Alas for those who are lost and are no
longer found!"

—Rabbi Nahman ben Simhah of Bratslav

Stories, it was once believed, offer a temporary reprieve from death. So Scheherazade stayed her execution at the hands of the sultan with fantasy, suspense, and eroticism enough to last a thousand and one years. So too the seven noble women and three amorous men who fled the plague-ridden city of Florence in 1348. While they did nothing to alleviate the collective horror, they managed to stave off their own fear of death in a ten-day long contest of bawdy and irreverent tales. But six centuries after Boccaccio, when the poet Itzik Manger assembled a minyan of ten Holocaust survivors in an imaginary bunker, each Jew hailing from another part of Europe, he could finish no more than two stories of this modern *Decameron.* The muse simply failed in the face of such catastrophe.[1]

How much redemptive weight can stories bear? For Walter Benjamin, storytelling was the answer to modern angst. Storytelling conjured up a world of communal listening, of young and old alike sharing and shaping the collective memory of the folk; a world where each individual storyteller, according to Benjamin, was a master of local traditions, rooted in the soil, or a mercurial figure just returned from his travels. Whether a master of local or exotic tales, Benjamin's storyteller inhabited a moral universe of "experience" rather than an alienated world of "facts." The storyteller used "transparent layers" of personal and collective experience, of wisdom and practical knowledge gained over centuries, in much the same way as a craftman used the tools and techniques passed down from master to apprentice. By choosing the Russian storyteller Nikolai Leskov (1831–1895) to occupy the center of this idyllic, preindustrial landscape, Benjamin implicitly repudiated the Nazi image of the past, complete with Teutonic knights and pagan bloodlust, and the Nazi vision of a racially purged Europe. As Benjamin tells it, the Slavic-born storytellers inherit the earth.[2]

Stories, however ephemeral and insubstantial, can stay the executioner's hand or offer a humane countervision in a world gone mad. But stories have never enjoyed autonomy within the Jewish tradition. Live audiences of today, whether they sign up for "The Oral Tradition: Jewish Stories for Adults" at the 92nd Street Y in New York or whether they attend the Annual Storytelling Festival in Jonesborough, Tennessee, have little in common with the orthodox practice of Jewish men studying sacred texts out loud. These men are not only heir to a learned tradition that devalued stories and storytelling but also are at work within a closed circle in which even the meaning of the tales is governed by strict rules of interpretation. The reason why one needs to learn the art of Jewish storytelling nowadays at community centers, conferences, and workshops is that stories were preserved—that is to say, recorded and revered—within the folio pages of a *seyfer,* a "sacred tome" in Hebrew-Aramaic, or not at all.[3]

The Torah was the Book of Life, the source of law *and* lore. So thoroughly did the rabbis accomplish their task of binding one to the other that the study of Halachah, the Jewish Law, was inconceivable without recourse to the lore of Aggadah, and vice versa. Some legal interpreters and commentators made free and frequent use of their favorite aggadic tales while others made do with a cryptic reference to folk traditions current in their own day.

The Mishnah (codified around 250 C.E.) teaches that a man may not be alone with two women but a woman can be alone with two men. The Gemara (codified in 450 C.E.) brings a *beraita* (a source contemporary with the Mishnah) that contradicts the Mishnaic ruling. Abba Saul taught that when a child dies within thirty days of birth there is no need of a coffin. The dead child may be carried out in one's bosom. But how many people should accompany the corpse? Abba Saul said, "Even by one man and two women!" The real argument, then, centers on human behavior in extremis. Abba Saul believes that in a period of intense mourning, man's lustful passion is inactive while the rabbis of the Mishnah believe precisely the opposite. And to prove their point they stenographically cite the following evidence: "Even as the story of [or the case concerning] a certain woman: it once happened that she took him out" (B. Kiddushin 80b).

Schooled in rabbinic shorthand, every Talmud student immediately turns to Rashi, the eleventh-century commentator, for elucidation. Rashi fills in the plot as follows: "A woman carried out a live child, pretending that it was dead, so that she might satisfy her lust unsuspected." His curiosity roused, the student turns next to Tosafot, Rashi's disciples, whose commentary appears on the opposite side of the folio page. Here the plot is finally laid out in graphic detail in the name of Hananel ben Hushi'el, a North African rabbi of the eleventh century. Once there was a widow who grieved terribly at her husband's grave. There happened to be a soldier nearby guarding a crucified corpse. After seducing the widow, he discovered that the corpse had been stolen from off the cross. The widow, now fully reconciled to her grief, urged him to replace the corpse with that of her husband. And so "she took him out" and hung him up instead. "This proves," concludes the commentator, "that even in a state of intense mourning, her passions got the better of her."

The rabbis did their job well, weaning the excitable Jewish mind away from too much fancy but providing just enough narrative for the story to function as a brainteaser. The Talmud student could care less that Rabenu Hananel probably heard the story in the garrison town of Kairouan that then stood at the crossroads of world folklore, or that ten centuries earlier the story was popularized by the Roman satirist Petronius Arbiter as "The Matron of Ephesus."[4] The important thing was to decide whether the story supported or disputed the privileged Mishnaic opinion.[5]

Stories that did legal duty in rabbinic texts were marked by a specific label, *ma'aseh* (from which the Yiddish *mayse* would later derive). Exactly like the Latin *gesta*, *ma'aseh* could mean either a factual occurrence or the account thereof. Thus the Hebrew phrase "*ma'aseh be*, . . ." usually rendered "a tale is told of, . . ." more plausibly means "a case concerning. . . ."[6] In order to rebut their opponent, Abba Saul, the rabbis cited case law, not folktale.

The *ma'asim*, or "deeds," recounted by the rabbis in their synagogue sermons and studyhouse debates, were never meant to stand alone, however dramatic they seem to us, however widely they may have circulated among the "folk." The wondrous death of the deadly lizard who dared to bite the praying Hanina ben Dosa, a first-century "man of deed," as the Mishnah called him (M. Sotah 9:15), was turned by the rabbis into an exemplary tale of how all Jews should pray with total concentration.[7] The personal trials and achievements of even the greatest rabbinic personalities, like Eliezer ben Hyrcanus, who sacrificed all for the sake of Torah, only to be excommunicated at the end of his career; or like Rabbi Akiva, whose grasp of the Torah was the envy of Moses himself, but who died at the hands of the Romans, some say, as a martyr—these and other extraordinary events were consistently downplayed. The stuff of epic, romance, farce, and fantasy, they were lost in the "sea" of the Oral Tradition. They were buried within complex "legal debates" called *sugyot* or scattered among the wordgames, creative philology, parables, and fables used by the rabbis to read each of their contemporary concerns out of and into the Torah.[8]

So long as invention meant the discovery of something already in Scripture, the story could never be fully "emancipated" from the Book of Books. The very concept of "emancipation"—the concern for each individual's autonomy, hence for tales that chart the self's journey through time, hence for narrative flow—is one among many modern constructs that is totally at odds with the self-understanding of rabbinic Judaism. If anything, the Jewish (re)turn to storytelling during the Middle Ages was made in the name of de-emancipation: it was a way of legitimating legendary motifs borrowed far and wide or a newer repertoire of tales about a local aristocracy by invoking the authority of the hallowed texts.[9]

The permanence of medieval Jewish culture was vouchsafed by the existence of the *seyfer*, the "weighty tome," the "canonical text," sanctified by virtue of its language (Hebrew-Aramaic), its subject matter (halachic, aggadic), its point of origin (Sinai, Yavneh, and the talmudic academy), and its intended reader (men). The medium of the Yiddish *mayse-bikhl* (the modest story- or chapbook that made its first appearance in sixteenth-century Italy) was its contrasting message: it was anonymous and cheap, contained a single narrative unit that could be read at a single sitting, and was written (and printed) in the vernacular. Jewish compilers seized upon the chapbook as a way of cutting the Hebrew giant down to salable size. They raided the classical collections for their juiciest items; removed these dramatic plots from their learned context, published each unit separately, and included just enough Hebrew-Aramaic "markers" to render the work kosher.[10] It was singularly in Yiddish that the ephemerality of storybooks became their chief virtue.

As the *seyfer* was seamless, timeless, and permanent, the flimsy *mayse-bikhl* was but a brief distraction. Ideally, those Yiddish chapbooks translated from the Talmud, Midrash, and the Apocrypha could be attached to a specific holiday: the Apocryphal Book of Macabees and Tobith to be read on Hannukah; the story of Rabbi Meir and the Ten Lost Tribes on Shavuoth; the Destruction of the Temple on Tisha b'Av.[11] It did not take long, however, for some enterprising editor to seek the more lucrative market of sanctioned reading for the Holy Sabbath, those fifty-two days in the year when Jews could reasonably be expected to look into a nonsacred book. Out of this desire came the famous *Mayse-bukh* (Basle, 1602), a blockbuster anthology of over 250 tales.

Here was a book for all seasons that tried to pass itself off as a *seyfer*. Why study Talmud and the legal commentaries, the Lithuanian-born bookpeddler Jacob ben Avrom went so far as to claim, when his *Mayse-bukh* could answer all rabbinic queries? "The rabbi and rabbi's wife and every man, all except someone really schooled in Talmud" could win friends and influence people simply on the strength of the midrashim and sacred tales that he, the faithful compiler, had assembled.[12] Even practical halachic issues, he had the gall to claim, could be settled by reference to his storybook. Still occupying the moral high ground, Jacob ben Avrom went on to excoriate such "licentious" secular reading material as the *Ku-bukh, Dietrich von Berne,* and *Meister Hilderbrant,* "that merely send you into a fever." It was a sin to have such books in one's possession, let alone to read them on the Sabbath.

Read skeptically, as every sales pitch should be, the printer's preface to the *Mayse-bukh* might lead one to conclude that the Renaissance had finally created a cultural climate in which the story no longer needed to function as the foundation of faith; it could live simply as narrative. Why, otherwise, did the printer protest so much? Unless he was hedging his bets, why did that selfsame printer go on to publish a Yiddish adaptation of a German best-seller, *The Seven Sages of Rome?* As for the *Mayse-bukh* itself, little more than half the tales actually derived from the Talmud, via the popular *Ein Ya'akov*, the original layperson's guide to the Talmud. A third were thinly disguised legends and novella of international provenance, and under a separate heading Jacob Ben Avrom introduced a cycle of early medieval tales about the life of the Founding Fathers of Ashkenaz, Rabbi Shmuel Hasid ("Samuel the Pious") and his son Rabbi Judah. If this did not signal the "emancipation" of Yiddish storytelling, then what did?[13]

The *Mayse-bukh* indeed became the Yiddish "folk book" par excellence, spawning many other story collections in its wake; and it gave future editors license to publish accounts, an amalgam of folklore and chronicle, which preserved the memory of local events, heroes, and heroines. And many a tale recorded in the *Mayse-bukh* made its way back to the Yiddish-speaking folk, which stripped it clean of all didacticism. But the medium of the *Mayse-bukh* in its own time and place heralded the integration of Yiddish into the Torah-centered world of Ashkenazic Jewry, a place where the *seyfer* was the source of all knowledge. What the Yiddish story lost in revolutionary potential it gained in restorative power.[14]

"They say that stories put you to sleep," he told his disciples, "but I say that through stories you can awaken people from their sleep." Rabbi Nahman ben Simhah of Bratslav (1772–1810) was the first Jewish religious figure to place storytelling at the center of his creative life. These were neither occasional tales, as retold intact by his great-grandfather, Israel Ba'al Shem Tov (the Besht), to illustrate the hidden workings of the Shekhinah, nor tales recounted *in praise of* the Besht, but tales of Nahman's own invention, some taking several sessions to complete. Devoid of the standard heroes, settings, and props of Jewish storytelling—no Elijah the Prophet working behind-the-scenes, no mythical Sambatyon River, no Sabbath or holiday—these stories were informed by Nahman's personal mythology, by his reading of Psalms and the Zohar, by his messianic striving.[15]

Born in a moment of despair, his tales have a tragic urgency. The hoped-for act of restoration, which is the goal of every seeker in every tale, is deadlocked, deferred, and only sometimes fully realized. These are stories of a world in crisis, of faith under siege. The present evil is ubiquitous, whether it comes from the geopolitical upheaval brought on by the Napoleonic wars, or from the primal sin of Sabbatianism, the root cause of the crisis of faith; whether the evil-doers are closer at hand, in the person of his archrival, the Shpoler Zeyde, who hounds his every move, or in the so-called *khokhem*, the "freethinker," who denies the existence of God.

Reb Nahman turned to storytelling when all else failed, when he could not reveal his messianic program outright, because the frontal approach had forced the hand of Satan. In 1806 Reb Nahman announced to his Hasidim, *"Ikh vel shoyn onheybn mayses dertseyln,* the time has come for me to begin telling stories," since all his other efforts had failed.[16] Thus modern Yiddish storytelling was born. And it was no easy birth, for a member of the Jewish elite did not simply stand up before his disciples one day and start telling fairy tales when everything in the system of traditional Judaism militated against it. There had to be a radical will and a hidden way.[17]

The events leading up to 1806 formed a three-act drama. The first was a period of frenetic activity, as Reb Nahman threw himself into the cause of universal redemption. His messianic calendar, from Rosh Hashanah 1804 onward, was cluttered with extraordinary efforts on all fronts: instituting rites of purification; collecting, editing, and disseminating his teachings; the birth of his son Shloyme Ephraim upon whom great messianic hope was now placed; Reb Nahman's mysterious journey to Shargorod; and finally the instruction to his disciples to don white garments.[18]

In the second act, the revolution failed. The mission of the disciples to proclaim the messianic era failed for lack of support; Shloyme Ephraim lay dead of a childhood disease; the Hasidic establishment openly attacked Reb Nahman for heresy, and the inner ranks of his disciples began to thin. It was to rouse those remaining disciples from their spiritual slumber, to reconsecrate them to the arduous task of redemption in a world alive with evil and tragedy that Reb Nahman began telling stories.

What was needed in the third act was a return to something elemental. Reb Nahman's discovery of a new symbolic language came after he had already mastered all the traditional forms of Jewish self-expression: the languages of prayer and song; of biblical, rabbinic, and kabbalistic exegesis; of ethical exhortation. Were it not for the present crisis that forced Reb Nahman to rechannel his redemptive faith into a more potent—albeit more hidden—medium, he would never have gone back to so primitive a form. But neither would he be content merely to retell what others had told before him. To serve as a proper vehicle for the revolution of the Jewish spirit, the fund of available stories had to be utterly transformed.

"In the tales which other people tell," he counseled his disciples in 1806,

> there are many secrets and lofty matters, but the tales have been ruined in that they are lacking much. They are confused and not told in the proper sequence: what belongs at the beginning they tell at the end and vice versa. Nevertheless, there are in these tales which other people tell lofty and hidden matters. And the Besht (may his holy memory be a blessing) could "unite unities" by means of tales. When he saw that the upper conduits were ruined and he could not repair them through prayer, he would repair and join them by means of a tale. (Y 7; E 32–33)[19]

Hasidism, to be sure, was a more fertile ground for "the tales which other people tell" than rabbinic Judaism had ever been. The idea of God's immanence in everything, no matter how lowly or trivial, was a central tenet of Hasidism, beginning with the Besht, the founder of Hasidism. Quoting Isaiah (6:3), Reb Nahman elaborated upon the same teaching. "*His presence fills all the earth!* God's glory is proclaimed even from tales told by the gentiles; as it is written [1 Chron. 16:24], *Tell of His glory among the nations.*"[20] The songs of shepherds, by the same token, or marching tunes, could likewise be a conduit to God, and Hasidism ushered in a musical revival among the Jews of Eastern Europe. But just as it took Rabbi Akiva to unlock the allegorical meaning of Solomon's Song of Songs, only a great zaddik, someone schooled in the hieroglyphics of the holy, could discover the divine emanations in the stories told even by lowly peasants.

In Bratslav the operative category was not immanence but *tikkun,* the myth of cosmic mending that went back to Isaac Luria (1534–1572). Reb Nahman was the first to suggest that the *shevirah,* the primal act of breakage that scattered the sparks of holiness throughout the profane universe, had affected even the tales that other people tell. Their internal order was destroyed and whatever secret and lofty matters were contained within them was lost as well. To merely retell them with proper *kavvanah* or "absorption" was therefore not enough. The *tikkun* could only work if the tales themselves were redeemed from their profane outer shell. Only then could the zaddik use the mended tale to reunite the *sefirot* and to awaken his disciples from their slumber.

Herein lay the blueprint for creative renewal. Reb Nahman was a kind of romantic philologist, like the Brothers Grimm, just then beginning their work some fifteen hundred kilometers to the west.[21] Whereas they looked to the German folk for a naïveté that would embody wholeness, Reb Nahman's restorative program was more cosmic and dialectical. He did not wish to create a seamless narrative out of disparate traditions—he ripped out all the seams and started over instead. To effect the perfect camouflage would be to defeat his purpose, which was to signal the real meaning of the tale. That meaning was coded into the story's deviation from the norm. The more difficult the tale—in its myriad details, its plotting, its bizarre symbolism—the more redemptive weight it carried. The more aberrant the tale, the more obvious the fact that it did have a hidden meaning.[22]

Reb Nahman made his task more difficult still by choosing precisely the type of story that the Germans call *Märchen* and that in English is usually rendered as "fairy tale." The more obvious choice would have been the legends, those wondrous "deeds" and histories recorded in the Talmud, the midrashim, and the *Mayse-bukh,* which bore witness to the contact of holy persons with God and the supernatural. Some were sacred tales of long ago; others were local legends set in Regensburg, Prague, and even as close to home as Okup, birthplace of the Besht. The *vunder-mayse,* in contrast, told of magic potions that changed a person's face;

of young men who turned into birds; of travelers who crossed the mythical Sambatyon River to the Jewish Neverland wherein resided the Ten Lost Tribes; of seduction and abduction; of marriages made in heaven that were frustrated here on earth. Miracles were commonplace, as was repetition, for the isolated episodes of the fairy tale made up a plot of action. They were generally regarded as fiction.[23]

How romantic to imagine Reb Nahman, scion of two Hasidic dynasties, roaming through the forests and soaking in the oral lore of Orthodox pilgrims and Ukrainian serfs! How else could he have come by "the tales which other people tell?" But Reb Nahman did not draw his inspiration directly from the folk, Jewish or Gentile; he turned to storybooks in Hebrew and Yiddish. Of magic potions he might have read at some length in "A Beautiful Story" [*Ayn sheyne historye*] *that Goes by the Name Bove Mayse,* a prosaic reworking of the Yiddish Renaissance classic by Elia Levita, *Bovo bukh* (Isny, 1541). Nahman's elaborate tale about "The King and the Emperor," which told of a bride and her three suitors, might easily have come from *Mordecai and Esther, A Beautiful and Wondrous Story about a Groom and a Bride,* the most popular Yiddish romance of the nineteenth century.[24] To cover his tracks, as it were, he eliminated the Jewish names, places, and temporal settings. Instead of the prophet Elijah helping Boruch the son of Rabbi Fridman, as in the story of the bride and groom, Reb Nahman's fairy-tale heroes were unnamed; their actions transcended natural laws and took place somewhere no more specific than a town, a palace or a desert. Within their new archetypal settings and intricate plots, these characters were meant to bear mystical meanings they had not borne before. By reinventing these tales so that they might yield their messianic and kabbalistic secrets, Nahman was restoring them to a pristine form they had never known within Jewish recorded time. No one less than the greatest zaddik of his generation could counteract the combined forces of Satan and the *shevirah.*

Thus Reb Nahman's return to fairy tales was only his point of departure, just as the Brothers Grimm were inspired by the study of modern German folklore to reassemble the scattered sparks of Teutonic mythology toward recovering primal myths that were still potent. In the light of what they discovered in the far distant past, they concluded that German fairy tales, even their own collection of *Household Tales,* were nothing more than "broken-down myths," narratives of belief that were crushed under the impact of European Christianity.[25] Reb Nahman took a different approach to closing the chasm between myth and mere story. He set out to *remythologize* many of these same fairy tales by reaching back to ancient times.

Adapting terms from the Zohar, Reb Nahman distinguished between tales "in the midst of days," which told of past but incomplete redemption, and the *Ur*-tale, "of the years of antiquity." The former told of God's beneficence in the past, such as stories of the Patriarchs or the Exodus, or even more recently, in the days of the Besht. The Ur-tale represented "the most archaic memories, hidden fears, and unspoken fantasies of the self, as well as those of the universe."[26] More concretely, these tales of the primal years predicted the great act of final redemption that for Nahman still lay in the future. Since that final redemption had not yet taken place and the Messiah had not yet come, these stories were usually left unfinished.[27] From mending the disorder of Jewish and European fairy tales, Nahman discovered the language of pure myth.

Reb Nahman enacted the three-act drama from radicalism, to crisis, to creative retrieval in just under two years. That left him only four years in which to master the neglected art of storytelling. As Nathan of Nemirov tells it, the master threw himself into it body and soul. Words could not express the profundity of these tales; even the most exact transcription could not do justice to the drama of their first live telling. "For by means of body movement—rocking his head back and forth, winking his eyes and hands gesticulating—it was by these means in particular that the learned [listener] was enlightened to understand just a little; he was amazed at what he beheld, and his eyes perceived from afar the wonders of the Lord and the greatness of his [Reb Nahman's] holy Torah" (p. 6).

As always in Judaism, when the Oral Torah was finally written down, it assumed canonical status. In this case, Reb Nahman left instructions to Nathan of Nemirov to issue the Tales with an exact Hebrew translation printed above the Yiddish original. When modern Yiddish storytelling made its public debut, therefore, it did so as a bilingual *seyfer,* not as a Yiddish *mayse-bikhl.* Nathan appended a Hebrew preface, a short biography of the author, and other teachings of the Master that threw some light on the hidden meanings of the tales.[28] And like every *seyfer,* this one too grew exponentially as each generation added its own commentaries and supercommentaries—from Nathan of Nemirov's detailed explication of selected tales, first published after Nathan's death in 1845, to the beautiful *Seyfer sipurey mayses* (Jerusalem, 1979) that I hold in my hands right now, updated to include a commentary from the beginning of the twentieth century.[29]

These commentaries bear out once again that context is nine-tenths of the meaning in the art of storytelling. Because they appreciated Reb Nahman's genius for deriving cosmic significance from incidental detail, his Hasidim paid careful attention to the structure, the repetitions, and the seeming redundancy of the tales. Because they studied his texts in exactly the same way as other sacred texts, they understood his tales as multivalent, as militating against a single and narrowly allegorical meaning. Because they were *di toyte khsidim,* the "dead Hasidim," who accepted no other teacher after Nahman, they knew him to be the hidden hero of his tales.

Among the many traditions that Bratslav Hasidism exploited to its advantage was the standard division of labor between Hebrew and Yiddish. Bilingual texts were always aimed at a differentiated Jewish audience. Because Hebrew remained the language of the learned Jewish male, the Hebrew record of Reb Nahman's stories, parables, and dreams was more complete and reliable than the Yiddish original.[30] The Yiddish was for *proste mentshn,* for the simple folk, especially female. They were far less likely to be alive to the multiple levels of Scripture, Talmud, and the Zohar operating beneath the narrative surface. They could be bought off instead with a delightful story and a straightforward moral.[31] Thus far, business as usual. But since, for the first time, the scribe felt mandated to preserve the *spokenness* of the Master's original, not deviating to the right or to the left; and since Hebrew had been used solely as a high literary language, Nathan had to invent a hybrid Hebrew style that would capture Nahman's spoken Yiddish as much as possible. Unlike the editor of the Hebrew *Shivhei haBesht* (In Praise of the Baʻal Shem Tov), Nathan did not try to compensate for the loss of vitality by making his Hebrew version resonate with scriptural and other learned echoes.[32] Instead, it was a Yiddish syntax and vocabulary that echoed throughout, oftentimes deviating from the grammar of rabbinic Hebrew—and from the elevated style of rabbinic speech.[33] How could a thinker and teacher of Nahman's caliber allow this to happen? Surely this quasi-colloquial style implied a learned author who, for mysterious reasons, had begun to tell stories that only an Ideal (male) Reader and disciple of the rebbe could understand.

The element of surprise in the Yiddish text, printed below the Hebrew, cut in the same direction. The tales of Nahman of Bratslav dispensed entirely with the archaic style that Yiddish editors and printers still almost universally employed and reproduced instead the Yiddish as actually spoken in Eastern Europe.[34] Here, for the first time, the oral quality of the text was the measure of its authenticity. Whatever learned Hebrew phrases echoed in Reb Nahman's telling were presumably put there by Reb Nahman himself, not by a scribe who was trying to raise the spoken narrative to a literary standard. The transparently idiomatic quality of the Yiddish implied a storyteller talking to a live audience.

Stories as told to, and as understood by, their several intended audiences necessarily carried a plurality of meanings. As the work of an artist who was using the entirety of Jewish tradition in a wholly personal way,[35] the tales cried out for the same kind of pluralistic interpretation that was normally reserved for Scripture. In mystical circles, the mnemonic for the fourfold reading of Scripture was PaRDeS, which stood for *peshat, remez, derash*[ah], and *sod.*[36] The PaRDeS model was never actually applied to the tales, but it could have been. The fourfold reading model goes a long way toward an understanding of both the traditional Hasidic commentaries and the modern critical research that came later.

The moment one takes Reb Nahman's poetic manifesto seriously, that there is a universal fund of motifs and plots that were scattered in the primal act of *shevirah,* then there is much to be learned from studying the structure and patterning of the tales in their mended, Bratslavian form. The peshat, or contextual, approach would take the "tales which other people tell" as its point of departure. The key to meaning is the deviant structure of the story, the discrepancy the reader feels based on hearing countless such tales told in the past. If the order of events within the body of the tale should be thus-and-so and that order is skewed in Nahman's retelling; or if the rule that all things in the folktale repeat three times is somehow violated; or if the standard motif of the Sleeping Beauty is turned on its head, then the secret of the story's *tikkun* surely lies there.

The derash, or homiletic, approach looks for one-to-one correspondences. When the stories are read as allegories, each element in the plot is explained in terms of another, fixed, meaning rooted in traditional sources and concepts. In this scheme, the literal meaning falls away. The merchant is no longer a merchant, but Satan in disguise. The king is read as God and the Kingdom of Lies as the world of human affairs. Sometimes Reb Nahman throws such allegorical clues into the stories themselves. More frequently, they appear at the end, in a highly abbreviated scriptural shorthand and in smaller print, presumably put there by Nathan. Some have argued that this is no more than a smoke screen, a conscious attempt to neutralize the highest level of reading, or sod.

Read as sod, kabbalistically, the tales do double duty. For every cruel reversal here on earth, for every arduous quest, there is a corresponding drama enacted simultaneously in the upper realms and the two are mutually dependent. The tales are about worlds in collusion and about the forces of Good and Evil fighting it out. Each individual motif is the derivative of the divine configuration of *sefirot,* while the sum of the plot recapitulates—in whole or in part—the Lurianic myth of *tsimtsum, shevirah,* and *tikkun.* This is a reading reserved for adult male initiates.

None of these structural, homiletic, and kabbalistic methods, however, directly addresses the existential drama of the storyteller himself, and through him, of every person listening to the tale. Thus one more approach to the tales is needed that does not depend on preexisting plot structures, scriptural and rabbinic sources, or on kabbalistic symbols. The subtext is Reb Nahman's own life and complex personality. This is the most difficult method of all, because the text is conditioned by Nahman's ever-unfolding life, rather than *being* his life.

While Reb Nahman was alive, the personal experience he brought to each subsequent tale kept changing. There was a year-and-a-half break between the telling of the eighth and the ninth tale, during which time Reb Nahman traveled to the city of Lemberg to be treated for tuberculosis. When he picked up his storytelling again in 1809, he was not the same person. The stories reflected that change in their length and extraordinary complexity. After his death the drama of discovery now centered on the written clues to his internal life scattered among all his other writings. As the reader learns more about Reb Nahman, the sum of the story's existential meanings changes too.

Informed by that biographical knowledge, the reader-listener discovers that

Reb Nahman is both the Wise Man *and* the Simpleton; both the zaddik whose prayers are efficacious and the leprous prince whom he finally heals. Most spectacularly, Nahman is revealed as all the Seven Beggars at once, and then some. Just as the purpose of the bilingual transcript is to conjure up the living presence of the Master in the very act of storytelling, so the existential-biographical reading tries to make contact with the living author for whom the written text is but an intermediary. When the audience discovers its own existential drama being played out in the storyteller's multiple personae, then and only then does the final barrier fall.

"On the way I told a tale (of such power) that whoever heard it had thoughts of repentance. This is it." Thus Reb Nahman re-creates the precise moment for the telling of his first tale that he now repeats for the benefit of his chief disciple. Nathan will later title this tale "The Loss of the Princess" and superimpose titles on the other twelve as well. Perhaps because it is the first, it still reads much like a "tale which other people tell." A princess is taken into captivity; a hero volunteers to set her free and undergoes severe tests until he does. Yet there is much happening on the peshat level of reading that already doesn't fit the mold. Reb Nahman gives the happy ending away at the very outset—but when the story does conclude, the climax is missing. "(And how he freed her he [Reb Nahman] did not tell.) And finally he [the viceroy] did free her." The viceroy-hero, moreover, fights no dragons and kills no witches. Instead, he undergoes three prolonged tests that involve much fasting, crying, and perseverance. There is no erotic element. After the viceroy fails the second time around, the princess awakens him from his sleep—the Sleeping Beauty motif in reverse—and when all is said and done, there is no hint that the triple ordeal will end in marriage.[37]

An allegorical reading makes sense of some, but by no means all, of these discrepancies. The king, as usual, is God, and the princess is the Shekhinah, the female aspect of God in His nearness to the world. Since the Destruction of the Temple, she accompanies Israel in exile. That leaves the viceroy as a stand-in for the people of Israel. With all three main characters accounted for, each of the viceroy's three trials translates into another phase of Israel's sacred history: like Adam, the viceroy tasted of the forbidden apple; like Noah, he drank of the forbidden wine, and his seventy-year-long sleep corresponds to the Babylonian exile. If Israel repents of its evil ways, then the Shekhinah will someday be restored to her proper place in God's Temple.

The story also offers an ethical lesson for each individual Jew. For instance, the viceroy at first has no trouble entering the palace where the princess is held captive, for this is the "Devil's habitat"—*dos ort vos iz nit gut,* in the words of the story. Anyone can enter, but getting out is something else. In contrast, the place of her last captivity, the pearly castle on a golden mountain, is very difficult to breach. In a place where "everything is very expensive," you need to bribe your way in and only the pure of heart can manage to save themselves from its corruption. That escape route is never mapped.

The precise redemptive calendar falls into place only on the next level of reading, for the king is none other than *Keter,* the "Crown," and his six sons are the lower *sefirot:* Power and Mercy, Majesty and Endurance, Beauty and Foundation.[38] The reason why the king favors his only daughter over them is that she is Sovereignty, the queen, the bride, whose reunion with the Godhead is the ultimate goal of cosmic *tikkun.* Once the reader is alerted to the messianic urgency of this tale, then the opposite, demonic forces come alive as well. It begins with an act of *tsimtsum,* of the king retracting his love for his daughter with the harsh words "*der nit guter zol dikh aveknemen;* may the Devil take you away!" Her sudden disappearance is the act of *shevirah* that follows. The viceroy's quest to return her to her proper place necessarily leads him into the world of evil and seduction. Only by purging the root of evil in one's soul can the redemptive process be completed.

Not everyone, of course, can hope to achieve this. That is why the viceroy is none other than Nahman, the *tsaddik hador,* the "champion of redemption." And that is why the storyteller lavishes so much attention on the viceroy's tears and prayers, which call attention to the hero's quest to overcome his bodily passions, his theological doubts, and his yearning for material wealth.[39] In this existential reading, the viceroy's debate with the three giants in the desert no longer seems like a stalling tactic, like mere repetition, but as the only way the hero's struggle can ever be resolved. Here as elsewhere in the tales, the desert is both a place of seduction and of purification.[40] Henceforth, the desert is the favored setting of radical self-confrontation in Reb Nahman's symbolic landscape.

Then there are the demons, who wear so many guises. They have been around in Jewish narrative at least since Job. There, at least, Satan worked behind-the-scenes and chose his victim with utmost care, but if to judge from the Talmud and midrashim, his emissaries were an everyday presence in all rabbinic households. The extreme asceticism of the thirteenth-century German pietists restored something of Satan's elite proclivities: Overcoming his temptations is what separated the true pietists from the mere sinners. Finally given free rein by the spread of kabbalistic teachings, a multitude of demons populated the sermons and ethical tracts of the Jewish Middle Ages.[41] Now, as Nahman's generation approaches the eleventh hour before the final redemption, the demons pull out all the stops. They work alone or in groups, in person or by proxy. The evil may be set in motion either by the demonic behavior of kings, princesses, and their maidservants (tales 4 and 11) or when the ruling elite has recourse to sorcerers who then carry out its nefarious plans (tale 5). Sometimes, there are whole kingdoms where evil and foolishness reign supreme (tales 6 and 12); other times, the demons in their separate habitations can be provoked to self-destruct (tale 3). The Devil himself may waylay the unsuspecting victims (tale 8). On rarer occasions he can be the rod of God's wrath (tale 9).

Were the hero or heroine to combat the evil alone, he or she would have little hope of success. Mortals may draw upon the powers of prayer and of introspection, but there are also unifying forces out in the universe that come to the aid of humans. There are giants who know every aspect of the world; one tree that if watered would destroy all the demons; an iron staff that grows at the place where the 365 courses of the sun all meet; a poem that can only be sung by one person completely and correctly; a magical instrument that can be exchanged for the knowledge of how to deduce one thing from another; a hand with a map of all the worlds and all the occurrences past, present and future; a blind beggar who can see through reality; and the True Man of Kindness who enables time to exist. As the demons are the agents of *shevirah,* the mystical unities are the agents of *tikkun.*

Walking the tightrope between these dialectical forces, the hero can fall and be destroyed; can reach his desired end; or, as in the case of "The Lost Princess," be left hanging in midair. These are heroes possessed of divine madness, of exemplary beauty and ugliness, of utter selflessness and gratuitous cruelty. The lyrical and passive princess of the first tale becomes the relentless egoist of the second, a princess who gets her suitors drunk before disposing of them; who kills an innocent prince when she sights him scrambling up a mast half naked.[42] No other form of self-expression—not prayer, not commentary, not ethical exhortation—could dramatize Reb Nahman's sense of life in extremis as effectively as these fantastically elaborated tales of anonymous kings, queens, courtiers, and wandering beggars. To give them names would delimit the scope of that universal crisis: not Ivan the Prince or Ivan the Fool; not Elijah the Prophet or the star-crossed lovers Mordecai and Esther; not the Besht and his famous disciples, but an unnamed aristocracy scheming, wandering, and suffering anywhere and everywhere. Instead of named cities, towns, and villages, a symbolic landscape of two thousand mountains, seven waters, singing forests, and enormous deserts. Instead of sabbaths and festivals, endless time punctuated by sudden disaster and joyous weddings.

What makes the crisis real within that rarefied world of symbolic and anonymous action is Reb Nahman's talent for historical realism, psychological insight, and social satire. The Napoleonic wars once caught Reb Nahman off the coast of the Land of Israel; back home in the Ukraine, he followed Napoleon's progress through Europe with keen interest.[43] These dramatic events must have quickened in Reb Nahman a sense of déjà vu: Had not the Jews of Spain and Portugal also succumbed to a king Ferdinand and queen Isabella who had wanted

to conquer the world? Had not Solomon Ibn Verga described the tragic consequences of the expulsion in his sixteenth-century chronicle, *The Sceptre of Judah*?[44]
Did not the repetition of conquest and apostasy augur ill for the Jews of Europe?

"Once there was a king who decreed for his country exile or conversion.
Whoever wanted to stay in the country would have to convert, and if not, he
would be exiled from the country." Some of the king's subjects abandon their
wealth, but others choose to remain and live the life of Marranos. "Secretly they
practiced the Jewish religion, but in public they were not allowed to do so." When
the king dies his son rules more cruelly still and the ministers plot to kill him. One
among them is a secret Jew who reveals the plot to the king and as a reward is
allowed to practice his religion freely, "to put on prayershawl and phylacteries in
public." Then the son dies too and is followed by a grandson who rules with
kindness. As a precaution against ever meeting up with his father's fate, he consults
with astrologers, who predict "that his seed would be destroyed unless he took
heed of the ox and the lamb." Thus it is recorded and then he dies.

The great-grandson who assumes the throne returns to the path of evil and
orders all oxen and sheep banished from his kingdom. In his drive to conquer the
world, he fashions a man out of metal that consists of all the seven kinds of metal
in the world, for each of the seven planets.

> And he placed him on a high mountain. All the seven planets shone on that
> man. When a person needed some advice, whether to make a certain deal or
> not, he would stand opposite the limb made from the kind of metal that
> corresponded to the part of the world where he came from, and would think
> whether or not to do it. If he was supposed to do it, that limb would light up
> and shine, and if not, the limb would darken. The king did all this, and
> thus, he conquered the entire world and collected much money. (Y 39; E
> 101)

But for the man of metals to function properly, however, the king has to "humble
the proud and exalt the humble," so the king, slavishly literal in all things, does
just that throughout his kingdom. The old Jewish minister suddenly finds himself
reduced once more to living the life of a Marrano.

One reversal works another. The king dreams that the constellations of
Taurus (the ox) and Aries (the lamb) are laughing at him—confirmation of the
terrible omen contained in the book of records. When the dream interpreters
cannot allay the king's fears, there appears a wise man whose father taught him
about an iron staff that grows at the crossroads of the sun's 365 courses. "When
whosoever was fearful came to this place, he was saved from his fear." Led by the
wise man, the king sets out with his wife and family until at the crossroads they

meet a destructive angel who maps out the obstacles that lie ahead. Finally they come upon a fire. And the king sees that "kings and Jews, wrapped in prayer shawl and *tefilin,* were walking through the fire." The wise man, armed with his father's warnings, will not proceed any further, but the king, seeing other kings walking safely through the flames, forges ahead with his wife and sons and all his seed and they are consumed in the flames.

Back in the palace, the Marrano minister explains this dramatic turn of events to the other ministers. "The astrologers saw," he now openly mocks, "and did not know what they saw." The omen has nothing to do either with real oxen and sheep or with their celestial counterparts. "From the skin of the ox one makes *tefilin,* and from the wool of the lamb one makes fringes for the prayer shawl, and through them he and his seed were destroyed. Those kings in whose country Jews lived dressed in *tallith* and *tefilin* walked through the fire, and were not harmed at all" (Y 42; E 103).

As historical legend, "The King Who Decreed Conversion" is familiar enough. Ever since Joseph became viceroy over Egypt and Mordecai bested Haman in King Ahasuerus's court, God has rescued His people through His chosen ministers. Reinforcing the surface plot of palace intrigue—and a folktale chronology of three-kings-plus-one—is another, more subtle, narrative strand about illusion and reality. In a kingdom where no one can be what he wants, Jews pretend to be non-Jews and traitors pretend to be loyal servants. Each king after the first is labeled truly *wise,* regardless of how he actually behaves. The great-grandson in turn becomes so very wise that "he fell upon a clever plan" to fashion a kind of metal golem. Reb Nahman undermines that pretense to wisdom by using the word *khokhme* for "clever plan," from the same root as *khokhem,* "wise man." The attribution of wisdom to each of the earthly rulers builds up contrapuntally to the appearance of a true *khokhem.* His knowledge, he repeatedly stresses, comes down to him by tradition from his father. And so the kingdom founded on lies, brute force, and false wisdom is finally destroyed by the combined force of traditional wisdom, simple piety, and sublime knowledge.

The allegorical reading confirms that the story is structured around the absolute dichotomy between the worlds of truth and falsehood. According to Nathan's cryptic comments at the story's end, all the story's astonishing symbols, including the wise man's mysterious itinerary, are rooted in the Torah, the Book of Truth. To be precise, the story can be read as a running commentary on the second chapter of Psalms, the book that Reb Nahman committed to memory from early on.[45] The nations that raged and the peoples who plotted against the Lord and against His anointed (verse 1) exclaimed, "Let us break the cords of their yoke, / shake off their ropes from us!" (verse 2). The Talmud in Avodah Zarah already identified the cords in this passage with the leather straps of *tefilin* and the ropes with the fringes of the prayer shawl. The Lord's response was to laugh at the blasphemers from His heavenly throne (verse 4), just as the constellations laugh at the last of the wicked kings. Then God spoke to them in anger, terrifying them in His rage (verse 5), just like the destructive angel at the crossroads. In demonic opposition to the king whom God enthroned on Zion, His holy mountain (verse 6), the evil king has installed a composite metal statue of all the earthly rulers whose advice was sought by all—instead of God's (verse 8). "You shall break them with an iron rod," said the Lord (verse 9)—and so it is.

For those who view Nahman as the precursor of Jewish modernism, such a homiletic reading is anathema. It turns the most exciting and mysterious passages in his tales into mere pablum for the pious. If everything is rooted in Scripture, and in the Psalter at that, then the Jewish story is not nearly "emancipated." But for those who wish to plumb the wellsprings of Reb Nahman's imagination, and to understand why his voice alone broke through the stodgy conventions of the learned tradition, such spadework is indispensable. For who else ever unpacked the tight rhetoric of the Psalms into a metahistorical plot that linked Joseph to Mordecai to the Spanish Inquisition to the Napoleonic conquest? Is this any less creative than the Master's radical messianic agenda that in any event had to be cloaked in unobjectionable terms?

Perhaps Nathan's commentary should have allowed that the grotesque description of the Man of Seven Metals placed by the last king atop a mountain owes more to *Adam Kadmon,* the "Primordial Man of the Zohar," than to Psalms 2:6. The secret world of the Godhead was manifested in the Primordial Man who drew together the seven *sefirot.*[46] In demonic contrast, the Man of Seven Metals embodies all that is base and corrupt in the world of illusion. Certainly he stands in counterpoint to the Destructive Angel who guards the iron rod at the crossroads of the sun's 365 courses. For just as the second act of *shevirah* in the story—the point at which the Jewish minister has to go into hiding once again—is ushered in by the fashioning of the all-knowing idol, the presence of the angel at the crossroads heralds the final fiery act of *tikkun.*

The most active agent of *tikkun,* it turns out, is not the wise man with his father's traditions but the minister who himself takes credit for the king's downfall and has the last triumphant word. And a fitting end it is for a man who was born into a kingdom of lies, after the exile of the faithful had already occurred. At great personal risk, he gambles and wins his freedom to pray as a Jew, only to have it snatched away at the whim of a mad king who considers himself a sage. The minister is thus forced to live most of his life in disguise and even when he is granted "freedom of religion" he can never pray with a requisite quorum of other Jews. He stands alone wearing prayer shawl and *tefilin* and surrounded by enmity, while they, in their simple piety, are off somewhere else protected by a wall of fire.

Could this be Reb Nahman, the zaddik as Marrano, a character with true visionary and introspective powers? Once, during that fateful voyage to the Land of Israel, at a moment when everything seemed lost, Reb Nahman resolved that should he be sold as a slave and prevented from living the ritual life of a Jew, he would still be able to observe the commandments in spirit.[47] That formative experience, now reimagined as a story, is resolved through a hero who can thwart the powers of darkness *only* by living in disguise. In the real world of idolatry, war, and falsehood, the way to achieve his goal is to cut himself off from his people, from prayer, and from public observance. The seeker's soul is born into a world of falsehood and that is where the redemptive struggle must be waged.

The hero as tightrope walker, as master dissimulator, as Marrano. These are versions of existential loneliness more terrifying than the typical "isolation" of the fairy-tale hero who, as hated stepchild or lone adventurer, invariably establishes a new and more lasting affiliation.[48] What happens to the viceroy after he returns the princess to her father? And what of the minister who can practice freely as a Jew once more but has left his coreligionists far behind? All the more terrifying, then, when the ending of the story is not deferred until a messianic tomorrow or righteously resolved in a punishing fire but is unequivocally tragic.

This brings us to "The Rabbi and His Only Son," the most overtly auto-biographical of Reb Nahman's thirteen tales. The story harks back to his earliest years gathering disciples in Medvedevke. Akin to such real-life figures as Dov of Cheryn, the rabbi's son must overcome both internal and external obstacles in order to find proper spiritual counsel. The fictional son who "felt that there was some imperfection in himself, but he did not know what it was, so he felt no delight in his study and prayer," corresponds to Dov, who fell into a state of inner turmoil and depression on the eve of his trip to see Reb Nahman.[49] In lieu of the stern rabbinic father who does everything he can to thwart his son's desire, Dov's own teacher had warned against having any contact with the young rebbe. Reb Nahman adds an overlay of generational conflict between the young, who are drawn to Hasidism, and the older, rabbinic elite who remain adamantly opposed.

Since the days of Isaac Luria such tales of *hitkarvut* carry obvious propaganda value. They celebrate and propagate the powers of the mystical hero to *draw close* the souls of those who have strayed.[50] Failed encounters, in this scheme, are equally fraught with messianic meaning. Such is the famous tale about the Besht seeking his Sephardic counterpart Rabbi Hayyim ibn Atar in order that the two of them together might bring the Messiah. Perhaps in allusion to this tale, Reb Nahman uses the kabbalistic code words *ma'or katan,* "the small light" (or the moon, Sovereignty), to describe the rabbi's son. And so hardly has the story begun than it reverberates with autobiographical, historical, and messianic echoes.[51]

It also reads like a conventional folktale in which everything is tripled. The story is divided into three main parts. The middle section describes three aborted attempts by the father and son to reach the zaddik as each time something happens to trip them up. After the third attempt, when the son dies, he appears to his father three times in a dream. The son is angry and instructs his father to visit the zaddik in order to discover why. Now the bereaved father sets out alone and, stopping at the same inn as before, he recognizes the merchant who convinced them to turn back. Here the story takes a surprising turn, even as it wraps all the loose ends together.

> And the merchant opened his mouth and told him: "Why, I can swallow you if you want me to."
> He [the father] said to him: "What are you talking about?"
> And he replied: "Do you remember? When you traveled with your son, first the horse fell on the bridge, and you returned. Then the axles broke. Then you met me and I told you the zaddik was frivolous. And now that I've done away with your son you're free to travel on. For your son was in the aspect of 'the small light,' and that zaddik . . . is in the aspect of 'the great light,' and if they had united, the Messiah would have come. But now that I have done away with him, you're allowed to travel."
> In the middle of his words he disappeared, and the rabbi had no one to talk to. The rabbi traveled to the zaddik and he cried: "*Gevald, gevald!* Help me! Oh help me! *Ḥaval 'al de'avdin velo mishtakḥin!* Alas for those who are lost and are no longer found!" (Y 61; E 137–138)

Lest there be any doubt as to the merchant's true identity, Nathan explains that he is Samael, the Devil. "For this is how the Evil One behaves. First he incites the person, and if the latter obeys, God forbid, he [the Devil] himself taunts the person and wreaks personal vengeance upon him for obeying. May the Lord blessed be He rescue us from his hands and return us to the real truth. Amen."

The classical story repertoire had its sublime and tragic moments—the excommunication of Eliezer ben Hyrcanus; the martyrdom of Rabbi Akiva; the deathbed scene of Isaac Luria; Joseph della Reina's last-minute failure to capture Satan; the Besht's failed intercession for the Martyrs of Pavlysh—but that moment was always somehow mitigated and neutralized. Even when the story was not embedded within a larger discussion (why a man may not be alone with two women but a woman can be alone with two men), God and His judgment remained inviolate. Human error, hubris, and heroism all confirmed the ultimate authority of God. If there were choices to be made, the wrong choice always proved illusory; biblical monotheism did not allow for two equally valid choices. Reb Nahman, while adhering to the compositional rules of telling a saint's tale and remaining within a believable historical setting, produces a story that is dead-ended.[52]

To begin with, there is the zaddik, falsely accused of being a *kal,* light-headed, and frivolous, and of having openly transgressed. There is veiled reference here to the bitter feud with the Shpoler Zeyde who stopped at nothing to link Reb Nahman's name with the Sabbatian heresy. In the story, the Devil comes cloaked as a traveling merchant. In real life he can live dangerously close to home.[53]

Then there is the son, who struggles on three fronts: with the authority of his father who disparages the zaddik's learning and seeks every excuse to return home; with the demonic obstacles laid in his path; and with his psychological obstacles to faith. He of the exalted soul, whose personal salvation might have brought the redemption of the world, is finally destroyed by the combination of the three.

Most tragic of all is the father who is neither devil nor saint. Nathan's homespun moral tacked on to the end tries hard to alleviate the pain, but the anguished cry—in Aramaic and Yiddish—is Reb Nahman's very last word. *Ḥaval 'al de'avdin velo mishtakḥin* is what is said to honor the memory of the dead. *"Gevald, gevald"* (which appears only in the Yiddish) is an outburst of unrequited grief. This is the cry of the storyteller himself whose only surviving son died of a childhood disease the year before. Though still an infant, Shloyme Ephraim loomed very large in his father's messianic plans. Yes, the devil was to blame, but no less than the father: guilty of overbearing pride, guilty of driving the unities of Beauty and Sovereignty apart, guilty of killing the very partner in redemption whom he himself had sired. Once, on Mount Moriah, a father's only son was spared by the intercession of an angel. There, too, the Midrash tells us, the devil was sent to frustrate the resolve of man.[54] Here, in contrast, a father succumbed and sacrificed his only son on the altar of his own self-interest.

Increasingly, Reb Nahman invented plots that center on a complex and dramatic contest between those who lived in a world of illusion and those who broke through to the truth of existence.[55] There were sound biographical reasons for such inventions. In the summer of 1807 Reb Nahman detected in himself the first signs of tuberculosis, the dread disease that had just killed his wife Sosia. That fall he left for Lemberg, a center of commerce and enlightenment, to seek medical treatment. Upon his return some eight months later, he came to view himself as a new kind of survivor, having entered the kingdom of falsehood and seen the modern heresy in all its scope. Rousing himself and his disciples to fight the great battle that lay ahead, he resumed his storytelling in the winter of 1809. All the longer tales (nos. 9–13) date from the intensely creative year that followed.[56]

Most memorable is the contest waged between "The Wise Man and the Simpleton," the *khokhem* and the *tam*. We already know from his earlier tales that *khokhme* can cut both ways, to be used for evil as well as for good. In traditional sources, however, the epithet of *tam* always carried positive associations. There was Jacob, "a *quiet man [ish tam]*, dwelling in tents" (Gen. 25:27); Job, who "was wholehearted *[tam]* and upright and one that feared God and shunned evil" (Job

1:1), and, of course, the third of the Four Sons in the Passover Haggadah. Like his namesake, the *tam* of Reb Nahman's story decides to stay put when his wealthy father lost everything but the parental house. Being of "a plain and common mind," the simpleton takes up shoemaking and settles down to an austere life, while his good friend and former classmate responds to his own father's impoverishment by setting out into the world seeking adventure and knowledge. Due to his restless nature and his hatred of physical labor, this wise man wanders from place to place and from one profession to another. In all, he masters seven wisdoms: goldsmithery, gem-cutting, medicine, Latin, writing, philosophy, and sciences, but with this vast fund of knowledge "the world began to seem like nothing in his eyes" (Y 65; E 145). So he decides to return home where he can at least show off what he has learned. "And he suffered greatly on the road, since he had no one to talk to because of his wisdom" (Y 65; E 146).

The simpleton, meanwhile, never fully masters the one craft of being a cobbler. Rather than pursue external goals and material gains, he is happy in his minimal existence. Though the object of ridicule, he always responds,

> "*Nor on leytsones,* Only no mockery!" And as soon as they answered him without mockery, he listened to them and began talking with them. He did not want to be overly shrewd *[ibertrakhtn khokhmes]* since it too was a mockery of sorts and he was a simple man. And when he saw that their intention was to mock, he used to say: "So what if you are more clever than I? You will still be fools!" (Y 68; E 148)

Though simple, he knows the difference between simplicity and folly, which is ultimately the difference between good and evil.[57]

The reunion of the two sons and neighbors concludes the first part of the story and draws the contrast between them ever so sharply. Though he ridicules his friend's behavior as that of a madman, it is the wise man's home that lies in ruins and the simpleton's house in which he seeks refuge at last. More acute still is his suffering for wanting to achieve perfection. He suffers because his mastery is put in question by local philistines and because he alone knows that the lauded work is flawed. Later, when the two friends debate the matter of foolishness, the simpleton not only holds his ground but goes so far as to predict, "With the Lord, blessed be He, everything is possible. And it is possible that in an instant I should attain your cleverness" (Y 71; E 150).

This sets the stage for the reversal of their fortunes. It happens that their epithets (The Wise Man and The Simpleton) become known to the king, who calls them for an audience. The simpleton's response is joyous and spontaneous. "No joke?" he asks, and when at each stage he is assured that the request is serious, he does what is required and rises at last to becoming a minister. The wise man's response is to deny the king's existence and to convince the king's messenger of the same. The two of them then set out together and soon become beggars. In this sorry state they eventually arrive in the domain of the new minister, where there lives a famous faith healer known as a *ba'al shem*. Naturally, the wise man (himself a doctor) ridicules the *ba'al shem*'s powers and is soundly beaten for such heresy. Seeking redress, he goes all the way up the ranks of the bureacracy until he comes before the simple minister himself. Thus they have come full circle, the wise man reduced to rags and the simpleton possessing wealth and practical wisdom.

Were this a folktale about Little Ivan and Big Ivan, it would end here, but Reb Nahman goes further. Only their external circumstances have changed, after all. The simpleton has merely been raised to a ministerial position while the wise man, though pauperized, is unrepentant. A true miracle is needed to alter the status quo. So, in the third and final episode, it is the devil who sets out to test them, not the king. Each acts exactly on cue: The simpleton rushes to the *ba'al shem* for a protective amulet while the wise man sets out for the encounter with military protection. The simpleton is saved while the wise man and his traveling companion are thrown into a muddy torture pit. "And they suffered excruciating torments for several years."

Then, accompanied by the *ba'al shem,* the simpleton minister discovers the wise man in the mire. "My brother," exclaims the wise man upon seeing his old friend. Despite years of prolonged torture, the latter still denies the devil his due. "See how they beat and torment me, those hooligans, for no reason!" he protests. Astounded by such stubborn denial, the simpleton minister appeals for the *ba'al shem* to perform a miracle, "and show them that this is the Devil and not men." Only when the mire disappears and the devil turns to dust does the wise man (and presumably his companion too) admit that there was a king, and a true *ba'al shem.*

So unlike the other stories, this one is stark, polemical, and gritty. Its dialogue and characterization are true to life, as are the specific issues of faith and denial. A Yiddish guide to popular medicine had recently appeared in the Ukraine, unremitting in its criticism of faith healers and old wives' remedies.[58] That was something Reb Nahman could not let pass, not because he had to protect his great-grandfather's reputation, but because once you placed your trust in science instead of in God, the door to apostasy was thrown open. In their differentiated response to the *ba'al shem,* the two major figures of the story act out their opposing worldviews. The rationalist believes only what the eye can see and has delved so deeply into philosophical matters that he denies the existence both of the king and the devil. The simpleton's path of joy and simple faith leads him to trust implicitly in the *ba'al shem*'s powers. The true path of faith is through serving the king and not through scientific inquiry. It is a faith that can alter the course of nature.

As charming and precise as is Reb Nahman's portrayal of religious sim-plicity, his counterportrait is surprisingly accurate.[59] It is clear that Reb Nahman has visited the seat of reason himself. Elsewhere he taught that only the zaddik can risk studying the "seven wisdoms," for any lesser mortal would surely stumble and fall.[60] In proscribing those "seven wisdoms" from his disciples, he did not differentiate between works of medieval Jewish philosophy and the newfangled heretical tracts. But where did that leave him? The zaddik too must "suffer greatly on the road, since he has no one to talk to because of his wisdom." Alone in his ivory tower of absolute perfection, tortured by knowledge and wisdom that he cannot share with anyone, constantly plagued by the fear of pollution, he desperately needs to be redeemed by the simple and the pure. "Only no mockery," says the simpleton, whose innocence saves him from doing evil. The wise man must first acknowledge that the devil is real before he can ever admit the error of his ways. As the one who has glimpsed, even for a moment, a universe devoid of the king—of God—he must live with that terror for the rest of his life.

What is happening in Reb Nahman's tales—the happy resolution of "The Wise Man and the Simpleton" notwithstanding—is that the contest between alternatives has become ever more extreme. He pits a life of utter denial against a life of boundless joy. There is no middle path. The stories are getting longer now, are becoming apocalyptic staging grounds for the final cosmic battle. Yet there is a concomitant burst of lyrical, fantastic, and ecumenical energy. Instead of sisters scheming against their brothers, husbands against their wives, and ministers against their king; instead of a father bereft of a son and a wise man bested by a simpleton, Reb Nahman finally releases his characters from their terrible isolation, enabling them to orchestrate the final redemption. In the final two tales, tales that account for nearly half of the volume, the cast of characters is infinitely more complex. Only a master storyteller can keep them all together; only an audience schooled in memorization can recall the half of it in proper sequence.

Far from human habitation there lives a Master of Prayer who establishes an order of holy hermits. Elsewhere there exists another "voluntary society" that is likewise sealed off from the outside but for diametrically opposite ends: A pagan hierarchy predicated solely on the acquisition of wealth.

To this first set of oppositions, Reb Nahman then adds another. There was a royal court with a king and a queen and a princess and a child, an orator and a wise man, a keeper of the king's treasure and a faithful friend, and a warrior and a master of prayer, one more wondrous than the next. But one day "there arose a great tempest in the world. And the tempest upset and confused the entire world. It turned desert into settlement and turned ocean into dry land" (Y 160; E 229). In this act of *shevirah* the royal court was dispersed and each court member lost contact with the others. There arose many factions and sects, each one devoted to another form of idolatry: one worshiped only honor, another celebrated destruction and murder; a third practiced sexual orgies; and so on. A modern commentator has mapped it out like this:[61]

| MEMBER OF COURT | REPRESENTATIVE OF: | DEBASED VIRTUE | HIGHER VIRTUE |
|---|---|---|---|
| King | God | Honor | Glory |
| Queen | — | Murder, destruction | Understanding |
| Princess | Shekhinah | Orgiastic fecundity | Divine abundance |
| Warrior | Precursor of Messiah | Physical prowess | Spiritual prowess |
| Faithful Friend | Abraham | Drunkenness | Unlimited love |
| Wise Man | Moses | Cleverness | Torah, wisdom |
| Treasurer | Aaron, high priest | Wealth | Blessing |
| Orator | King David, Levites | Verbosity | Praise of God |
| Infant | Messiah | Health, care of body | Perfection |
| Master of Prayer | Elijah, zaddik of generation | Prayer (not debased) | Prayer |

In the vast orchestration of *tikkun* that follows, each member of the royal entourage is acclaimed by another idolatrous sect that then submits to purification. The "debased virtue" is turned back into its "higher virtue." The Master of Prayer, too, is acclaimed king over a band of zaddikim who had engaged only in prayer, "but now the Master of Prayer opened their eyes until they became venerable *zaddikim*" (Y 174; E 238). Though the Master of Prayer remains distinct from the others, he no longer operates alone. He has his own group of zaddikim, receives tactical guidance from the Warrior, and succeeds in reuniting all the lost members of the royal court whom the storyteller now calls *der heyliker kibuts*, the "Holy Community."

Yet the combined force of cosmic *tikkun* fails to crack the hardest nut of all—the Land of Wealth. When the Master's disciples go off on their own to convert the Land of Wealth, having overheard the Master sigh despondently, "Who knows how far they can go astray this way?" (Y 144; E 217), the disciples try to replicate the way the Master originally proselytized sinners. The disciples begin, as he did, with the "lowly people," and try to work their way up the social ladder. And they use the identical argument, "saying that money was not the purpose of life, but that the chief purpose of life was worship of the Lord" (Y 144; E 218). Yet their pleas fall on deaf ears, for this is a country whose hierarchy and cosmology are based on wealth. These people actually perform human sacrifice in order to insure greater wealth and they have instituted an elaborate system of checks and balances to insure that only the truly wealthy are honored. When the disciples bring back a report that the inhabitants have established idols of the truly wealthy, the Master's worst fears are confirmed. He decides to take action himself.

But he fails to win over even the lowliest of those who guard the perimeter of the fortified city; when he gains easy entry, he finds the inhabitants obsessed with the impending attack of the Warrior. The Warrior wants only their submission, not their wealth, but precisely because he disdains what they worship, to capitulate would be tantamount to conversion. Out of fear, they begin sacrificing the least wealthy people (whom they call *khayelekh*, "little beasts") to the gods. They take out their wrath on the Master of Prayer, too, for disparaging the latest rescue plan to seek aid from a neighboring and supremely wealthy kingdom. Nothing thus far in this world of mammon in any way violates the laws of human folly. Only at this point, a third of the way through, does the storyteller introduce a dimension beyond time and space (as the Master hints at some hidden knowledge about the Warrior). "At the palace of the King with whom I stayed," says the Master of Prayer, "was a hand, that is, there was a picture of a hand with five fingers and with all the lines which are on a hand. And this hand was a map of all the worlds. And everything which has been from the creation of the heavens and the earth until the end of time, and will be afterwards was drawn on that hand" (Y 155; E 225). It was by means of that hand, he goes on to explain, that he gained entry into the fortified city and that he could foretell the downfall of the neighboring wealthy kingdom. Convinced of the hand's prophetic powers, the inhabitants press the Master for more details, and he launches into the tale of the royal court and its tragic dispersion.

When the story of the Land of Wealth finally picks up again many pages later, the Master has already joined forces with the Warrior, whom he recognizes as a lost member of the royal court. The Warrior explains that the only cure to the passion for money is through the drastic measure of his magic sword. They, meanwhile, have returned to their folly with a vengeance, and despite everything they've heard, they send messengers to the neighboring kingdom to rescue them from the Warrior. On the way the messengers meet someone carrying a cane studded with precious diamonds. So awestruck are they by his wealth that they kneel down before him and prostrate themselves. The man says that this is nothing compared to the king's treasure which, when displayed before them, inspires even greater awe.

> However they made no sacrifices (according to their opinion, this man was a God and they would surely have sacrificed themselves to him) because the emissaries were ordered not to make sacrifices along the way, for they feared that if they wanted to make sacrifices along the way, not one of them would remain. For if one might find a treasure along the way, or if one of them went to the outhouse and found a treasure there, he would begin to sacrifice himself and no one would remain among them. (Y 175; E 239–240)

What an exquisite parody of religious fanaticism! Brainwashed into worshiping everything that glitters and glows, these people have to protect themselves from their own religious fervor, lest they martyr themselves to the cause. The grotesque spectacle of dying for wealth inside a foul outhouse is not incidental detail. It is all explained in the marvelous scatalogical climax. Here the Warrior employs a kind of behaviorist treatment to cure the emissaries of their passion for wealth. He leads them through a controlled experiment in which one wind whets their appetite while the countervailing wind carries a stench. Several repetitions later the Warrior says, "Can't you see that there is nothing here that should stink? It must be you yourselves who stink." When they are finally fed the desired food, it brings on a veritable orgy of self-repugnance.

> No sooner had they eaten from the foods than they threw away their money. Each one dug a pit and buried himself in it out of great shame, because they felt that their money stank exactly like excrement, for they had tasted of the food. They tore at their faces and buried themselves and could not lift up their heads at all. Each was ashamed of the other. (Y 190; E 249)

Purged of their lust for money, they are ready as a group to be cleansed by prayers of penitence. "And the King became ruler of the whole world, and the whole world returned to God and all engaged only in Torah, prayer, repentance, and good deeds. Amen. May it be His will."

Scatology as eschatology, one might say. As Reb Nahman lets out all the stops, perhaps feeling that time is running out, he chooses new down-to-earth settings in which to enact the final messianic drama. Just as the members of the royal court—symbolic stand-ins for the *sefirot*—must get their hands dirty in the gross idolatries of pride, murder, sex, drunkenness, and the like, so must the zaddik resort to extreme forms of shock treatment and group therapy in order to break down the human passion for money. How simple was the viceroy's task in liberating the kidnapped princess when compared to this vast mobilization of cosmic and earthly forces.

Everything has become more complex, dense, and demanding in these tales: the plot, the characters, and the figure of the storyteller. For as the first of the Yiddish storytellers, Reb Nahman is also the first to invent a persona, a double, a fictional role that justifies how and why he came to tell stories in the first place. That persona is the Master of Prayer, and the key to his complexity lies in the name itself.

In Yiddish he is merely a *baal-tfile*, a Jewish "Everyman" who leads the congregation in prayer. He need not be learned, need not be rich, but in order to lead, his piety should be beyond reproach. Indeed, he must humble himself before the Lord in order to make his prayers efficacious. As it happens, the English equivalents, "Prayer Leader," and "Master of Prayer," are quite misleading, since they suggest precisely the opposite: someone who stands above and beyond the pious flock.[62] Such figures have appeared in earlier tales—the Prince of Jewels, the unreachable zaddik (the Great Light), the Marrano minister—but as a Jewish folk type the *baal-tfile* is a cousin to the *tam,* the cobbler of simple faith and minimal demands. The *baal-tfile* empowers others by virtue of his own self-negation.

Yet as the story unfolds we discover his membership in the elect Holy Community who hold the restoration of the cosmos in their hands. Like the other nine, he has been forced to descend into the cesspools of human depravity in order to effect *tikkun.* Unlike the others, he is seized with a sense of apocalyptic urgency. He works all fronts. He forms a fellowship of disciples who learn his ways but still cannot do what he alone can do. They fail to move the idolatrous Kingdom of Wealth, thus forcing him to leave their utopian community and to stand before kings and their ministers and to debate even with the palace guards. Out there in the world of power and greed, his message of piety and purgation meeting with universal scorn, he must prove his mastery, reveal his hidden knowledge, and reunite the cosmic forces that have been torn apart.

All this proseletyzing, agitating, and organizing has, of course, served a clearly defined goal: a *baal-tfile* cannot pray alone. He needs a quorum. He cannot remain an ascetic saint living in his tower of perfection. Without the others, without the profane, his prayers are nothing. Without them, even his intense piety will not bring the words on the page alive before God. He is much like the storyteller, then, who carries the divine spark but who operates here on earth with standard phrases, fixed plots, and cannot be effective unless there are at least nine other people present to answer: Amen. Like the divinely inspired storyteller, the power of his words are such that they can rouse a whole world to penitence even as they consecrate a tiny group of disciples to the building of utopia.

If there is catharsis to hearing such a difficult story through to its finale, there is perhaps even greater pathos in a complex tale that never ends. The "Tale of the Seven Beggars" is Reb Nahman's unfinished symphony and a grand replay of all his major themes. Here too there is a hero (a prince) who falls into heresy through a misguided quest for wisdom; here too there is a primal disaster that confounds the world; here too there are contests between those who seem to be gifted and those whose deformity is a mask of the sublime; here too the setting for *tikkun*—the joyous wedding of the lost children—is a pit; and here too it takes the combined efforts of seven wondrous beggars to restore the prince to his throne. So much has been written about this tale, and so often has it been stylized, that it would take another book to do it justice.[63] Yet the section from this story that has most excited the Jewish imagination deserves to be cited, at least in part, for it marks both the culmination of everything in Reb Nahman's storytelling art and the beginning of the Jewish storytelling renaissance to come.

It is the third day of the wedding feast in the pit and in response to the cries and longing of the newlyweds, the stuttering beggar appears with his own gift. Like the blind and deaf beggars who preceded him, his deformity is but a mask. He stutters only when he mouths the worldly words that are not praises of the Holy One and are imperfect. Otherwise, he "can recite riddles and poems and songs so marvelous that there is no creature in the universe who would not wish to hear them. And in these songs lies all wisdom." There is a True Man of Kindness *(der emeser ish khesed)* who can vouch for his miraculous powers, but therein lies a story.

The story takes the same narrative form as with the two beggars before, that of a boasting contest. This time wise men are sitting around boasting of their scientific and metallurgical inventions. Then comes one who claims to be as wise as the day, to which the stutterer counters, "Like which day are you wise?" With that question the stutterer is proclaimed the wisest of them all. Why? Therein lies another story.

This last story has to do with the creation of time. Time is created through the deeds of true kindness that the stutterer collects and brings to the True Man of Kindness.

> Now there is a mountain. On the mountain stands a rock. From the rock flows a spring. And everything has a heart. The world taken as a whole has a heart. And the world's heart is of full stature, with a face, hands, and feet. Now the toenail of that heart is more heart-like than anyone else's heart. The mountain with the rock and spring are at one end of the world, and the world's heart stands at the other end. The world's heart stands opposite the spring and yearns and always longs to reach the spring. The yearning and longing of the heart for the spring is extraordinary. It cries out to reach the spring. The spring also yearns and longs for the heart. (Y 211; E 268)

The heart suffers both from without and within: without, because it is being scalded by the sun, within, because of its yearning. When the first becomes too much to bear, a large bird flies overhead and shields it from the sun with its wings. But even during that brief respite, the heart continues to long for the spring. And there is no possible resolution for this yearning because if the heart approaches the hill, it can no longer see the peak or look at the spring. Not to see the spring even for an instant would destroy the heart entirely. "And how could the world exist without its heart?"

As for the spring, it does not exist in consecutive time. "The only time the spring has is that one day which the heart grants it as a gift. The moment the day is finished, the spring, too, will be without time and it will disappear," thus destroying the heart as well. To mark the day's passing, they begin to express their mutual longing by singing riddles and poems and songs. And that is the moment the True

Man of Kindness is waiting for. Just as the day is about to end, he grants the gift of a new day to the heart who then gives it over to the spring. And so another day is secured.

Now each new day arrives with its own distinct poems and music, depending on what day it is. The time that the True Man of Kindness has to grant derives from the stutterer himself, who travels around collecting the good deeds. So, the stutterer is the wisest of all because he alone initiates the process of time through his actions, and knows the riddles and songs appropriate to each new day.

Again one can point to a chapter of Psalms that may have inspired some of Reb Nahman's imagery.

> Hear my cry, O God,
> heed my prayer.
> From the end of the earth I call to You;
> when my heart is faint,
> You lead me to a rock that is high above me.
> For you have been my refuge,
> a tower of strength against the enemy.
> O that I might dwell in Your tent forever,
> take refuge under Your protecting wings.
>
> (Ps. 61:2–5)

But this would only reveal the degree to which the storyteller has transformed the biblical text and context. The parable itself is not a prayer or a psalm. Rather, it recasts the *experience* of prayer, the awesome and unbridgeable gap between the worshiper and God, into a language at once personal, poignant, and poetic. It is no surprise that Reb Nahman composed many songs of his own—*niggunim* without words and haunting melodies set to Hebrew and Yiddish lyrics—which would take on a life of their own, wherever and whenever Jews were in despair.[64]

Once again there are kabbalistic substitutes for the symbols Reb Nahman employs—the heart is the Shekhinah is the true zaddik longing for God—but the sense of wounded passion in this tale-within-a-tale-within-a-tale is utterly new. The yearning for an intimacy that cannot come to be. The paradox of a dialectical faith that cries out for God's distance rather than His presence, for without distance there is no longing, and without longing there is no faith. The cosmic struggle not to bring back the unities but to commingle moments of particularized time and the primal source of Time, which exists outside time. All this is unique to Reb Nahman's theology and artistic vision.[65] It is the true match between the existential struggle of the storyteller and the materials of his story.

Reb Nahman was the first modern Jewish classicist, the sum of everything that came before and the harbinger of the revival to come. He changed the way his immediate audience listened to a Yiddish story; the way future generations of Jewish writers were to view the art of storytelling; the way we, in retrospect, read Jewish tales; and the way we write about them. Were it not for Reb Nahman, the story of Yiddish storytelling would begin with Ayzik-Meyer Dik in the 1850s or with I. L. Peretz in the 1890s. Instead, it must begin with the closing of the biblical canon, and even before that, with the primal catastrophe that brought the world into being.

The cultural significance of these tales cannot be exaggerated. They are the great watershed, from which the many streams of Jewish creativity—scriptural, liturgical, rabbinic, and kabbalistic—are drawn all at once. By reaching back to the "primal years" both of his own psyche and of the collective unconscious, Reb Nahman made the fairy tale speak—both to the tragic finality of death and to the joy of communal and cosmic healing. By bridging Hebrew and Yiddish, the scholars and the folk, mythical past and historic present, Reb Nahman invented a new form of Jewish self-expression. Bringing his passion and learning to bear upon the act of storytelling, he made the evanescent tale into the stuff of a *seyfer*. The learned storyteller turned his craft into a source of prayer, into a numinous text to be recited by the faithful. There had been stories that the sages told about the patriarchs, prophets, and priests; there had been stories that disciples spread about their saints. Not until Nahman ben Simha of Bratslav was there a rabbi-poet-preacher-mystic who made himself the mythic hero of tales of such power that they might awaken the world.

### Notes

1. See Manger's Afterword to *Noente geshtaltn un andere shriftn* [Intimate Figures and Other Writings] (New York, 1961), p. 516.

2. Walter Benjamin, "The Storyteller: Reflections on the Works of Nikolai Leskov" (1936), in *Illuminations,* trans. Harry Zohn, ed. Susan Sontag (New York, 1968), pp. 83–109.

3. For the Jewish presence at Jonesborough festival, see Peninnah Schram, "Telling Stories at NAPPS," *The Jewish Storytelling Newsletter* 1:2 (Winter 1986): 7.

4. Haim Schwarzbaum provides all the relevant variants in *The Mishle Shu'alim (Fox Fables of Rabbi Berechiah Ha-Nakdan: A Study in Comparative Folklore and Fable Lore* (Kiron, 1979), pp. 394–408.

5. Baruch M. Bokser, "Wonder-Working and the Rabbinic Tradition: The Case of Hanina ben Dosa," *Journal for the Study of Judaism* 16 (1985): 77.

6. See on this, Dan Ben-Amos, "Generic Distinctions in the Aggadah," in *Studies in Jewish Folklore,* ed. Frank Talmage (Cambridge, Mass., 1980), pp. 66–67; and M[enahem] E[lon], "Ma'aseh," *Encyclopedia Judaica* 11: 641–649.

7. Bokser, "Wonder-Working and the Rabbinic Tradition, pp. 42–51.

8. Eliezer ben Hyrcanus, *The Fathers According to Rabbi Nathan,* chap. 6; and *Midrash Pirkei de Rabbi Eliezer,* trans. Gerald Friedlander (New York, 1981; rpt. of London, 1916), chap. 2. This last is a sustained (and relatively late) cluster of biographical tales and traditions, which do not, however, build up to a climax. The account of Eliezer ben Hyrcanus's excommunication is entirely absent.

On Rabbi Akiva, see my book, *Against the Apocalypse: Responses to Catastrophe in Modern Jewish Culture* (Cambridge, Mass., 1984), pp. 27–30.

9. The major exponent of the emancipation theory of Hebrew narrative prose is Joseph Dan, in *Hasippur ha'ivri biymei habenayim* [The Hebrew Story in the Middle Ages] (Jerusalem, 1974), and the précis thereof in "Fiction, Hebrew," in *Encyclopedia Judaica,* vol. 6, pp. 1261–1271. For a follow-up, see his "Letoldoteha shel sifrut hashvaḥim," *Jerusalem Studies in Jewish Folklore* 1 (1981): 82–100. In contrast, folklorists Heda Jason, Sara Zfatman, Tamar Alexander, and Eli Yassif stress the interplay of oral and written sources, learned and folk traditions, and Hebrew and vernacular languages. Once they account for the strict conventions of folk literature and the conservative nature of any textual tradition, the desire or ability of medieval Jewish editors and compilers to achieve a free-flowing, "original" narrative appears greatly diminished. A third approach, exemplified by Jacob Elbaum, is to trace the subtle reworking of discrete motifs within their dense and immediate textual setting. See, for example, "From Sermon to Story: The Transformation of the Akedah," *Prooftexts* 6 (1986): 97–116.

10. Sara Zfatman-Biller, "Hasipporet beyidish mireshitah 'ad 'Shivḥei haBesht' (1504–1814)" (Ph.D. diss., Hebrew University, 1983), vol. 1, pp. 9, 116–121.

11. Ibid., p. 97.

12. For the full text, see Sarah Zfatman, *Yiddish Narrative Prose from Its Beginnings to "Shivhei ha-Besht" (1504–1814): An Annotated Bibliography* (Jerusalem, 1985), 17.

13. Though neither a scholarly nor a complete edition, Jacob Meitlis's annotated translation of the *Mayse-bukh* into modern Yiddish conveniently groups the stories into literary-historical clusters and refers the reader to alternative sources. See vol. 38 of the *Musterverk fun der yidisher literatur* (Buenos Aires, 1969). For a (bowdlerized) English ed., see *Maaseh Book,* ed. Moses Gaster (Philadelphia, 1934), 2 vols.

14. See Eli Yassif, "What Is a Folk Book?" *International Folklore Review* 5 (1987): 20–27. For but one example of the refolklorization process, compare "Eliyohu Hanovi un di dray zin" (Meitlis, no. 37; Gaster, no. 157) with "Der

vortzoger," *Yidishe folks-mayses,* ed. J. L. Cahan (Vilna, 1940), no. 23. Both are variants of "The Lazy Boy," AT 675. On the integration of Yiddish within the culture of medieval Ashkenaz, see Max Weinreich, *History of the Yiddish Language,* trans. Shlomo Noble and Joshua A. Fishman (Chicago and London, 1980), chap. 3.

15. The quotation is from *Sefer ḥayyei MOHaRaN hamenukad* (Jerusalem, 1985), sec. 25. On the place of the tale in Beshtian Hasidism, see Joseph Dan, *Hasippur haḥasidi* [The Hasidic Tale] (Jerusalem: Keter, 1975), pp. 40–46; Mendl Piekarz, *Ḥasidut Braslav* [Braslav Hasidism] (Jerusalem, 1972), pp. 104–105; and esp., Chone Shmeruk, *Prokim fun der yidisher literatur-geshikhte* [Yiddish Literature: Aspects of Its History] (Tel Aviv, 1988), p. 253.

Much has been written about the putative sanctity of the Hasidic tale. Arguing for the absolute sanctity of the tale within all of Hasidic tradition is Gedalia Nigal in *Hasipporet haḥasidit: toldoteha venos'eha* [The Hasidic Tale: Its History and Topics] (Jerusalem, 1981), pp. 57–80. Piekarz (pp. 85–101) and Shmeruk (chap. 6), on the other hand, take a more casual view, one most recently corroborated by Yehoshua Mondshein in his facsimile and variorum edition of *Sefer shivḥei haBesht* (Jerusalem, 1982), pp. 52–57. The debate is extremely well summarized by Ada Rapoport-Albert in "Hagiography with Footnotes: Edifying Tales and the Writing of History in Hasidism," *History and Theory Beiheft* 27 (1988): 153–155. A new critical ed. of *Shivḥei haBesht* was published (posthumously) by Avraham Rubinstein (Jerusalem, 1991).

16. These words are quoted in Yiddish in Nathan of Nemirov's first Hebrew preface to the tales. All Yiddish quotations (abbreviated Y) are from *Seyfer sipurey mayses* (Jerusalem, 1979), a bilingual edition of the tales based on the first edition of 1815. This beautiful volume is the closest thing to a scholarly edition of the tales that is now available and is the first in 164 years to restore the Yiddish to its original, southeastern dialect.

Professional Yiddishists and Bratslav Hasidim refer to the town as "Breslov" or "Braslav." See, for instance, the note "On Breslov" appended to Aryeh Kaplan's *Gems of Rabbi Nachman* (Jerusalem, 1980). I adopt the more common spelling.

17. Arthur Green, *Tormented Master: A Life of Rabbi Nahman of Bratslav* (Alabama, 1979), chap. 5; Yehuda Liebes, *"Ha-Tikkun Ha-Kelali* of R. Nahman of Bratslav and Its Sabbatean Links," in his *Studies in Jewish Myth and Jewish Messianism,* trans. Batya Stein (Albany, 1993), pp. 115–150; and Yoav Elstein, *Ma'aseh ḥoshev* [Studies in Hasidic Tales] (Tel Aviv, 1983), chap. 6.

18. Green, *Tormented Master,* chap. 5.

19. *E* stands for Arnold Band's translation, *Nahman of Bratslav: The Tales* (New York, 1978). To simplify matters, all page references are to this translation, even when I deviate therefrom.

20. *Sefer siḥot haRaN,* ed. Nathan Sternherz (Jerusalem, 1978), sec. 52. For a discussion, see Piekarz, *Hasidut Braslav,* p. 111.

21. The analogy between Reb Nahman and the Brothers Grimm was first drawn by Arnold Band. See his edition of *The Tales,* pp. 29–30. Cf. also *The Brothers Grimm and Folktale,* ed. James M. McGlathery (Urbana and Chicago, 1991).

22. I owe this insight to an unpublished paper by the late Seth Brody on the kabbalistic symbolism of Reb Nahman's tales.

23. On the basic distinction between *Sage* (Legend) and *Märchen* (Fairy Tale or Folktale), introduced by the Brothers Grimm and now universally recognized, see Max Lüthi, *Once Upon a Time: On the Nature of Fairy Tales,* trans. Lee Chadeayne and Paul Gottwald, ed. Francis Lee Utley (Bloomington, 1976); and William Bascom, "The Forms of Folklore: Prose Narratives," *Sacred Narratives,* ed. Alan Dundes (Berkeley, 1984), pp. 5–29.

24. See David G. Roskies, "The Genres of Yiddish Popular Literature 1790–1860," *Working Papers in Yiddish and East European Jewish Studies* (February 1975), pp. 1–15. *Alerley mayse-bikhlekh,* an anthology of Yiddish chapbooks (Sudilkov, 1834), offers the best sampling of the kind of stories, popular chronicles, and ethical wills that circulated in the Ukraine in the decades immediately following Nahman's death. See also, Zalmen Reisen, "Tsu der geshikhte fun der yidisher folks-literatur," *YIVO-bleter* 3 (1932): 240–259; esp. 248–249. An exotic *historye*—originally the term that denoted a non-Jewish narrative source—did not carry the same belief status as the more familiar *mayse.* See Zfatman-Biller, "Hasiporet beyidish mireshitah 'ad 'Shivḥei haBesht,'" vol. 1, p. 27.

The first to recognize that Reb Nahman drew not from folklore but from literary sources was Meir Weiner. See his *Tsu der geshikhte fun der yidisher literatur in 19tn yorhundert* [To the History of Yiddish Literature in the Nineteenth Century], 2 vols. (New York, 1945): 1:34–35. Yoav Elstein identifies a thirteenth-century Spanish kabbalistic work as the possible Hebrew source for some of Reb Nahman's motifs. See *Pa'amei bat melekh* [In the Footsteps of a Lost Princess: A Structural Analysis of the First Tale by Rabbi Nachman of Braslav] (Ramat-Gan, Israel, 1984), pp. 161–188, 235–237.

25. Dan Ben-Amos, Introduction to *Folklore Genres* (Austin, 1981), p. xxii; Jack Zipes, "Once There Were Two Brothers Named Grimm," Introduction to *The Complete Fairy Tales of the Brothers Grimm* (Toronto, New York, and London, 1988), vol. 1, pp. xx–xxii.

26. Green, *Tormented Master,* p. 347.

27. Band, Introduction to Nahman of Bratslav, *The Tales,* pp. 34–35; Piekarz, *Hasidut Braslav;* p. 121; Liebes, *"Ha-Tikkun Ha-Kelali,"* p. 188 n. 11.

28. This rare first edition is described by Piekarz, *Hasidut Braslav,* on pp. 184–185.

29. See ibid., chap. 5 and Elstein, *Pa'amei bat melekh,* chap. 1.

30. "The Yiddish original." There is much debate on whether Nathan recorded the stories in Yiddish first, and then translated them into Hebrew, or the reverse. The question was first raised by Samuel H. Setzer in his Yiddish edition of the Tales, *Sipurey mayses (vunder mayses) fun Rabi Nakhmen Braslaver* (New York, 1929), pp. xxxiv–xlii. It was picked up again years later by Piekarz and Shmeruk. The unfortunate effect of this scholarly debate has been to obscure the narrative power of the Yiddish and to promote the Hebrew as the primary source.

31. All this is stated explicitly in Nathan of Nemirov's "Hakdome af taytsh" (Yiddish Preface) to the *Seyfer sipurey mayses,* pp. 15–16.

32. See Jacob Elbaum, "HaBesht uvno shel R. Adam—'Iyyun besippur mi*Shivḥei haBesht,"* *Jerusalem Studies in Jewish Folklore* 2 (1982): 66–75.

33. The newest edition of *Seyfer sipurey mayses* (Jerusalem, 1990), in which, for the first time, the entire Hebrew text is vocalized, contains a one-page apologia (p. 27), partially attributed to Nathan of Nemirov, for occasional lapses into ungrammatical, colloquial, style. (The examples given—*vena'asah brogez aleha, velakah et 'atsmo el hashtiyah*—are extremely tame.) As the apologia makes clear, however, such "lapses" underscore the unique and hidden qualities of Nahman's teaching.

34. See David Roskies, "Yidishe shraybshprakhn in 19tn yorhundert," *Yidishe shprakh* 33 (1974): 1–11. Returning to Reb Nahman's Yiddish original these many years later, I hear it as far more idiomatic than I did then.

35. Green, *Tormented Master,* p. 4.

36. See Gershom G. Scholem, *On the Kabbalah and its Symbolism,* trans. Ralph Manheim (New York, 1965), pp. 57–62; and Moshe Idel, *Kabbalah: New Perspectives* (New Haven and London, 1988), chap. 9.

37. See Shmeruk, *Prokim,* pp. 251–252; and Liebes, *"Ha-tikkun Ha-Kelali,"* p. 137.

38. Since Scholem's *Major Trends in Jewish Mysticism,* 3rd ed. (New York, 1954), the sefirotic system has become common knowledge. For a lucid explanation in English, based on a kabbalistic source known to Reb Nahman, see Louis Jacobs's Introduction to *The Palm Tree of Deborah* by Moses Cordovero (1960; New York, 1974), pp. 20–37.

39. See Elstein, *Pa'amei bat melekh,* pp. 199–222 for an extended analysis. He was the first to note the precise sequence of events in this story.

40. Ibid., pp. 205–211; Jacob Elbaum, "Tavniot mishtarsherot venishberot be'Ma'aseh miberger ve'ani'vleR. Nahman miBraslav," *Jerusalem Studies in Hebrew Literature* 4 (1983): 76.

41. The standard source is still Joshua Trachtenberg's *Jewish Magic and Superstition: A Study in Folk Religion* (1939; rpt. Cleveland and Philadelphia, 1961). See, more recently, Sara Zfatman, *Nisu'ei adam veshedah* [The Marriage of a

Mortal Man and a She-Demon: The Transformation of a Motif in the Folk Narrative of Ashkenazi Jewry in the Sixteenth–Nineteenth Centuries (Jerusalem, 1987); Tamar Alexander-Frizer, *The Pious Sinner: Ethics and Aesthetics in the Medieval Hasidic Narrative* (Tübingen, Germany, 1991); and Gedalyah Nigal, *Magiyah, mistikah vehasidut* [Magic, Mysticism and Hasidism] (Tel Aviv, 1992).

42. For a brilliant analysis of this tale in its relation to the first, see Green, *Tormented Master,* pp. 350–355.

43. Ibid., pp. 69, 186. Cf. the Hasidic folklore brought by Samuel Zanvel Pipe in "Napoleon in Jewish Folklore," *YIVO Annual of Jewish Social Science* 1 (1946): 297–302.

44. For a convenient English sampling of this extremely popular chronicle, see my *Literature of Destruction: Jewish Responses to Catastrophe* (Philadelphia, 1989), nos. 30–33.

45. Green, *Tormented Master,* p. 28.

46. On Primordial Man, see Scholem, *On the Kabbalah and its Symbolism,* pp. 104–117.

47. Green, *Tormented Master,* p. 74.

48. See Max Lüthi, *The Fairytale as Art Form and Portrait of Man,* trans. Jon Erickson (Bloomington, 1984), chap. 5.

49. Green, *Tormented Master,* p. 44.

50. See *Sefer toldot haAri,* ed. Meir Benayahu (Jerusalem, 1967), esp. tale nos. 5–8. Tales of how the Ba'al Shem Tov "drew close" ever new disciples play a central role in the *Shivḥei haBesht* (1815). See, on this, Joseph Weiss, "A Circle of Pneumatics in Pre-Hasidism," in his *Studies in Eastern European Jewish Mysticism,* ed. David Goldstein (Oxford and New York, 1985), pp. 27–42; and Avraham Rubinstein, "Sippurei hahitgalut besefer 'Shivḥei ha Besht,'" *'Alei sefer* 6:7 (1979): 157–186.

51. On the historical and messianic dimensions of the story, see Shmeruk, *Prokim,* pp. 256–258. For the failed meeting between the Besht and Hayyim ibn Atar, see *Sefer shivḥei haBesht,* ed. S. A. Horodetzky (Tel Aviv, 1960), pp. 188–189.

52. The incompatibility of biblical monotheism and tragedy in the classical Greek sense is something that obviously requires systematic study. I draw my conclusions from two discussions on the subject with my friend and colleague, Raymond P. Scheindlin.

53. The first to make this identification was Weiss, the pioneer of all modern research on Nahman. See his *Meḥkarim baḥasidut Braslav* [Studies in Braslav Hasidism], ed. Mendl Piekarz (Jerusalem, 1974), pp. 22–23.

54. Louis Ginzberg, *The Legends of the Jews* (Philadelphia, 1968), vol. 1, pp. 276–278.

55. On the prevalence of this motif in "The Burgher and the Pauper," see Yaakov Elbaum's brilliant analysis in *Jerusalem Studies in Hebrew Literature* 4 (1983): 59–85.

56. See Green, *Tormented Master,* chap. 6.

57. See *Beggars and Prayers: Adin Steinzaltz Retells the Tales of Rabbi Nachman of Bratslav,* trans. Yehuda Hanegbi, Herzlia Dobkin, Deborah French, and Freema Gottlieb, ed. Jonathan Omer-Man (New York, 1985), p. 135. Steinsaltz provides a sustained, and nuanced, allegorical reading of the tale on pp. 133–147 of his retelling.

58. This was Moyshe Markuze's *Seyfer refues hanikro eyzer yisroel* (Poryck, 1790). For a full description of this work, the first written in Eastern Yiddish, see Khone Shmeruk, *Sifrut yidish beFolin* [Yiddish Literature in Poland: Historical Studies and Perspectives] (Jerusalem, 1981), pp. 184–203. On Nahman's rebuttal, see pp. 201–202.

59. Steinzaltz (p. 134) finds the depiction of the simple man "rather flat" and "stereotypical," while the clever man "is treated with greater depth and understanding."

60. *Likutey MOHaRaN tanina,* p. 22.

61. Steinzaltz, *Beggars and Prayers,* pp. 109–110, with minor changes to conform to Band's translation.

62. See Cynthia Ozick's delightful rumination on this subject in "Prayer Leader," *Prooftexts* 3 (1983): 1–8.

63. The most intelligent guide to the multiple interpretations of this tale and to the many works of modern literature that it inspired is a two-volume high school curriculum edited by Zecharia Goren. See *Be'ikvot shiv'at hakabtsanim lerabi Nahman miBraslav* [In the Footsteps of Rabbi Nahman of Braslav's Seven Beggars] (Oranim and Tel Aviv, 1986).

64. Too many songs attributed to Reb Nahman have been issued of late by his Hasidim in Israel to constitute the authentic core. Cassette tapes titled *The Songs of Rabbi Nachman of Breslav* and sung by Rabbi David Raphael Ben-Ami are available at local Bratslav and Judaica bookstores. Many of them were probably composed by his Hasidim rather than by the rebbe himself. For a more reliable source, see *Old Jewish Folk Music: The Collections and Writings of Moshe Beregovski,* ed. Mark Slobin (Philadelphia, 1982), p. 300, and nos. 130, 134, 146, 150 of the "Textless Songs" published on pp. 449–490.

65. See Green, *Tormented Master,* pp. 301–304; and Steinzaltz, pp. 180–181.

# 3

## The Cut That Binds
### *Time, Memory, and the Ascetic Impulse*

### *Elliot R. Wolfson*

i needed so much
to having nothing to touch—
but i've always been greedy that way
—Leonard Cohen

### Memory, Mindfulness, and Masculinity

Throughout the ages commentators have given a host of explanations to account
for the significance of circumcision, arguably one of the most important rites in
the history of Judaism when viewed from both the anthropological and theological
perspectives. A rather innovative attempt to characterize circumcision is found in
David M. Levin's study on phenomenological psychology, *The Body's Recollection of
Being: Phenomenological Psychology and the Deconstruction of Nihilism* (1985).[1] In
the context of discussing the correlation of bodily limbs and the "body" as a
"primordial text," Levin casts his attention to the part of the blessing of grace that
is traditionally uttered after one eats a meal with bread, the *birkat ha-mazon,*
which mentions the covenant of circumcision that God "has sealed into our flesh."
Constructing a midrashic reading of this liturgical text in an obvious Derridean
vein,[2] Levin observes, "'Sealed' protects the truth of which circumcision would
remind us, viz., that the ancestral body of the Jewish people was created by grace of
a primordial incision or inscription: the writing and attesting of the divine signature, the grammatology of the original divine de-cision."[3] Reflecting further on
the use of the expression to circumcise the foreskin of the heart in Deut. 10:16,
Levin notes that "circumcision is symbolic of a process of opening," indeed "the
very *essence* of circumcision—the heart of the matter, as it were—lies in the fact
that the *incision opens.* Circumcision therefore corresponds to the breaking open of
a path."[4]

This act of incision/inscription sealed upon the sexual organ, resulting in
what Levin aptly calls the "breaking open of a path," in turn constitutes an act of
re/membering, for it reminds the male Jew of the sign imprinted upon his member, the seal inscribed upon the flesh that bespeaks the consecrated union between
God and the community of Israel that must be realized in time but that is not

essentially of time. Circumcision, therefore, "initiates the ancestral body into a spiritual process which Jews call 'remembrance.'"[5] The remembrance spoken of here obviously is not the common everyday memory of isolated experiences that are time-bound, the capacity to retain images in the present of that which is past to help one anticipate events of the future, but it is rather a recollection that transcends the linearity of time by gathering together past, present, and future in the circular resumption of what has never been, a calling to mind that allows one "to see old things with a newer, farther look."[6] Circumcision is the cut that opens the flesh of the spirit to the reminiscence of a primordial bond, a kind of memorial thinking,[7] which involves concentration on the point in which consciousness in its entirety is ground, a return, that is, to one's origin.[8] In a word, circumcision is a *rite de retour,*[9] a retrieval of the beginning that stands not in the past but unfolds always in the future, the breaking open of the path that engenders memory across the divide of time.

Nowhere in the biblical or classical rabbinic texts, so far as I am able to surmise, is the ritual of circumcision connected specifically with the words *memory* or *remembrance.*[10] At best, it may be argued that, inasmuch as the rite of circumcision is referred to as a "sign of the covenant" (Gen. 17:11) and the nature of a sign is such that it brings to mind,[11] there is an implicit connection between the covenant of circumcision and memory. Such is the case explicitly in several biblical verses with reference to the word *covenant.* For instance, in the narrative regarding the sign established by God with Noah after the deluge, the rainbow, the word for memory is used in conjunction with the word *covenant* (see Gen. 9:15 and 16).[12] Or again, in Lev. 26:42, we read of God guaranteeing that He will remember the covenant that he made with each of the three patriarchs, Abraham, Isaac, and Jacob.

Notwithstanding these and other pertinent examples that could have been mentioned,[13] there is no specific correlation in the traditional sources between the covenant of circumcision and the word *remember,* let alone a substantiation of the idea that circumcision initiates a spiritual process of remembrance. To be sure, in the immense body of literature produced by Jewish thinkers through the centuries one can find textual evidence for the interpretation of circumcision as a sign that fosters the memory of the covenantal relationship between God and Israel. An interesting example of such an approach is found in the tenth-century commentary on *Sefer Yeṣirah* by Dunash ben Tamim who interpreted the statement, "a covenant of oneness set in the middle, [expressed] in the circumcision of the tongue and in the circumcision of the foreskin," as a reference to the fact that "God made the circumcision as a memorial of the unity *(zikkaron ha-yiḥud)* since Abraham was the first of the circumcised and of those who believed in one God."[14] According to this interpretation, Jewish males bear the sign of circumcision on their flesh as a reminder of God's unity that was originally proclaimed by

Abraham, the first to enter the covenant of circumcision. The rationale for circumcision is projected here from the philosophical standpoint, which is developed further by Maimonides in the second of the two reasons he offers in the *Guide of the Perplexed* to explain this rite.[15] The incision on the penis, according to Maimonides, is the "bodily sign" that fosters a social alliance among the sons of Abraham who enter the covenant that "imposes the obligation to believe in the unity of God." The sign of circumcision is the physical cut that binds together the community of Israel through the fundamental tenets implicit in the monotheistic faith, to wit, the belief in God's oneness, incorporeality, and utter dissimilarity to all other beings.

In medieval kabbalistic sources, we find an elaborate application of the correlation of circumcision and memory in an altogether distinctive tone. The special relationship that pertains between the two is suggested by the symbolic identification of the *membrum virile* as the seat of memory. This connection is based in kabbalistic texts, beginning already in *Sefer ha-Bahir*,[16] on a word play between *zakhor*, "to remember," and *zakhar*, "masculine."[17] The play on words suggests an ontological connection between masculinity and memory, that is, that which most singularly marks the male Jew, the circumcised penis, which bears the scar that affords him access to the site of memory in the Godhead, to enter the mystery of faith.[18] The link between masculinity and memory was further strengthened by thirteenth-century kabbalists, primarily from northern Spain, who identified *zakhor* as the divine potency that corresponds specifically to the phallus.[19] Basing themselves on the supposed linguistic correlation between *zakhar* and *zakhor*, the kabbalists refer to this divine gradation by the names *zikkaron* and/or *zekhirah*,[20] "memory," for it is the masculine potency par excellence.[21] Moreover, insofar as this gradation corresponds to the phallus, and the latter is the focal point of the covenant of circumcision, the former is referred to metonymically as the "upper covenant."[22]

In a plethora of kabbalistic sources, a connection is established between masculinity, memory, and circumcision. The circumcised phallus is the epitome of memory,[23] for what is remembered most basically, that is, what is recollected at the root, is the mark of circumcision, the sign of the covenant, the letter *yod* inscribed on the corona of the phallus (*'ateret berit*) that is exposed as a result of the peeling away of the foreskin (*peri'ah*). The exposure of the sign through the cut of the flesh calls forth to memory the attribute of God that corresponds to the phallic sign disclosed as a result of the circumcision, a sign that betokens the initiatory bond that links the divine to the male members of the community of Israel. This memory, however, is not only a retrospective glance back to the beginning, but it is also a foreboding glimpse ahead to the future, for the mark of circumcision is symbolically interchangeable with the messianic sign of the rainbow that will appear in the cloud, the portent of peace beheld by Noah after the deluge. Exile is repeatedly depicted in kabbalistic texts as a time when the divine phallus is covered by the shells of demonic impurity, collectively symbolized by the foreskin, whereas redemption is heralded by a removal of this covering to expose the corona of the phallus, the semiotic seal of the covenant incised upon the penis, a disclosure of disclosure occasioned by the showing of what appears in the guise of that which is not-shown. The dissimilitude is sharply conveyed by the image of the rainbow, the appearance of which is caused by the refraction of the rays of sunlight in the drops of rain. The bow of prismatic colors is naught but image, indeed an image of an image, the doubling of vision that renders visible the invisible in the invisibility of the visible, a revelation that reveals itself in the laying bare of that which is withheld.[24] According to the kabbalistic interpretation, the (un)seeing of the phallic sign is the fulfillment of the prophetic promise of the vision of the ancient glory in the end of days.[25] To anticipate the future, then, is to retrieve the past, not, however, as a factual event that transpired in time, but as the originary evocation that sends one forth on the temporal path that leads beyond time.

### Returning Beyond: Recollecting the Future
### in Anticipation of the Past

In this study, I will explore the nexus of the rite of circumcision as the inscription of the covenantal sign on the body and the spiritual process of memory in the thought of Nahman ben Simhah of Bratslav (1772–1810).[26] In particular, I will focus on the depiction of circumcision as the ceremony that fosters the recollection of the future through anticipation of the past, the retrieval of what has never been in the time-consciousness that overcomes the consciousness of time, remembering the sign in the phallic gratification of the ascetic impulse.[27]

In one of his expositions on circumcision in the collection, *Liqqutei Halakhot*,[28] Nathan of Nemirov (1780–1845),[29] the leading disciple and personal secretary of Nahman, sets out to explain this rite in terms of his master's teaching concerning the illusion of time and the knowledge of that which is above time. The "ultimate purpose" of circumcision, Nathan writes, is "that one should merit perfect knowledge," *da'at shalem*.[30] Nahman taught, however, that the perfection of knowledge was dependent upon consciousness of "that which is above time,"[31] for temporal sensibility ensues from the absence of knowledge. "Know, however, that the essence of time *('iqqar ha-zeman)* is only due to the fact that we do not understand, that is, on account of our small minds. As the mind becomes greater, time becomes smaller and is more abolished."[32] As an illustration of this principle, Nahman notes that in a dream state, when reason *(sekhel)* is absent and one has only the faculty of imagination *(koah ha-medammeh)*,[33] a short interval of time may seem very long. Similarly, what we consider to be a long period of time in a higher state of consciousness is very short. Nahman thus depicts the ascent of the soul from a state of imagination in which the illusion of time dominates to a state of mind in which time is considered as nothing at all: "And so higher and higher until there is a mind *(sekhel)* so high that all of time in its entirety is not considered at all, for on account of the greatness of the mind all of time is nothing and absolutely non-existent."[34] Not only is God characterized by this quality, but the Messiah, says Nahman, is one who possesses this expanded consciousness, an idea that is suggested by the verse, "You are my son, this day I have begotten you" (Ps. 2:7). Although the Messiah (referred to as God's son) is coeval with the creation of the world,[35] it is as if he were created anew each day, for in his consciousness all time is abolished. According to another passage, Nahman assigns this quality of transcending temporality to Moses who is equated with the "unity of times" *('aḥdut ha-zemanim),* for the Hebrew letters of his name are decoded as *mah she-hayah hu' she-yihyeh,* "what was is what shall be."[36]

The consciousness that transcends time underlies Nathan's statement that a "great principle" *(kelal gadol)* taught repeatedly by Nahman is that "a person should begin each time anew."[37] Moreover, Nathan indicates that the quality of constantly being reborn was a hallmark of Nahman's own comportment in the world. In fact, not only did Nahman actualize this principle by starting from the outset repeatedly, but on some days he actually experienced several initiations, which Nathan further depicts in terms of the older rabbinic idea (linked exegetically to Deut. 6:6) that it is incumbent upon the Jewish male to consider the Torah as if it were given anew each day so that he can enter afresh into the covenantal relationship.[38] From this vantage point it is detrimental to view oneself as an old person *(zaqen),* for this would result in the loss of hope in the possibility of genuine change in the future, which is based on the prospect of always beginning at the beginning. Indeed, the key to repentance, the mystery of *teshuvah,* is the turning back by looking ahead, a re/turn that is predicated precisely on the awareness of constant renewal, a secret that is indicated by the verse "Take us back, O Lord, to yourself, and let us come back; renew our days as of old" (Lam. 5:21). The act of repentance affords one the opportunity to transcend the limitations of time. "On the day that a person repents he is above time, and he elevates all the days above time, and thus Yom Kippur is above time . . . for repentance is the aspect of the nullification of time *(biṭṭul ha-zeman),* that is, time is unified, that is, time ascends and it is bound and contained in the aspect of that which is above time."[39] The essence of pious worship is to abrogate time by elevating it and binding it to that which transcends time. In order to achieve this state, it is necessary for one to approach each temporally bound ritual action *(miṣwot zemaniyyot)* as an opportunity to start over again from the beginning. Even for one who is completely righteous it is not good to worship as an elder, for such a focus sustains the evil inclination, which is called the "old and foolish king" (Eccles.

4:13).[40] To combat the strategy of the demonic potency to paralyze human hope by forcing one to focus on the misfortunes of the past, it is necessary to cultivate the sense that each venture is truly a new beginning.[41] In Nahman's own words,

> When a person falls from his gradation, he should know that it is from heaven, for keeping distant is the beginning of drawing near *(hitraḥaqut teḥilat hitqarevut)*.[42] Thus he fell so that he might be more aroused to draw close to God, blessed be he. His advice is that one should begin anew to enter into the worship of the Lord as if he had never started before. This is a great principle in the worship of the Lord, that it is verily necessary to begin each day anew.[43]

Nahman's pietistic teaching is predicated on the existential belief that the only time that matters spiritually is the beginning; indeed time in its phenomenological essence is naught but the beginning since each moment is marked by the recurrence of that which has never been before, a paradox that can be expressed as well as the return of that which has remained, for only that which has remained may return.[44] The way forward, as T. S. Eliot insightfully remarked, is the way back.[45] Nahman expresses the matter in the following way in another context:

> The essence of all things is the beginning, for "all beginnings are difficult,"[46] since one goes out from one opposite to the other. Thus, each and every time that one travels to the righteous man, he must envision it as if each time he comes anew, not as if he were already by the righteous man and now he is coming a second time, but it should be as if he were never by the righteous man, and he is with him anew in the present as if it were the first time. The essence is the beginning, for "all beginnings are difficult," . . . Hence, the essence of the potentiality of worship on each of the days is only in the beginning . . . and in accordance with the power and enthusiasm of the beginning so does his worship progress and unfold, for the essence is in the beginning. Thus, one must start each time anew . . . and one must come to the righteous man anew with the potency of great enthusiasm and renewed vigor in the worship of God, blessed be he, so that his worship will be appropriate according to the power of the beginning.[47]

For Nahman, the only segment of time that is real is the present, for the past is no longer and the future is not yet. If the moment is the only time that is not illusory, then the life of piety requires that one always begin again at the beginning.[48] In this connection it is of interest to recall Nathan's explanation of his choice of the title *Ḥayyei MoHaRaN* for the biography of Nahman. "For he was a man of life in truth of which there is no copy, and he lived constantly a true life, and each time he lived he lived a new life *(ḥayyim ḥadashim)* as I heard from his holy mouth, for one time he said, 'Today I lived a life that I have never lived before,' and then he began to reveal a bit of the chapter headings of Torah . . . and the principle is that the essence of life is the true life, which is the true wisdom."[49] In a similar vein, Nathan wrote in another context, "I have seen and I have heard several times from the mouth of our master, blessed be his memory, that he lived a new life *(ḥiyyut ḥadash)* every time, as I heard him say several times 'Today I lived a life that I have never lived like it before.'"[50] An essential aspect of Nahman's teaching is that spiritual existence requires a renewal of consciousness *(hithadshut ha-moḥin)* on each and every day, for no day has any vitality but that very day.[51] " 'O, if you would but heed his voice this day' (Ps. 95:7). This is the great principle in the worship of the Lord that he should not place before his eyes anything but that very day . . . for a person has nothing in his world except for that very day and that very hour in which he stands, for the next day is an entirely different world."[52] Building upon this dictum of Nahman, Nathan explains the ritual of counting the forty-nine days of *'omer* between Passover and Pentecost as well as the nature of the Sinaitic revelation itself in terms of this principle.

> It is forbidden for a person to procrastinate from day to day, but he should well know that this day shall not be again all the days of his life, for another day is an entirely different matter. . . . It is as our master and our teacher, blessed be his memory, said with respect to the verse "O, if you would but heed his voice this day" (Ps. 95:7), for the essence of worship of the one who wants to heed his voice and to cleave to him is to know that the essence is that day, "this day" precisely. This is the aspect of the commandment of counting the *'omer*, which is the beginning and the preparation for receiving the Torah, to demonstrate that it is impossible to receive the Torah unless it is known that the essence is the very day in which a person stands. . . . This is the aspect of "O, if you would but heed his voice this day," that is, if you want to heed his voice and to receive the Torah, you cannot receive except by means of the aspect of today.[53]

The mandate is to begin each day anew, to see oneself reborn in every moment. However, the nature of the beginning implies a paradox[54] that Nahman expresses in his explanation of the rabbinic dictum that "all beginnings are difficult." The beginning is difficult because it marks the transition from one state to its opposite. But if the beginning is understood in this way, then the beginning presupposes a state of affairs that exists prior to the beginning. Alternatively expressed, the notion that the beginning is a changeover entails that origin involves duplicity.[55]

Authentic worship is predicated on an awareness of the paradox of beginning at the beginning that is itself a shift from what has already been. The truth of the beginning exemplifies a duplicitous nature insofar as no beginning can begin without already having begun. As I have noted, this is precisely the paradox that Nahman assigns to the Messiah who is said to be beyond time. The savior is reborn each day, but to be reborn each day he has to have already existed. To be beyond time, therefore, implies this confluence of novelty and repetition.

From another statement of Nathan we learn, moreover, that the righteous in general are characterized by this messianic quality: "The essence of hope is by means of the aspect *(beḥinah⁵⁶)* of that which is above time which the righteous comprehend for they are in the aspect of Messiah."⁵⁷ In the continuation of that passage, Nathan revealed that close to his departure from this world *(samukh le-histalquto)*, Nahman disclosed the meaning of the teaching from *Liqquṭei MoHaRaN* concerning the Messiah's posture as one who is above time. "It is impossible," writes Nathan, "to explain this matter in writing at all."⁵⁸ From the remainder of the passage, however, the implication seems to be that the attribute of transcending time attributed to the Messiah was in fact applicable to Nahman himself in his function as one who sought to redeem souls.⁵⁹ His messianic efforts were somewhat thwarted by the limitations of corporeality, but in the end "we will all return in truth to God, blessed be he, and to the former days, for all time will be abolished and everything will be contained in the aspect of that which is above time, and there everything will be perfected."⁶⁰ In the present state of existence, the inwardness of Torah is concealed by the polarity of night and day, the love that is marked by temporality *('ahavah she-ba-yamim)*, the love of God for Israel that is actualized on a daily basis. By contrast, in the future, the Torah of the ancient concealed one will be revealed and, consequently, the secrets of Torah will be disclosed without any garments. This disclosure is depicted, moreover, as the love that is beyond the division of time and the delimitation of measurement, the love that is strictly in the mind *('ahavah she-ba-da'at)*, which is the love that God has for Israel before the creation of the world when they existed only as a potentiality in thought. In a reversal of the standard philosophical orientation, Nahman's distinction between the two kinds of love is predicated on the assumption that potentiality is greater than actuality, for the latter, in contrast to the former, is limited by specific forms that are determined by temporal and spatial laws. In this state of potency prior to creation, which is retrieved in the eschaton beyond nature, there is no day or night, but only the perfection of peace that transcends all strife and discord.⁶¹

The conception of time underlying Nahman's eschatological view of redemption as the promise of the future that resurrects the past in the ever-recurring present bears a remarkable similarity to the following phenomenological description of time offered by Emmanuel Levinas:

For the production of an instant of time cannot come from an infinite series; it can cut the Gordean knot of time without untying it. It can be, out of itself. That way for an instant to be is to be present. The present is an ignorance of history. In it the infinity of time or of eternity is interrupted and starts up again. The present is then a situation in being where there is not only being in general, but there is a being, a subject. Because the present refers only to itself, starts with itself, it refracts the future. . . . Of itself time resists any hypostasis; the images of current and flux with which we explain it are applicable to beings in time, and not to time itself. Time does not flow like a river. . . . The present is a halt, not because it is arrested, but because it interrupts and links up again the duration to which it comes, out of itself. Despite its evanescence in time, in which alone it has been envisaged, or rather because of that evanescence, it is the effectuation of a subject. It breaks with the duration in which we grasp it.[62]

According to Nahman, the sequential flow of temporality—the succession of seconds, minutes, hours, days, weeks, months, years, and so on—is naught but illusion for one who has achieved a level of cognition appropriate to God or what may be called "messianic consciousness." To express the matter in terms of the formulation of Levinas just cited, the evanescence of time gives way to the duration of eternity, the world that is to the world that is coming, for that which comes eternally is always on the way to becoming what it is. Messianic hope lies, paradoxically, in remembering the future, which is the return of the present that has never been past.[63] In that present, time is conquered by the memory of the past that lies ahead as the future that lies behind.[64]

Nathan applies Nahman's teaching concerning the awareness of that which transcends time to the rite of circumcision. The commandment to circumcise the child is to be carried out on the eighth day, for the seven days preceding the day of circumcision represent the aspect of time, the weekly cycle, and the eighth, by contrast, is the dimension beyond time.[65] For Nahman, temporal consciousness is really a lack of consciousness and supratemporal consciousness is perfected consciousness. Circumcision is the means by which one attains knowledge, which is the perspective of being beyond time, a seemingly impossible state of mind for consciousness to comprehend in its temporal deportment. In Nathan's words,

> It is impossible for one to attain the aspect of that which is beyond time, which is the perfection of knowledge, until one passes first under time, which is the aspect of the lack of knowledge. . . . Then he will merit through time itself to ascend and be contained in the aspect of that which is beyond time. This is the aspect of the cutting and removal of the foreskin, which is the rectification of the phallus *(tiqqun ha-berit)*, that is, the perfec-

tion of knowledge *(shelemut ha-da'at)*. This is merited precisely after the passing of seven days, which are the totality of time *(kelal ha-zeman),* for all time is contained in the seven days of the week. Then does one merit the aspect of that which is above time, which is the perfection of knowledge, by virtue of circumcision on the eighth day, for that is the aspect of that which is above time. The eighth day is the aspect of that which is above time, for it is the aspect of *Binah,* the world-to-come,[66] which is above time, above the "seven days of the edifice,"[67] which comprise the aspect of time.[68]

Perfection of knowledge, which entails the transcendence of time and the abolition of temporal limitations, is the esoteric intent of the rite of circumcision. To clarify this matter, we must embark on a deeper path by undertaking an excursion into the notion of time in the thought of Rebbe Nahman.

### Perfection of Memory, Rectification of the Phallus, and the Conquest of the Eros of Time

Knowledge is in an inverse relation to temporality. But what is it about time that leads Nahman to characterize knowledge as the negation of time? Let us recall Nahman's homiletic reflection on the verse, "But you shall be to me a kingdom of priests and a holy nation. These are the words that God shall speak to the children of Israel" (Exod. 19:6). "It is written, 'Reproach breaks my heart' (Ps. 69:21), that is, acts of shame and disgrace break the heart of a person. The rectification *(tiqqun)* comes about by his binding his heart to the point that belongs to his heart in this moment. By means of this the shame will be nullified."[69] Nahman decodes the meaning of his opening remark in the balance of the homily. The heart is identified as the "aspect of the *waw*" and as the "aspect of the tablets," terms that no doubt symbolically signify the masculine element or, more specifically, the phallic gradation. The shamefulness that breaks the heart refers to illicit sexual relations, the evil passions *('ahavot ra'ot)* that seduce a man, the aspect of fallen and broken love *('ahavah nefulah u-shevurah)*, also identified as the foreskin of the heart *('orlat ha-lev)* and as the broken tablets *(shivrei luḥot)*.[70]

In another passage, the broken heart *(lev nishbar)* is described as the heart that is warmed by the fallen passions *('ahavot nefulot)*. The rectification for this state of brokenness is the *shevarim,* the broken sounds of the *shofar* blowing.[71] The linkage of spiritual breakage and sins related to the penis is a motif expressed in much older kabbalistic sources. For instance, in one passage in *Tiqqunei Zohar,* the matter is expressed in terms of the association of the word *basar,* which denotes the flesh in general but that relates specifically to the male organ, and *shever,* a word that means both "fracture" and "corn" (or "grain"):

What is the secret of this flesh *(basar)?* It is as it is written, "since he too is flesh" *(beshaggam hu' vasar)* (Gen. 6:3). This secret has been transmitted to the wise of heart. The [letters of the word] *basar* can be transposed into *shever,* concerning which it says, "your starving households" *(shever ra'avon bateikhem)* (ibid. 42:19). If they are meritorious, the flesh is holy *(basar qodesh)* concerning which it says, "From my flesh I will see God" *(u-mibesari 'eḥezeh 'eloha)* (Job 19:26), and if they do not guard this flesh, the sign of the covenant is transposed for them into a calamity *(be-shever)*.[72]

If one is sexually pure, then the male organ is the locus of beatific vision for one beholds God from that place, but if one is impure, then this very location is transformed into a source of affliction and misery. When the heart is overwhelmed by the feeling of disgrace brought about by sexual transgression, the soul is dominated by the evil inclination and the demonic shells, which originate from the shattering of the vessels of mercy *(shevirat kelei ha-ḥesed)*. The brokenhearted man can rectify his condition only by binding his heart to the point of the *yod*, which is identified as the *ṣaddiq*.

When the heart is sunk in shame, which is the foreskin of the heart, the aspect of the broken tablets, then "Reproach breaks my heart" (Ps. 69:21). But when he binds the heart, which is the aspect of the *waw*, to the *yod*, that is the point, which is the aspect of the *ṣaddiq*, wherein the light of the holy love dwells, for the light of mercy remains in the foundation of the emanation *(yesod de-'aṣilut)*, then the evil passions will be abrogated . . . for the *ṣaddiq*, who is the point wherein the holy love dwells, shines upon the *waw*, which is the aspect of the heart, and the shame is nullified.[73]

In the same context, Nahman expresses this symbolism in slightly different terms. The *waw*, which is the heart, refers to the males of Israel, the supporters of Torah *(tomkhei 'oraita')* or the hooks of the posts *(wawei ha-'ammudim)*, and the *yod* alludes to the righteous, the sages of the community *(ḥakhmei ha-'edah)*.[74] From one perspective the former support the latter, but from another the latter the former. Hence, the heart that is broken, imaginatively represented by the shattered tablets and/or the divided *waw*, is healed (in the sense of being made whole) by attaching itself to the *yod*, the phallic point of the *ṣaddiq*. "The point is the aspect of the *ṣaddiq* in relation to his comrade *(ḥaveiro)*, and this point illumines the heart of his comrade, which is called *waw*."[75] The brokenhearted individual finds his healing by attaching himself to the righteous one and receiving the illumination that radiates from him into his heart. The *ṣaddiq* serves as a conduit through which the divine influx flows and he is thus called the "mouth that is full," *male' fum*.

The intent of the attribution of this expression to the *ṣaddiq* is clarified from another passage wherein Nahman relates *male' fum* to the grammatical idiom *mela'fum,* which is another name for the vowel *shuruq*. "And this is the aspect of *mela'fum, male' fum.* The matter is that *mela'fum* consists of *yod waw,* and this [*yod*] is the aspect of the ten knockings, which correspond to the ten commandments . . . and the *waw* is the aspect of drawing the spirit *(hamshakhat ha-ruah)* . . . for by means of drawing the spirit the lack is perfected."[76] The *yod* and the *waw* together signify the double aspect of the phallic gradation to which the *ṣaddiq* is attached. The *yod* is the sign of the covenant, which is linked to the corona of the penis that is disclosed by the act of *peri'ah,* the splitting and pulling down of the membrane in the rite of circumcision. In this passage, the *yod* is related to the ten knockings that correspond to the ten commandments, which represent the spirit that is in the Torah, and the *waw* is the elongation of the penis that is associated with the drawing forth of the spirit. How so? The *ṣaddiq* manifests the phallic potency of the divine, which is the creative energy of the universe, through his speech, the drawing forth of the spirit/breath.[77] The words of the righteous come forth from the dissemination of the vital spirit that breathes life into the world. The special power of the *ṣaddiq* thus lies in the fact that the "full mouth," *male' fum,* constitutes the perfection of what is lacking, *shelemut ha-ḥissaron.* Nahman interprets the prophetic dictum that all the people of Israel are righteous (Isa. 60:21) in light of this quality of the *ṣaddiq* as one who possesses a mouth that is full. Each male Jew has the capacity to repair the broken heart by means of the power of the mouth of the *ṣaddiq,* which is expressed through prayer and Torah study.[78]

One of the characteristic features of Nahman's thought, and Hasidism more generally, is the identification of these two verbal activities, although priority is given to prayer such that the words of Torah study are themselves transformed into liturgical utterances.[79] As Nahman puts it in one context, "With respect to all of the Torah that a man learns in order to observe and to practice, all of the letters are sparks of the souls, and they are garbed within the prayer, and they are renewed there in the aspect of impregnation."[80] Or, in the language of another passage, "In each and every level, as in each and every world, there is an aspect of 'Let us do and let us hear' (Exod. 24:7), for each one in accordance with its gradation has an aspect of 'Let us do,' the aspect of the Torah, that is, those things that are revealed to him, and the aspect of 'let us hear,' which is the aspect of the hidden things, the aspect of prayer."[81] According to this passage, then, the aspect of prayer is higher than that of Torah study since the former corresponds to the esoteric dimension, which is correlated further with the religious response of contemplation, whereas the latter corresponds to the exoteric dimension, which is correlated with action. In a third passage, however, the hierarchical relationship between prayer and Torah study is described in somewhat different terms since the highest kind of prayer is liturgical utterance that is composed of words of Torah. "It is also good to make prayer out of the Torah, that is, when one learns or hears some discourse on Torah from a veritable righteous man, then he should make from this a prayer, that is, to entreat and to beseech before the blessed One with regard to everything that was said there in that very discourse. . . . The matter of this speech rises to a very high place, and especially when he produces prayer out of the Torah. From these very great delights *(sha'ashu'im)* are made above."[82]

The quality of transforming every speech utterance into a liturgical act endows the *ṣaddiq* with messianic potentiality, which is related more specifically to the sexual purity attained by the *ṣaddiq* in virtue of the phallic gradation of the divine that he embodies.[83] In Nahman's own words,

> The essence of the weapon of the Messiah is prayer . . . and this weapon he must receive by means of the aspect of Joseph, which is vigilance with respect to the phallus *(shemirat ha-berit)*. . . . And every man must intend in his prayer to bind himself to the righteous ones of the generation, for each righteous one of the generation is the aspect of Moses the savior *(mosheh mashiah)*. . . . And each and every prayer that every man prays is the aspect of a limb of the *Shekhinah*.[84]

By joining oneself to the *ṣaddiq* through prayer one ontologically transmutes the words of worship into a part of the body of the divine presence; indeed, one is justified in speaking of the imagistic construction of the divine body (or, according to the accepted idiom of the ancient esoteric tradition, the *shi'ur qomah)* out of the words of prayer of the *ṣaddiq,* which comprise the prayers of all those who attach themselves to him. In another context, Nahman makes explicit the connection between the letters of prayer, the garments of the *Shekhinah,* the colors of the rainbow, and the remembering of the phallic covenant.

> "When he saw that they were in distress, when he heard their cry, [he was mindful of his covenant and in his great faithfulness relented]" (Ps. 106:44). By means of music the judgments are sweetened. As it is written in the holy *Zohar,*[85] the rainbow is the *Shekhinah*. The three colors of the rainbow are the patriarchs, and they are the garments of the *Shekhinah*. When she clothes herself in the luminous garments, then "I will see it to remember the everlasting covenant" (Gen. 9:16), and, consequently, "the king's fury abated" (Esther 7:10). This may be compared to a king who was angry at his son, but when the king sees the queen in luminous garments, he has pity on his son. The letters of prayer are the *Shekhinah,* as it is written, "O Lord, open my lips" (Ps. 51:17), for the speech is the name "Lord" *('adonai),* and it is called the rainbow. . . . The sound of music consists of the three colors

of the rainbow, for in the voice there is fire, water, and spirit, which are the three patriarchs, for the patriarchs are the three luminous colors, concerning which it says "I will see it to remember the everlasting covenant." Thus, the one who musically plays the letters of prayer, with a voice of the melody that is meritorious and in great clarity, clothes the *Shekhinah,* that is the letters, in luminous garments, and the blessed holy One sees her and then "the king's fury abated." . . . [This occurs] as well by means of belief in the sages, for the one who believes that all of their words and actions are not simple, but there are secrets in them, thereby clothes the rainbow in luminous garments, and [consequently] "I will see it to remember the everlasting covenant," for the *ṣaddiq* is the aspect of the rainbow.[86]

Nahman explains the sweetening of judgment by means of the voice of song in terms of the zoharic theme of the appeasement of God's anger by means of His looking upon the sign of the covenant manifest in the colors of the rainbow. Interestingly enough, the aspect of the rainbow is assigned to both the feminine *Shekhinah* and to the masculine *Yesod.* Following closely the intent of the zoharic symbolism, Nahman asserts that initially the rainbow is the *Shekhinah,* but the garments in which she is cloaked are the three patriarchs who correspond respectively to the three central emanations, *Ḥesed* (Abraham), *Din* (Isaac), and *Raḥamim* (Jacob). Nahman adds that these luminous garments are made up of the letters of prayer. Only when the bow is cloaked in these garments, which arises as a consequence of the theurgical activity of prayer, does it become the everlasting covenant remembered by God, which signifies as well the transformation of the bow into the phallic sign. In this sense, the bow signifies the *ṣaddiq,* the earthly manifestation of the gradation of *Yesod,* which corresponds to the phallus. The aptitude for prayer, in particular, is expressive of the righteous man's phallic potency, which has messianic implications as well. "By means of the rectification of the phallus *(tiqqun ha-berit),* which is the rainbow, he can bring forth the arrows, which is the prayer that consists of the eighteen liturgical blessings, which are the three *wawin,* the aspect of the arrows, and their place is in the phallus in the aspect of 'My covenant with him shall endure' (Ps. 89:29). Faith is the aspect of prayer in the aspect of 'thus his hands remained steady' (Exod. 17:12), and as a result there is the beginning of the uplifting of the horn of the Messiah in the aspect of 'There I will make a horn sprout for David' (Ps. 132:17) in the aspect of 'rays proceed from his hand to him' (Hab. 3:4), this is the aspect of prayer."[87]

 The special efficacy of the speech of the *ṣaddiq* in terms of both prayer and the study of Torah, which is by no means unique to Bratslav Hasidism,[88] is predicated ultimately on the correlation of the mouth (or, more specifically, the tongue) and the phallus, a motif that is one of the fundamental principles—or what I would call a "ground concept"—of Jewish esotericism.[89] To cite but one representative passage where Nahman articulates the point by drawing the analogy between rectification of the phallus *(tiqqun ha-berit)* and perfection of the sacred language *(leshon ha-qodesh)*, an analogy that is dependent on the aforementioned homology between the phallus *(berit)* and the tongue *(lashon)*,

> By means of the sacred language the lust of temptation for adultery is tied up and bound. . . . The rectification of the phallus is dependent on the sacred language, for from the aspect that is here illicit sexual relations where prohibited for them. The one without the other cannot possibly be, that is, the rectification of the phallus and the perfection of the sacred language are dependent on one another . . . for the one who blemishes the phallus destroys the sacred language.[90]

Given the correspondence between the tongue and the phallus, it follows that sins committed with respect to the latter may be rectified by means of the former, and specifically through the utterance of the sacred language in acts of study or prayer. In one passage, the link between the sacred language *(leshon ha-qodesh)* and the rectification of the phallus *(tiqqun ha-berit)* is presented as the secret intention of circumcision *(sod kawwanat milah)*.

> The sacred language comes from above, but it is still lacking rectification, for there is still a need to elevate the good from the Aramaic translation *(targum)*, and this is the secret intent of circumcision . . . for the sacred language is the aspect of the rectification of the phallus that comes from above, but it is still lacking rectification, for the essence of its rectification is from below in this world by means of the fact that we elevate the good in the Aramaic translation and complete the sacred language.[91]

The final perfection of the phallus, which is connected to the sacred language, is based on the elevation of the good from the sensual plane, which is represented by the Aramaic translation, a mixture of good and evil. *Tiqqun ha-milah* thus relates to the transformation of the sexual impulse, *tiqqun ha-berit*, which is brought about by the perfection of the Hebrew language through Aramaic. For many, however, the mending of the heart, which is shattered by the yielding of the flesh to sexual temptation, comes only by way of cleaving passionately to the words that come forth from the mouth of the *ṣaddiq*[92] by means of which the *yod* completes the *waw*, an act that clearly has (homo)erotic overtones in Nahman's teaching,[93] reflecting a much more widespread phenomenon in Hasidic thought based on earlier kabbalistic literature wherein the relationship between the master and the disciple is portrayed in terms of the constitution of the androgynous unity of the divine located symbolically in the phallus.[94] As Nahman explicitly states, the obligation of being bound to the righteous man, *hitqasherut la-ṣaddiq,* is a kind of love that even exceeds the love of a man for his wife.[95] If the attachment to the *ṣaddiq* is appropriately depicted in erotic terms, it follows that the reception of the words of the *ṣaddiq* would be experienced and described in the language of marriage and sexual intercourse, as we find in the following passage:

> It is impossible to come to the truth except by coming close to the righteous *(hitqarevut la-ṣaddiqim)* in order to go in the way of their advice, and on account of receiving their advice the truth is engraved in him. . . . The advice he receives from them is the aspect of matrimony *(nissu'in)* and conjugality *(ziwwug).* Receiving advice from the wicked is the aspect of matrimony with the shell. . . . And why is advice called by the aspect of matrimony? For the kidneys give counsel,[96] and the kidneys are the instruments of procreation, the instruments of the semen. It follows that receiving advice from a person is like receiving semen from him, and everything is in accordance with the person, whether he is wicked or righteous . . . and the advice of a righteous man is entirely truthful semen.[97]

To be conjoined to the *ṣaddiq* is comparable to sexual mating, for the words uttered by the *ṣaddiq* are like drops of semen that he ejaculates into the ear of the recipient.[98] Analogously, to receive words from an evil person is a form of illicit copulation. In a second passage, Nahman repeats this point:

> Know that the words of the wicked who is without knowledge produce adultery in the listener, for the acts of copulation proceed from knowledge, as it is written, "And Adam knew his wife" (Gen. 4:1), and it is written, "every woman has known a man" (Num. 31:17). However, there are two types of copulation, the copulation of holiness, which is attachment *(hit-qasherut)* to the righteous, to the Torah, and to the Lord, blessed be he, and this proceeds from the knowledge of holiness *(da'at di-qedushah),* but the transgressive acts of copulation proceed from the knowledge of the shell *(da'at di-qelippah).* Speech is the disclosure of the mind, for what is in the mind cannot be known except through speech.[99]

The seminal teaching that comes forth from the full mouth of the *ṣaddiq* sustains the one who receives it in the manner that the semen that oozes from the penis fertilizes the egg in the act of physical intercourse between a man and his wife.

> Know that the essence of the living spirit is received from the righteous one and the master of the generation, for the essence of the living spirit is in the

Torah . . . and the righteous cleave to the Torah, and thus the essence of the living spirit is with them. When one is bound to the righteous one and the master of the generation, and one sighs and extends one's breath, then one draws forth the living spirit from the righteous one of the generation *(ṣaddiq ha-dor)*,[100] for he cleaves to the Torah wherein is the spirit.[101]

The rectification of illicit sexuality is by means of attachment to the righteous soul, an attachment that occurs in "this moment," *'et ha-zo't.* The cleaving to the *ṣaddiq* must be realized fully in the present, in the perpetuity of the eternal now, the moment of the centered point that grounds and stabilizes the ceaseless flux of time. For Nahman, chronological succession—with its continuous ebb and flow—structurally resembles carnal desire, which likewise is characterized by impermanence and incompleteness. The fulfillment of such desire—which is always in and of the moment—is never anything but temporary, and hence time-bound.[102] Time is overcome by the genuine moment in which the disciple cleaves to the master. In this moment, the momentariness of time is redeemed by the fullness of the present, which is concurrently a recovery of the end and an anticipation of the beginning.

The revocation of time by the consciousness of the moment that is timeless is occasioned by cleaving to the *ṣaddiq,* for the latter represents the mastery of eros, which constitutes the unending and boundless duration of time. The *ṣaddiq* attains pure consciousness, which does not signify empty mindedness, but purification from all guilt related to sexual improprieties. The cessation of physical (especially sexual) desire eventuates in the nullification of time, which is the perfection of knowledge. This is the intent of Nathan's claim that the rectification of sins related to the phallus, *tiqqun ha-berit,* is identical with the perfection of knowledge, *shelemut ha-da'at.* That is, the cutting of the foreskin, long considered in Jewish sources to be a symbolic suppression of sexual desire,[103] is the precondition for the attainment of supratemporal (or messianic) consciousness.[104] However, to attain the aspect of that which is beyond time, symbolized by the number eight, one must pass through the seven days of the week, collectively symbolizing the aspect of time or the imperfect state of consciousness. According to Nathan, this is the esoteric meaning of the verse, "And Abraham was old" (Gen. 24:1). Abraham merited the aspect of elderliness, which is the aspect of "acquiring wisdom,"[105] that is, the "perfection of knowledge," which is, in turn, "the aspect of transcending time." Abraham merited such a state for he was the "first of those circumcised," and "by means of the commandment of circumcision we merit to abolish time and to be contained in the aspect that transcends time, which is the essence of elderliness."[106] Abraham was the first elderly person ever to exist, for only through the rite of circumcision can one merit the aspect of elderliness that is the abolishment of time. This sense of elderliness is to be distinguished from the negative connotation of this term related to one who is incapable of perceiving the potential novelty of each moment, a condition that was just discussed. The old man who transcends time, by contrast, is perpetually reborn.[107] The paradox embraced by the one who is authentically elderly is that he is ancient because he is always new, but he is always new because he is ancient.

Nathan further identifies this perfection of knowledge as the perfection of memory, *shelemut ha-zikkaron*. "The perfection of knowledge is the aspect of the perfection of memory. . . . for memory is the aspect of knowledge and forgetfulness the aspect of folly.[108] Thus memory is the perfection of knowledge, which is the aspect of that which is above time."[109] Insofar as memory is depicted as the state of knowledge of that which is beyond time, and, as we have seen, this state is achieved by means of circumcision, it follows that memory itself is attained through the act of circumcision. Nathan thus forges a clear link between memory and circumcision. The essence of memory is the abolishment of temporal consciousness (imagination-desire), and the concomitant perfection of knowledge by means of which one is cognizant of the aspect that is beyond time. But it is precisely the ritual of circumcision that allows one to reach this state, for the very nature of circumcision is such that it negates the natural instincts that are time-bound and connects the individual with the spiritual root in a dimension above time. According to Nathan, moreover, this idea of memory as the abolishment of time provides the key for interpreting Nahman's tale "The Seven Beggars." Although it is beyond the confines of this study to discuss all the intricate details of this tale, it is necessary to summarize it briefly before proceeding to the part that is relevant to our analysis.

The tale[110] begins with the episode of a transference of power from a king to his son. The king, who predicts the downfall of his son, nevertheless gives him advice concerning the need to always be joyous[111] even—or especially—in the loss of royal power. We are then told about the son's being led to apostasy through his attachment to rational wisdom. The narrative then shifts[112] to an account of a mass flight from a certain country in the course of which two children get lost in a forest. The children are sustained by the graciousness of seven beggars, each of whom has a particular physical deformity. The first beggar is blind, the second deaf, the third a stutter, the fourth possesses a twisted neck, the fifth a hunchback, the sixth is without hands, and the seventh without feet. In due time the two children, who have survived the forest ordeal, get married. Six of the seven beggars make an appearance at the wedding to offer gifts to the couple. The presentation of each of the gifts is accompanied by the telling of circuitous tales that purport to illustrate that the given beggar's apparent deformity is actually a virtue connected with his particular gift. Indeed, we learn that these deformities are, in truth, no deformities at all, but are perceived as such only from a limited perspective. What appears to be blindness appears as such only to one who cannot truly see; what appears to be deafness appears as such only to one who cannot truly hear; and so on. As Nahman of Cheryn, one of Nathan's disciples, expressed the matter in his commentary on Nahman's tales, the fact that the beggars appeared to the world as physically deformed was due to both the "superlative distinction of the perfection of their level and stature," and to the great measure of "concealment and hiddenness of the truth in this world."[113] Or, as a contemporary writer has put it: "In general, the six beggars who appear to present gifts are similar in one respect: They demonstrate, as delightful raconteurs, that the world of reality we live in is really an illusion."[114] The truly real world is a negation of this world: The blind man in truth sees, the deaf man hears, the one who stutters is an extraordinary orator, the one with a twisted neck in fact has a perfectly straight and handsome neck, the hunchback is one who truly carries a heavy load for he is characterized as "the little-that-holds-much,"[115] and the one without hands in truth has extraordinary power in his hands to perform miraculous deeds through the playing of music.

The tale ends abruptly after the appearance of the sixth beggar, and we are not told at all about the arrival of the seventh beggar, the one without feet. The seventh beggar, it seems, represented the completion of the wedding feast, the ultimate rectification and hence the coming of the Messiah.[116] Logically, of course, one would not expect the beggar without feet to arrive on his own at the celebration. His inability to walk, however, is only apparent: he does not come because it is not time for him to come and not because he cannot come. His deformity, as that of the others, is only such for those who cannot penetrate beneath the surface. Yet, whereas the other six beggars can reveal the truth of common illusions, the seventh beggar cannot. In truth, he is the "consummate dancer"[117] and if the world were ready for his coming he would have arrived, or better yet, the world would have already perceived his absent presence rather than his present absence.[118]

For our purposes the section dealing with the first beggar is of central importance. The first of the seven beggars, who is blind, bestows the following gift upon the couple: "You should be as old as I." He then proclaims, "Do you think that I am blind? Not at all. It is just that the entire world does not amount to an eye's wink (moment) for me. . . . For I am very old and yet I am still young. I haven't even begun to live , yet I am very old."[119] The beggar explains his rather cryptic remarks with the following story: Once after a storm a group of people assembled in a tower. They began to converse and decided that each one had to "recite an old tale, one he remembered from his earliest recollection, that is, what he remembered from the inception of his memory."[120] Each of the eight men, the eldest first, related an "ancient story" concerning some prenatal memory, ranging from the first who recalled the time of his birth (the "cutting of the apple from the branch") to the last who recalled the coming-to-be of the higher spirit before birth (the "appearance of the fruit before it was on the fruit"). The younger the person the more ancient the memory. The blind beggar, who at the time was an infant, spoke last. "I remember all of these tales and I remember nothing [*ich gedenk gor nicht*]."[121]

As Nathan already pointed out,[122] the first beggar possessed that level of knowledge that Nahman himself attributed to the Messiah, a state of mind in which time is abolished. Like the Messiah, moreover, the beggar was at one and the same time the youngest and oldest of all those present.[123] Since time was negated in his consciousness, it was as if he were born again each day—hence, he was the youngest; yet, he was the oldest, for his memory reached further back than the rest, indeed to a point where memory itself was not appropriate. "I remember all these tales and I remember nothing." The first beggar was thus truly old—and hence truly young—for he lived beyond time.[124] This is the meaning of his wedding gift to the couple "You should be as old as I am." His old age, as his youthfulness, was rooted in the spiritual awareness of that which transcends time.

This "transcending of time" holds the key to understanding the beggar's blindness. "He looked like a blind man because he did not look at the world at all, since the entire world did not amount to an eye's wink for him. Therefore seeing and looking at this world did not pertain to him." That is, all time was illusory to him for he was fundamentally beyond time.[125] His blindness is only apparent—to one who is truly blind—for his vision is a true vision, a seeing without temporally bound objects.[126] A similar reversal is applicable to his memory, which may be characterized as the epitome of remembrance and forgetfulness. That is, his memory extended to the highest and deepest reaches possible where he remembered "nothing," that is, he remembered the very source of memory, the nothing that lies beyond time and therefore beyond anything memorable. Here we may have, as Nathan maintained,[127] an allusion to *Keter*, the first of the ten divine emanations, identified in the standard theosophical symbolism of the kabbalists as the absolute nothing.[128] If that interpretation is correct, then Nahman's point is that the blind beggar, as the Messiah himself, is able to reach *Keter* where the supernal source of his soul is to be found. The one whose memory stretches this far back indeed remembers *gor nicht*, that is, the nothing that is the root of all things. Paradoxically, the most sublime memory—*ich gedank gor nicht*—turns out to be a state of forgetfulness, for in such a frame of mind nothing (but Nothing) can be remembered.[129] As we shall presently see, this positive ideal of forgetfulness, which in some sense is identical with memory, is to be contrasted with another negative view of forgetfulness found in Nahman's writings. According to the latter view, rooted in earlier kabbalistic documents,[130] forgetfulness is the force of the demonic side.

Ascetic Renunciation and the Eschatological Triumph Over Time

Memory is, for Nahman, the perfection of knowledge.[131] But knowledge is perfected only when the phenomenal world is transcended and the somatic desires nullified, when one becomes fully aware of that which is beyond time, beyond the limitations of eros.[132] In one passage, Nahman expresses this idea in terms of the opposition of forgetfulness and the miraculous, which is also identified as the aspect of prayer *(tefillah)* and the aspect of faith *('emunah)*.

> Prayer is the aspect of faith, and this is the aspect of miracles, for the miracle transcends nature, and for this one needs faith. . . . On account of this prayer is effective for memory *(mesuggal le-zikkaron)*, for prayer is the aspect of faith . . . and forgetfulness is related to having something before us that is forgotten, and it passes from us. . . . The miracle is the opposite of forgetfulness, for miracles are the aspect of prayer, the aspect of faith, which is the opposite of forgetfulness.[133]

The access to that which transcends nature, the infinite will of God,[134] is prayer, but only one who has faith in the possibility of the impossible can pray.[135] Prayer is effective for memory, for prayer itself is a miraculous event, an act of faith, predicated on the impossible, whereas forgetfulness is an obscuring of the sign of the covenant that calls forth to memory. This notion is expressed in another passage in the following way: "We must protect the memory so as not to fall into forgetfulness, the aspect of the death of the heart. The root of memory is to remember the world-to-come always."[136] What is intended in this passage is rendered clear in another context wherein the connection between memory and the world-to-come is described as follows: "It is fitting for a person to accustom himself to be in the world-to-come, that is, to be separated from desires as it is in the world-to-come in which there is no eating and no drinking[137] and none of the other ephemeral animal desires of this world . . . And surely if one will remember well the pleasures of the world-to-come, then he could not at all endure the life and pleasures of this world."[138]

Memory is linked to the consciousness of the world-to-come, an openness to time beyond time, to the day that never begins because it could not end. In this time, which is without time, the order is reversed, and that which served as the vessel will rise to serve as the crown. "This is [the import of the verse] 'After two year's time, Pharaoh dreamed etc.' (Gen. 41:1). 'Two year's time' is the aspect of the cycles of days and the cycles of years . . . which are the aspect of the world-to-come, for it is a day that is entirely long,[139] for there the order of temporality *(seder ha-zemanim)* is the aspect of the encompassing *(maqqifin)* . . . which are all the pleasures and delights of the world-to-come."[140] The joy of the world-to-come is expressed primarily in terms of the image of the encompassing light, a spatial metaphor employed by the kabbalists to denote the aspect of the female, which is usually depicted as that which is encompassed, that has been assimilated and integrated into the male. In other words, the aspect of the female that encompasses the male relates to the masculinized feminine. However, only the feminized male, the male that has subdued the sexual drive by ascetic renunciation, can experience the ecstasy of the world-to-come, which is related to the aspect of the encompassing light, the female that has been restored to the male in the form of the *'ateret tif'eret,* the "crown of splendor."[141]

As Nahman emphasizes in another context, the eschatological ecstasy is experienced by those who proffer innovative insights in the study of the ritual laws of the Torah, "for when halakhah is renewed, the intellect and knowledge are renewed, and knowledge is the essence of the joy of the world-to-come *(sha'ashua' 'olam ha-ba')*."[142] The process of creating new textual insights captures the paradox of that which is new being new insofar as it is old. Only that which is ancient can be novel. In another passage, Nahman remarks that the spiritual pleasure of the world-to-come *(ta'anug 'olam ha-ba' ha-ruhani)* cannot be attained fully by human beings in their limited state of embodiment since this pleasure is without limit. Even in this context, however, Nahman follows the long-standing rabbinic tradition[143] by asserting that the delight of Sabbath *(oneg shabbat)* affords one an opportunity to experience something of the texture of the spiritual bliss of the world-to-come. "The rabbis, blessed be their memory, said, 'The one who takes delight on the Sabbath receives an inheritance without bounds,'[144] that is, without limit. Therefore, the essence of the eternal life of the future-to-come is the aspect of the pleasure of the world-to-come, and this will pertain only to the lowliness of every one, for humility and modesty are the aspect of that which has no boundary, for it is the aspect of the actual nothing *('ayin mamash),* and it has no boundary since it is the ultimate modesty, and the essence of the eternal life of the world-to-come is only in the aspect of the boundless."[145] Partaking of the pleasure of Sabbath affords one the opportunity to have a foretaste of the spiritual beatitude of the world-to-come, an eternal state that exceeds the boundary of time. To experience the rapture that has no limit it is necessary for one to transcend the limitations of one's own embodied condition, but the only way that one attains this transcendence is by becoming that which has no limit, which is the divine nothing, the first of the sefirotic emanations. The means to become this nothingness, which is designated by the paradoxical expression *'ayin mamash,* the "actual nothing," that is, the nothing that is actual, indeed the wellspring of all that is real, is through the nihilation of self that results from being meek and submissive. One procures the expansiveness of that which is beyond all limit, the joy of the world-to-come, by diminishing oneself in the world of physical limitation. Excessive delimitation fosters the aggrandizement of consciousness such that one is transformed into the nothing that is everything, the *'ayin mamash.*

In a reversal of logic so typical of Hasidic thought in general, reinforced by Nahman's particular psychological disposition, he states that the "essence of greatness is debasement," *'iqqar ha-gedullah hi' shiflut.*[146] By viewing humility as the measure of greatness, Nahman is following the pietistic ideal expressed in much older kabbalistic sources. To be humbled is to be exalted, or, in the words of the *Zohar,* "he who is small is great."[147] Even more to the point, the idea expressed by Nahman reflects the nexus between the virtue of humility and the first of the divine attributes, *Keter,* which is identified as the nothing. To emulate the quality of divine nothingness, one must humble oneself to the point of becoming nothing.[148] In becoming nothing, one experiences something of the bliss of the world-to-come since this is a state of consciousness that transcends all limitation and boundary and thus is technically nothing. Nahman maintained that prayer afforded the individual an opportunity to achieve this utter abnegation of self, which he described further (in a somewhat unusual way) as union with Ein-Sof, that which has no limit. "Worship of the heart is prayer, that is, conjunction *(devequt)* to Ein-Sof, for Ein-Sof is the aspect of that which cannot be comprehended, and inasmuch as he has no comprehension of this, he is in the aspect of prayer, which is conjunction, that is a complete nullification *(bittul)* in Ein-Sof."[149] As a consequence of being contained within the Infinite *(keshe-nikhlal be-'ein sof),* one is transformed into the Torah of God and into the prayer of God.[150] In this mystical state of union, there is no distinction between the finite and Infinite, the limited and limitless. The individual will is so completely annihilated in the unity of Ein-Sof that every action on the part of the individual is perceived as an execution of the divine will, and since the latter is not confined by spatial and temporal limitations, the soul in this unitive condition also transcends these very limitations and thereby experiences the world-to-come, which is beyond space and time.[151] A prolepsis of this state is experienced as well on the Sabbath, a day whose spiritual essence transforms the physical acts in such a manner that satisfying corporeal desires is akin to the ascetic renunciation appropriate to eschatological consciousness. Thus, in contrast to an unambiguous negative attitude toward physical eating, Nahman associates the pleasure of Sabbath *(oneg shabbat)* with eating in holiness *('akhilah bi-qedushah).* Not only is this eating an act of complete holiness with no admixture of evil, but it facilitates the demise of the demonic, which is usually effected by fasting. "In the [act of] eating related to the six weekdays the Other Side also derives pleasure from it, but in the eating of Sabbath there is no portion for the Other Side whatsoever. . . . [In the case of] the eating of Sabbath, holiness and the complete divinity are attained without an admixture of refuse whatsoever. He may achieve through eating on Sabbath what he achieved by means of a fast."[152]

When we become, as the first beggar, "blind" to the sensible world, we share in the experience of memory; when, however, we are overtaken by the faculty of imagination, the animal power of the soul, our memory is impaired and we fall into forgetfulness. The unfettered imagination brings about a flawed condition that Nahman calls the evil eye *(ra' 'ayin)*[153] or the death of the heart *(mitat ha-lev)*, that is, the strengthening of desire, especially of a sexual nature, which in turn causes a defect in memory.

> In order to protect the memory one must be careful not to fall into the aspect of the "evil eye," the aspect of the death of the heart, for the essence of memory is dependent on the eye, as it is written "for a memorial between your eyes" (Exod. 13:9), and forgetfulness comes by means of the "evil eye," by means of the death of the heart, in the aspect of "I am forgotten as one dead to the heart" (Ps. 31:13) . . . and the death of the heart is the aspect of the broken tablets, the heart is the aspect of the tablets, in the aspect "inscribe them on the tablet of your heart" (Prov. 3:3), and forgetfulness is by way of the broken tablets, according to the saying of the sages, blessed be their memory, "Had the first tablets not been broken, there would not have been forgetfulness in the world."[154] It follows that the essence of forgetfulness is by way of the evil eye, which is the aspect of the death of the heart, the aspect of the broken tablets, for from there is the essence of forgetfulness.[155]

The heart overcome by sensual lust is governed by the "evil eye" of desire, which brings about a state of spiritual oblivion, forgetfulness of the covenant, and breaking of the tablets. Only one who masters the "evil eye" overcomes the death of the heart. Guarding the mind from acting on the sexual impulse, therefore, fosters the memory of the covenant. Thus, commenting on the tale of the seven beggars in another context, Nathan identifies the blind beggar with the "aspect of phylacteries," the latter constituting the "aspect of memory," as it is written in Scripture, they shall be as a "memorial between your eyes" (Exod. 13:9). "A 'memorial between your eyes' precisely, for the essence of memory is dependent on the repair of the eyes *(tiqqun ha-'einayim)*, as is clear from the tale, for the blind [beggar] was completely blind to this world . . . and this is the essence of the perfection of the eyes. He merited the final perfection of memory *(takhlit shelemut ha-zikkaron)* beyond which there is no perfection."[156] In one passage, Nahman himself contrasts the efficacy of the phylacteries, which are the beauty and truth that emanate from the aspect of Jacob, and the desire to eat, which is representative of the physical appetites more generally: The former is associated with illumination of the face and the latter with hiding the face. The mystical effect of donning the phylacteries, therefore, is to break the craving for food.[157]

The function of the sign of circumcision similarly is to protect one against the evil eye of sensual lust that results in spiritual amnesia. Just as the sinfulness of sexual temptation is linked especially to the eyes, so the rectification of this sin is dependent on the covenantal sign of the head phylacteries that lies as a memorial between the eyes.[158] The one who resists temptation of the flesh is illumined from the divine light and is thereby protected from the wrath of the demonic force. "By means of the rectification of the holy phallus *(tiqqun berit qodesh)* he is saved from the face of the Other Side, and by means of the blood of circumcision the blood of menstruation is rectified, the desire for money[159] . . . for by means of this he is bound to divinity and he is separated from the worship of idols, as it is written, 'From my flesh I will behold God' (Job 19:26), for by means of the rectification of the phallus he illumines himself with the light of the face of the living king."[160]

The act of memory, therefore, is an act of becoming aware of that which is beyond the confines of the physical world. For Nahman, one attains this state of reexperiencing the world-to-come by freeing oneself from the ocular yearning of the imaginative faculty[161] and from the base animal desires that are generated by it.[162] The soul that controls the imagination and erotic passions through ascetic renunciation can perfect its knowledge in such a way as to remember. This very subjugation of animal desire and the consequent attainment of a state of knowledge that epitomizes the perfection of memory is the mystical significance of circumcision. With this in mind we can appreciate better a remark of Nahman reported by Nathan.

> He also said that the copulation of the true *ṣaddiq* is a matter that is hard for him, and it is not enough that he has no pleasure at all, but on the contrary he has actual sufferings from this like the sufferings of the infant in the time of circumcision. For the *ṣaddiq* has actual sufferings in the moment of copulation, and he has more, for the infant has no consciousness, and thus his sufferings are not so great, but the *ṣaddiq* has consciousness, and his sufferings are greater than the infant.[163]

It is in light of this pietistic ideal of abrogation of carnal desire that Nathan interprets the section of Nahman's tale concerning memory in the context of a discussion on circumcision, for only by means of the latter can one merit the former. "The perfection of memory," writes Nathan, "is by means of the abolishment of time that is merited through the perfection of knowledge. And this we must perfect by means of circumcision. For we must perfect memory, that is the aspect of masculinity *(zakhar),* that is [related to] the word 'memory' *(zikkaron),* and is the root of the commandment of circumcision."[164] In the final analysis, the phallus is the locus of memory for control over the libido typifies control over the passions in general, and precisely such control is characteristic of the nature of existence in the world-to-come, the transcendent source of memory. Nathan thus connects his own interpretation with the older kabbalistic linkage between "memory," *zikkaron,* and "masculinity," *zakhrut.* In a wonderful reversal, so characteristic of Hasidic thought, the place of the most intense sexual desire becomes the most powerful symbol of memory that is realized only through the sublimation of eros.

Through circumcision, then, one enters the world beyond this world; that is the significance of the ritual being held on the eighth day, the day that exceeds the cycle of seven that symbolizes nature, time, corporeality. Hence, the perfection of knowledge, which is the recollection of that which is above time, can be acquired only through circumcision. This is the hidden meaning of the beggar's tale. The eight other participants represented the eight days of circumcision. Each one had abolished time to the degree to which his given memory reached. But the first beggar, the most ancient and the youngest of them all, abolished time to the utmost degree. Insofar as this beggar represents otherworldliness and thus completely transcended time, his memory was the most perfected. The rite of circumcision is an act of participating in this source, of attaining expanded consciousness of that which transcends time, in a word, of remembering. By virtue of circumcision, therefore, one becomes like the first beggar, "blind" to the world of space and time, but all the while beholding the supramundane realm of divine verities. For Nathan, Rebbe Nahman's teaching affirmed that one who is circumcised is initiated into the spiritual process of remembrance. But this is an event that must be constantly relived. In the reliving of circumcision—primarily through the subduing of sexual desire—one again remembers the source whence all memory is derived and all time overcome.

## Notes

1. David M. Levin, *The Body's Recollection of Being: Phenomenological Psychology and the Deconstruction of Nihilism* (London, 1985).

2. See ibid., p. 363 n. 77, where the author cites Jacques Derrida's *Of Grammatology.* The issue of circumcision, which indeed may be viewed as a trope for the method of deconstruction as the cut that binds, is found in a number of Derridean compositions. See idem, "Shibboleth," in *Midrash and Literature,* eds. G. H. Hartman and S. Budick (New Haven, 1986), pp. 307–348; idem, *Glas,* trans. J. P. Leavey Jr. and R. Rand (Lincoln and London, 1986), pp. 41–46; idem, *Jacques Derrida,* trans. G. Bennington (Chicago, 1993), pp. 59–60, 65–74, 87–88; and the analysis in J. D. Caputo, *The Prayers and Tears of Jacques Derrida: Religion without Religion* (Bloomington and Indianapolis, 1997), s.v. circumcision.

3. Levin, *Body's Recollection of Being*, p. 202.

4. Ibid., p. 203 (author's emphasis).

5. Ibid.

6. The remark of Heidegger reported by Paul Shih-yi Hsiao, as cited in R. May, *Heidegger's Hidden Sources: East Asian Influences On His Work*, trans. G. Parkes (London and New York, 1996), p. 3.

7. I have borrowed this expression from a remark of Heinrich Wiegand Petzet cited in ibid. For a different English rendering of the relevant remark as "mindful thinking," see H. W. Petzet, *Encounters and Dialogues with Martin Heidegger 1929–1976*, trans. P. Emad and K. Maly (Chicago and London, 1993), p. 73.

8. My formulation is based on the description of memory in M. Heidegger, *What Is Called Thinking?*, trans. J. Glenn Gray (New York, 1968), p. 145.

9. V. Crapanzano, *Hermes' Dilemma and Hamlet's Desire: On the Epistemology of Interpretation* (Cambridge, Mass., 1992), p. 261, applies this term in his examination of the ritual of circumcision as performed by Moroccan Arabs (see pp. 265–280).

10. In Babylonian Talmud, Menaḥot 53b, the verb "to remember" is connected with *berit milah,* for Abraham says to God on behalf of the people of Israel at the time of destruction of the temple, "You should have remembered the covenant of circumcision." Even in this context, however, no essential relationship between memory and circumcision is advocated.

11. See, e.g., Exod. 13:9 where the words sign *('ot)* and memorial *(zikkaron)* are used synonymously.

12. See Babylonian Talmud, Berakhot 59a. According to one rabbinic opinion, the blessing to be uttered at the occasion of seeing a rainbow is "Blessed is the one who remembers the covenant."

13. See, e.g., Lev. 26:45; Ezek. 16:60; and Ps. 105:8 (1 Chron. 16:15), 106:45. Cf. also the prayer in the traditional liturgical service for each morning, "Master of the universe, let it be your will, the Lord our God and God of our ancestors, to remember on our behalf the covenant of the patriarchs."

14. *Sefer Yeẓirah with the Commentary of Dunash ben Tamim,* ed. M. Grossberg (London, 1902), p. 26.

15. Maimonides, *The Guide of the Perplexed,* trans. S. Pines (Chicago, 1963), III. 49, pp. 609–610. For an illuminating study, see J. Stern, "Maimonides on the Covenant of Circumcision and the Unity of God," in *The Midrashic Imagination: Jewish Exegesis, Thought, and History,* ed. M. Fishbane (Albany, 1993), pp. 131–154. The second reason offered by Maimonides is linked to the presumed weakening of the sexual drive affected by the cut of circumcision. See n. 103.

16. D. Abrams, *The Book Bahir: An Edition Based on the Earliest Manuscripts* (Los Angeles, 1994), § 124, p. 207 (Hebrew). See G. Scholem, *Origins of the Kabbalah,* ed. R. J. Zwi Werblowsky, trans. A. Arkush (Princeton, 1987), pp. 142–

143, 158–159; I. Tishby, *The Wisdom of the Zohar,* trans. D. Goldstein (Oxford, 1989), p. 1223; E. K. Ginsburg, *The Sabbath in the Classical Kabbalah* (Albany, 1989), pp. 107–108. The bahiric correlation is based in turn on a talmudic statement (Babylonian Talmud, Berakhot 20b and Shavu'ot 20b) that identifies *zakhor* with the positive time-bound commandment to sanctify the Sabbath day over wine and *shamor* with the prohibitions that are to be observed on the Sabbath. Insofar as the former category generally applies to males and the latter to females as well as males, there is an implicit correlation of *zakhor* with the masculine and *shamor* with the feminine. This rather terse remark of the *Sefer ha-Bahir* became a cornerstone of subsequent kabbalistic exegesis. For instance, in thirteenth-century Spanish kabbalah, beginning with the Gerona circle, the correspondence of *zakhor* (remember) to male and *shamor* (keep) to female was used as a basis to explain the fundamental rabbinic division of the commandments into positive and negative. For a more complete discussion of this theme, see E. R. Wolfson, *The Book of the Pomegranate: Moses de León's Sefer ha-Rimmon* (Atlanta, 1988), pp. 63–71 (English section).

17. On the connection of memory and phallus, and the supposition that the two terms derive from the same Hebrew root, see J. Kristeva, *Tales of Love,* trans. L. R. Roudiez (New York, 1987), p. 87.

18. Particularly poignant are the passages of Moses de León translated and discussed in E. R. Wolfson, "Woman—The Feminine as Other in Theosophic Kabbalah: Some Philosophical Observations on the Divine Androgyne," in *The Other in Jewish Thought and History: Constructions of Jewish Culture and Identity,* eds. L. J. Silberstein and R. L. Cohn (New York, 1994), pp. 186–187.

19. *Zohar* 1:48b; 2:92a *(Piqqudin),* 118b *(Ra'aya' Meheimna'),* 138a; 3:80b. For various ramifications of this symbolic motif, see Wolfson, "Re/membering the Covenant: Memory, Forgetfulness, and the Construction of History in the Zohar," in *Jewish History and Jewish Memory: Essays in Honor of Yosef H. Yerushalmi,* eds. E. Carlebach, D. M. Myers, and J. Efron (Hanover, NH 1998), pp. 214–246.

20. See *Zohar* 1:159b; 2:70a, 200a; J. Gikatilla, *Sha'arei 'Orah,* ed. J. Ben-Shlomo (Jerusalem, 1981), 1:105. See also Nahmanides' commentary to Lev. 23:24 (ed. C. Chavel [Jerusalem, 1981], pp. 153–154), and the supercommentary on Nahmanides by Isaac of Acre, *Sefer Me'irat 'Einayim,* ed. A. Goldreich (Jerusalem, 1981), p. 107; *Book of the Pomegranate,* pp. 147–148, 152 (Hebrew section).

21. It should be noted, however, that kabbalists writing in the later part of the thirteenth century, such as the authorship of the *Zohar* and Gikatilla, distinguish between two senses of memory, *peqidah,* corresponding to the feminine *Shekhinah,* the tenth *sefirah,* and *zekhirah,* corresponding to the masculine *Yesod,* the ninth *sefirah.* Cf. *Zohar* 1:115a, 159b, 160a; 3:163a; *Book of the Pomegranate,* pp. 152–153; *Sha'arei 'Orah,* 1:105; Isaac of Acre, *Sefer Me'irat 'Einayim,*

p. 128. See, in particular, the following remark of Moses Cordovero in *Shi'ur Qomah* (Warsaw, 1843), chap. 44, p. 102:

> Even though we have decreed that *zekhirah* refers to the masculine and *peqidah* to the feminine, this is only in a general way. For more specifically both aspects are in the masculine and both in the feminine. Thus it is written, "And Elohim remembered" *(wa-yizkor)* (Gen. 30:22), even though the name Elohim refers to the feminine [*Shekhinah*] and the word *zekhirah* to the masculine. Similarly, it is written, "And the Lord remembered *(pa-qad)* Sarah" (ibid., 21:1), even though the name Lord [i.e., the Tetragrammaton] refers to the masculine and the word *peqidah* to the feminine. And this is because the masculine is in the feminine and the feminine in the masculine . . . And thus *zekhirah* will be in the feminine that is within the masculine and *peqidah* in the masculine that is within the feminine.

22. See *Zohar* 1:95b, 96b; 2:92b, 116a; 3:14a, and elsewhere. The symbolic correspondence of this gradation to the covenant of circumcision predates the period of the *Zohar.* It should also be noted that in the *Zohar* the word *berit* (covenant) corresponds symbolically to either *Yesod* or *Shekhinah,* the underlying assumption being that the covenant comprises in its totality masculine and feminine aspects. See G. Scholem, "Colours and Their Symbolism in Jewish Tradition and Mysticism," *Diogenes* 109 (1980): 69. For example, see *Zohar* 3:115b: "*Ṣaddiq* [i.e., *Yesod*] and *Ṣeddeq* [i.e., *Shekhinah*]: [both] refer to the covenant and they are called covenant. . . . Therefore *zakhor* and *shamor* are bound together, *zakhor* in the day and *shamor* in the night." Gikatilla, *Sha'arei 'Orah,* 1:114–117, distinguishes three symbolic usages of the word *berit* referring respectively to *Binah, Yesod,* and *Shekhinah.* See E. R. Wolfson, *Circle in the Square: Studies in the Use of Gender in Kabbalistic Symbolism* (Albany, 1995), p. 153 n. 81.

23. See *Zohar* 2: 26a, 92b; Moses de León, *Shushan 'Edut,* ed. G. Scholem, in *Qoveṣ 'al Yad,* n.s. 8 (1976): 363; *Book of the Pomegranate,* p. 128 (Hebrew section).

24. This, in a nutshell, is my thesis regarding the visual imaging of the imageless God in kabbalistic sources, which I presented in *Through a Speculum That Shines: Vision and Imagination in Medieval Judaism* (Princeton, 1994). See especially pp. 273–275, 306–317, 336–345, 348–355, 357–368, 386–392, 397. For a more in-depth discussion of the hermeneutic of not-showing in zoharic literature, see E. R. Wolfson, "Occultation of the Feminine and the Body of Secrecy in Medieval Kabbalah," in *Rending the Veil: Concealment and Secrecy in the History of Religions,* ed. E. R. Wolfson (New York and London, 1999), pp. 113–154.

25. On the phallic signification of the symbol of the rainbow, see *Zohar* 1:72b, 117a; 3:215a; *Tiqqunei Zohar,* ed. R. Margaliot (Jerusalem, 1978), §§ 18,

36a–b, 37, 78a. See the discussion of this seminal zoharic symbol in Wolfson, *Through a Speculum that Shines,* pp. 274, 286, 334 n. 30, 337–338 n. 40, 340–341 n. 48, 361, 368–369 n. 149, 386–387; idem, "Re/membering the Covenant," pp. 228–231; and the latter reverberation of this symbol in idem, "*Tiqqun ha-Shekhinah:* Redemption and the Overcoming of Gender Dimorphism in the Messianic Kabbalah of Moses Hayyim Luzzatto," *History of Religions* 36 (1997): 326–329. See also the remark of A. Elqayam, "The Rebirth of the Messiah," *Kabbalah: Journal for the Study of Jewish Mystical Texts* 1 (1996): 143 n. 72 (Hebrew). For a recent attempt to challenge my claim that prevalent in kabbalistic sources is a phallomorphic understanding of the rainbow as the sign that characterizes the phenomenological texture of visionary experience, see M. Fishbane, *The Exegetical Imagination: On Jewish Thought and Theology* (Cambridge, Mass. and London, 1998), p. 214 n. 41. Although Fishbane readily admits that the rainbow can be interpreted as symbolic of the male sexual potency, he contends that the "arc of colors is perceived as the whole divine Glory in a form like a Man. It is this anthropomorphic configuration as a whole that enters the Kingdom *(Malkhut)* of the beloved, symbolized by the cloud." In my judgment, the notion of body as it appears in the classical kabbalistic literature is predicated on the assumption that the body itself is metonymically the phallus since the kabbalists maintained that the phallus is the glory *(kavod,* which should be deciphered in terms of its philological root, *kaved,* weightiness, that which impresses itself upon the surface of another) of the body inasmuch as it comprises all of the energy of the body. The point is epitomized in the expression, *guf u-verit ḥad hu',* "the body and the phallus are one," which appears in a passage in *Sefer ha-Bahir* wherein the limbs of the divine anthropos are delineated. See Abrams, *The Book Bahir,* § 114, p. 199. The phallic nature of the body as such is also expressed in the anatomic presumption well attested in kabbalistic sources that the male organ comprises the energy of all the limbs, which is the implicit significance of the designation of the phallus (in both the human and the divine realms) by the term *kol,* the "all." See, for example, Moses de León, *Book of the Pomegranate,* p. 227 (Hebrew section), "You must know that the secret of this limb is the secret of all the limbs that are placed in him from the head to his feet, for all of them exist through its foundation. . . . Thus you should know that it is the containment of all the limbs of the body *(kelal kol 'eivarei ha-guf).*" Similar language is used by idem in his *Sod 'Eser Sefirot Belimah,* ed. G. Scholem, *Qoveṣ 'al Yad* n.s. 8 (1976): 381, "The phallus . . . is called *kol,* for it is the containment of all the limbs *(kelal kol ha-'eivarim)* and the containment of the entire body *(kelal kol ha-guf).*" And see *R. Moses de León's Sefer Sheqel ha-Qodesh,* ed. C. Mopsik (Los Angeles, 1996), p. 50 (Hebrew): "For the secret of the phallus is the foundation of the whole body *(qiyyum kol ha-guf)* in desire and inclination, and all the limbs in an abundance of yearning and love are aroused in relation to it, and they are joined in the union of inclination and love in accord with its will." Even if one brackets this phallic conception of the male body, I am not sure how we can (following Fishbane) speak of the whole anthropomorphic configuration entering the feminine without privileging the phallic potency, which is, after all, the mechanism by which the male penetrates the space of the female, here depicted symbolically by the bow appearing in the cloud. The texture of the theosophical symbolism employed by kabbalists is based on the phenomenal contours of the embodied conditions of human experience. If in the human sphere it is impossible to imagine the male cohabiting with the female except through phallic penetration (and this is not to deny other forms of contact or intimacy, but only to focus on cohabitation in the most technical sense), then it is impossible to conceive of the theosophical symbol in the manner suggested by Fishbane. Finally, the remark that the arc of colors refers to the whole anthropomorphic form neglects the subtle nuance of the relevant kabbalistic passages to which I have referred in previously published scholarship, and many more examples that I could add, according to which the manifestation of these colors through the prism of the *Shekhinah* signifies her transformation and restoration into the masculine potency in the image of the corona or the sign of the covenant that makes visible that which is concealed. Consider the unambiguous formulation of de León in *Sheqel ha-Qodesh,* p. 76, "How delightful it is to contemplate the notion that this sign of the covenant is the secret of the corona that is known in the secret of the covenant that is inscribed and sealed," *u-mah neḥmad ha-'inyan lehaskil bihyot zo't 'ot ha-berit she-hi' sod ha-'aṭarah ha-yedu'ah be-sod ha-berit re-shumah we-ḥatumah.* This is precisely the point of the symbol of the bow in the cloud, which, in my judgment, is one particular way of expressing the highly complex idea that the *Shekhinah* is the visible image that renders the invisible image of the masculine phenomenologically accessible. See Wolfson, *Through a Speculum that Shines,* pp. 315–316. Regarding the phallic nature of the symbol of the rainbow, see, in particular, the passage from de León's *Shushan 'Edut,* cited in Wolfson, "Re/membering the Covenant," pp. 230–231. The rainbow as the sign of the covenant, which is associated more particularly with the disclosure of the corona, is also emphasized in de León, "*Sefer ha-Mishkal:* Text and Study," ed. J. Wijnhoven, Ph.D. diss., Brandeis University, 1964, pp. 132–133. Finally, consider *Tiqqunei Zohar,* § 37, 78a, wherein it is stated explicitly that the three colors of the rainbow correspond to the three colors of the eye, which correspond to the three shells of the foreskin surrounding the *Shekhinah,* or the three shells of the nut. Precisely through these colors the *Shekhinah* assumes the title "pupil of the eye," *bat 'ayin,* the point that is the sign of the covenant concerning which it is said "I will see her to remember the everlasting covenant" (Gen. 9:16). On the symbol of the *bat 'ayin* in zoharic sources, see Wolfson, "Weeping, Death, and Spiritual Ascent in Sixteenth-Century Jewish Mysticism," in *Death, Ecstasy, and Other Worldly Journeys,* eds. J. J. Collins and M. Fishbane (Albany, 1995), pp. 241–242

n. 69. Redemption is depicted as the time in which the three shells are removed so that the sign of the covenant, which is identified further as the letter *yod* of the phallic inscription, is disclosed through the three luminous garments of the *Shekhinah,* a mystery related exegetically to the verse "Then your master will no longer be covered, but your eyes will see your master" (Isa. 30:20). For a parallel to this passage, see ibid., § 58, 92a-b. See texts cited at nn. 86–87.

26. The motif studied here is one example of the phallocentric orientation of Nahman, which is consistent with the dominant symbolic approach of the kabbalists through the ages. For an attempt to retrieve a feminist sensibility in Nahman's teachings, see O. Wiskind-Elper, *Tradition and Fantasy in the Tales of Reb Nahman of Bratslav* (Albany, 1998), pp. 103–114. It lies beyond the scope of this study to respond in detail to Wiskind-Elper's analysis, but let me simply state in general terms that it suffers from an inability to evaluate the use of gender terms in a contextually nuanced way. Nahman's references to the feminine cannot be lifted out of context in order to argue that he was positively disposed toward the female. Each of the references to the female, especially those that are drawn from the repository of kabbalistic symbols, have to be evaluated carefully in terms of the gender valence that is implicit in the particular literary tradition. The author herself alludes to such a problem on p. 260 n. 104 after citing Arthur Green's uncritical affirmation of feminine images in rabbinic and kabbalistic literature, but she fails to heed her own caution in the presentation of her thesis. Indeed, she relies on this very essay of Green as support for her claim that Nahman's "intuitive sense of the female" is continuous with an "interest in experiences unique to women" that is "intrinsic in Jewish mystical thought as a whole" (p. 104). In my judgment, as I have argued in a variety of studies, this is a very problematic and questionable characterization of the images of the feminine in the traditional kabbalistic sources. Finally, let me note that it is remarkable that in a book on Nahman there is no sustained engagement with the motif of *shemirat ha-berit,* "guarding the covenant," applied in an essential way to the *ṣaddiq* as an antidote to *pegam ha-berit,* the "blemish of the covenant," which refers to sexual transgressions. Also conspicuous is the lack of attentiveness to *tiqqun ha-kelali,* the "comprehensive rectification," which refers to Nahman's unique remedy for the sin of spilling semen in vain, which he considered to have soteriological significance. Regarding this seminal theme in Nahman's messianic orientation, see Y. Liebes, "R. Nahman of Bratslav's *Ha-Tiqqun Ha-Kelali* and his Attitude towards Sabbatianism," *Zion* 45 (1980): 201–245 (Hebrew); English translation in idem, *Studies in Jewish Myth and Jewish Messianism,* trans. B. Stein (Albany, 1992), pp. 115–150. Consider, for example, the words of R. Nahman in *Liqquṭei MoHaRaN* (Benei-Beraq, 1972), I, 10:4, "This is the essence of Israel's coming close to their Father in heaven, that is, by means of the rectification of the covenant *(tiqqun ha-berit).* By means of this is the essence of Israel's coming close to their Father in

heaven in the aspect of 'I bore you on eagles' wings and brought you to me' (Exod. 19:4). The eagle is the comprehensive rectification *(tiqqun ha-kelali)*, which is the aspect of 'He declared to you the covenant' (Deut. 4:13) . . . that is, the rectification of the covenant." See ibid., I, 10:5–10, 205; II, 92. And in *Liqqutei 'Esot* (Jerusalem, 1976), s.v. berit, § 25: "By means of the comprehensive rectification, which is the rectification of the phallus, the [states of] consciousness *(mohin)* are exalted, for the essence of the rectification of knowledge is in accordance with the rectification of the phallus, and the essence of Israel's closeness to their Father in heaven is by means of guarding the phallus." See ibid., § 38, "When one rectifies the sign of the holy phallus, then his consciousness is in perfection, and he can comprehend the words of the righteous man, for one's comprehension is in accord with one's rectification, for this is a great principle that no man can comprehend and grasp the word of the righteous man if he has not first rectified the sign of the holy phallus as is appropriate." Given the overwhelming preponderance of phallic images in Nahman's teachings, it is truly astonishing that a whole book on Nahman could be written with no reference to the patent phallomorphism. Even if one were to grant that there is a genuine voice of the female to be retrieved from Nahman's discourses and tales, it would be reasonable to expect at least some mention of the phallocentric elements in an effort to present a more balanced picture. I would contend that the positive images of the feminine in Nahman (as well as in Hasidic sources more generally) have to be examined very carefully in order to discern if the female as such is valenced in a positive way or rather, as I suspect, the female is accorded value when she is transposed into the male. I concur with Wiskind-Elper's observation that in the worldview of Nahman, "'masculine' and 'feminine' do not designate qualities that belong, respectively, to men and women but rather are ontological valences simultaneously inherent in all of reality—from the world of the *sefirot* to human beings and even to 'inanimate' things" *(Tradition and Fantasy,* p. 261 n. 108). What Wiskind-Elper ignores, however, is that these ontological valences even in Nahman's thinking reflect a gender hierarchy that is evident as well in the social sphere. For a more accurate account of the status of the feminine in Hasidic literature, see A. Rapoport-Albert, "On Women in Hasidism, S. A. Horodecky and the Maid of Ludmir Tradition," in *Jewish History: Essays in Honour of Chimen Abramsky,* eds. A. Rapoport-Albert and S. J. Zipperstein (London, 1988), pp. 495–525. For a response to Rapoport-Albert, see N. Polen, "Miriam's Dance: Radical Egalitarianism in Hasidic Thought," *Modern Judaism* 12 (1992): 1–21. Polen's study suffers from the same criticism that I leveled against Wiskind-Elper: No attention is paid to the cultural dimension of the gender construction, which at least raises questions about the presumed correlation of biological sex and gender attribution.

27. The ascetic and anti-erotic tendencies in Eastern European Hasidism, which in some measure approximate the Christian monastic renunciation of

sexuality, have been well noted by D. Biale, *Eros and the Jews: From Biblical Israel to Contemporary America* (New York, 1992), pp. 121–148. Biale briefly, but incisively, discusses the specific case of Nahman on pp. 135–136. The recognition of the ascetic aspect of some of the key proponents of Beshtian Hasidism is an important corrective to the one-sided portrayal of this phenomenon as essentially nonascetic in contrast to earlier forms of hasidic asceticism linked to the kabbalistic ethos. For a recent articulation of this position, see M. Rosman, *Founder of Hasidism: A Quest for the Historical Ba'al Shem Tov* (Berkeley, 1996), pp. 30, 33–35, 37–38, 115. On the affirmation as well as the qualification of mystical asceticism in Eastern European sources prior to the rise of Hasidism, see M. Piekarz, *The Beginning of Hasidism: Ideological Trends in Derush and Musar Literature* (Jerusalem, 1978), pp. 37–39, 48–49, 62–63, 74, 78, 113, 153, 157, 168, 230–231, 262, 339–340 (Hebrew). For a balanced analysis of the ascetic and anti-ascetic tendencies in Beshtian Hasidism, and the attitude toward physical pleasure, see A. Nadler, *The Faith of the Mithnagdim: Rabbinic Responses to Hasidic Rapture* (Baltimore and London, 1997), pp. 80–87. On the ascetic tendencies in Nahman, see A. Green, *Tormented Master: A Life of Rabbi Nahman of Bratslav* (Alabama, 1979), pp. 27–28, 35–40. See also M. Mantel, "The Meaning of Suffering according to Rabbi Nathan of Nemirov," *Da'at* 7 (1981): 109–118 (Hebrew). On the intrinsic connection between asceticism and the spiritual ideal of communion with God *(devequt)* in early Hasidic sources, see M. Krassen, *Uniter of Heaven and Earth: Rabbi Meshullam Feibush Heller of Zbarazh and the Rise of Hasidism in Eastern Galicia* (Albany, 1998), pp. 55, 108–121. Particularly interesting is a passage in *Liqquṭei MoHaRaN* II, 68, wherein the clash between the ascetic ideal of the abrogation of the body and the traditional norm of procreation is applied to the specific case of the *ṣaddiq*. Even though it is necessary for the righteous man to repudiate physical needs and sensual desires, his perfection depends on his leaving progeny above in the spiritual plane and below in the physical world. See ibid., II, 71, where it is stated that by means of producing offspring the glory of God is augmented insofar as the essence of this glory is revealed only by man.

28. *Liqquṭei Halakhot* (Jerusalem, 1974), Yoreh De'ah: Milah, IV:2.

29. For a detailed account of Nathan of Nemirov, see J. Weiss, *Studies in Braslav Hasidism* (Jerusalem, 1974), pp. 66–83 (Hebrew). See also Green, *Tormented Master,* index, s.v. "Nathan Sternharz."

30. *Liqquṭei Halakhot,* Yoreh De'ah: Milah, IV:2. Knowledge in the thought of Nahman does not signify a discursive, abstract knowing but rather a mystical or spiritual awareness that may lead to *unio mystica.* Cf. *Liqquṭei MoHaRaN,* I, 4:4, 21:11, 53, 58:5, 255; II, 1:5, and see the comments of Green, *Tormented Master,* pp. 320–322.

31. *Liqquṭei MoHaRaN,* II, 61.

32. Ibid. For an alternative translation and analysis, see Green, *Tormented Master*, pp. 321–322. For a negative characterization of a spiritual state in which there is neither time nor intellect, a state that is depicted as the constant thirst for God, see *Liqqutei MoHaRaN*, I, 76. The means to rectify this condition is through cleaving to the righteous. By drawing close to the righteous one attains the form of worship that is in the aspect of vision, which has a fixed boundary and time.

33. This term reflects medieval philosophical usage. See Weiss, *Studies in Braslav Hasidism*, p. 48 n. 17. On Nahman's complex and contradictory views regarding the role of the imaginative faculty in religious faith, see Green, *Tormented Master*, pp. 341–342. The negative depiction of the imaginative faculty, *koah ha-dimyon*, is well-attested in Hasidic literature, in large measure following the view of Maimonides, perhaps as mediated through the writings of Abraham Abulafia. See, e.g., Jacob Joseph of Polonoye, *Sofnat Pa'aneah*, ed. G. Nigal (Jerusalem, 1989), p. 176. For another negative assessment of the *mundus imaginalis* ('olam ha-dimyon) in Hasidic literature, see Israel Dov Baer of Weledniki, *She'erit Yisra'el* (Brooklyn, 1985), Sha'ar ha-Zemanim, 4c. For the possible Sufi background of this conception in earlier kabbalistic writings, which were influenced by the ideas and practices of Abulafia, see M. Idel, *Studies in Ecstatic Kabbalah* (Albany, 1988), pp. 73–90.

34. *Liqqutei MoHaRaN*, II, 61. On the "unreality of time" in Nahman's tales, see Wiskind-Elper, *Tradition and Fantasy*, pp. 53–54, 57–58.

35. The preexistence of the Messiah is an old Jewish apocalyptic idea that had an important influence on subsequent Christological and rabbinic speculation. See H. A. Wolfson, *The Philosophy of the Church Fathers* (Cambridge, Mass., 1956), pp. 156–165. See, in particular, *Midrash Tehillim*, ed. S. Buber (Vilna, 1891), 2:9, 14b, where Ps. 2:7 is interpreted as a reference to the preexistence of Messiah. See, in contrast, Acts 13:33 where the same verse is cited as a prooftext for the resurrection—rather than the preexistence—of the Messiah.

36. *Liqqutei MoHaRaN*, II, 79.

37. *Liqqutei Halakhot*, Yoreh De'ah: Basar be-Halav, IV:1.

38. Nathan alludes to *Sifrei Deuteronomy*, ed. L. Finkelstein (New York, 1969), sec. 32, p. 59, which is paraphrased by Rashi in his commentary on this verse (as Nathan himself notes). The connection between the present, which is the only aspect of time that is real, and divine worship in Nahman's thought is highlighted in Mordecai Menahem Mendel Kossowsky, *'Emunat 'Ittekha* (Piotrków, 1914).

39. *Liqqutei MoHaRaN*, II, 79.

40. The image of the "old and foolish king" (Eccles. 4:13) is related to the evil inclination in older rabbinic sources. See *Ecclesiastes Rabbah* 4:9; *Midrash Tehillim* 9:5, 41b; *'Avot de-Rabbi Natan*, ed. S. Schechter (Vienna, 1887), version

B, chap. 16, 18b; and *Pesiqta' de-Rav Kahana'*, ed. B. Mandelbaum (New York, 1962), p. 460.

41. Based on the line from T. S. Eliot, "Four Quartets," in *The Complete Poems and Plays: 1909–1950* (New York, 1971), p. 128.

42. Cf. *Liqquṭei MoHaRaN*, II, 45: "When a person enters into the worship of the Lord, the way that is shown to him is keeping a distance *(hitraḥaqut)*, and it seems as if they keep him at a distance from above, and they do not allow him at all to enter into the worship of the Lord. In truth, all of the distancing is only entirely a drawing near *(hitqarevut)*." On the possible influence of the Psalms in engendering the terms *hitqarevut* and *hitraḥaqut* to characterize Nahman's devotional states, see Green, *Tormented Master*, p. 28.

43. *Liqquṭei MoHaRaN*, I, 261.

44. Here my language is indebted to M. Heidegger, *Discourse on Thinking*, trans. J. M. Anderson and E. Hans Freund, with an Introduction by J. M. Anderson (New York, 1966), p. 68, "But remaining is a returning." See n. 124.

45. "Four Quartets," p. 134.

46. *Mekhilta' de-Rabbi Yishma'el*, eds. H. S. Horovitz and I. A. Rabin (Jerusalem, 1970), Bahodesh, chap. 2, p. 208, and see commentary of Rashi to Exod. 19:5.

47. *Liqquṭei MoHaRaN*, I, 62:6.

48. This conception of time realized in pious worship, which points to the world-to-come that lies beyond time, is implicit as well in the following remark in *Liqquṭei MoHaRaN*, I. 38:1: "Every man must examine himself in every moment *(be-khol 'et)* if he is conjoined to God, blessed be he. The sign of conjunction is the phylacteries because the phylacteries are a sign regarding conjunction." The emphasis that Nahman placed on innovating words of Torah must be understood in this context as well. See *Liqquṭei MoHaRaN*, I, 262; II, 21, 118. The same idea is implicit in ibid., p. 246, where the greatness that a man achieves is related to the task of forgetting all the wisdom that he previously acquired. The need to begin anew constantly is related to Nahman's method of dialectical negation according to which each attainment is perceived only as a rung on the ladder leading to a higher attainment; every form of knowledge is perceived, accordingly, as ignorance. See Green, *Tormented Master*, p. 294. Also relevant here are the words attributed by Nathan to Nahman himself in *Ḥayyei MoHaRaN* (Brooklyn, 1974), *Shivḥei MoHaRaN:* Gedullat Hassagato, § 6, "Thus you know the substance of the world now. Had the world not been as it is, I would have been a novelty *(hayyiti ḥiddush)*, that is, had there not been the corporeality and density of the events of the current world, which greatly conceal and hide him, everyone would have seen the distinctiveness of his wonders, for he is a wondrous novelty *(ḥiddush nifla')*, awesome and exalted." Liebes, "*Ha-Tiqqun Ha-Kelali*," p. 201 (English translation, p. 115), cites this comment in support of his claim that the "messianism of

Bratslav contrasts sharply with Judaism's traditional messianic views." Leaving aside the thorny problem of ascertaining in an unambiguous manner the "traditional messianic views" of Judaism, I would counter that the operative understanding of *ḥiddush* in the view expressed by Liebes as a total innovation that breaks with everything that proceeded it simply does not take into account the paradoxical nature of Nahman's view that what is new is new only because it is old. For an explicit formulation of this paradox, consider the passage from *Shivḥei MoHaRaN* cited in n. 123. In more general terms, the monolithic and dogmatic presentation of Nahman's position on the part of Liebes fails to take into account the profound sense of paradox (see n. 54) that he embraced and the identification of the logical antinomies that ensue therefrom. Particularly relevant to the passage that Liebes cites, not only is it the case that what is new is new because it is old, but what is revealed is revealed because it is concealed. Thus, when Nahman speaks of his being hidden by the density of the corporeal world, this must be decoded as the ultimate sign of the manifestation of his unique and superior holiness. Consider *Liqqutei MoHaRan*, I, 243: "Know that there is a very great *ṣaddiq*, and the world cannot endure his holiness. Thus, he is greatly concealed, and concerning him no one sees any holiness or additional abstinence, and this is on account of the greatness of his holiness." In the continuation of this passage, the disclosure of the holiness of the *ṣaddiq* through his concealment is ingeniously related to the rabbinic idea that the Song of Songs is the holy of holies. That is, the one book in which there is ostensibly no reference to matters of cultic purity is deemed to be the most sacred book. The apparent lack of holiness is directly proportionate to its supreme sanctity. See as well *Liqqutei MoHaRaN*, I, 63:1, where the paradox of concealment and disclosure pertaining to the *ṣaddiq* is related to the secret intent of circumcision. On the necessity for the *ṣaddiq* to become a simpleton *('ish pashut)*; see ibid., II, 77.

49. *Ḥayyei MoHaRaN*, 2b.

50. *Liqqutei Halakhot*, 'Oraḥ Ḥayyim: Tefillin V.5.

51. *Liqqutei MoHaRaN*, I, 76. Nahman's notion of renewal can also be expressed in terms of drawing down mercy to ameliorate judgment, an act that reproduces the pattern operative in the creation of the world. See *Liqqutei Halakhot*, Ḥoshen Mishpaṭ: Hilkhot Matanah V.1.

52. Ibid, I, 272.

53. *Liqqutei Halakhot*, Ḥoshen Mishpaṭ: Piqqadon, IV.5.

54. In this study, I recurrently use the term *paradox* to characterize Nahman's thinking. On the role of paradox in Nahman, see Weiss, *Studies in Braslav Hasidism*, pp. 109–149; and idem, *Studies in East European Jewish Mysticism,* ed. D. Goldstein (Oxford, 1985), pp. 49, 53–54.

55. Here my formulation is indebted to Derrida, "Faith and Knowledge: the Two Sources of 'Religion' at the Limits of Reason Alone," in *Religion,* eds. J.

Derrida and G. Vattimo (Stanford, 1998), p. 17, "Since everything has to be said in two words, let us give two names to the duplicity of these origins. For every origin is duplicity itself, the one and the other."

56. On the use of this technical term in Nahman's writings, see Green, *Tormented Master,* pp. 286–287.

57. *Ḥayyei MoHaRaN,* Siḥot MoHaRaN, 'Avodat ha-Shem, § 137, p. 68.

58. Ibid.

59. Liebes, *"Ha-Tiqqun Ha-Kelali,"* p. 202 n. 7 (English translation, pp. 185–187 n. 7).

60. *Ḥayyei MoHaRaN,* Siḥot MoHaRaN, 'Avodat ha-Shem, § 137, p. 68.

61. *Liqquṭei MoHaRaN,* I, 33:5.

62. E. Levinas, *Existence and Existents,* trans. A. Lingis (Dordrecht, Netherlands, 1978), p. 73. Consider as well the reflections of E. Husserl, "The World of the Living Present and the Constitution of the Surrounding World External to the Organism," in *Husserl: Shorter Works,* eds. P. McCormick and F. A. Elliston (Notre Dame, 1981), p. 239,

> The entire physical perceptual field as a constituted manifold of things that appear in perspectives is a harmonious unity of perspectivity; one perspectival style governs and continues to govern throughout the changing perceptual field. . . . Furthermore it governs not just in each instantaneous present, but in the concrete and flowing present with its continuous synthesis. This synthesis is also concerned with the perspectival coexistences and successions as they pass over into one another and thereby suitably fit together with one another.

63. A similar observation about time in Nahman's thinking, particularly as it relates to his conception of the story, is offered by Wiskind-Elper, *Tradition and Fantasy,* pp. 142–143.

64. Here, too, one is reminded of a stanza in the first of Eliot's "Four Quartets," pp. 119–120, "Time past and time future / Allow but a little consciousness. / To be conscious is not to be in time / But only in time can the moment in the rose-garden, / The moment in the arbour where the rain beat, / The moment in the draughty church at smokefall / Be remembered; involved with past and future. / Only through time time is conquered." According to my interpretation of Nahman, consciousness similarly involves being beyond time, but the only way to be beyond time is through the memory in the present of the future that is past, the end that is the beginning.

65. This symbolic significance of the number eight may underlie Nahman's positive attitude toward the spiritual value of music whose basic structure is the octave. It is particularly noteworthy that Nahman, according to a report of

Nathan, affirmed that the effectiveness of songs is dependent upon the capacity to "despise the sexual desire." See reference cited in M. Piekarz, *Studies in Braslav Hasidism* (Jerusalem, 1972), p. 45 (Hebrew); and Liebes, "*Ha-Tiqqun Ha-Kelali*," p. 236 n. 125 (English translation, p. 206 n. 121); and, most recently, Wiskind-Elper, *Tradition and Fantasy*, pp. 90–103, 195–199. As will be seen from our following discussion, the symbolic rationale for circumcision is also predicated upon the eradication of the sexual drive. On the eschatological significance of the number eight in earlier rabbinic sources, see the reference in the following note. Let me remark, finally, that the *ṣaddiq* is also related by Nahman, following the standard kabbalistic symbolism, to the number six insofar as this attribute comprises the lower six emanations of the divine, which correspond to the six days of the week. See *Liqquṭei MoHaRan*, I, 63:1, where the phallus is depicted as comprising the six potencies, but it is also equated with the Sabbath, which is the seventh.

66. Already in early kabbalistic literature, *Binah* is identified as the eschatological world-to-come. See, e.g., *Zohar* 1:49a; 2:27b, 115b, 204a, 225a; 3:278a; and Gikatilla, *Sha'arei 'Orah*, 2: 65–66. *Binah* is associated with the number eight, moreover, for it is the eighth of the ten emanations when counting from below. On the eschatological significance of the number eight in rabbinic haggadah, see L. Ginzberg, *The Legends of the Jews* (Philadelphia, 1968), 5: 130–131 n. 142, 6: 262 n. 81. Especially important for an appreciation of Nahman's messianic symbolism is the rabbinic idea (mentioned by Ginzberg) that the harp to be used in messianic times consists of eight strings compared to the seven-stringed harp of David (although some maintained that David's harp had ten strings). On the comparable significance of the number eight in Christian gnosis, see C. G. Jung, *Mysterium Coniunctionis: An Inquiry into the Separation and Synthesis of Psychic Opposites in Alchemy*, 2nd ed., trans. R. F. C. Hull (Princeton, 1977), pp. 403–404.

67. That is, the *sefirot* from *Ḥesed* to *Malkhut*. This terminology likewise can be traced back to early kabbalistic sources. The seven lower emanations are called "seven days of the edifice," for the structure of the cosmos is fashioned out of these seven archetypes. See G. Vajda, *Le commentaire d'ezra sur le cantique des cantiques* (Paris, 1969), pp. 169–170.

68. *Liqquṭei Halakhot*, Yoreh De'ah: Hilkhot Milah, IV:3.

69. *Liqquṭei MoHaRaN*, I, 34:1.

70. Ibid., I, 34:7.

71. Ibid., II, 13.

72. *Tiqqunei Zohar* § 16, 41b.

73. *Liqquṭei MoHaRaN*, I, 34:7.

74. Ibid., I, 34:6.

75. Ibid., I, 34:8.

76. Ibid., I, 8:9. See ibid., I, 66:1, where Nahman says that the student who attaches himself to the *ṣaddiq* in the manner of the branches to the tree experiences the ups and downs that characterize the life of his spiritual mentor.

77. It should be noted, however, that in ibid., I, 64.3, the *ṣaddiq*, who embodies the attribute of Moses, is identified further as the aspect of silence *(beḥinat shetiqah)*. See ibid., I, 64.5, where silence is related to the song of the righteous man *(niggun shel ṣaddiq)*, who is identified as the supernal faith *('emunah 'elyonah)* or the "head of faith" *(ro'sh 'emunah)*, which is the gradation of thought that is above speech. On the nexus between silence and thought, which is related to the saying attributed to God in response to the query of Moses regarding the fate of Aqiva, *shetoq kakh 'alah ba-maḥshavah*, "Be silent, for thus it arose in thought" (Babylonian Talmud, Menahot 29b), see *Liqquṭei MoHaRaN*, I, 234, 251; II, 8. On the symbolic identification of silence and the lower point, which is the *Shekhinah*, see ibid., 6:5.

78. Ibid., I, 34:3–4. Compare ibid., 73. In that context, the vessel that facilitates the conjunction of thought and speech through prayer is the *'ani*, the "I," which consists of the *ṣaddiq* represented by the *'alef*, speech *(dibbur)* or *Malkhut* represented by the *nun*, and thought *(maḥshavah)* represented by the *yod*. In the word *'ani*, therefore, is encoded the unity of the sefirotic potencies. The vessel is constructed by means of the prayer of every Jewish male, and it is in this sense that Nahman understands the prophetic claim that all of Israel are righteous. The converse of this relationship is Nahman's claim that one who sins sexually, and thereby blemishes the phallic covenant *(pogem bi-verit)*, cannot pray properly; see ibid., I, 50. Although Nahman placed great emphasis on the auditory aspect of hearing and receiving the words spoken by the *ṣaddiq*, his overall theory of language was such that he privileged the written over the verbal; indeed, he viewed the latter as a species of the former. See, for instance, *Liqquṭei MoHaRan*, I, 17:5, where Nahman describes in elaborate fashion the engraving of the "words of faith of the truly righteous one," *dibburei 'emunah shel ha-ṣaddiq ha-'emet*, in the air in a manner comparable to the graphic inscription of letters in a book.

79. On the Hasidic inversion of the hierarchy of prayer and study of Torah and the response of the Lithuanian rabbinic elite, see Nadler, *Faith of Mithnagdim*, pp. 50–77.

80. Ibid., I, 2:6. See I, 44, "By means of prayer the secrets of Torah are revealed."

81. Ibid., I, 22:10.

82. Ibid., II, 25. On the delights *(sha'ashu'im)* that God derives from human actions below, see ibid., II, 7:4. The principle that the master's teachings can be transformed into prayers is applied to Nahman's own discourses in Nathan's *Liqquṭei Tefillot* as is evident from the introduction to this work. See Idel, *Hasidism* p. 239.

83. On Nahman's personal struggles to conquer erotic desire and his interpretation of the role of the *ṣaddiq* as one who attains sexual purity, see Green, *Tormented Master*, pp. 37–39. I am not sure I agree with Green's suggestion that Nahman's "teachings on the conquest of sexual desire" reflect "am emphasis far beyond that of other Hasidic writings" on account of his "youthful trials." While I would not quibble with Green's surmise regarding Nahman's personal torment, I would argue that the conquest of sexual desire, and especially the act of spilling semen in vain, lies at the phenomenological core of Hasidism, a task that is related to the distinctive role of the *ṣaddiq*. See the remark of Eliezer Zweifel cited by Green, *Tormented Master*, p. 61 n. 79, regarding the predominance of sexual sins in the confessions offered before the *ṣaddiq* according to early Hasidism. Green suggests that Zweifel had Bratslav sources in mind from which he generalized about Hasidism. Perhaps this suggestion is correct, but it seems to me that Zweifel touched upon a central nerve in the Hasidic movement, which indeed is marked by an obsessive attitude toward *shemirat ha-berit* or avoiding sexual offenses, and especially the act of masturbation, which is consonant with the intense focus on this topic in the moralistic and pietistic works (betraying the ascetic influence of the kabbalistic orientation) written by rabbinic figures in the seventeenth and eighteenth centuries. See Biale, *Eros and the Jews*, pp. 113–118, 123–130. One cannot understand the social and religious function of the *ṣaddiq* in Hasidism unless one appreciates this obsession.

84. *Liqquṭei MoHaRan*, I, 2:1–2, 6. On the designation of Israel as the "parts of the *Shekhinah*," see ibid., I, 260.

85. *Zohar* 3:215a.

86. *Liqquṭei MoHaRan*, I, 42.

87. Ibid., II, 83.

88. The pairing of Torah study and prayer is found frequently in Hasidic sources, and it is even transmitted as a direct teaching of the Besht. See Weiss, *Studies in East European Jewish Mysticism*, p. 59. The insight concerning the intricate connection between prayer and Torah study as a mystical-magical praxis in Hasidic sources underlies the analysis in M. Idel, *Hasidism: Between Ecstasy and Magic* (Albany, 1995), pp. 147–188.

89. Thus, in *Sefer Yeṣirah* 1:3, a correspondence is made between the covenant of the foreskin and the covenant of the tongue. For select references to this motif, see Wolfson, *Circle in the Square*, pp. 149–150 n. 59, 150–151 n. 62. An important source, which I neglected to mention in previous studies, is *Esther Rabbah* 7:11. In that midrashic context, circumcision and Torah are described respectively as the "covenant in their flesh" and the "covenant in their mouths." The reference to the two covenants in *Sefer Yeṣirah* has been repeatedly interpreted by kabbalists as an allusion to circumcision and the Torah.

90. *Liqquṭei MoHaRaN*, I, 19:3. See *Liqquṭei 'Eṣot*, s.v., *berit*, §§ 11–12,

The essence of the subjugation and the abrogation of all desires, and in particular the desire for adultery, for this is the main one that needs to be abrogated, is by means of the holy language, that is, by means of the multiplication of sacred words, which consists of Torah, prayer, and the conversation between himself and his Creator. . . . The rectification of the phallus *(tiqqun ha-berit)* and the perfection of the holy language *(shelemut leshon ha-qodesh)* are dependent on one another: Inasmuch as they increase the articulation of holy words, which are in the aspect of the holy language, they also merit the rectification of the phallus, and in accordance with the rectification of the phallus they merit the perfection of the holy language.

The nexus between speech and the phallus also underlies another passage in *Liqquṭei MoHaRaN,* II, 5, "The perfection of speech *(shelemut ha-dibbur)* is the aspect of the sacred language *(leshon ha-qodesh)* . . . and the sacred language is bound to the Sabbath. . . . When we merit the aspect of the sacred language, which is bound to the Sabbath, we draw by means of it the holiness and the joy of the Sabbath to the six days of the week." On the phallic connotation of the Sabbath in Nahman's thought, see n. 65.

91. *Liqquṭei MoHaRaN,* I, 19:9.

92. *Liqquṭei 'Eṣot,* s.v., *berit,* § 17,

The essence of the perfection of the holy language, which is the essence of the rectification of the phallus that comprises the rectification of all the desires and attributes, cannot be received except from the mouth of veritable righteous men. On account of this it is necessary to travel to the veritable righteous man to listen to [what comes from] his mouth precisely . . . for the essence of the perfection of speech, which is the aspect of the perfection of the holy language, which is the essence of the rectification, cannot be received except from his holy mouth itself precisely, for there is the source of fear, which is the perfection of the holy language, which is the rectification of the phallus that is comprised of all the rectifications.

93. Nahman's struggle with, and rejection of, homosexuality are noted by Green, *Tormented Master,* pp. 51–52. See also Green's interpretation, ibid., pp. 71–72, of the puzzling incident of Nahman and the young Arab during the former's sojourn in Haifa. Despite Nahman's unequivocal rebuff of homosexuality, the relationship of the *ṣaddiq* and his Hasidim is depicted in explicitly phallo-centric and homoerotic terms.

94. See Wolfson, *Through a Speculum That Shines,* p. 371 n. 155. Biale, *Eros and the Jews,* p. 122, duly notes the eroticized nature of the Hasidic community, which is based on "male companions" organized "around a charismatic leader." His concern, however, is not with the implicit homoeroticism, but with

the displacement of erotic desire from carnal sexuality to the passionate love of God. For a discussion of some facets of the use of erotic symbolism in Hasidic sources, see L. Jacobs, *Hasidic Prayer* (New York, 1973), pp. 60–61, 127–129; and Idel, *Hasidism: Between Ecstasy and Magic*, pp. 133–140. On the pious eros of Hasidic spirituality and the consequent model of feminized masculinity, see D. Boyarin, *Unheroic Conduct: The Rise of Heterosexuality and the Invention of the Jewish Man* (Berkeley, 1997), pp. 55–68. As one might expect from a predominantly heterosexual culture, the homoerotic relationship of the master to the disciple is depicted in terms that reflect the accepted norm. One striking illustration of this is found in *Liqqutei MoHaRaN*, I, 185: "By means of the desire and the will to travel to the *ṣaddiq,* the impression of the vessel is made, just as when a craftsman wants to make a vessel, he must first form and etch out the impression and the shape of the vessel, and afterwards he can make the vessel. Similarly, the will to travel produces the shape and the impression of the vessel, and afterwards when he comes to him the vessel is made." The disciple is thus characterized as the vessel who receives the overflow from the master. In the continuation of this passage, the union of master and disciple is signified by the word *'adam,* for the first two letters, *'alef* and *dalet,* spell *'ed,* that is, the vapor that rises as the female waters, which is also identified with the pietistic quality of fear, and the final letter, *mem,* is the vessel that contains that which overflows. Here, too, we see that the bonding of the male disciple to the male master constitutes the completion of the anthropos.

95. *Liqqutei MoHaRaN*, I, 135. The principle of gender, which is derived from much older sources, is the simple binary correlation of the masculine with the power to overflow and the feminine with the desire to receive. Consider ibid., I, 73: "It is known that the one who receives pleasure from another is called female. . . . Thus when God, blessed be he, receives pleasure from the prayers of Israel, he becomes, as it were, female in relation to Israel. This is [the intent of] what is written 'an offering by fire of pleasing odor to the Lord' (Num. 28:8), for by means of the pleasing odor that God, blessed be he, receives from the prayers of Israel, he becomes the mystery of the woman [ *'ishshah,* which is the same consonants as the word *'ishsheh,* the fire offering mentioned in Num. 28:8]. 'And the female surrounds the man' (Jer. 31:21). If so, the inwardness becomes external." On the feminization of God vis-à-vis Israel, see also *Liqqutei MoHaRaN,* I, 219. In that context, the operative image is that of God becoming humble and impoverished, that is, diminishing and constricting himself, in order to disclose his kingship and his fear. The qualities of humility and poverty, as well as those of kingship and fear, are related to the attribute of *Malkhut,* the feminine potency of the divine. The homoerotic bond between master and disciple is predicated on a similar gender transformation of the party that receives into the female in relation to the male. I assume that the gender transposition is implicit as well in *Liqqutei MoHaRaN,* II, 72, where Nahman notes that by means of envisioning oneself with

the *ṣaddiq* one receives a sense of greatness, but the "essence of greatness is humility," *'iqqar ha-gedullah hi' shiflut.* That is, attachment to the *ṣaddiq* elevates and aggrandizes the individual, but true greatness is docility. To express the matter in gender terms, the Hasid who cleaves to the *ṣaddiq* is phallically empowered, but that empowerment is expressed through diminishing the power of the phallus by means of ascetic renunciation, which is the ideal of the feminized masculine. The nexus between attachment to the righteous master and sexual abstinence is affirmed in other Hasidic sources as well. Consider the passage from Menahem Nahum of Chernobyl cited and analyzed by Biale, *Eros and the Jews,* pp. 129–130. For a discussion of erotic imagery employed in Hasidic texts to depict the relationship between the masculine God and the feminized soul of the male, see Idel, *Hasidism,* pp. 133–140. Idel does not engage the evidently homoerotic implications of the relevant material wherein the soul of the male is feminized in relationship to the male potency of the divine.

96. Babylonian Talmud, Berakhot 61a.

97. *Liqquṭei MoHaRaN,* I, 7:3.

98. On occasion Nahman describes the task of cleaving to the *ṣaddiq* in a way that places the emphasis on the need of the individual to bind himself to the words of prayer or Torah that issue forth from the mouth of the *ṣaddiq.* For instance, in *Liqquṭei MoHaRaN,* I, 9:4, Nahman writes that each person *(kol 'adam,* which for him means every male Jew) must tie his prayer to the righteous one of the generation, for only he has the knowledge and capacity to lift up the prayers to their appropriate celestial gates. See ibid., I, 10:10, where Nahman mentions the prideful ones, *ba'alei ga'awah,* who consider themselves righteous and thus try to dissuade others from going to the true *ṣaddiqim* to ask them to pray on their behalf.

99. *Liqquṭei MoHaRaN,* I, 43.

100. On this technical expression in Nahman's writings, which is likely based on the description of Noah in Gen. 6:9, see Green, *Tormented Master,* pp. 19, 116–122, 143, 159, 169, 186, 191–196, 201, 205.

101. *Liqquṭei MoHaRaN,* I, 8:2.

102. This characterization of eros as inherently insatiable and transient in nature has its roots in ancient Greek philosophy. See B. S. Thornton, *Eros: The Myth of Ancient Greek Sexuality* (Boulder, 1997), pp. 127–134.

103. The symbolic interpretation of the cutting of the foreskin as a weakening of sexual desire is to be found in earlier sources such as Philo of Alexandria as well as Judah ha-Levi and Maimonides. See R. Hecht, "The Exegetical Contexts of Philo's Interpretation of Circumcision," in *Nourished with Peace: Studies in Hellenistic Judaism in Memory of Samuel Sandmel,* eds. F. Greenspahn, E. Hilgert, and B. Mack (Chico, Calif., 1984), pp. 51–79; Judah ha-Levi, *Sefer ha-Kuzari,* I. 115; and Maimonides, *Guide of the Perplexed,* III. 49. See also the use of this motif in the Provençal figure, Isaac ben Yedaiah, discussed by M. Saperstein, *Decoding the*

*Rabbis: A Thirteenth-Century Commentary on the Aggadah* (Cambridge, Mass., and London, 1980), pp. 97–98.

104. On the struggle to eradicate the sexual impulse in Nahman's teaching, see Green, *Tormented Master,* pp. 167–170.

105. According to the talmudic explanation (see, e.g., Babylonian Talmud, Qiddushin 32a), the word *zaqen* is an acrostic for *zeh sheqanah ḥokhmah,* "this one who has acquired wisdom."

106. *Liqquṭei Halakhot,* Yoreh De'ah: Hilkhot Milah, IV, 4.

107. See *Liqquṭei MoHaRaN,* I, 60. In that passage, wealth is associated with the rectifications of *'Atiq,* the first of the *sefirot,* and it is also identified as the aspect of the length of days or the aspect of elderliness. Since Abraham merited the aspect of being elder, or the length of days, he also merited wealth, a point exegetically supported by Gen. 24:1.

108. Cf. *Liqquṭei MoHaRaN,* I, 37.

109. *Liqquṭei Halakhot,* Yoreh De'ah: Hilkhot Milah, IV, 5.

110. Nahman's stories have been translated in several editions. For the purpose of this study I have made use of the standard Hebrew-Yiddish edition, *Sippurei Ma'asiyot* (New York, 1949), and of the English translation, *Nahman of Bratslav: The Tales,* (Ramsey, N.J, 1978). All translations are taken from the latter volume.

111. The need to be joyous is one of the fundamental themes of Nahman's teachings. See, e.g., *Liqquṭei MoHaRaN ,* I, 5:3; II, 10, 12, 23–24; and *Liqquṭei 'Eṣot,* s.v. *simḥah; Siḥot ha-RaN* (New York, 1972), §§ 20, 41–45, 131. See the remarks of Green, *Tormented Master,* p. 50; and Liebes, "*Ha-Tiqqun Ha-Kelali,*" pp. 236–237 (English translation, pp. 139, 206–207 n. 128), who emphasizes that joy for Nahman connotes in particular the overcoming of sexual desire. On this point, see *Liqquṭei 'Eṣot,* s.v. *berit,* § 54, "The essence of the blemish of the phallus *(pegam ha-berit)* is through sadness and melancholy, and analogously the essence of the guarding of the covenant *(shemirat ha-berit)* is through joy." See ibid., s.v. *simḥah,* § 7, "Joy is the aspect of the faces that are illuminated, the aspect of truth and faith, and by contrast sadness is the aspect of idolatry, the faces that are dark, death. The essence of joy is merited in accordance to the rectification of the phallus *(tiqqun ha-berit),* and in accordance to one's drawing close to the truly righteous men who are the joy of all Israel. By means of this he binds himself to God, blessed be he, and he merits 'to see the splendor of the Lord' (Ps. 27:4), and he illumines himself by the 'light of the face of the living God' (Prov. 16:15)." On the role of joy in the spiritual comportment of Nahman, see, more recently, Fishbane, *Exegetical Imagination,* pp. 168–172, 173–184.

112. For a possible explanation of this shift, see Band's commentary, *Nahman of Bratslav,* pp. 322–323. Band, relying on Joseph Dan's interpretation, suggests that the opening sequence is representative of the twin-process of withdrawal *(ṣimṣum)* and the breaking-of-the-vessels *(shevirat ha-kelim),* two processes

that form part of the Lurianic myth of creation. The second sequence, beginning with the flight and the meeting of the two children in the forest, signals the start of the process of rectification *(tiqqun),* the final stage in the Lurianic myth. See Dan, *The Hasidic Story—Its History and Development* (Jerusalem, 1975), p. 147 (Hebrew). While I cannot analyze this interpretation in detail here, it seems to me that the spontaneity of the shift in the tale is left unexplained by this reliance on the "cosmic cataclysm" and its "rectification" according to Lurianic myth. Perhaps it is not even desirable to try to explain the narrative's structure along such systematic lines. Was Nahman's sudden shift an intentional ruse to confound the reader's power of reason and argumentation? After all, the faux pas of the king's son was his admiration of the rational sciences!

113. *Rimzei Ma'asiyot,* published in the standard edition of Nahman's *Sippurei Ma'asiyot,* p. 124.

114. Band, *Nahman of Bratslav,* p. 253. See also Dan, *Hasidic Story,* pp. 153–154; H. Hidenberg and M. Oron, *The Mystical World of R. Nahman of Bratslav* (Tel Aviv, 1986), pp. 123–124 (Hebrew).

115. The expression, *mu'aṭ ha-maḥaziq 'et ha-merubbeh,* has its origin in rabbinic sources. Cf. *Genesis Rabbah,* 5:7, eds. J. Theodor and C. Albeck (Jerusalem, 1965), p. 36; and *Leviticus Rabbah,* 10:9, ed. M. Margulies (Jerusalem, 1972), p. 216; see also the commentary of Rashi to Lev. 8:3.

116. In the standard edition of the tales there is a postscript that explains, "The end of the story, i.e., what occurred on the seventh day concerning the beggar without feet, as well as the end of the first part of the story concerning the king, we have not merited to hear. . . . We will not merit to hear it until the Messiah comes." On the messianic implications of the tale's ending, see Dan, *Hasidic Story,* p. 169; Liebes, "*Ha-Tiqqun Ha-Kelali,*" pp. 207 nn. 22, 237 (English translation, pp. 139, 190 n. 22). Cf. also *Liqquṭei Halakhot,* 'Oraḥ Ḥayyim: Tefillat ha-Minḥah, VII, 93, where Nathan states that the Messiah, son of David, is comprised of the seven true righteous ones, *ṣaddiqei ha-'emet,* who are further identified with the seven beggars of Nahman's tale. The Messiah, says Nathan, is the "aspect of *malkhut,*" a reference to the last of divine emanations, the *Shekhinah.* All the beggars were involved in the rectification of the world which was not, however, completed. The *ṣaddiq* on the level of the Messiah is further identified with the blind beggar who reaches the level of the divine Nothing, the first *sefirah* of *Keter.* Prima facie, it would seem that there is a contradiction here between saying, on the one hand, that the Messiah is the aspect of *malkhut* (the tenth *sefirah)* and asserting, on the other hand, that the Messiah is on the level of the one who reaches the Nothing (the first *sefirah).* In fact, however, there is no contradiction because the ultimate *tiqqun* involves the unification of the last and first *sefirot,* divine action and thought. To realize this unification is the task of the Messiah and the true *ṣaddiq.* In Nathan's words, "Thus the completion of the rectification *(shelemut ha-tiqqun)* is by means of the aspect of the kingship of the Messiah *(beḥinat malkhut mashiaḥ)* . . . which is to draw forth the

end of action from the beginning of thought *(sof ma'aseh mi-maḥshavah teḥilah)* [a statement that is based on a verse in the kabbalistic hymn, *Lekhah Dodi,* composed by Solomon Alkabets in the sixteenth century]. The end of action [*Malkhut*] is the aspect of the revelation of his kingship *(hitgalut malkhuto)* that first arose in thought [*Keter*] . . . And the great *ṣaddiq,* who is the aspect of Messiah, merited to purify himself to such a degree that from the inception of thought and the beginning of all the grades that are above thought and above *nefesh, ruaḥ,* and *neshamah,* until the final end of action, he stood in war in all the aspects until he merited to reveal his kingship in completion. But there is no king without a nation, and it is necessary to inform all people in the world of his kingship. Therefore the essence of the rectification of everyone, in general and in particular, is by means of him [the *ṣaddiq* on the level of Messiah]." The unification of the first and last *sefirot* is an idea expressed in much earlier kabbalistic sources, ultimately based on the description of the ten *sefirot* in *Sefer Yeṣirah* 1:7, "their end is fixed in their beginning and their beginning in their end." On the dynamic connection between *Keter* and *Malkhut,* see, for example, *The Book of Mirrors: Sefer Mar'ot ha-Ẓove'ot,* ed. D. C. Matt (Atlanta, 1982), pp. 26–27 (Introduction). A detailed study, tracing this theme from the writings of the zoharic circle to the Lurianic texts and then beyond into Hasidic sources, would prove instructive.

117. Band, *Nahum of Bratslav,* p. 253. And see reference to Dan in the preceding note.

118. Cf. the remark of Kafka in *Parables and Paradoxes* (New York, 1971), p. 81: "The Messiah will come only when he is no longer necessary; he will come only on the day after his arrival; he will come, not on the last day, but on the very last."

119. Band, *Nahman of Bratslav* p. 259.

120. Ibid., p. 260.

121. Ibid., p. 261.

122. See *Liqquṭei Halakhot,* 'Oraḥ Ḥayyim: Hilkhot Tefillat ha-Minḥah, VII, 93, where Nathan explicitly identifies the first beggar with the Messiah. See n. 57.

123. On the possibility that Nahman described himself in these very messianic terms, specifically in the context of his polemic with Aryeh Leib of Shpola, see Weiss, *Studies in Braslav Hasidism,* p. 48; Piekarz, *Studies,* p. 142; Dan, *Hasidic Story,* p. 155; and Liebes, "*Ha-Tiqqun Ha-Kelali,*" p. 204 n. 11 (English translation, p. 188 n. 11). Leib was known as the Zeide, that is, the Elder, but it was the younger Nahman who asserted that he was truly the "eldest of the elders" *(sabba' di-sabbin).* See *Ḥayyei MoHaRaN,* II, 32. Nathan already connected this remark of Nahman with the description of the first beggar in the "Tale of the Seven Beggars": he was at once the oldest and the youngest. On the relationship of Nahman and the Shpoler Zeide, see Green, *Tormented Master,* pp. 100–115. And cf. *Ḥayyei MoHaRaN, Shivḥei MoHaRaN,* Gedullat Hassagato, § 24, where Nahman reportedly said, "I

will lead you in a novel way that never existed before *(derekh ḥadash shelo' hayah me-'olam),* even though it is an ancient way *(derekh ha-yashan mi-kevar)* it is entirely new *(hu' ḥadash legamrei)."* The description of Nahman's method of teaching involves the same paradoxical convergence of what is old and what is new that is found in the description of the first beggar. See Liebes, *"Ha-Tiqqun Ha-Kelali,"* 211–12 n. 38 (English translation, p. 193 n. 38).

124. See Hidenberg and Oron, *Mystical World of R. Nahman,* p. 124. See, however, Liebes, *"Ha-Tiqqun Ha-Kelali,"* p. 212 n. 38 (English translation, p. 193 n. 38). According to Liebes, the paradoxical description of the first beggar as the oldest and youngest should not be explained "as an expression of eternity beyond time, but precisely as life in the present, renewed each moment." Liebes's interpretation of Nahman's aspect of that "which is above time" is reminiscent of Nietzsche's doctrine of the eternal recurrence of the same in which the incessant flow of time and becoming is broken not by an escape to some transcendental eternity (Being) beyond time and space, but by experiencing and willing the ever-returning present in the here and now. See F. Nietzsche, *The Will to Power,* ed. W. Kaufmann (New York, 1967), § 617, "To impose upon becoming the character of being—that is the supreme will to power. . . . That everything recurs is the closest approximation of a world of becoming to a world of being:—high point of meditation." And ibid., § 708, "Becoming must be explained without recourse to final intentions; becoming must appear justified at every moment . . . the present must absolutely not be justified by reference to a future, nor the past by reference to the present." See M. Harr, "Nietzsche and Metaphysical Language," in *The New Nietzsche,* ed. D. Allison, *New Nietsche,* pp. 24–34; G. Deleuze, "Active and Reactive," in Allison, *New Nietsche,* pp. 85–86, 102–103; P. Klossowski, "Nietzsche's Experience of the Eternal Return," in Allison, op. cit., pp. 107–120. See also J. Stambaugh, *Nietzsche's Thought of the Eternal Return* (Baltimore, 1972), pp. 13–16; M. Heidegger, *Nietzsche Volume II: The Eternal Recurrence of the Same,* trans. D. Krell (New York, 1984), pp. 211–233. It is not clear to me, however, that such a reading is appropriate for Nahman who affirms the transcendental realm of divine emanations in general, and particularly the third emanation, *Binah,* which is the eighth when counting from the bottom up, when he speaks of the aspect beyond time. The issue is not a constantly renewed lived moment, but rather a supratemporal grade that is the ontological source of Messiah, the blind beggar, and the true *ṣaddiq.* In light of that source, one can speak of the paradox of the eternal return of that which has never been.

125. For a similar explanation, see Wiskind-Elper, *Tradition and Fantasy,* pp. 203–204.

126. On the nexus between faith, vision, and consciousness, see *Liqquṭei MoHaRaN,* I, 225. On the depiction of vision in terms of the limitation of boundary and time, see ibid., I, 76.

127. See *Liqqutei Halakhot,* 'Oraḥ Ḥayyim: Hilkhot Tefillin, V, 3; and Tefillat ha-Minḥah, VII, 93.

128. See Dan, *Hasidic Story,* pp. 154–155; Liebes, "*Ha-Tiqqun Ha-Kelali,*" p. 208 n. 26 (English translation, p. 190 n. 26); and Hidenberg and Oron, *The Mystical World of Rabbi Nahman of Bratslav,* p. 125. On occasion Nathan applied this symbolism of the divine nothing *(Keter)* to Nahman himself; see Piekarz, *Studies,* pp. 142–143. On Nahman's self-identification with *Keter,* see also M. Verman, "Aliyah and Yeridah: The Journeys of the Besht and R. Nachman to Israel," in *Approaches to Judaism in Medieval Times,* vol. 3, ed. D. R. Blumenthal (Atlanta, 1988), 3:164–165. For a useful discussion of the symbol of nothing in kabbalistic sources, see D. C. Matt, "Ayin: The Concept of Nothingness in Jewish Mysticism," in *The Problem of Pure Consciousness: Mysticism and Philosophy,* ed. Robert K. C. Forman (New York, 1990), pp. 121–159.

129. The paradoxical coincidence of memory and forgetfulness in Nahman's description of the blind beggar has already been noted by Liebes, "*Ha-Tiqqun Ha-Kelali,*" p. 208 n. 26 (English translation, p. 190 n. 26 ibid). On forgetfulness as an ideal in Nahman's thought, see Liebes, op. cit., p. 211, and references in n. 38 (English translation, pp. 121, 192–193 n. 38).

130. See Wolfson, "Re /membering the Covenant," pp. 227–228.

131. In *Liqqutei MoHaRaN,* I, 37:2, Nahman sets up the following antinomies: body and soul, animal and human, matter and form, folly and sagacity, darkness and light, death and life, forgetfulness and memory, external (or foreign) sciences and the wisdom of Torah. Forgetfulness is thus the realm of materiality, ignorance, and darkness. For a discussion of the concept of forgetfulness in Nahman, particularly with reference to his interpretation of the talmudic dictum "the sage who has forgotten his learning" (Babylonian Talmud, Sanhedrin 96a), see Weiss, *Studies in Braslav Hasidism,* pp. 47–54. On forgetfulness as a distinguishing characteristic of the demonic realm, *Sitra' 'Aḥra',* in zoharic theosophy, cf. *Zohar* 1:193b; 3:14b.

132. On ascetic renunciation *(perishut)* as an antidote for the blemish of the mind *(pegam ha-da'at),* see the statement of Nahman in *Liqqutei MoHaRaN,* II, 78.

133. *Liqqutei MoHaRaN,* I, 7:5. On the correlation of prayer, miracles, and the land of Israel, see ibid., I, 9:5. On the eschatological power of the prayer of the *ṣaddiq* to overturn the natural order, see ibid., I, 62:6, "When the righteous man through his prayer abrogates some necessity of the order of constellations, then it is known from what is disclosed about what is hidden that God exists, for he listens to the prayers of the righteous man, and he destroys the orders, and he changes nature. All this will be in the future." On the overturning of nature by means of prayer, see ibid., I, 216. And see ibid. I, 250, where the people of Israel are described as being governed solely by divine providence *(hashgaḥah),* for by nature

they are "above nature," but in the exile they follow the ways of the idolatrous nations who are controlled by the natural forces. In the messianic future, nature will be entirely abrogated.

134. In *Liqqutei MoHaRaN*, II, 4:5, the "philosophers of nature" *(ḥakhmei ha-ṭeva')* are identified as the "evil beasts" who do not hear the sound of the Torah reading of the Jewish festivals, the aspect of the holy scripture *(miqra' qodesh)*, for they (mistakenly) claim that everything happens according to nature *('al pi ha-ṭeva')* as if there were no will of God unrestrained by the limitation of time and the circumscription of space. On the description of the miracle of the splitting of the Reed Sea as a nullification of time *(biṭṭul ha-zemanim)*, see the words of Nahman in *Liqqutei MoHaRaN*, II, 79.

135. In *Liqqutei MoHaRaN*, I, 62:5, Nahman relates the ostensible absurdity of faith to the paradoxical depiction in *Zohar* 2:95a of the body of the beautiful maiden as hidden and revealed, "She is hidden, for if you ask the one who believes for a reason for faith, he certainly will not know to offer you a reason in response, for faith belongs only to that which has no reason. Even so she is revealed, that is, in relation to the believer the matter is revealed as if he saw with his eyes the thing in which he believes on account of the greatness of his complete faith."

136. *Liqqutei MoHaRaN*, I, 54:1.

137. See Babylonian Talmud, Berkahot 17a.

138. *Siḥot ha-RaN*, § 96. Nahman goes on to say, however, that only by means of forgetfulness, a vice in itself, can one survive in this world. Hence, memory belongs essentially to the world-to-come whereas forgetfulness is germane to this world. See also *Liqqutei 'Eṣot*, s.v. zikkaron, § 4.

139. Babylonian Talmud, Qiddushin 35b; Ḥullin 142a; *Midrash Tehillim* 23:7, 101b.

140. *Liqqutei MoHaRaN*, II, 7:12. On the rich implications of the notion of *maqqifin* in Nahman's thought, see Green, *Tormented Master,* pp. 292–320.

141. *Liqqutei MoHaRaN*, II, 21:8.

142. Ibid., II, 2:2.

143. For references to both primary and secondary sources related to the motif of the Sabbath being in the pattern of the world-to-come, see E. R. Wolfson, "Coronation of the Sabbath Bride: Kabbalistic Myth and the Ritual of Androgynisation," *Journal of Jewish Thought and Philosophy* 6 (1997): 307 n. 19.

144. Babylonian Talmud, Shabbat 118a. On the use of the idiom "inheritance without boundary" to denote the eschatological reward, see Babylonian Talmud, Berakhot 51a.

145. *Liqqutei MoHaRaN* II, 72.

146. Ibid. For a more in-depth context of this statement, see n. 95.

147. See *Zohar* 1:122b and parallel in 3:168a-b. On the virtue of humility in zoharic sources, see Tishby, *Wisdom of the Zohar,* pp. 1330–1331.

148. Moses Cordovero, *Tomer Devorah* (Venice, 1589), p. 9a; Elijah de

Vidas, *Reʾshit Ḥokhmah ha-Shalem* (Jerusalem, 1984), Shaʿar ha-ʿAnavah, chap. 1, p. 480. For the impact of these texts on early Hasidism, see B. Sack, "The Influence of Reshit hokhmah on the Teachings of the Maggid of Mezhirech," in *Hasidism Reappraised,* ed. A. Rapoport-Albert (London, 1996), pp. 253–254. See also Idel, *Hasidism: Between Ecstasy and Magic,* pp. 109–111. On the *via passiva* in early Hasidism, see Weiss, *Studies in Eastern European Jewish Mysticism,* pp. 69–94; and R. Schatz Uffenheimer, *Hasidism as Mysticism: Quietistic Elements in Eighteenth Century Hasidic Thought,* trans. J. Chipman (Princeton, 1993), pp. 67–79, 168–188. On Nahman's interest in ethical works, and particularly the *Reʾshit Ḥokhmah,* see the evidence adduced in *Shivḥei ha-RaN* (New York, 1972), I.7; and the comments of Green, *Tormented Master,* p. 30.

149. *Liqquṭei MoHaRaN,* I, 22:9.

150. Ibid., 22:10.

151. See Green, *Tormented Master,* pp. 319–320; and Idel, *Hasidism,* pp. 239–240.

152. *Liqquṭei MoHaRaN,* I, 57:5. On the role of fasting as a rectification of speech *(tiqqun ha-dibbur),* which is related more generally to the overcoming of physical desires, see ibid., I, 62:5. On the positive valence of eating as a means to unite the masculine and the feminine potencies of the divine in the case of one whose faith is perfect, see ibid., 62:6. On this theme is Hasidism, see L. Jacobs, "Eating as an Act of Worship in Hasidic Thought," in *Studies in Jewish Religious and Intellectual History Presented to Alexander Altmann on the Occasion of his Seventieth Birthday,* eds. S. Stein and R. Loewe (Alabama, 1979), pp. 157–166.

153. The expression is derived from Prov. 23:6, 28:22. Cf. the rabbinic expressions *ʿayin raʾah* and *ʿayin ha-raʿ* (Mishnah, ʾAvot 2:9, 11). In both cases, as in the biblical contexts just noted, the meaning is avarice or selfishness. But cf. *ʾAvot de-Rabbi Natan,* version A, chap. 16, p. 31b, where the latter expression is explained in two ways: to hold others in contempt or to give grudgingly (see the translation of J. Goldin, *The Fathers According to Rabbi Nathan* [New Haven, 1955], p. 82). Nahman's use of the term, however, comes closest to the Aramaic equivalent, *ʿeina bishaʾ,* in Babylonian Talmud, Berakhot 20a. The expression is used there as a synonym for the evil inclination, but from the context it is evident that the sexual urge in particular is meant. It seems to me that for Nahman as well the "evil eye" refers to desire in general, but to the sexual instinct in particular. See n. 155. Moreover, in *Zohar* 2:225a, the demonic force, *Siṭraʾ ʾAḥraʾ,* is called precisely by the name, *raʿ ʿayin.* Cf. also *Zohar* 2:3a, for an interpretation of Prov. 23:6 that has a definite sexual emphasis. On the connection between *semen virile* and light of the eyes, see Maimonides, *Mishneh Torah,* Hilkhot Deʿot, 4:19.

154. Babylonian Talmud, ʿEruvin 54a. The precise wording of the talmudic text reads as follows: "R. Eleazar said: Why is it written '[the writing] was the writing of God engraved upon the tablets' (Exod. 32:16)? Had the first tablets not been broken, the Torah would not have been forgotten in Israel." This is not

the place to elaborate, but within the rabbinic saying a link is forged between breaking the tablets and obfuscation of Torah.

155. *Liqquṭei MoHaRaN*, I, 54: 4. Nahman emphasizes that there are various forms of the "evil eye," but it is clear that the root core of this is sexual desire. Cf. *Liqquṭei MoHaRaN*, I, 7:4, and *Liqquṭei 'Eṣot*, s.v. *zikkaron*, § 6, s.v. *'einayim*, § 4.

156. *Liqquṭei Halakhot*, 'Oraḥ Ḥayyim : Hilkhot Tefillin V, 3.

157. *Liqquṭei MoHaRaN*, I, 47. On the nexus between the desire for food and the concealment of the face and, conversely, the diminution of this desire and the uplifting of the face, see ibid., 67:2–3. An important exception to Nahman's negative attitude toward physical eating is his explanation of eating on Sabbath; see n. 152. On Nahman's struggle with eating, see Green, *Tormented Master,* pp. 28, 39, 49.

158. In *Liqquṭei MoHaRaN*, I, 7:4–5, Nahman presents the mystical rationale for the commandment of the ritual fringe garment *(ṣiṣit)* as a protection against adultery *(shemirat le-ni'uf)*, which is the aspect of the protection of the phallus *(shemirat ha-berit)*, which is the gradation of *Yesod*, represented symbolically by the figure of Joseph. The logic employed here is that the biblical formulation of this commandment involves the explicit gesture of gazing upon the fringe garment, and the eyes are connected in an essential manner with sexual improprieties.

159. Nahman relates the desire for money to the side of holiness inasmuch as material wealth originates in the same source as the vital soul *(nefesh)*, which is the attribute of *Malkhut*, or the *Shekhinah*. From that perspective one can account for the special connection between the people of Israel and money. As the emanations overflow, however, this desire takes on the darker and coarser form of avarice, which is related as well to anger, an attribute that befits the demonic potency. See *Liqquṭei MoHaRaN*, I, 68–69.

160. *Liqquṭei MoHaRaN*, I, 23:2.

161. Ibid., I, 54:5, "One must protect the eye from the imaginative faculty, and even one who is of the good eye must be on guard against this as we see that even the one who has good vision can err on account of the fact that he sees from a distance and what appears to him is the opposite of truth."

162. Ibid., 25:4, where the desires generated by the imagination are depicted as the demonic shells that need to be conquered.

163. *Shivḥei ha-RaN*, I.17, cited in a different translation by Green, *Tormented Master,* p. 39. See also Biale, *Eros and the Jews,* p. 135.

164. *Liqquṭei Halakhot*, Yoreh De'ah: Hilkhot Milah, IV, 6.

# 4

## Adorning the Souls of the Dead
### *Rabbi Nahman of Bratslav and* Tikkun Ha-Neshamot*

### *Yakov Travis*

[Rabbi Nahman's] whole purpose in coming to Uman, and
choosing it as the place from which to depart this world and in
which to be buried, was to accomplish the rectification of souls
from the past several hundred years that needed mending. For
Uman had been the scene of the slaughter of innumerable souls,
and tens of thousands of children had been killed there before
their time. His intentions were evident from the words he spoke in
Uman, some of which have been recorded elsewhere.

—*Hayyey MoHaRaN*

### Introduction

Death is a veil separating the land of the living from the world of souls. This does
not, however, prevent the human spirit from reaching beyond its bounds—to
influence those in the realm beyond the grave, or to reach back from that realm to
touch the lives of the living. This interchange between the living and the dead is
richly expressed in various religious traditions.[1] Judaism is no exception; the
permeability of the two realms, while muted somewhat in the Bible, is vividly
represented in rabbinic and kabbalistic literature.[2] It is especially prominent
within Hasidism, the spiritual revival movement of eighteenth-century Eastern
Europe. Hasidic stories, teachings, and practices vividly portray the flow of influence between the living and the dead.

The interconnection between the living and the dead takes center stage in
the life and teachings of Rabbi Nahman ben Simhah of Bratslav (1772–1810)
more than in any other school of Hasidism. As R. Nahman's spiritual leadership
matures, and as an intractable illness threatens his own life, he turns his attention
from his small community of living disciples toward the countless disembodied
souls in the congregation of the dead. And subsequently, since R. Nahman's death
almost two centuries ago, generations of followers have developed a vibrant and
influential form of Hasidism that revolves around the vital power of the discarnate
rebbe, earning them the name "the dead Hasidim." In R. Nahman we hear
testimony of the power of the living to influence the souls of the dead, as well as

the powerful impact that the dead can have on the souls of the living. Our primary focus here, however, will be on R. Nahman's work with the souls of the dead. We will first establish the centrality of R. Nahman's caring for the dead during the final months of his life and then trace the development of his interest in this endeavor. In so doing, we will examine some of the experiences and ideas that likely influenced him and how they came to be articulated in his teachings. Our interest here is to present a thorough portrait of a critically important, but not well-known, element in R. Nahman's self-perception of his role as "spiritual leader," or *tsaddik*.[3] While R. Nahman's extraordinary claims may invite psychoanalytic consideration, such analysis is beyond the scope of this chapter.

Our inquiry into this well-documented aspect of R. Nahman's life will not only contribute to a better understanding of the *tsaddik* from Bratslav, but it will also provide insight into an important, but elusive dimension in the vocation of many early Hasidic "masters," or *tsaddikim*. Bratslav literature on R. Nahman's work with the dead offers perhaps the most vivid portrait available of the mysterious and idiosyncratic practice of *tikkun ha-neshamot,* the *tsaddik's* rectification of the souls of the dead.[4] This discussion of *tikkun ha-neshamot* seeks to augment Moshe Idel's recent reexamination of Hasidic leadership by focusing our attention in a completely different direction. While Idel has emphasized the *tsaddik's* role in "drawing down" supernal influence to the carnal community,[5] a complete portrait must also accentuate the *tsaddik's* involvement with "raising up" the community of discarnate souls. An appreciation of the centrality of *tikkun ha-neshamot* in R. Nahman's life, grounded as it is in BeSHTian doctrine and lore, is therefore a critical key for broadening our perspective of the parameters of Hasidic spirituality.

More is known about the life of R. Nahman than any other *tsaddik* in the first generations of Eastern European Hasidism thanks to Rabbi Nathan of Nemirov, his chief disciple, whom he trusted to be the editor of his writings. Besides editing his major work, *Likkutey MoHaRaN* ("The Collected Teachings of Rabbi Nahman") and *Sefer Ha-Middot* ("The Book of Moral Qualities"), brief teachings on living a virtuous life begun by R. Nahman in his youth and completed a few years before he died, the devoted disciple independently recorded with great care biographical information as well as other sayings and teachings he considered essential for understanding the spiritual path of his rebbe. These are found in the hagiographic works *Shivhey ha-RaN* ("The Praises of Rabbi Nahman") and *Hayyey MoHaRaN* ("The Life of Rabbi Nahman"); in R. Nathan's own autobiography, *Yemey MaHaRaNaT* ("The Days of Rabbi Nathan"); and in a collection of shorter teachings and statements entitled *Sihot ha-RaN* ("Conversations of Rabbi Nahman"). These primary sources are saturated with relatively trustworthy biographical data, and our examination of R. Nahman's work with the dead will rely heavily upon them.[6] The relevant quotations are numerous and often repetitive. While we will often quote only the key sentences of lengthy passages, occasionally we will quote an entire passage, that may include certain themes previously mentioned, which will better convey the prominence, importance, and mystery surrounding this aspect of the *tsaddik*'s life in Bratslav literature.

### Rabbi Nahman and the Souls of the Dead

With death at his door after a three-year bout with tuberculosis, R. Nahman decided to leave Bratslav and spend the last of his days in the nearby city of Uman. R. Nathan's account of his rebbe's life from the move in early May of 1810 until his death in mid-October of that same year makes it clear that he was drawn to Uman to be near two very different groups of people: a small group of Jewish heretics called *maskilim* (enlightened ones), and the many thousands of Jews martyred in the Gonta massacres of 1768 who lay buried in a mass grave in the Uman cemetery.[7] While scholarship on this final chapter in R. Nahman's life has concentrated, almost exclusively, on his unconventional attraction to the *maskilim*,[8] our focus here will be on the *tsaddik*'s care for the souls of the martyrs. As we shall see, R. Nahman considered his work with the martyrs to be the pinnacle of his career as a *tsaddik*.

While warning his readers about the difficulty in understanding its significance, R. Nathan explains R. Nahman's primary occupation while living in Uman. Reflecting upon the last few months of his master's life, he writes,

> As for the Rebbe's sojourn in Uman—it is impossible for us to ever fully comprehend its meaning from the few words we heard from his holy mouth, or from whatever flashes of insight we may have gleaned from the hints he gave us. *For during the course of the summer that he dwelt in Uman, [the rebbe] brought about the most wondrous and awesome rectifications (tikkunim), and he became more and more involved with the rectification of souls.* This was the implication of the story he told as he entered Uman. Just before he departed this world,[9] he mentioned the story again, asking me, "Do you remember the story I told you?"[10]

Elsewhere, R. Nathan recounts that as they were about to enter Uman, the rebbe reminded him of an anecdote about R. Israel Ba'al Shem Tov (the BeSHT), the first central figure of Hasidism and R. Nahman's maternal great-grandfather. It is worth noting that R. Nahman's framing of his one-way journey to Uman with the telling of this tale functions as an important "hint" from the master to the disciple about the true meaning of his final months.

One time the Ba'al Shem Tov, may his memory be a blessing, came to a certain place and became extremely depressed . . . for in that very place there were souls from the past three hundred years that had not yet ascended on high. And when the Ba'al Shem Tov came there they all gathered together before him for they had been continuously awaiting such a man as he who would be able to rectify them. He became heavyhearted; the matter weighed so heavily upon him because it was impossible to rectify them except by means of his own death. This was very difficult for him, and for that reason he became depressed. . . .[11]

Note that in the story about the BeSHT, the souls were connected to a particular place and had been seeking a redeemer to come to them for hundreds of years. R. Nathan reports that his rebbe experienced a similar phenomenon.

While in Uman [the rebbe] said that there were tens of thousands of souls there that he needed to elevate . . . and the day before his passing he asked me: "Do you remember the story that I told you?" I said to him: "Which story?" He responded: "The story about the BeSHT that I told you as I entered Uman?" I answered: "Yes." He in turn said: *"For a long time now these* [souls] *have been looking to get me here."* Then he said: "There are not a thousand souls here, but tens of thousands! Tens of thousands! Tens of thousands! And that night he also spoke of this matter. . . .[12]

In yet another passage, we learn that, like in the story of the BeSHT, some souls had been in need of this for centuries.

His whole purpose in coming to [Uman], and choosing it as the place from which to depart this world and in which to be buried, was *to accomplish the rectification of souls from the past several hundred years that needed mending.* For Uman had been the scene of the slaughter of innumerable souls, and tens of thousands of children had been killed there before their time. [The rebbe's] intentions were evident from the words he spoke in Uman, some of which have been recorded elsewhere. . . .[13]

The BeSHT apparently found an alternative means to mend and elevate those souls, but as Arthur Green has noted, the point of the story is apparently "that the BeSHT had nearly paid with his life for his willingness to take part in this task; R. Nahman seems to be telling R. Nathan that his own final task, that for which he will die, is to be the redemption of the sainted dead in Uman."[14]

R. Nahman's involvement with the souls of the dead can be traced back much earlier than his stay in Uman. Four years before, the tragic death of his year-old son prompted him to start publicly discussing his interest in *tikkun ha-neshamot*.

> In the summer of 5566 [1806] in the month of Sivan his young son Shlomo Ephraim died. *When we came to [the rebbe] after the little boy's death, he began speaking with us about the rectification of souls, about the "Master of the Field."*[15] [He told us] of a field in which souls grow, how they require the Master of the Field to tend them, and how one who girds his loins to become Master of the Field has to endure countless troubles and suffering. . . . *From this time on he spoke a great deal about the rectification of souls,* especially after his return from Lemberg and even more so as he entered Uman. . . .[16]

At this time the rebbe also revealed to R. Nathan that while living in Zlotopolye (September 1800–August 1802), several years before discussing the subject, he had already begun learning how to rectify the souls of the dead.[17] The following passage relates how R. Nahman's ability to talk about *tikkun ha-neshamot* resulted, not surprisingly, from much in-depth study of the phenomenon over a protracted period of time. We are also told how, long before arriving in Uman, the *tsaddik* was contemplating and discussing the rectification work he felt called to do specifically with the souls that had lived there.

> Once when he was living in Uman he was sitting and talking with us when he said: "Do you remember when I first started talking of Uman?" I told him: "I remember." . . . Our Rebbe responded: "You don't know, therefore you don't remember. I had certainly been talking about it before then![18] . . . *by then I had gone far in my grasp of the matter and was well-advanced in the subject, for I already had the power to bring this into conversation and make it relevant to that which was being spoken."* . . . And he also said that, even during the previous winter, when he spoke of wanting to travel around the region, *his primary intention was to stay here* [in Uman] *for a time. . . . From all he said on the subject it was clear that he had a very great and awesome purpose in coming to Uman, and that it had been a long time since he first began to grasp the significance of this mission.* He had a comprehensive understanding of it that was very deep. *Long before he came to Uman, when he was still in Bratslav and only talking about this matter, he was already well-advanced in his grasp of the subject.* How much more so now that he was already here [in Uman]! But it is impossible to express whatever glimpses of insight we may have concerning this matter, for in all [the rebbe] did his intentions were so very deep. This is especially true of his journey to Uman in order to depart the world from there. "It is deep, deep. Who will find it?" (Eccles. 7:24)[19]

Toward the end of his life R. Nahman came to understand, in retrospect, that all of his great troubles were necessary for him to be able to accomplish what he now considered his major task.

> [The rebbe] was able to grasp the significance of all these matters. The whole purpose of his many wanderings and the suffering he had endured was to rectify the worlds and mend the souls of the living *and, even more so, the dead. He became more and more involved with the latter as he reached the end of his days.* He said quite explicitly that the work he did with us was something small for him, and this was what we ourselves needed to do, *for he needed to work on the rectification of the souls of the dead, for there are some souls that are literally naked. . . .*[20]

Here, as in other sources that we will discuss further on, R. Nahman feels compelled to work with the souls of the dead because of their "nakedness." The notion of "naked souls," mentioned sporadically in Bratslav teachings, is an important element of the afterlife teachings in classical Kabbalah. In order to understand R. Nahman's involvement with the dead, it is first necessary to briefly survey these classical teachings.

### The Postmortem Garments of the Soul

According to *Sefer ha-Zohar,* the most important kabbalistic work, in postmortem existence each of the three aspects of the soul is clad in a different garment *(levush)* appropriate to its particular experience.[21] While these aspects of the soul are distinct, there is clearly an interconnectedness through which the lower aspects yearn for, and access, the experience of the divine light with which the higher ones are privileged.[22] But to enter into these more sublime realms, the lower aspects of the soul must first be cloaked within the robes of the higher ones.

Upon death, most individuals first suffer the temporary purgations of the nether world called *Gehinnom* (Gehenna)[23] during which the *nefesh,* that lowest aspect of the soul that animates the body and is thus most attached to the physical, "goes forth roaming the world and visiting its grave until it is garbed in its garment." Ordinarily, after thirty days, and sometime within the next twelve months, the higher aspects of the soul complete their purification and are robed in the garments appropriate for their respective destinations in the two levels of *Gan 'Eden* (Garden of Eden).[24] The aspect of the soul above *nefesh,* called *ruah,* ascends to the "terrestrial" or "lower" *Gan 'Eden,* while the higher aspect of the soul, *neshamah,* rises to "upper" *Gan 'Eden.*

Upon release from *Gehinnom,* the *nefesh* binds itself with, and is illuminated by, *ruah*. Enwrapped in *ruah*'s garment, the individual delights in "lower" *Gan 'Eden*.[25] The *Zohar* describes the garment as "woven from the light of supernal resplendence" by the good deeds done during one's life.[26] This garment of righteousness is essential for existence in "lower" *Gan 'Eden*,[27] but cannot be donned until death removes the physical body that garbs the soul in the corporeal world.[28] While *ruah*'s vestment is indeed regarded as precious, its form is considered earthly in comparison with that destined for *neshamah* in the "upper" *Gan 'Eden*.[28]

The *neshamah*, if it so merits, ascends, and is taken into the "delight of delights" of the "upper" *Gan 'Eden* to bask more directly in the divine light.[30] This may take some time, and meanwhile "the *neshamah* is enwrapped and clothed within *ruah*"[31] in the lower paradise, limited by a garment suited to *ruah*.[32] On the Sabbath and on other holy days, the *neshamah* casts off this garment and temporarily ascends.[33] But, for the *neshamah* to dwell in the "upper" *Gan 'Eden*, "garments . . . of a more exalted order" are provided for it, "made of the devotion *(r'auta)* and intentionality *(kavannah de-liba)* which characterized its study of the Torah and its prayer."[34] Adorned with light, the *neshamah* is enabled to gaze at the Glory of God.[35] Those righteous, "who know the mystery of their Master *(raz'a de-M'areyhon)*, cleaving to Him every day," rise further and enter the *innermost* gates of the supernal *Gan 'Eden*.[36]

The naked souls requiring rectification, to which R. Nahman so often refers, are primarily those which, due to a lack of good deeds, were not able to weave their soul's celestial garments.[37] Leaving behind their physical bodies, but without meeting the conditions for entrance into the spiritual realms, these souls roam about in a liminal state; drifting back toward their graves and longing for the inaccessible delights of *Gan 'Eden*. For many, the only remedy is to return to the earthly realm to acquire the garment through a new incarnation. In the *Zohar* we read,

> Truly, all souls must undergo transmigration; but men do not perceive the ways of the Holy One, blessed is He, how the revolving scale is set up. . . . They perceive not the many transmigrations and the many mysterious works which the Holy One, blessed is He, accomplishes with many naked souls, and how many naked spirits roam about in the other world for they cannot enter within the veil of the King *(le-paragod'a de-malkh'a)*. *Zohar* II, 99b

It's very likely that R. Nahman had these zoharic teachings in mind as he sensed the presence of thousands of "naked" souls in Uman. The draw to this particular locale is perhaps more comprehensible if we recall that R. Nahman was attracted to the dead of Uman particularly because many were "children that had been killed there before their time."[38] In such a circumstance these unfortunate souls would not have had the opportunity to perform many good deeds, thus lacking in the fulfillment of the commandments through which the soul weaves its celestial garment.[39]

## Early Influences on R. Nahman's Bond with the Dead

While R. Nahman's care of the dead was viewed as the mature fruit of his spiritual leadership and the result of intense contemplation on the subject during his later years, the *tsaddik's* fascination with, attraction to, and comprehension of the life of the souls of the dead are to be found much earlier in his career.

R. Nahman's enchantment with the dead began in his early childhood.[40] In R. Nathan's biographical sketches of his rebbe's youth, he recounts how the aspiring *tsaddik* would ask God to perform wonders for him. The young Nahman once requested to see a dead person's soul.[41] God granted his request but it was more than the youth could handle and he reacted hysterically. When speaking of his rebbe's later work with the dead, R. Nathan explained this initial experience as follows:

> [The rebbe] said that the dead person in question had been an evil-doer and that was why he had been so very terrified. . . . Subsequently, he saw many, many souls of the dead and he was never afraid, especially in the latter days when he became "Master of the Field" and thousands upon thousands of souls came to him for their rectification. For he was intensely involved in rectifying the souls of the dead and the naked souls which had never entered a body at all. . . .[42]

When we are told of this early wish to behold a dead soul and of the subsequent ease with which he could encounter so many souls of the dead, we should not be so surprised. After all, in the intensely spiritual milieu of early Hasidism in which the young Nahman was raised, the dead were very much alive. We must remember that as a boy R. Nahman lived in the home of his deceased great-grandfather, the revered BeSHT. Following centuries-old custom, countless Hasidim would visit the grave of the BeSHT to pray for material and spiritual blessings. Hasidic lore is filled with talk of the great influence *tsaddikim* wield from beyond the grave. *Shivhey ha-RaN*, R. Nathan's account of the rebbe's youth, relates how important such visits were for the young Nahman, and conveys the vitality of the dead *tsaddikim* in his life. "From his early childhood, [the rebbe] frequently ran off to visit the grave of the holy Ba'al Shem Tov to ask that he help draw him close to God."[43]

R. Nathan also relates that when the rebbe left Medziboz to live with his father-in-law, there were still occasions when he wanted to speak with his great-grandfather. Since he could not actually visit his grave, he would go to the grave of the renowned Rabbi Isaiah of Yanov[44] in the nearby city of Smela. He would ask this *tsaddik* to transmit his request to the BeSHT.[45]

More important for our inquiry, however, are the early Hasidic tales of the work that *living tsaddikim* did on the souls of the dead that surely had a profound impact on the young Nahman. For example, in *Shivhey Ha-BeSHT* ("The Praises of the Ba'al Shem Tov"),[46] a collection of hagiographic folk tales about the founder of Hasidism, one finds a story about why it took the BeSHT so long to complete the afternoon *Minhah* prayer recited prior to the beginning of the Sabbath. Explaining the reason to his brother-in-law, R. Gershon of Kutov, he said, "When I got to the words 'revives the dead,' I contemplated *yihudim* [unifications of the divine names][47] and then souls of the dead came to me by the tens of thousands."[48]

From his subsequent description of how he cared for each soul, we get a glimpse of how it could be so very time-consuming. "I need to speak with each and every one concerning the reason why it was rejected, and I do a rectification for it and pray on its behalf, and raise it up . . . there are so many that if I wanted to raise them all my prayer would last three years!" R. Gershon attempted to do the same but he became overwhelmed when he saw "that the dead came to him like a great flock of sheep."[49]

The phenomenon represented in this tale of encountering numerous souls of the dead and assisting them in their ascension to *Gan 'Eden* is also evidenced in two other, more trustworthy, literary sources. An early Hasidic commentary to Psalm 107, attributed to the BeSHT and published under the title *Sefer Katan* (Zhitomir, 1805),[50] interprets the psalm as a thanksgiving prayer for the naked souls, who with the arrival of the Sabbath are raised up from the netherworld through the descent of the *tsaddikim* to that realm.[51] Rivkah Schatz-Uffenheimer's study of this cryptic work clearly demonstrates its connection to the early Hasidic phenomenon of *tikkun ha-neshamot* during the *Minhah* prayer preceding the Sabbath.[52] In concert with his own practice of *tikkun ha-neshamot*, the BeSHT instituted the custom of reciting Psalm 107 before *Minhah* on the eve of the Sabbath, a practice observed by Hasidim to this day.

The other source is a letter from the BeSHT written to R. Gershon around 1750 and published during R. Nahman's youth.[53] Therein he describes one of his mystical ascents during which he again encounters numerous souls of the dead who need his assistance in their ascent to the upper reaches of *Gan 'Eden*.

On Rosh Hashanah in the year 5507, I used Divine names to bring about the ascension of my soul, as you know, and in my vision I saw wondrous things—things I had never seen before. It is impossible to describe the things I saw and learned during my ascension or to discuss them with anyone else, but when I returned to the "lower" Garden of Eden *(Gan 'Eden ha-Tahton) I saw the souls of some who are dead and some who are alive,* some whom I know and some whom I do not know, *countless in number,* moving up and down in their attempt to ascend from world to world by means of the pillar that is known to scholars of the Kabbalah. They were rejoicing in a great happiness that no human mouth can describe and no mortal ear can hear. . . . They were all rejoicing greatly as they participated in these ascensions. All of them together addressed me at great length. "Your honor," they implored, "because of your standing in Torah, God has given you a special intelligence that enables you to understand and know these things. Please ascend with us and give us your help and support." Because of their great happiness, I was about to ascend with them. . . .

This extraordinary practice must have made a great impression early on in R. Nahman's life. In *Sefer ha-Middot,* which contains much of his early thought, we already find epigrammatic statements that reflect this. For example, one reads, "The *tsaddik* is able to raise the dead to a very great [spiritual] level."[54] Another is a little more dramatic. "With his utterance, the *tsaddik* is able to send one person to *Gan 'Eden,* and another to *Gehinnom.*"[55]

R. Nahman was not only a direct descendant of the BeSHT, but he saw himself as a spiritual heir par excellence. In pursuing the practice of *tikkun ha-neshamot,* he clearly believed that he was following in the path of the BeSHT. Before we turn to R. Nahman's own teachings on the rectification of the dead, we will first outline in broad parameters the practice as found in early Hasidism.

### Toward a Phenomenology of *Tikkun ha-Neshamot* in Early Hasidism

According to the twentieth-century *tsaddik,* R. 'Arele Roth, conversing with the dead and rectifying their souls was a unique practice that distinguished those who followed the spiritual path of the BeSHT.

The ultimate attainment . . . is when the [deceased's] soul itself recounts all of its deeds to the *tsaddik*. This is the level of the disciples of the holy Ba'al Shem Tov, may his merit protect us, who spoke with the souls of those who came to them and revealed to them what had happened to them since they were on the earth, and what was defective in their previous transmigrations, and the root of their correction. This is widely known among all the congregation of Hasidim and in the books of the *tsaddikim*.[56]

While the phenomenon may have been widely known, the technique of *tikkun ha-neshamot* was largely a secret reserved for kabbalistic adepts.[57] Extant descriptions of the procedure are transmitted in quite an obscure manner and require a sound grasp of kabbalistic cosmology and psychology. Moreover, it is only reasonable to assume that, even if it were fully disclosed, the average person lacks the experiential attunement to the spiritual matters discussed that would enable real comprehension of this practice. Nevertheless, from the stories in *Shivhey ha-BeSHT,* and from the comments in *Sefer Katan* and other Hasidic sources, we can trace the contours of *tikkun ha-neshamot* to recover a somewhat intelligible outline of the basic methodology.

We have already seen that the propitious time for *tikkun ha-neshamot* is the Sabbath eve, and that the souls flock to the *tsaddik* when he engages in the mystical meditations of *yihudim* during the *Minhah* prayer service.[58] These meditations apparently involve drawing down from the light of *Ein Sof,* the infinite essence of the Divine, through the four planes of existence unto the lowest plane, the World of Action, for the purpose of raising this lowest realm of existence up to its source.

> And we must rectify them and lift them higher and higher to *'Ein Sof,* as is known of the ascents of the Sabbath eve which we draw down through the *Minhah* prayer: from Emanator [*'Ein Sof*] to [the World of] Emanation, and from Emanation to [the World of] Creation, etc., and afterwards we lift up from [the World of] Action to [the World of] Formation, etc.—up to the Emanator.[59]

While the practice was not limited to Sabbath Eve, the *tsaddikim* usually engaged in *tikkun ha-neshamot* only when souls "came to them" during their meditations or prayers. R. Nathan relates that during R. Nahman's first few days in Uman, while he was absorbed in prayer, a certain heretic came to the *tsaddik's* mind *(b'a 'al da'ato),* "so that he would act on his behalf, to rectify him."[60] Perhaps, as the language in this passage suggests, for a *tsaddik* in a heightened state of consciousness, thoughts of the deceased are tantamount to a needy soul's appeal for *tikkun.* For the adept, thoughts of another may actually represent a tangible rendezvous of souls.

Two different stories in *Shivhey ha-BeSHT* shed some light on what occurs when the souls eventually come to the *tsaddik.* According to one account, the procedure involves three consecutive stages: (1) speaking with each soul individually and getting to the "root" of its rectification, (2) doing the actual rectification for the soul's imperfection, and (3) praying for the soul.[61] The other account describes the basic psychodynamics involved in the actual moment of rectification. Describing the BeSHT's attempt to rectify the soul of Shabbetai Tsvi, R. Joel of Nemirov states, "the *tikkun* is achieved through binding *nefesh* (life force) with *nefesh, ruah* (spirit) with *ruah, neshamah* (soul) with *neshamah.* . . ."[62] Apparently, the *tsaddik* attaches these three aspects of the deceased's soul with his own, and is thereby able to work with that soul in rectifying its deficiency. Since individuals have different deficiencies, the heart of each *tikkun* is presumably different.

As a secret practice of the *tsaddikim*, we should not be surprised that Hasidic literature does not appear to offer further details. To go beyond this point and to attempt to explain more precisely how a *tikkun* is achieved is to enter the realm of speculation. Nevertheless, it seems that the *tsaddik's* practice of *tikkun ha-neshamot* is related in some sense to two other phenomena that involve a precise operation executed in the realm of the *tsaddik's* thoughts while in an elevated state of consciousness. One serves to bring about good; the other rights a wrong. First, we must consider the phenomenon of *contemplative* fulfillment of the *mitsvot* at their supernal "root," already evidenced in early kabbalistic texts.[63] Recalling the practice of the Kozniter Maggid, his son R. Moshe 'Elyakim Beri'ah explains that the *tsaddikim* perform the commandments while the "essence of their thought" is united with the "supernal secret" of each commandment.[64] He writes, "and when the *tsaddik* wants to perform some good deed for the sake of Israel, such as a remedy or similar action, he is elevated up to the supernal essence and root of the thing and he operates there, and automatically it is done also below, as is known to the perfectly righteous."[65] Once we shift focus to the souls of the dead, it is not too hard to imagine a *tsaddik* doing the same sort of practice for the benefit of an individual soul, lacking in the perfection associated with a particular *mitsvah*.

The other phenomenon is the Hasidic practice of "elevating strange thoughts." Early Hasidism emphasized this technique for dealing with impure thoughts that enter one's mind, particularly during prayer. Instead of suppressing a disturbing lustful, arrogant, or idolatrous thought, the ideal response was to contemplate the inner holy essence from which it must derive its existence, thus "elevating" the profane to its source in holiness. A lustful thought, for example, is a lowly degraded form of a holy yearning to cleave to God. Rather than push such a thought out of the mind, one raises it to its spiritual "root." This technique, which involves dwelling on the impure thought, is consequently fraught with spiritual danger. Many considered it inappropriate for the layman, restricting its practice to the *tsaddikim* whose minds were mostly pure and thus suitable for such an approach. According to some teachings, a true *tsaddik's* mind is so completely pure, that the "strange" thoughts that enter therein are viewed as originating not from within him, but rather from one of the many souls that are attracted to him.[66] If a *tsaddik* can rectify the degenerate thoughts of the living in such a manner, it is not hard to imagine him doing something similar when confronted by the disembodied souls of the dead seeking *tikkun* for thoughts or deeds of the past.

After first "conversing" with the deceased's soul to discover its particular blemish, and then consciously binding the three aspects of that soul to his own, it is conceivable that the *tsaddik* is then able to work on that soul's imperfection as though it were his own. We might imagine that, once this melding of souls is achieved, the *tsaddik* could either contemplatively fulfill the appropriate commandment at its "root" on high, or contemplatively amend a particular sin by "raising" it to its "root" in holiness.

Before we continue, let us briefly review some similar phenomena in traditional rabbinic practice and consider what seem to be the innovative elements in this Hasidic practice. The ancient phenomenon of *living* next-of-kin engaging in Torah study, charity, and prayer (i.e., *Kaddish*) on behalf of their deceased relatives to elevate their souls is, of course, well-known and continues to this day.[67] But this is far from the Hasidic practice in which the *tsaddik* actually *encounters* souls of the dead, *previously unknown to him*, who are *drawn toward him*, often in *great multitudes*. While in the Talmud we do find examples of those who were able to release a soul from Gehinnom and elevate it, their restorative efforts were on behalf of a single individual with whom there was a close relationship.[68] Moreover, in the Hasidic practice the *tsaddik* elevates the deceased soul through *conversing* with it, and upon diagnosis, *fixing its particular blemish*.

The underlying theory regarding the soul's need for rectification after death, the *tsaddik's* role in the process, and twilight of Sabbath eve as the most auspicious time for the soul's restoration, are indeed already articulated in zoharic and Lurianic texts. However, in these sources, to the best of my knowledge, we do not find evidence of the Hasidic practice in which a *living tsaddik* enters into the realm of the dead *at regular intervals* to elevate *countless* individual souls.[69] Such a new venturesome, and rather pretentious, practice gave additional cause for the Mitnaggedim's fierce opposition to the leaders of the nascent Hasidic movement.[70]

## *Tikkun ha-Neshamot* in the Teachings of Rabbi Nahman

### *The Master of the Field*

To better understand R. Nahman's work with the dead we will now examine his own words on the subject. While his early interest in this subject intensified in his late twenties through private study and secret practice, R. Nahman was reticent to speak about it until the age of thirty-four when his infant son's sudden death gave occasion for the teaching of the "Master of the Field" mentioned in a few of the previous quotations. It is of some interest to note that this was the summer of 1806, less than a year after the publication of *Sefer Katan*. The teaching is presented in *Likkutey MoHaRaN*, I:65:1–2, the only place in R. Nahman's own writings where he elaborates on the matter of *tikkun ha-neshamot*. The discourse is entitled "And Boaz said to Ruth" (Ruth 2:8) because it ultimately reaches a conclusion with an esoteric interpretation of Boaz's instruction to Ruth with regards to gleaning from the "field." R. Nahman begins by explaining just what kind of a field Boaz is speaking about.

> Know that there is a field. Extraordinarily beautiful trees and herbs grow there. The beauty of the field and what grows there is so very precious—it is beyond words. Trees and herbs—these are but representations of *(behinat)* the holy souls growing there. There are many, many naked souls wandering about outside of the field awaiting their rectification in order to be able to return and take their place.

While R. Nahman notes that many of these wandering souls are naked, this particular problem is not the focus of the teaching.[71] Here, his major concern is the exile of souls from "their place." These souls are portrayed as consciously anticipating their rectification while wandering about outside the "field." The "field" to which these souls yearn to return is R. Nahman's symbol of choice for what is most commonly referred to as *Gan 'Eden.*[72] His vision of *Gan 'Eden* takes the metaphor of the garden quite seriously; it is a place where beautiful souls are *growing.* Later in this teaching, he even portrays the Master of the Field as a gardener who is "in charge of constantly watering the trees and growing them, as well as tending to the other needs of the field."

The teaching continues. "Sometimes, even a great soul upon which other souls depend goes out of the field and finds it hard to return." R. Nahman's expression, "a great soul upon which other souls depend" is an echo of a Lurianic teaching prominent in the early Hasidic thought. The first Hasidic book, R. Jacob Joseph of Polnoye's *Toldot Ya'akov Yosef,* already speaks of the *tsaddik's* calling "to lift up the levels of the people who are his sparks and his branches, to repair them all."[73] The danger of not returning from such a mission is also addressed in this earlier work. "But when he descends to repair *(le-takken)* others, he does not wish to descend—because he fears he may not return, but come to sin, Heaven forbid—until he is promised that he will not come to sin. . . ."[74] Elsewhere, R. Jacob Joseph, warns, in the name of the BeSHT, that without the requisite spiritual purity one may not return from the descent.[75]

R. Nahman continues with his portrait of the Master of the Field, which is understood in all subsequent Bratslav literature to be nothing other than a self-portrait.[76] He depicts the necessary qualifications and the labor involved in caring for the field in anything but pastoral language.

> All of them expectantly await the Master of the Field whose efforts are capable of fulfilling the demands of their rectification. There are some souls that are rectified by the death of another person, or by someone else's

*mitsvah* and worship. Whoever desires to gird his loins to become the Master of the Field must be a powerful warrior, and wise, and a very great *tsaddik*. He must be a great man, a person of exceptional caliber.[77]

Understanding the next passage self-referentially, we hear R. Nahman's disclosure that his sufferings were essential to accomplish his work with the dead and that his own death might be necessary for him to achieve his purpose as the Master of the Field.

> And there is one who is not able to complete the task except through his own death. Even to accomplish this, one must be very great for there are many eminent people who will not realize this even through their death. Only a great person on an extraordinarily high level can accomplish all that he needs to in his lifetime, for he must suffer many troubles and difficult experiences. But because of his towering greatness he passes through all these experiences and he labors in the field as is necessary.

As we have seen, and will explain more fully in the next section, R. Nahman believed that a *tsaddik's* death can be a powerful rectification for the souls of the dead. According to R. Nathan's detailed account of his rebbe's death, he clearly viewed his own death as a necessity for accomplishing his work as Master of the Field.

> On that Monday evening, the eve of the last day of his life, his disciples R. Naftali and R. Shimon stood before him . . . and he again spoke of the souls that longed to be redeemed, and how many there were in this place. Naftali answered him, saying, "But didn't you tell us in the teaching "Boaz said to Ruth" that the truly great *tsaddik* could do it all within his lifetime?" He replied, "But then I only revealed a part of the thing to you; *really one has to die to do this.*"[78]

The teaching continues, ambiguously connecting the rectification of souls to the subject of rectified prayer. "Then, when he merits to rectify the souls and to bring them back into the field, [they] can pray, for prayer has then been rectified." A long exposition on "perfected" prayer that goes far beyond the scope of this study is the subject of the remainder of this teaching. While R. Nahman does not articulate this, a possible connection between these two motifs is the zoharic notion, which was just discussed, that for the soul's elevation—or in this metaphor, for her entrance into the field—a gleaming garment must be woven from the devotion and intentionality of one's *prayers*. As Master of the Field, R. Nahman's main task seems to be to rectify the prayer life of the dead.[79]

Other Bratslav works also shed important light upon the *tsaddik's* care for the dead. True to his emphasis on prayer, R. Nahman taught that what is learned through Torah study should also be expressed through prayer. He, therefore, instructed R. Nathan to transform every teaching in *Likkutey MoHaRaN* into liturgical form. In the compilation of R. Nathan's prayers, entitled *Likkutey Tefillot* ("A Collection of Prayers"), we find a supplication based upon this teaching that proclaims the importance of the Master of the Field for both the dead *and the living.*

> my soul wanders off. It has distanced itself and has now become driven away from the Holy Field where all the holy souls are growing. . . . And now that I am so far from my true soul, how can someone as coarse and confused as I speak the words of the living God? My only hope of coming back, of attaining grace, is through the true Master of the Field. . . . Arouse Your love and compassion for my severely blemished soul, and for all the bare souls who go about naked. . . . Have compassion on our souls and on all Your people, the House of Israel, and on all the *neshamot, ruhot* and *nefashot* of the living and the dead. Send us a true Master of the Field who can take upon himself the rectification of our *nefashot, ruhot* and *neshamot.* And may he have the strength to mend all the souls of the living and the dead, to bring in all the souls from outside into the Holy Field, and to attend to all their needs, sowing and planting, watering, tending and cultivating them. . . . Show your great compassion to all the true *tsaddikim*—the Masters of the Field—who are working to repair the Holy Field. . . . Show compassion to all the oppressed souls who have not received rectification even after so many hundreds of years. They have endured so many incarnations. They have gone through so much suffering in each one. Have pity on these tired, persecuted souls, and especially all the naked souls that cannot even be clothed in a body. You know how pitiful they are. Have pity— observe their tears, heed their cries, their sighs and groans. Take heed of their bitter anguish, their unbearably difficult wanderings.[80]

Toward the end of his life (October 1809), R. Nahman considered the work that he did with these disembodied souls far more important than his leadership of the living. In the following teachings, recorded in *Sihot ha-RaN,* he explains his rationale:

> [The rebbe] said, "What I do with you is a very small thing for me. It is what you yourselves need to do." . . . I stood there dumbfounded, for according to our understanding there is nothing greater than bringing people close to

God! [The rebbe] then said: *"There are naked souls that cannot enter a body at all; these souls are to be pitied so very much more than anyone alive,* for the living are embodied and they are able to raise children and observe God's commandments. *But these naked souls are so very, very pitiful for they cannot ascend on high, nor can they clothe themselves in a body.*⁸¹

R. Nahman returned to the theme of the naked souls time and time again. In the following teaching he conveys how his own spiritual vision compels him to respond to naked souls with the same pity one would show to the unclothed in this world:

[The rebbe] responded: Everyone perceives worldly pity, and therefore pursues worldly things. For they see those who are hungry or thirsty and feel great compassion for them. And great is the pity on those who go about without clothing or shoes. *But who has eyes that can perceive the great compassion we must have on the souls in the next world?! For in the next world there are souls that go about literally naked, but it is impossible to show them any pity.* In this world, if a person lacks clothing, others can take up a collection and buy him something to wear. But in the next world, if one walks about naked it is impossible to show him any pity . . . for what kind of garments does one need there? Only those woven from Torah and good deeds! And for these, pity has no recourse. *But he who had the merit of drawing close to a true tsaddik* [in this world] *will be able to make a run for the tsaddik and get from him whatever garment he might need.*⁸²

*The Power of the* Tsaddik—*After Death*

According to R. Nahman, one who was close to the *tsaddik* in *this* world can "run to the *tsaddik* and garb himself" in the *next* world. In other words, an individual's close relationship with a true *tsaddik* while living, assures that his soul will receive a complete rectification after death. As Master of the Field, R. Nahman came to believe that he could have a greater effect upon his disciples after their death, when they would be divested of their free will, than he could by means of his spiritual guidance during their lifetime. Toward the end of his life, R. Nahman was not only busy fixing the souls of the dead, but he was preparing his disciples for the rectification he would do for their souls—after his own death—when they too would eventually cross over into the realm of the dead. Comforting them about his impending death, he said, "Why should you worry yourselves? I am going before you. Those of our people that have already died, they had cause for concern, but you? Since I am going before you, you don't have to worry at all. And if [these] souls that never knew me at all are anticipating my *tikkunim,* then, of course, so will you!"[83]

Even R. Nahman's involvement with the *maskilim* of Uman may be better understood in terms of his preparation to influence them *after his own death.*[84] His warm relations, and apparently idle encounters with the *maskilim* confounded both enemies and disciples. Why would the true *tsaddik* waste precious time in his final days engaged in frivolous conversation, and even playing chess with these heretics? It is likely that one of his reasons for "descending" to their level was to make it easier for them to draw close to him. For R. Nahman believed that their souls could only be rectified in the *next* world if they had some connection with him in *this* world.

Amongst the many teachings in *Sefer ha-Middot* concerning the importance of being close to a *tsaddik,* some emphasize the residual benefits that will be reaped particularly after death. While R. Nahman writes, in general terms, that "closeness to the *tsaddikim* is good in this world and the next,"[85] he also states, more specifically, that "those who are close to the *tsaddik* while he is alive, will be close when they are dead."[86] More to our point, he warns, "In this world, all who want to draw close [to the *tsaddik*] may do so, but only those who already drew close [before death] can do so in the next world."[87]

Besides R. Nahman's deep involvement with the dead martyrs of Uman, he was engaged in drawing close to himself the living heretics of that city. Even while contrasting the holiness of the martyrs to the baseness of the *maskilim,* he would explain that "they too possess precious sparks that need to be purified."[88] Although he sometimes referred to the *maskilim* as "wicked" or "heretics," he avoided any confrontation or debate, but befriended them—believing that this would enable him to eventually purify and uplift the sparks of their souls. In one teaching he clearly states that even one "on the absolute lowest level . . . at the bottom of Hell *(Sh'eol)*" can return to God through the "vitality" *(hiyut)* of the Torah he will receive through his connection with a true *tsaddik.*[89]

Alongside R. Nahman's assurances to his adherents, he also explained that, just as in life, there are many powerful obstacles preventing a person from coming to the true *tsaddik* for *tikkun* even after death. He stressed the need to strengthen one's resolve to draw close to the *tsaddik,* not only in this world, but also in the next. By way of example he related a story concerning a devoted follower of the *tsaddik,* R. Menahem Mendel of Vitebsk (d. 1788), who died while on a journey back to Europe to raise funds for his Rebbe's community in the Holy Land. R. Nahman describes in great detail how the follower was deceived into believing that he was still alive and on his way to Leipzig. But, being that he was so attached to the *tsaddik,* he told his servant and wagon-driver he wanted to return. They dissuaded him, but he persisted. They dissuaded him again, but he was unyielding. This went on for some time until finally,

They told him the truth: that he was already dead, and that they were Angels of Destruction *(malakhey habalah)* who were leading him about and fooling him. He said, "Now I really beg of you—take me to my master, the *tsaddik*, at once!" They said, "Now we really refuse! and they argued the matter vigorously. Finally, the case came before the heavenly court. The court ruled that he was in the right—they must take him to his master immediately. And so it happened. They brought him to R. Menahem Mendel of Vitebsk, who was still alive and in the land of Israel. When this man entered the house of the *tsaddik*, one of the Angels of Destruction entered with him, and the *tsaddik* was so frightened that he fainted. After they revived him, he spent about eight days working on this man until he rectified him. Then the *tsaddik* told the community that the messenger had died, for they still had not learned of it. And he told them the entire story.[90]

### The Obstinate Living versus the Impressionable Dead

With his proficiency in *tikkun ha-neshamot*, R. Nahman seemed to lose patience with the drudgery of being a rebbe for the living—even the great *tsaddikim* among them. While R. Nahman was motivated primarily by the dire need of the dead, he also came to realize how much more worthwhile it would be to devote his numbered days to them.

> [The rebbe] said, "Have we not already spoken about this? It requires spending so much time and energy to help even a righteous person serve God—to raise him up to his highest potential—while he is still embodied in this world. *It is so much harder than helping and raising up thousands of sinners in the spiritual realm—that is, to rectify their souls.* For it is very difficult to work with someone who has free will, to detach him from his own chosen path and lead him to the true one. *For, even the greatest of sinners, once he has passed on, we can do whatever we want with him: whatever he is ordered to do he will do, even if he is a very great sinner.* On the other hand, *even the greatest tsaddik, so long as he is still in his body and possesses free will, it would be very hard to work with him, should the need arise, to turn him away from some* [false] *matter and lead him to the truth.*"[91]

In an obvious attempt to counterbalance the this-worldly pessimism of this passage, R. Nahman of Cheryn added these encouraging parenthetical remarks:

> By his own account [the rebbe] was occupied with rectifying thousands upon thousands of souls that had fallen long ago. This was his main task, and for this reason he wondered if he should not completely relinquish his

leadership of the earthbound. If he hesitated it was because there was no doubt that, if he could help someone with free will to come back to God— it was a great matter, of incalculable value.[92]

While R. Nahman made it clear that, as Master of the Field, he preferred to spend his numbered days tending to the souls of the dead, his chief disciple found that hard to accept and argued in vain for the value of the living.

> Then I said to [the rebbe]: "Surely if you help a living person who *does* have free will it is a very worthwhile accomplishment." The Rebbe replied: "Certainly! It goes without saying. What you forget is how time-consuming it is!" And by his holy gestures he expressed that it was an achievement of inestimable worth . . . His holy intent was that, although it was certainly precious, even invaluable, to work with a person possessing free will, it took so much time. And even then it was still doubtful whether one would succeed, because it is so difficult to help someone with free will. *All of this time could be used to elevate the souls of the dead by the thousands, and even by the tens of thousands.* This was why the Rebbe had such doubts. . . ."[93]

The unequivocal move to Uman for what he knew would be the last months of his life made R. Nahman's choice apparent to all.

### *The Death and Burial of Rabbi Nahman*

As we mentioned at the beginning of this inquiry, R. Nahman's telling of the story about the BeSHT was meant to hint that his very death was necessary to effect the *tikkunim* for the tens of thousands buried in Uman. In fact this was considered his ultimate task. "Everything [the rebbe] had spoken of was fulfilled: In Uman he departed this world. . . . Then everyone saw and was amazed! (Ps. 48:6) They understood that the whole purpose of his coming to Uman was to depart the world from there, just as we had heard him say explicitly so many times."[94] We have also seen how R. Nahman taught that in certain circumstances a Master of the Field cannot accomplish the necessary rectifications except by means of his own death. In other teachings, R. Nahman spoke about the great benefit resulting from the death of a *tsaddik,* in the realms of both the dead and the living.[95] He reassuringly taught that a *tsaddik's* death was a spiritual boon for his disciples[96] and particularly for those present at the moment of his death.[97]

    In dying for such a holy purpose, R. Nahman was able to fulfill his most cherished childhood dream.

> [The rebbe] once told us that in his youth he was very much afraid of death, and whenever this fear became very intense, *he would then beg of God that he*

*be privileged to die a martyr's death, in sanctification of His Name.* He followed this practice for a long time. He did not remember how long, but it was for at least a year. *All during this time, in spite of his great terror of death, he would not say a prayer without also asking that he depart this world in sanctification of God's Name.*[98]

R. Nahman had longed to die in sanctification of God's name. In casting his lot with the martyrs of Uman, he had finally found his place.

> After this, the Rebbe spoke with me about his present home, saying how Uman was so very good for him. If he wanted to be anywhere, it was best for him to be here. *And he said that it would also be good for him to depart the world from here—when his time had come and his days were complete— because in Uman there had been a martyrdom which brought about a tremendous sanctification of God's Name.* Tens of thousands of Jews were killed here, as is known. Many died quite literally in sanctification of God's Name because the gentiles tried to make them convert and they died as martyrs rather than doing so. But even Jews who were killed without being asked to convert, their deaths were also a sanctification of the Name, as is known.[99] They suffered all kinds of tortuous deaths. Little children and suckling babies were killed in the thousands—all this is a sanctification of the Name.[100]

Finally, R. Nahman desired not only to die in Uman, but also to be *buried* amongst the martyrs laid to rest there. According to R. Nathan, his rebbe already remarked that Uman would be a good place to be buried while passing through the city eight years previous to making it his home. And while living in Uman, he spoke often about how he would like to be buried there.

> When [the rebbe] first arrived, a local man came to see him . . . [The rebbe] pointed outside with his finger and said, "Have you seen how good and beautiful this garden is!?! How do you like the garden?" The visitor assumed [the rebbe] was referring to the garden in front of the windows. But [the rebbe] pointed to the cemetery, which was visible in the distance through the windows, directly facing him. "This is the garden I'm talking about," the Rebbe said. "You have no idea how precious this holy cemetery is—it is so precious and holy!"

Time and time again [the rebbe] used to tell people about the cemetery of Uman, praising it in the most glowing terms, for it was the resting place of the tens of thousands of martyrs who had fallen there in the great slaughter [of 1768]. On many different occasions the Rebbe had told both me and many others . . . how pleased he would be to be buried there because of the great sanctification of God's Name which came about at that very place.[101]

But it is naive to think that his yearning to be buried in Uman was due merely to some sort of romantic identification with those who died as he wished he could have. Consistent with his general purpose, R. Nahman very likely had in mind the further good he could do for the martyrs by also being buried amongst them. As R. Nathan wrote,

His whole purpose in . . . choosing [Uman] as the place from which to depart this world *and in which to be buried,* was to accomplish the rectification of souls from the past several hundred years that needed mending. . . . [The rebbe's] intentions were evident from the words he spoke in Uman, some of which have been recorded elsewhere. . . .[102]

The burial site of the true *tsaddik* is a holy center to which the living Hasidim, especially Bratslaver Hasidim, make regular pilgrimages. But in the end of history, when the resurrected dead make their pilgrimage to the Holy Land, they too will derive benefit from the *tsaddik's* presence among them. R. Nahman taught that "Because of *tsaddikim* who are buried outside of the land of Israel, all the other dead will merit *gilgul mehilot.*[103] Perhaps this was one of R. Nahman's considerations. Presumably, there were others.

## Conclusion

Through the impassioned pen of the devoted disciple, eager to relate the greatness of his master, we have learned how R. Nahman's care for the souls of the dead was considered to be the climax of his life as a true *tsaddik.* In probing the master's own terse and allusive teachings, as well as some of the ideas that nourished them, we have attained a better grasp of both the meaning and the method of his work with the dead. But, in the final analysis, we are still severely limited by R. Nahman's reticence to explain more fully, and perhaps even more so, by our empiricist culture's distance from dealings with the realm of the dead. Well aware of his readers' limitations, R. Nathan, nevertheless, told his rebbe's story because he believed that the telling itself had the power to uplift the soul.

We heard no more than a drop in the ocean about this, and even the little [the rebbe] did kindly share with us—it is impossible to explain except in the most allusive manner. Nevertheless, I did not hold back from recording what I could, for the sake of those who sincerely yearn and wait at [the rebbe's] doors. It will benefit them greatly to know what befell him and what came forth from his holy mouth concerning these matters. The enlightened who look into what I say with eyes of truth will understand a little of the greatness of the Creator and of the *tsaddikim,* and the pain and suffering the *tsaddikim* endure for the sake of mending our souls. Perhaps we will be inspired by this to follow [the rebbe's] holy ways that he taught us in his holy books, and truly return to God.[104]

In spite of the self-professed limitations of R. Nathan's writings, his presentation of R. Nahman's work with the souls of the dead is still a greater witness to the phenomenon than any other body of Hasidic literature, providing us with a greater understanding of the *tsaddik*'s vocation in early Hasidism.

## Notes

*This chapter is dedicated in memory of my father, Raphael ben 'Aharon ha-Kohen, whose passing inspired my research on this subject. I wish to express my gratitude to several mentors, colleagues, and friends for the many insights received from critical readings of earlier drafts of this essay or from discussions with them on its subject matter. These include Alan Brill, Shai Cherry, Gedaliah Fleer, Yehuda Gellman, Daniel Gil, Pinchas Giller, Marc Gopin, Arthur Green, Avraham Greenbaum, Nachum Gruenwald, Samuel Heilman, Naftali Lowenthal, Shaul Magid, Nehemia Polen, Simcha Raphael, Meir Sendor, and my wife Elisa Travis. A synopsis of this chapter was presented at the Twelfth World Congress of Jewish Studies in Jerusalem, July 1997. Participation in the conference was made possible by grants from the Graduate School of Brandeis University and from the Faculty Research Council of the University of Massachusetts, Amherst.

1. For a broad survey of related phenomena, see the collection of articles from *The Encyclopedia of Religion,* in *Death, Afterlife and the Soul,* ed. Lawrence E. Sullivan (New York and London, 1989). For cross-cultural studies on the phenomena that is the focus of this chapter, namely, the salvific work of the living in the realm of the dead, see Anna-Leena Siikala, "Descent into the Underworld" in ibid., pp. 117–123; and John G. Bishop, "The Hero's Descent into the Underworld," in *Journey to the Other World,* ed. Hilda R. Ellis Davidson (Totowa, N.J., 1975), pp. 109–129, esp. pp. 116, 120–121. The kabbalistic practice of *tikkun ha-neshamot* may be instructively compared to similar practices in shamanistic cultures. The shaman's journey to the underworld in order to escort the soul of the dead is a well-attested phenomenon in cross-cultural accounts of shamanism. Although such journeys may be seen as serving a similar purpose, there are,

however, many important differences in their respective objectives and methods. On this aspect of shamanism, see Mircea Eliade's "Shamanism: An Overview," in *The Encyclopedia of Religion,* ed. Eliade (New York, 1987), vol. 13, pp. 202–208, esp. pp. 205–206.

2. To the best of my knowledge, there are presently no studies that focus on this phenomenon in Judaism. At present there is also no historical-critical survey of afterlife teachings in classical works of Jewish literature. Isaiah Tishby's intention to treat the subject in his projected third volume of *Mishnat ha-Zohar* ("Wisdom of the Zohar") was, unfortunately, never fulfilled. However, for a wide-ranging annotated anthology of afterlife teachings from the perspective of a transpersonal psychologist, see Simcha Paull Raphael, *Jewish Views of the Afterlife* (Northvale, N.J., 1994). Also of interest is the unedited manuscript of Raoul Nass, published as *The Road to Eternal Life and to Resurrection from Death, After Death* (Montpellier, Vt., 1976), pp. 241–150.

3. *Tsaddik* (lit.: righteous one; plural: *tsaddikim*) is the honorific title given to a spiritual leader, also called "Rebbe," of a Hasidic community. The highly developed doctrines and practices revolving around the *tsaddik* are pivotal in Hasidic thought and ethos. On the *tsaddik* in Hasidism, see Arthur Green, "The Zaddiq as Axis Mundi in Later Judaism," reprinted in *Essential Papers on Kabbalah,* ed. Lawrence Fine (New York and London, 1995), pp. 291–314; idem, "Typologies of Leadership and the Hasidic Zaddiq," in *Jewish Spirituality,* ed. Green (New York, 1987) vol. 2, 127–156; and Ada Rapoport-Albert, "God and the Zaddik as the Two Focal Points of Hasidic Worship," in *Essential Papers on Hasidism,* ed. Gershon Hundert (New York and London, 1991), pp. 299–329. On the *tsaddik* in Bratslav Hasidism, see Green, *Tormented Master: The Life and Spiritual Quest of Rabbi Nahman of Bratslav* (1979; Woodstock, Vt., 1992), pp. 14 ff., 116–122, 135–175; Yehuda Leibes, *"Ha-Tikkun ha-Kelali* of R. Nahman of Bratslav and Its Sabbatean Links," in idem, *Studies in Jewish Myth and Jewish Messianism* (Albany, 1993), pp. 115–150. For a traditional hagiographic treatment of the subject by a Bratslaver Hasid, see Shmuel Chechik, *Meshekh Ha-Nahal* (Jerusalem, 1964).

4. *Tikkun ha-neshamot* (lit.: rectification of the souls) is the *tsaddik's* proxy fulfillment of the Hasidic ideal of *tikkun.* In the normative application of this Hasidic ideal, the purpose of life is to reinstate one's own soul within the original cosmic soul of Adam by self-rectification, not only through practicing the mitsvot, but also by constantly cleaving to God in the particular circumstances of one's unique life situations. On the Lurianic roots and Hasidic manifestations of *tikkun,* see Gershom Scholem, *Major Trends in Jewish Mysticism* (1946; New York, 1974), pp. 278–286, 327–330; idem, *The Mystical Shape of the Godhead,* trans. Jonathan Chipman (1976; New York, 1991), pp. 241–250; Lawrence Fine, "The Contemplative Practice of Yihudim in Lurianic Kabbalah," in *Jewish Spirituality,* ed.

Green, vol. 2, pp. 65–70; Louis Jacobs, "The Uplifting of Sparks in Later Jewish Mysticism," in ibid., pp. 106–108. On R. Nahman's particular approach to *tikkun*, see Leibes, "*Ha-Tikkun ha-Kelali* of R. Nahman of Bratslav and Its Sabbatean Links," pp. 115–128.

5. Moshe Idel, *Hasidism: Between Ecstasy and Magic* (New York, 1995), esp. pp. 103–227. Idel focuses on what he calls the "anabatic mystico-magical" model of Hasidic mysticism as opposed to the "katabatic-redemptive" model that would include the practice of *tikkun ha-neshamot*. On Idel's definition of these two models, see ibid., pp. 103–104.

6. On the general reliability of R. Nathan's biographical writings, see Green, *Tormented Master,* pp. 4–16. For more details on the Bratslav works cited in this chapter see the bibliography. On the full range of literary sources for R. Nahman's life and teachings, see ibid., pp. 4–9, 20–21. Most of the primary source materials are available in the easily readable and fairly reliable English translations of the Breslov Research Institute. Nevertheless, I found it necessary to significantly revise, or translate anew, most of the passages in this chapter for greater accuracy and consistency. I have also italicized specific phrases or sentences in order to focus the reader's attention on aspects of a passage that are most critical for our purposes. The chapter numbers follow the designation currently used in the Hebrew and English editions of the Breslov Research Institute. The numbers in parentheses follow the designations of Green, *Tormented Master,* pp. 75–76.

7. The Gonta Massacre of 1768, named after the Cossack commander Ivan Gonta, resulted in the death of approximately 20,000 Jews. For sources concerning the Gonta pogrom, see Jonas Gurland, *Le-Korot ha-Gezerot 'al Yisra'el* (1887; Jerusalem, 1972); Green, *Tormented Master,* p. 272 n. 57; and Aryeh Kaplan, *Until the Mashiach: The Life of Rabbi Nachman* (Jerusalem, 1985), pp. 188, 277–284.

8. The *tsaddik's* peculiar relationship with the *maskilim* has already received the serious attention it warrants from the major historians of Bratslav Hasidism. The first study of this relationship was Hayyim Lieberman's "Reb Nahman Bratslaver un di Umaner Maskilim," *Yivo Bleter* 29 (1947). A translation of that article appeared in *Yivo Annual of Jewish Social Science* 6 (1951): 287 ff. The most extensive discussion is found Mendel Piekarz, *Hasidut Bratslav,* 2nd ed. (1972; Jerusalem, 1995), pp. 21–55. In an entire chapter devoted to R. Nahman's life in Uman, Piekarz completely ignores the *tsaddik's* involvement with the dead! See nn. 84, 91. See also Joseph G. Weiss, *Mehkarim be-Hasidut Bratslav,* ed. Mendel Piekarz (Jerusalem, 1974), pp. 61–65, 172–180; and Green, *Tormented Master,* pp. 180 n. 66; 251–265.

9. Throughout this chapter the Hebrew verb *lehistalek,* and the corresponding noun *histalkut,* are translated in the sense of "departure from this world" instead of the more simple "death." While the texts translated here do utilize the

conventional Hebrew words conveying "death" or "dying," from the verb *lamut,* they are never used in reference to R. Nahman or to any other *tsaddik.* When speaking of *tsaddikim* in Hasidic literature, including the Bratslav corpus, the terminology of *histalkut* is used quite consistently. Whereas "death" and "dying" imply the end of life, this term implies a progression, an ascent that necessitates taking leave of the earthly realm.

10. *Hayyey MoHaRaN,* 217 (8:33). A detailed account of his rebbe's death is found in R. Nathan of Nemirov, *Yemey MaHaRaNaT* (Beney Berak, 1956), pp. 71 ff., esp. pp. 79–89. For an English translation, see Green, *Tormented Master,* pp. 275–282 (for the reference to the BeSHT, see pp. 278–279).

11. *Hayyey MoHaRaN,* 190 (8:6). The *tsaddik's* death as a requirement for *tikkun* is discussed in more detail toward the end of the chapter. For parallel teachings in R. Nahman and earlier sources, see nn. 95–99.

12. *Hayyey MoHaRaN,* 191 (8:7).

13. *Hayyey MoHaRaN* 151 (6:1). See ibid., p. 197 (8:13). Cf. *Yemey Ma-HaRaNaT,* pp. 48–49. There is a problem here in identifying these "innumerable" souls from "the past several hundred years" only with those killed in the Gonta massacre because the massacre occurred only forty-two years previous to this remark. There are two approaches one can take to this problem besides attributing the expression "several hundreds of years" to gross exaggeration. It is possible that the souls that were seeking redemption in Uman included those that were mar-tyred in the many pogroms or "judgments" of previous generations. See *Hayyey MoHaRaN,* 191 (8:7 end) where R. Nahman is quoted as speaking of "many judgments *(mishpatim)* and many martyrs." R. Nahman may be recalling, for example, the martyrs from the Chielmenicki pogroms of 1648. Alternatively, the souls that died in Uman were, perhaps, hundreds of years old and their lifetime in the late eighteenth century was only a recent incarnation. With an awareness of the prominence given to reincarnation in Hasidic thought, and from the other Bratslav writings, one can easily understand the comment in this latter sense. See, for example, the prayer of R. Nathan quoted, n. 80.

14. Green, *Tormented Master,* p. 252. On R. Nahman's interpretation of the spiritual reasons for the BeSHT's own death, see *Likkutey MoHaRaN* I: 207. See Leibes's analysis of this teaching in his "*Ha-Tikkun ha-Kelali* of R. Nahman of Bratslav and Its Sabbatean Links," pp. 129–134, 140.

15. The teaching of "The Master of the Field" in *Likkutey MoHaRaN* I: 65: 1–2 is quoted and discussed in the next section.

16. *Hayyey MoHaRaN* 151(6:1). Shlomo Ephraim was R. Nahman's first son. Cf. *Yemey MaHaRaNaT,* p. 21. See Green, *Tormented Master,* pp. 211–213 for a discussion of Ephraim's death as a turning point in R. Nahman's messianic strivings.

17. *Hayyey MoHaRaN* 151 (6:2).

18. R. Nathan became a disciple of R. Nahman in the fall of 1802 (*'Elul,* 5562), only after the rebbe had left Zlotopolye, and thus after he was already deeply involved in *tikkun ha-neshamot.* See *Yemey MaHaRaNaT,* p. 12.

19. *Hayyey MoHaRaN* 192 (8:8).

20. *Hayyey MoHaRaN* 151 (6:1). See, ibid., p. 228.

21. *Zohar* I, 224b; *Zohar* II, 141b–142a. See also *Zohar* II, 150a that explains that these garments are those with which the soul was clad before its descent to earth. As the soul ascends, it largely retraces the stages that it went through in its descent from the "upper" *Gan 'Eden* to the corporeal world. On the soul's journey of descent, see Tishby, *Wisdom of the Zohar,* vol. 2, pp. 749–754. Cf. *Zohar* III, 13a end. Besides these spiritual "garments," or, perhaps synonymous with them, is the zoharic notion of an ethereal "body." *Zohar* III, 88b, for example, teaches that the *neshamah* cannot ascend until it receives a "body" of light. Similarly, *Zohar* II, 150a describes the *ruah* as "garbed" in a "body" appropriate for *Gan 'Eden.* See also *Zohar* I:20b, where the physical body of a holy person is considered a garment of sorts. Cf. *Zohar Hadash* 78c. In some passages, the *Zohar* describes the souls of the righteous as garbed in the ethereal "atmosphere" (*'avirin*) of *Gan 'Eden.* See, for example, *Zohar* III, 169b. See also *Zohar Hadash* 90b that speaks of the *'avirin* of the "inner" Garden. Related to this motif is a passage in *Zohar* I, 66a that interprets Moses' entrance into the "cloud" at Sinai as a garbing in order to experience the Divine. On the history of the soul's garments in Jewish literature, see Gershom Scholem, "Levush ha-Neshamot ve-Haluka de-Rabbanan" *Tarbiz* 24 (1955): 290–306. Of related interest is Scholem's "Tselem: The Concept of the Astral Body," in *The Mystical Shape of the Godhead,* pp. 251–273, esp. p. 316 n. 32. See also, Dorit Cohen-Alloro, "The Secret of the Garment in the Zohar" (Hebrew) (Jerusalem, 1987), esp. pp. 50–67. In English, see Raphael, *Jewish Views of the Afterlife,* pp. 278–313. On the tripartite division of the soul in zoharic Kabbalah, see Tishby, *The Wisdom of the Zohar,* vol. 2, pp. 677–722, 749–776. esp. 2:684–698; Scholem, *Kabbalah* (Jerusalem, 1974), pp. 152–164.

22. *Zohar* I, 226b; *Zohar* II, 142a–b.

23. *Zohar* I, 225a–b; *Zohar* II, 141b. In rabbinic literature there are seven names given to the purgatory of the nether world (T.B. *'Erubin,* 19b; *Midrash Shohar Tov,* 11:16). Whereas in biblical literature the locale of postmortem tribulations was predominately called 'Sheol,' by rabbinic times the term *Gehinnom* prevailed. Kabbalistic writing, drawing from both bodies of literature, frequently interchanges these names.

24. *Zohar* II, 210a–b. It appears that the minimum period of transition is seven days. See *Zohar* III, 205a (end)–206a (beg.) for the case of R. Yossi of Pikin who reports on his exceptional near-death experience. In this passage R. 'Eleazar states that "for seven days after the *neshamah* leaves the body, it goes about naked."

25. *Zohar* I, 226a–b. On the association of *ruah* and "lower" *Gan 'Eden,* see *Zohar* I, 81a *(Sitrey Torah)*; II, 97b; III, 159b; *Pardes Rimonim, Sha'ar ha-Neshamah,* 31:5.

26. *Zohar* II, 229b: "the *good deeds ('uvdin tavin)* which a person does in this world weave a garment drawn from the light of the supernal resplendence *(mashkhey me-nehor'a de-zivv'a 'il'ah levush'a)* with which he will be prepared *(le-'itetakn'a)* for that realm to appear before the Holy One, blessed is He. Appareled in that raiment, he is in a state of bliss and feasts his eyes [on the Divine] through the "illuminated mirror" *('aspaklaria'a de-nehor'a)*. . . ." Cf. *Zohar* I, 65b–66a; II, 210a–b. Note the usage of the Aramaic equivalent for *tikkun,* suggesting both "fixing" and "dressing." On the relationship between good deeds and the soul's garments, see also *Zohar* I, 130b, 224a; II, 210a, 229b, 247a; III, 101a. See also R. Moses Cordovero's *Pardes Rimonim, Sha'ar ha-Neshamah,* 31:5–6 and his commentary on *Zohar* II, 99b in *'Or Yakar* (Jerusalem, 1991), vol. 21, p. 26. The latter explains how each of the 248 positive mitsvot clothes one of the 248 "limbs of the soul." One of the primary reasons for which a soul is reincarnated is to complete whichever of the 248 positive mitsvot the soul had yet to fulfill.

27. *Zohar* II, 141b.

28. *Zohar* III, 159b.

29. *Zohar* I, 7a. See *Zohar* II, 11a; *Zohar Hadash* 82d, where *ruah*'s garment is similar in form to its earthly body.

30. *Zohar* I, 226a–b. See *Zohar* II, 97b that intimates that the *neshamah* of the righteous, purified in its lifetime, ascends to paradise right away. See also *Zohar* II, 97b where the garment of *neshamah* shields it from malevolent forces seeking to hinder the its ascent. On the association of *neshamah* and "upper" *Gan 'Eden,* see *Zohar* II, 97b; and *Pardes Rimonim, Sha'ar ha-Neshamah,* 31:5.

31. *Zohar* II, 99b.

32. *Zohar* I: 38b; II, 210b; *Zohar Hadash* 18b. But see also *Zohar* II, 141b–142b, which states that the *neshamah* ascends immediately, and that the other aspects of soul depend on this to find their rightful places. The Zohar itself notes that this schema "appears" contrary to the main doctrine. Note that this "alternative" schematization is presented as an allegory to the inner dynamics of the Divine realm. According to R. Moses Cordovero *('Or Yakar* on *Zohar* II, 229b), the *neshamah* is adorned with this garment only until it acquires one fitting for the "upper" *Gan 'Eden* that is the "world of *neshamot.*" The *ruah,* however, remains with this garment in the lower paradise until the final resurrection.

33. *Zohar* II, 156b end, 210a end; *Zohar* II, 97b, 141b–142a; *Zohar Hadash* 82d–83a.

34. *Zohar* II, 210a–b. Cf. *Zohar* II, 229b. See Zohar I, 7a where the ascents of the righteous to the upper *Gan 'Eden* are described as occasional journeys, which include entering into the "Heavenly Academy" *(Metivta de-Rakiya')*. See

*Pardes Rimonim, Sha'ar ha-Neshamah,* 31:5–6. See also Scholem, "Levush ha-Neshamot," p. 289.

35. *Zohar* I: 38b; III, 214a.

36. *Zohar* I, 130b. It should be noted that Abraham is frequently presented as the exemplar of such righteousness. Associated with this level is emphasis on the perfection of each and every day, where the focus seems to be not so much the wholeness of the individual, but on the wholeness of his days. See the interpretation of Jacob's ascension in *Zohar* I, 224a–b.

37. *Zohar* II, 150a–b. On "naked" souls, see also *Zohar* I, 14b, 224a–b; II, 99b–100b, 275a–b (Raz'a de-Razin); III, 206a, 278a; *Zohar Hadash* 36d–37b; and *Tikkuney ha-Zohar* 6 (23b beg.), 26 (72a end). On the distinction between the naked souls of the dead and those naked souls that were never embodied at all, see n. 42. Note that, in the *Zohar,* the term *'artylayin* (naked) in reference to spiritual bareness has a range of meanings. For example, while *Zohar* I, 14b speaks of the destructiveness of the "naked" *ruhot* of the wicked, in *Zohar* II, 205b "nakedness" refers only to ignorance of the meaning of a specific verse in the Torah. Another usage is found in *Zohar* I, 208b where the term refers to the weekly disrobing of the *nefesh* when the *ruah* leaves it at the close of the Sabbath.

38. *Hayyey MoHaRaN,* 110 (4:7).

39. Although they did fulfill the supreme *mitsvah* of *Kiddush ha-Shem* (Sanctification of the Divine Name) through their martyrdom, this would not mediate their plight. On *Kiddush ha-Shem* through martyrdom in Bratslav thought, see n. 99.

40. See Green, *Tormented Master,* p. 36.

41. The supersensory ability to "see" the souls of the dead was apparently one of the psychic powers sought after by potential Hasidic leaders, even in their youth. See, for example, the autobiographical account of R. Yitshak Isaac of Komarno in his *Megillat Setarim,* reprinted in *Sefer Imrei Kodesh* (Jerusalem, 1996), pp. 6a ff.

42. *Hayyey MoHaRaN,* 110 (4:7). See also, *Sihot ha-RaN,* 195, quoted in the next section. There is an important distinction between the naked souls of the dead and those naked souls "which had never entered a body at all." While the two were very interrelated in the mind of R. Nahman, as this and other sources indicate, the latter appears to be secondary in importance, and thus not the focus of this chapter. However, a few words of explanation are in order.

The notion of naked souls that have never been embodied is based on aggadic legend that during the 130 years in which Adam was separated from Eve, he begat spirits *(ruhin, shadin,* and *lilin)* through wasteful seminal emissions. See *Bereishit Rabbah* 20:11, 24:6; T.B. *'Erubin* 18b; *Zohar* I, 19b. But, see also *Tikkunei ha-Zohar* 6 (23b beg.) which speaks of souls without bodies since the "six days of creation." According to the *Zohar,* when sin strengthens the forces of evil in the supernal realm, souls continue to be created without bodies, or are entrapped by that which is under the domain of these forces. Such souls are among those described as oppressed *('ashuk)*. See *Zohar* II, 95b, 113a–b. According to Lurianic doctrine, wasteful seminal emissions, in particular, continue to create these unembodied spirits. See *Pri 'Ets Hayyim*, "Kriat Shm'a 'al ha-Mitah," chap. 5 and the interpretation of R. Tsaddok Ha-Cohen, *Tsidkat ha-Tsaddik*, #245 (Beit El, 1988), pp. 160b–163a. For the *tsaddikim* of early Hasidism, extricating the oppressed souls from their entrapment in the realm of evil, and elevating them, is an ongoing task of major importance. See, for example, the BeSHT's *Commentary to Psalm 107*, discussed in the next section, which focuses on this matter. See also R. Moshe Ephraim's *Degel Mahane Ephraim*, "Mikets," p. 61a, where, in the name of his grandfather, the BeSHT, he explains that a *tsaddik's* own ascent is secondary in relation to his raising up of many "oppressed" souls. See also, ibid., p. 164a. On R. Nahman's use of this terminology, see *Likkutey MoHaRaN* I:39, 82. See also R. Nathan's *Likkutey Tefillot* I: 65, II: 8. Note that the importance of this practice to two of the BeSHT's progeny may attest to an established family tradition.

43. *Shivhey Ha-RaN*, 19. The continuation of the passage speaks of R. Nahman's visits to the grave even from the age of six.

44. On the identity of R. Isaiah, see Green, *Tormented Master*, p. 56 n. 44.

45. *Shivhey Ha-RaN*, 20. In his later years as well, R. Nahman would pray at the BeSHT's grave in times of great need.

46. Originally compiled by Dov Ber ben Samuel of Linitz and printed in 1814. For a critical edition, see *Shivhey Ha-BeSHT*, ed. Avraham Rubinstein (Jerusalem, 1991). On the creditability of this work, compiled some fifty years after the BeSHT's death, as a source for reconstructing a portrait of the BeSHT, see now Moshe Rosman, *Founder of Hasidism: The Quest for the Historical Ba'al Sham Tov* (Berkeley and Los Angeles, 1996), pp. 143–155, 279–280. The earliest manuscript is dated ca. 1810, the year of R. Nahman's death. Although it is unlikely that he actually read the work, we may assume that he was familiar with such stories about his illustrious great-grandfather.

47. On *yihudim*, see Fine, "The Contemplative Practice of Yihudim in Lurianic Kabbalah," pp. 64–98.

48. *Shivhey Ha-BeSHT*, pp. 96–98. On the BeSHT's attempt to rectify the soul of the infamous false messiah, Shabbetai Tsvi, see *Shivhey Ha-BeSHT*, pp. 133–134. On the similarities of these stories to the hagiographic accounts of the 'ARI, R. Isaac Luria, see Joseph Dan, *Ha-Sippur Ha-Hasidi* (Jerusalem, 1975), pp. 68–74. On the 'ARI's dialogue with the souls of the dead, see Meir Benyahu, *Sefer Toldot ha-'ARI* (Jerusalem, 1967), pp. 236–237; and R. Ya'akov Hillel, *Shivhei ha-'ARI: Ha-Shalem u-Mevu'ar* (Jerusalem, 1990), p. 89.

49. *Shivhey Ha-BeSHT*, p. 98.

50. See Rivkah Schatz-Uffenheimer, "The Ba'al Shem Tov's Commentary

to Psalm 107: Myth and Ritual of the Descent to She'ol," in *Hasidism as Mysticism: Quietistic Elements in Eighteenth Century Hasidic Thought,* trans. Jonathan Chipman (Princeton, 1993), pp. 342–381. The original Hebrew article, including a critical edition of the commentary, was published in *Tarbiz* 42 (1973): 154–184. The attribution is widely accepted as authentic among the Hasidim and Schatz-Uffenheimer concurs with this view. Scholem doubted the attribution based on, among other evidence, a manuscript copy of the commentary that attributes it to Menahem Mendel of Bar, around 1760, the year of the BeSHT's death. See Gershom Scholem, *The Messianic Idea in Judaism* (1971; New York, 1995), p. 189. See now Rosman, *Founder of Hasidism,* pp. 122–123. While Rosman concurs with Scholem, he is careful to point out that the manuscript does demonstrate that the commentary's ideas were in circulation within the circles of the Hasidim as early as the 1760s.

51. The Sabbath eve setting of the folktale about the BeSHT is no coincidence. There is a rich rabbinic and pre-Hasidic kabbalistic literature describing the Sabbath eve release of the souls from Gehinnom. See *'Otsar ha-Midrashim,* "'Aseret ha-Diberot" 10; *Midrash Tanhuma* (Warsaw) "Ha'azinu" 1; Rashi on T.B. *Sanh.* 65b; *Zohar* I, 237b; II, 136a, 150b–151a, 203b; R. Hayyim Vital, *Sha'ar ha-Kavannot* (Jerusalem, 1985), vol. 2, "*Mizmor Shir le-Yom ha-Shabbat,*" 50a; and idem, *Pri 'Ets Hayyim, "Sha'ar ha-Shabbat,"* chap. 8, s.v. "ve-nahzor" that discusses the descent of Moses, along with other deceased *tsaddikim,* every Sabbath eve, to elevate the souls of the dead and the living, who cannot ascend on their own merit. On the ascension of souls every Sabbath, see *Zohar* I, 205b. On the motif of the *tsaddik's* descent in early Hasidic literature, Mendel Piekarz, *Be-Yemey Tsmihat ha-Hasidut* (Jerusalem, 1978), pp. 280–302. On the Sabbath as the time of ascent and descent, see ibid., p. 287 n. 34; and Schatz-Uffenheimer, "The Ba'al Shem Tov's Commentary," pp. 361–362, 367.

52. "The Ba'al Shem Tov's Commentary," pp. 356, 359, 364–365, 368, 371, 374–376, 379.

53. The Epistle of the BeSHT was first printed in the appendix of Jacob Joseph of Polnoyye, *Ben Porat Yosef* (Korets, 1781). This English translation is found in Joseph Dan, *The Teachings of Hasidism* (New York, 1983), p. 96. Different versions of the letter have come to light and there is much debate among scholars on the recension history of the letter. The authenticity of the printed edition has been reexamined most recently in Rosman, *Founder of Hasidism,* pp. 99–113. Rosman concludes (p. 104) that the original letter probably did not include the quoted vision of the dead in the "lower" Garden of Eden. In the version he holds to be most authentic, there is no report of the BeSHT's descent from the higher realms where departed souls seek the *tsaddik's* assistance to ascend. There the BeSHT does, however, report on his experiences with the departed righteous in these upper reaches of Heaven. While the matter is far from resolved,

the image of the BeSHT presented in the quoted passage clearly reflects early Hasidic teachings that were widely associated with the BeSHT's practices already in R. Nahman's youth.

54. *Sefer ha-Middot, Tsaddik,* 1:26.

55. Ibid., 1:54.

56. R. Aaron (Arele) Roth, *Shomer 'Emunim* (Jerusalem, 1959), "Gilgulim," 141a. On the dialogue with the soul, see n. 48.

57. This is reflected in the story of the BeSHT and R. Gershon Kutover, just cited (n. 47) where the BeSHT gives his brother-in-law a piece of paper with the special *yihudim* written upon it.

58. Note that the special importance of the Sabbath in this regard, as well as the BeSHT's encounter with the souls of the dead on Rosh Ha-Shanah, is consistent with, and likely influenced by, an awareness of, the *Zohar's* teachings, which was just discussed, concerning the elevation of souls on the Sabbath and other holy days.

59. *Sefer Katan,* in Schatz-Uffenheimer, "Ba'al Shem Tov's Commentary to Psalm 107," p. 356. These "ascents of the Sabbath eve" are likely referring to the Lurianic meditations described in *Sha'ar ha-Kavannot;* "Tevillat 'Erev Shabbat," vol. 2, 26b–28a. On the four planes, see Jacobs, "The Uplifting of Sparks in Later Jewish Mysticism," pp. 99–107.

60. *Hayyey MoHaRaN,* 203 (7:19). See Weiss, p. 63. It should be noted that, in this case, R. Nahman seemed intent from the start on rectifying this particular soul. Before arriving in Uman, R. Nahman had arranged to live in the estate of this deceased *maskil,* who—much to his delight—was known by the name Nahman Nathan. Many of the disciples apparently thought that R. Nahman's main objective in coming to Uman was the *tikkun* of this soul. But while discussing his purpose there, he disabused them of that notion. As R. Nathan writes, "Once when he was living in Uman . . . he said: 'Do you remember when I first started talking of Uman? . . . You think it's all connected with Nahman Nathan.' In point of fact, he said, this was no more than an infinitesimal fraction of the purpose of his coming." *Hayyey MoHaRaN,* 192 (8:8). Another example of seeking out a specific soul, is the story of the BeSHT attempting to rectify the soul of Shabbatei Tsvi, discussed below.

61. *Shivhey Ha-BeSHT,* pp. 96–98. See n. 48. See also *Likkutey MoHaRaN* I:4: 5 where R. Nahman, interpreting T.B. *Sotah* 7b, discusses how Moses effects a *tikkun* for Judah when he first recalls Judah's confession of sin, and then prays for his acceptance on high.

On the Lurianic conception of the "root" of the soul, see R. Hayyim Vital's *Sha'arey Kedushah,* 3:5. The Lurianic teachings do discuss in some detail how a mystic adept can identify and help rectify the spiritual blemishes of the *living*. See, for example, Vital's *Sha'ar Ruah ha-Kodesh* (Tel Aviv; 1962–63), *Drush* 1, pp. 9–20. For an analysis of this phenomena, see Lawrence Fine, "The Art of Metopo-scopy: A Study in Isaac Luria's Charismatic Knowledge," reprinted in *Essential Papers on Kabbalah*, ed. Fine, pp. 315–337. It is worth noting that in *Sha'ar Ruah ha-Kodesh, Drush 1*, p. 17b, Vital explains that the 'ARI would speak directly to an individual's soul to understand that soul's particular blemish only when a reading of the individual's forehead was deemed insufficient for such diagnosis. But for the rectification of the *dead*, reading the forehead is apparently not an option, there-fore one proceeds directly to dialogue with the soul.

62. *Shivhey Ha-BeSHT*, p. 133. This method of binding souls is reminis-cent of the Lurianic practice in which one binds the holy soul of a deceased *tsaddik* to his own in order to attain some enlightenment. This is usually performed while prostrating on the *tsaddik's* grave. See Hillel, *Shivhei ha-'ARI: Ha-Shalem u-Mevu'ar*, pp. 94–99. See also Vital's *Sha'ar Ruah ha-Kodesh, Tikkun* 27, Intro-ductions 1–2, pp. 74–75; Introductions 1–5, pp. 107a–110a. For an introduc-tion to the kabbalistic doctrines underlying these practices, see Fine, "Contempla-tive Practice of Yihudim in Lurianic Kabbalah," pp. 79–82.

63. See, for example, R. Ezra of Gerona's "Mystery of the Tree of Knowl-edge," trans. in Scholem's *Mystical Shape of the Godhead*, pp. 66–67.

64. R. Moshe 'Elyakim Beri'ah, *Be'er Moshe* (New York, 1953), p. 28b–c, trans. in Idel, *Hasidism*, pp. 190–191. See also Arthur Green, *Devotion and Commandment: The Faith of Abraham in the Hasidic Imagination* (Cincinnati, 1989), esp. pp. 16–18.

65. Ibid.

66. On the Hasidic practice of "elevating strange thoughts," see Louis Jacobs, *Hasidic Prayer* (New York, 1978), pp. 104–121. For R. Nahman on the *tsaddik* "elevating" both strange (or evil) thoughts and souls, see *Likkutey MoHaRaN* II: 83. Cf. *Likkutey MoHaRaN* I: 96. On an interesting connection between the elevation of strange thoughts and *tikkun ha-neshamot*, see *Tsidkat ha-Tsaddik*, #239, 153b–154b. On R. Nahman's *tikkun* of Sabbateanism, involving affinity with the heretical teachings, terminology, and practices, see Leibes's analy-sis in "*Ha-Tikkun ha-Kelali* of R. Nahman of Bratslav and Its Sabbatean Links," pp. 130–134, 141–146, 148–150.

67. The earliest rabbinic source for the dependence of the dead on the practice of the living is *Sifrey Devarim*, Deut. 21:8.

68. For example, see the *aggadot* concerning R. Meir and his disciple Elisha ben 'Abuyah (T.B. *Hagigah* 15b) and King David and his son Absalom (T.B. *Sotah* 10b). Note that while R. Meir redeems Elisha only after his own death, King David is alive when he redeems Absalom. However, there is no indication that King David enters into the realm of the dead to achieve this. Another example is

the *aggada* concerning Abraham who always descends to Gehinnom to raise up from there even the sinful souls of Israel (T.B. *'Erubin* 19a). Note that Abraham's is a postmortem occupation.

69. While Piekarz traces the general motif of the *tsaddik's* descent to pre-Hasidic literature, he cites no evidence from these sources pertaining to the phenomenon of living *tsaddikim* descending into the nether world and rectifying the souls of the dead. The after death descent of *tsaddikim* into the nether world to elevate previously unknown souls is first found in pre-Hasidic kabbalistic sources. See Piekarz, *Be-Yemey Tsmihat ha-Hasidut,* pp. 280–288. On the zoharic sources, see Tishby, *Wisdom of the Zohar,* vol. 3, pp. 1425–1426, 1457 nn. 157–160. Of course, realizing that *tikkun ha-neshamot* is a somewhat secretive practice, we cannot claim that lack of written evidence implies absence of practice. However, see Schatz-Uffenheimer, "Ba'al Shem Tov's Commentary to Psalm 107," p. 367 who views the Hasidic practice as a definite departure from Lurianic ritual.

70. Such opposition is likely in the background of R. Jacob Joseph's polemic against those who were contemptuous of *tikkun ha-neshamot* practitioners, those "sages who descend to the level of Gehenna in order to raise up souls of the evil-doers from there." See *Toldot Ya'akov Yosef* (Jerusalem, 1966; rpt. Korets, 1780), "Tsav," 78d (trans. in Schatz-Uffenheimer, pp. 379–380).

71. We have already seen in *Hayyey MoHaRaN* that R. Nahman's involvement with the dead stemmed from his conviction that so many souls of the dead were "literally naked." We will return the matter of naked souls further on.

72. One of the many symbols for the *Shekhinah* in the *Zohar* is field *(hakel'a)*. See, for example, *Zohar* I, 224b. See also *Pardes Rimonim, Sha'ar ha-Kinnuim* 23:21, s.v. "Sadeh." *Gan 'Eden, Shekhinah,* and the Souls of Israel are all interrelated, and it is thus not unusual in kabbalistic literature for all of them to be implied in one symbol. The *tsaddik* is the central figure who nurtures all of them. See *Tikkuney ha-Zohar* 14, p. 30a, which depicts the "lower" *Shekhinah* with a similar image as that presented here.

73. "Hayyey Sarah," p. 18c–d (quoted in Schatz-Uffenheimer, p. 375).

74. Ibid.

75. Ibid., "Shemot," p. 36a. See also *Degel Mahane Ephraim,* p. 80a–b, where Jacob's fear of descending into Egypt is understood in this light. In general, those accounts of biblical heroes descending into Egypt paradigmatically illustrate the need for, and the danger associated with, spiritual descent. On the danger that the BeSHT encountered in attempting to rectify the soul of Shabbetai Tsvi, see *Shivhey Ha-BeSHT,* pp. 133–134.

76. This is stated explicitly in *Hayyey MoHaRan,* 110 (4:7). The symbolization of the ninth *sefirah,* yesod, as both *tsaddik* and "gardener" is already found in *Zohar,* II, 166b–167a which, according to R. Nahman (*Sihot ha-RaN,* 252), refers

also to the "true" *tsaddik*. See also *Pardes Rimmonim*, 8:26. Compare *Likkutey MoHaRaN* II: 67, that speaks of the true *tsaddik* as the master of the "house." In *Yemey MaHaRaNaT*, pp. 59–60. R. Nathan explains that in this teaching, as in others, R. Nahman was speaking self-referentially. See Weiss, p. 176 end, 198 n. 18; Piekarz, *Hasidut Bratslav*, pp. 77–78, 80–81; and Green, *Tormented Master*, pp. 212–213.

77. See Abraham Hazan, *Kokhvey 'Or* (1896; Jerusalem, 1987), *Hokhmah U'Binah*, par. 20–21, pp. 148–149, which interprets "The Valorous Wife" of Prov. 31:10–31 as an allusion to R. Nahman's spiritual leadership. Referring to the verses 16–17, "She sets her mind on a field and acquires it; From the fruit of her hands, she plants a vineyard. With strength (Be-'OZ) she girds her loins and fortifies her arms." R. Abraham writes "and [R. Nahman] acquired the Holy Field to water and to tend the trees which are the souls of Israel called [in Isa. 5:7] by the names 'field' and 'vineyard'." And with strength he girded his loins and fortified his arms *to complete all the tikkunim that were necessary. . . .*" See also *Likkutey Halakhot, Hashkamat Ha-Boker*, 4:18, which interprets the entire passage as referring to R. Nahman.

78. *Yemey MoHaRaNT*, pp. 79–80 (English translation, Green, *Tormented Master*, 279). See also, *Yemey MaHaRaNaT*, pp. 66–67.

79. *Zohar*, II, 210a–b. On the superiority of prayer in R. Nahman, see *Likkutey MoHaRaN*, II: 111 that concludes, "If a dead person would be allowed to return to this world, he would certainly pray very beautifully, with all of his strength."

80. *Likkutey Tefillot* I: 65. On the souls "which cannot even be clothed in a body," see n. 42.

81. *Sihot ha-RaN*, 195. On the souls "that have never entered a body," see n. 42.

82. *Sihot ha-RaN*, 23.

83. *Hayyey MoHaRaN*, 191 (8:7). Cf. *Yemey MoHaRaNT*, p. 80 (English translation, Green, Tormented Master, p. 279).

84. On R. Nahman's befriending of the *maskilim*, see Piekarz, *Hasidut Bratslav*, pp. 27–55. See also Green, *Tormented Master*, pp. 255–259. Piekarz's thesis concerning R. Nahman's purpose in Uman is that he was predominately focused on "tangible descent *(yeridah muhashit)* to the sinners . . . to bring them to repentance" (ibid., p. 27, cf. ibid., pp. 38, 52). Since Piekarz overlooks R. Nahman's involvement with the dead, it is not surprising that he does not consider the *tsaddik*'s association with the *maskilim* as preparatory for a future *tikkun*. See also n. 91.

85. *Sefer Ha-Middot, Tsaddik*, 1:53. See *Likkutey MoHaRaN* I:4:5–9 that discusses the three major ways of drawing close to a *tsaddik:* beholding the *tsaddik*'s

face, giving him alms, and confessing one's sins to him. On the particular quality of attachment to the *tsaddik* in R. Nahman's thought, see Leibes, *"Ha-Tikkun ha-Kelali* of R. Nahman of Bratslav and Its Sabbatean Links," pp. 117–118, 127–128.

86. Ibid., 1:74.

87. Ibid., 1:86. A possible zoharic source for this teaching is *Zohar Hadash, Lekh Lekha,* 25b *(Midrash Ha-Ne'elam).* Tishby noted that in this passage, as in *Tikkuney ha-Zohar, Tikkun* 32, 76b, the *tsaddik* only redeems evildoers in the next world if they had a personal connection with him in this world. See *Wisdom of the Zohar,* pp. 1425–1426; 1457 nn. 159, 160. Tishby's use of the passage from *Tikkuney ha-Zohar* is, however, based on a questionable reading of the text.

88. *Hayyey MoHaRaN,* 197 (8:13).

89. *Likkutey MoHaRaN* II: 78 end.

90. *Hayyey MoHaRaN,* 101(3:21). Note the length of time it took this *tsaddik* to rectify the soul of even one devoted disciple! In a parenthetical comment to this passage, R. Nahman of Cheryn (R. Nathan's disciple and the publisher of *Hayyey MoHaRaN*) explains, "even after a person passes away, as long as he does not yet merit to go in wholeness to his place of rest, he is still not in the World of Truth. Just the opposite! The essence of his punishment and suffering is brought about through Angels of Destruction that lead him along in the World of Confusion *('Olam haTohu)* where it appears to him as though he is still in this world. And they deceive him with many deceptions, as is well-known from the [holy] books.

91. *Hayyey MoHaRaN,* 197 (8:12). While the phrase, "whatever you tell him to do he will do" may point to R. Nahman's method of *tikkun,* it is more likely just a figure of speech. Note the contrast between R. Nahman's confidence in his power to affect the dead and his uncertainty concerning the strength of the dead to overcome the postmortem obstacles to drawing close to a *tsaddik,* which was just mentioned.

Piekarz (*Hasidut Bratslav,* p. 41), in his only reference to the martyred dead of Uman, misreads this passage, interpreting it as expressing R. Nahman's doubts about directing so much energy to the *maskilim* living in Uman. But when R. Nahman speaks here of the living, he is clearly referring, not to the sinful heretics, but to his righteous followers. He is not doubting his efforts with the *maskilim,* but expressing the utter futility of guiding any living person, even a "great *tsaddik."* This passage, and those cited in the next section, clearly emphasize this point. Moreover, it seems to me that the statement, "But even the greatest of sinners, once he has passed on . . . whatever you tell him to do he will do. . . ." expresses R. Nahman's confidence in his efforts with the *maskilim,* as they are preparatory for his work with them in the "spirit realm."

92. Ibid.

93. *Hayyey MoHaRaN,* 197 (8:12). The passage continues, "For him, this was an issue of, 'the day Moses added on his own initiative.'" This expression refers to the rabbinic notion, cherished by R. Nahman, of God allowing for ambiguity in spiritual leadership because He desires that sages employ their own wisdom and take the initiative in determining the proper course of action. See T. B. *Shabbat* 87a. This is the central motif of *Hayyey MoHaRaN,* 197–198 (8:12,13) and *Likkutey MoHaRaN* I: 190. See the comments of Green, *Tormented Master,* p. 273 n. 72. Cf. *Sefer ha-Middot,* 131. See Abraham J. Heschel, *Torah Min Ha-Shamayim be-'Ispaklaria' shel ha-Dorot* (Hebrew) (London and New York, 1965), vol. 2, pp. 128ff.

94. *Hayyey MoHaRaN,* 217 (8:33).

95. For the effect of a *tsaddik's* death on the dead, see *Likkutey MoHaRaN* I:20: 5. Cf. *Sefer ha-Middot, Tsaddik* 1:76; R. Nathan of Nemirov, *Likkutey Halakhot* (Jerusalem, 1991) *Hoshen Mishpat, Nezikin* 3:8–9, vol. 8, p. 520 (quoted also in Chechik, ed. *Meshekh Ha-Nahal,* pp. 79–81). For the positive effects on the living, see *Likkutey MoHaRaN* I:207 concerning the death of the BeSHT as a "sweetening" of the *gevurot.* In the BeSHT's day, the *gevurot* were the defamations of Oral Torah resulting from the Shabbetai Tsvi debacle. Cf. *Likkutey MoHaRaN* II: 83 end. But R. Nahman also spoke of the negative consequences. See *Sefer ha-Middot, Tsaddik* 1:73, 164; *Sihot ha-RaN,* 197. R. Nahman was undoubtedly influenced by the rabbinic and zoharic sources. Already in the Talmud we find the death of the righteous as an atonement for the generation. See T. B. *Shabbat* 33b, *Moed Katan* 28a. For zoharic sources, see Tishby, *The Wisdom of the Zohar,* vol. 3, pp. 897, 1494–1496. See Bracha Sack's discussion of this subject in her "Kiddush ha-Shem" (Hebrew) in idem, *The Kabbalah of Rabbi Moshe Cordevero* (Jerusalem, 1995), pp. 230–246. Concerning the *Zohar's* emphasis on the great *tikkun* resulting from R. Shimon bar Yohai's death, see Yehuda Leibes, "Messiah of the Zohar," in idem, *Studies in Zohar* (Albany, 1993), pp. 61, 63–65, 188 n. 182, 191 n. 209 and Zohar sources cited therein.

96. See *Likkutey Halakhot, Yoreh De'ah, Reishit ha-Gaz,* 3:8, vol. 5, pp. 519–520, where R. Nathan writes that a *tsaddik* lives forever because his *da'at* (perception), the "essence of his life," remains even after his ascension. He explains that this is because "his soul *(nishmato)* is enclothed within his *da'at* which he infuses into this world through his children and his disciples."

97. *Likkutey MoHaRaN,* I:66:1–2. See also *Yemey MoHaRaNT,* p. 86 where R. Nathan, grasping for words to convey the power of that moment, writes,

Only those who know a bit of his greatness, who have read his holy books or have heard his stories, will begin to realize that his death was completely unique. There was never any like it, nor will there ever be. How shall we speak? What shall we say? What shall I say to the Lord, who gave me the gift of being there as his holy soul passed out of him? Had I only come into the world for the sake of this moment, it would have been sufficient." (English translation, Green, *Tormented Master,* pp. 281–282)

98. *Sihot ha-RaN,* 57. See Green, *Tormented Master,* pp. 32–33, 212–213, 254; and Weiss, pp. 172–178.

99. See *Likkutey MoHaRaN* I:80. On death, especially the mass murders of the pogroms, as *Kiddush ha-Shem* (Sanctification of the Divine Name) in Bratslav thought, see also *Likkutey MoHaRaN,* I:260; *Likkutey Halakhot, Hoshen Mishpat, Hovel Be-havero,* 3:7–9, vol. 8, pp. 280b–281c. See the passages in *Zohar* I, 38b–39a, 41a that assign a special place for such martyrs in the fourth of the seven chambers *(heikhalot)* of *Gan 'Eden.* See also T. B. *Bab'a Batr'a* 10b. On the kabbalisitic theology of martyrdom relating to the pogroms of 1648 in Eastern Europe, see Yehuda Leibes, "Mysticism and Reality: Towards a Portrait of the Martyr and Kabbalist R. Samson Ostropoler," in *Jewish Thought in the Seventeenth Century,* ed. I. Twerski (Cambridge, Mass, 1987), pp. 249–253.

100. *Hayyey MoHaRaN,* 197 (8:13).

101. *Hayyey MoHaRaN,* 217 (8:33). Cf. 191–192 (8:7–8).

102. *Hayyey MoHaRaN,* 151 (6:1).

103. *Sefer Ha-Middot,* 1:45. *Gilgul mehilot* is the underground journey of the dead to Israel at the time of resurrection. See T. B. *Ketubot* 111a.

104. *Hayyey MoHaRaN,* 151 (6:1). One wonders whether R. Nathan himself practiced *tikkun ha-neshamot,* particularly after the rebbe's death when he took over the mantle of leadership. While Bratslav literature is silent on the matter, some evidence of a continuation is found in a *pinkas* (record book) from the Bratslav Hasidim living in Berditchev (after R. Nathan's death in 1844), recently published by a new traditionalist Hasidic periodical. It presents a story that describes R. Nathan teaching another how to see a dead person. The story concludes, "our Rebbe returned to his study, locked himself in, and labored in the *tikkun* of that dead person." See Shaul Shimon Deutsch, "The Pinkas of Chasidei Breslov of Barditchev," *The Chasidic Historical Review* 1:2 (1996): 10–12.

# 5

## Rabbi Nahman of Bratslav
### *The Zaddik as Androgyne*

#### *Nathaniel Deutsch*

Rabbi Nahman ben Simhah of Bratslav (1772–1810) may be viewed as a bridge between the beginnings of Hasidism and the movement's flowering in the Ukrainian heartland. As a great grandson of the Baal Shem Tov, Nahman represented a physical link with the founder himself, and this "noble lineage," or *yihus,* played a significant role in Nahman's life. Nahman's relationship with his illustrious great grandfather, like all aspects of his life, was highly ambivalent. There is an old saying that those who translate prose are slaves, while those who translate poetry are competitors. R. Nahman approached the Besht's life and teachings like a translator of poetry. From an early age, Nahman identified with the Besht and appears to have consciously patterned much of his behavior on that of his great grandfather. Yet Nahman also suggested that he had surpassed the Besht in certain respects and would complete the redemptive mission that his ancestor had only begun.

The implicit tension between Nahman and the Besht hints at a widespread concern within Hasidism at the end of the eighteenth and beginning of the nineteenth centuries, namely, how to achieve a transition from a group of founding fathers and their immediate followers to a widespread movement involving the masses of Eastern European Jewry. The creation of an oral biographical tradition and eventually the development of Hasidic hagiography, such as *Shivhei Ha- Besht,* helped to achieve this transition. The Besht, the Maggid of Mezeritch, and other early figures continued to "live" in the tales told and written about them. An important function of the growing number of Hasidic rebbes was transmitting these traditions to their followers, thereby establishing themselves as the legitimate interpreters of early Hasidism, a goal that was also achieved by establishing dynasties based on physical links with the founding fathers of Hasidism.

At the same time, in order to attract and maintain followers, as well as for their own well-developed senses of self, Hasidic rebbes had to find ways of distinguishing themselves from both their illustrious ancestors and their contemporary rivals. Thus the greatest rebbes treated Hasidic traditions like translators of poetry rather than prose, and Rabbi Nahman was the most poetic translator of all.

Indeed, Nahman's translations—in the form of tales and sermons, not to mention the story of his own life—were so powerful that after his death they took the place of a line of physical descendants. Alone among the early Hasidic groups, the Bratslaver Hasidim have functioned for the last two hundred years without a physical rebbe. For this reason, they are known in Yiddish as the *toyte hasidim,* that is, the "Dead Hasidim," although this name obscures the vibrancy that the movement's small number of adherents have maintained up to the present day. As Lieb Berger, a contemporary executive director of the World Bratslav Organization declared, "They call us 'the dead,' but we are alive and well. And with us lives Rab Nahman, whose writings and teachings we follow always."[1]

The most persistent aspect of R. Nahman's life-long inner struggle involved his sexuality.[2] Although a few studies on Nahman and his doctrines have explored issues of sexuality and the related topic of gender, much more work in these areas remains to be done. In this chapter I will make a small dent in this potential mountain of research by examining two clusters of themes in the writings by and about R. Nahman: one, the topic of motherhood and the related tropes of menstruation, pregnancy, and nursing, and two, the topic of circumcision and its relation to sexuality. These two thematic clusters are in turn related in Bratslaver literature by a series of ingenious semiological links between nursing and insemination, menstrual blood and milk, milk and semen, menstruation and circumcision, and circumcision and sexual intercourse. By focusing on these specific issues, this discussion will hopefully open at least a few doors onto Bratslaver conceptions of sexuality, gender, and kabbalistic symbolism.

In Nahman's collection of homilies, *Liqqutey MoHaRan,* he describes the Zaddik of the Generation *(Zaddik Ha-Dor),* that is, R. Nahman himself, as a nursing mother:

> There are three aspects of attachment to Zaddikim, by means of which everything is rectified *(nittaqen ha-kol);* and these are the three aspects: The first aspect is when one sees the Zaddik. . . . For the Zaddik of the Generation is called Mother *(aym)* because he nurses Israel with the light of his Torah, and the Torah is called milk, as it is written, "Honey and milk are under your tongue, (Song of Songs 4:11).[3]

The same maternal imagery is employed by Nahman's disciple and literary secretary R. Nathan of Nemirov to describe the beginning of his relationship with his master: "And he [R. Nahman] grabbed my hand and brought me close with his great compassion and raised me up 'like a nurse raises an infant'" (Numbers 11:12).[4]

It may surprise some to see a male figure depicted in such explicitly female terms, that is, as a nursing mother. In fact, the history of religions provides other examples of male religious leaders who are described as mothers who nurse their followers with the milk of their wisdom or teachings. The midrashic collection on the Song of Songs called *Shir Ha-Shirim Rabbah* preserves one of the most striking examples of this image from the Jewish tradition. Commenting on the biblical phrase (Song 4:5) "Your breasts are like two fawns," the text declares,

These [the breasts] are Moses and Aaron. Just as the breasts are the beauty and the ornament of a woman, so Moses and Aaron were the beauty and ornament of Israel. Just as the breasts are the charm of a woman, so Moses and Aaron were the charm of Israel. Just as the breasts are the glory and pride of a woman, so Moses and Aaron were the glory and pride of Israel. Just as the breasts are full of milk, so Moses and Aaron filled Israel with Torah. Just as whatever a woman eats helps to feed the child at the breast, so all the Torah that Moses our master learned he taught to Aaron.[5]

Leaving aside for the moment medieval depictions of Jesus as a nursing mother, Christian sources also provide examples of this phenomenon including St. Francis of Assisi, whose followers referred to him as "dearest Mother,"[6] and Bernard of Clairvaux, who wrote to a wayward monk, "And I have said this, my son, . . . to help you as a loving father. . . . I begot you in religion by word and example. I nourished you with milk. . . . You too were torn from my breast, cut from my womb. My heart cannot forget you."[7]

In similar fashion, Sufi texts employ the Arabic term *mashrab* or "the place where one drinks" to describe the source of one's religious tradition or lineage and traditionally depict the Sufi master, or shaykh, as a mother who nurses his pupils, as the contemporary Shaykh Ahmad Abu'l-Hasan (d. 1994) described his relationship to his teacher Ahmad Radwan of Luxor (d. 1967), "I stayed with the shaykh, drawing nourishment from his milk and being illuminated by his lights, until he met the Highest Companion."[8] A medieval Sufi text makes the relationship even more explicit.

Just as the infant drinks milk at the breast of its mother or wetnurse, receiving from them the sustenance without which it would perish, so too the infant of the spirit drinks the milk of the Path and the Truth from the nipple of the mother or prophethood, or the wetnurse of sainthood *(wilayat)*, receiving from the prophet or the sheikh—who stands in place of the prophet—that sustenance without which it would perish.[9]

The central image in all of these sources is of nourishment: the zaddik, priest, or shaykh nourishes his disciples with the "milk" of knowledge and tradition. The power of the descriptions derives from their physicality. That is, they hypostatically transform the typically abstract concept of wisdom into the concrete substance of mother's milk. The teachings of the holy man are linked to him organically; they are, in fact, an extension or even a product of his very body. In their own way, these descriptions belong to the ancient Logos tradition, whereby the word is given physical substance or hypostastized, whether into Jesus, the Torah, mother's milk, or as we will see shortly, semen.

The gender issues raised by the depictions of R. Nahman as a nursing mother are highly complex.[10] I will argue that in Bratslav thought, the nursing mother, the pregnant woman, and the cirmcumcised man, while biologically female or male in nature, are symbols of androgyny. Both categories, the pregnant and the nursing woman, exhibit characteristics that sharply and, in the Bratslaver view, positively differentiate them from other women. Chief among these differences is that according to Bratslav conceptions, not only do pregnant women cease to menstruate, but after giving birth the menstrual blood of nursing women is transformed into milk. Drawing on earlier Jewish traditions of menstrual taboos, Bratslaver writings emphasize the negative, polluting character of menstruation. The menstruating woman signifies the most extreme expression of female negativity. Why? Because her flow symbolizes her active independence from the male, in other words, she is a female who has not been transformed by a male via insemination. Put differently, menstruation is the most potent symbol of purely female identity.

From a kabbalistic perspective, menstruation is particularly problematic because it is an overflow, an activity generally conceptualized as masculine rather than feminine. Thus, as the divine effluence *(shefa')* descends downward through the sefirot (divine aspects), each sefirah is characterized as feminine when it receives the flow and masculine when it overflows into the sefirah below it.[11] With this model in mind, menstruation may be viewed as the negative mirror image of the positive, masculine flow of divine effluence, which, not surprisingly, is characterized as semen in both kabbalistic and Bratslaver sources. In short, menstruation, like ejaculation, is an active process, but one that is uniquely female and therefore in both kabbalistic and Bratslaver conceptions, dangerous.

In R. Nahman's own works, the idea that menstruation symbolizes the dangerous independence of the female from the male is cast in terms of the separation of the Shekhinah (the female aspect of God) from the Holy One Blessed be He (the male aspect): "But the wicked, through their sins, cause a separation between the Holy One Blessed be He and his Shekhinah, because they generate menstrual blood in her, and then she is called the 'city of blood' (Ezekiel 22:2). And by virtue of this, the wicked are called 'men of bloodshed'" (Ps. 55:24).[12] Nahman's text emphasizes that menstruation causes the female to be separated from the male within the theosophical realm, a situation that parallels the relationship between human males and females, as required by the laws of *niddah*. In the kabbalistic worldview, the separation (read: independence) of the female Shekhinah is considered the major catastrophe in the sefirotic realm. Thus, for example, the kabbalistic significance of the sins of both Adam and the rabbinic archheretic Aher was that they separated the Shekhinah from the other sefirot, that is, "cutting the shoots" *(kitsets ba-netiyot).*[13] Menstruation, therefore, symbolizes sexual differentiation and, more specifically, the violent and bloody separation of the female from the male. By contrast, as the research of Elliot Wolfson has shown, the ideal state of being for the Kabbalah and, as I will argue in the following pages, for R. Nahman and his circle is that of an androgyne, in which the masculine element incorporates the feminine.[14]

Indeed, without this androgynous ideal in mind it is basically impossible to understand Bratslaver writings on gender, including the previously cited descriptions of R. Nahman as a nursing mother. From one perspective, Nahman is feminized in these passages: he is, after all, symbolically engaged in an activity limited to biological females. Yet, I think the underlying message of these texts is quite different, even opposite to this surface understanding. The deeper significance of these passages is the symbolic androgenization of the image of the nursing mother. This interpretation jibes with R. Nahman's theosophical writings on the relationship between menstrual blood, mother's milk, and semen.

According to the Talmud, from the time a woman conceives a child until after she weans it, the flow of her menstrual blood is inhibited and actually transformed into milk. R. Nahman draws on this tradition when he exhorts his followers to perform actions that will convert the redness of menstrual blood into the whiteness of milk within the sefirotic realm. "And it is necessary to subdue the evil handmaid, who is 'a bad time,' as in (Eccl. 9:8) 'At all times let your garments be white,' 'at all times,' specifically. 'Your garments be white,' that is, without a stain. This is the concept of purifying the *Shekhinah* from her impurity [menstruation], corresponding to (BT Bekhorot 6b), 'The blood is decomposed and turned into milk.'"[15] In this passage, Nahman enjoins his followers to always maintain white garments, meaning to avoid sin, itself symbolized by the red stain of menstrual blood. By living a righteous life, the individual helps to purify the Shekhinah of its pollution by transforming the menstrual blood into mother's milk, a process, I suggest, of symbolic androgenization.[16] While it may be argued that mother's milk is as much a symbol of femaleness as menstrual blood, this is not the Bratslaver understanding. Indeed, as the following passages illustrate, R. Nahman symbolically identifies the nursing female with the ejaculating male, and mother's milk with semen.

According to Nahman, the 365 prohibitive commandments in the Torah correspond to the 365 blood vessels *(gidim)* in the human body. When people transgress these commandments, they "arouse menstrual blood in the Shekhinah."[17] In order to rectify these blood vessels, it is necessary to "draw whiteness to them, as in, 'The blood is decomposed and converted into milk.' And this is [the meaning of]: 'At all times let your garments *[bigadekha]* be white'— specifically, in your blood vessels *[bigidekha]*, to draw whiteness into them."[18] Thus, the sins human beings commit theurgically influence the sefirotic organism, literally flowing through its veins in the form of impure blood, while good deeds turn this impure blood white.

The problem is that correcting all the sins/blood vessels individually is a monumental task. This difficulty is overcome by achieving sexual purity or, in

Nahman's terms, rectifying the *berit,* that is the phallus that functions as the generality *(klaliut)* of all the *gidim.* Nahman's description of this process is peppered with complicated linguistic puns on sexual and theosophical images. It appears within a lesson delivered by Nahman on Shavuot 5566 (May 23, 1806) in Bratslav. For the first time, Nahman dressed in white and expanded upon his concept of the "General Remedy" or *tiqqun ha-kelali* for sins, which he had introduced about a year earlier.[19] The context of the lesson was a period of intense messianic activity within the Bratslav community, focused on R. Nahman, himself.[20] The holiday of Shavuot is significant because it celebrates the giving of the Torah, which is likened to milk (BT Hagigah 13a); for this reason, at the Shavuot morning *kiddush* it is customary to eat dairy products.

> It is therefore necessary to rectify the generality of the *gidim,* as in (Deut. 4:13), "And he announced *[va-yaged]* to you His covenant *[berito]*." And so, by means of the rectification of the covenant *[tikkun ha-berit],* which is the generality of the *gidim,* all the transgressions are rectified, and whiteness is drawn into them. Because of this, the generality of the *gidim,* which is the holy covenant, is called *Shaddai,* because it shoots *[shaday]* and fires like an arrow—whiteness and *tikkunim* to each and every place as needed, and even to the narrow and tiny places. For there are narrow and tiny places which no *tikkun* can reach except by means of the General Tikkun *(tikkun ha-klali).* . . . Now this whiteness is drawn from the mind, as in (Song of Songs 4:15), "flowing from Lebanon *[levanon],*": "from the whiteness *[libuna]* of the mind," (Zohar III, 235b). . . . These are the mentalities *[mohin]* which are father in *Hokhmah* [wisdom] and mother to *Binah* [understanding]. This is the meaning of (BT Berakhot): "An infant nurses from the breasts *[mi-shday]* of his mother." "An infant" alludes to the immature mentalities, for he nurses and is raised from his immaturity by means of the General Remedy, which shoots *[shaday]* and fires like an arrow. And thus, "his mother" signifies the gathering [of Israel], as it is written (Proverbs 23:22), "Do not despise your mother when she is old." [Your mother] Rashi interpreted is "your gathering," for there all the rectifications are gathered and included.[21]

Unpacking this extremely technical text requires a thorough grounding in both kabbalistic and Bratslaver symbolism. The focus of the text is the divine phallus, which by means of its ejaculation transforms the red menstrual blood into white semen and rectifies the entire divine corpus, even the "tiny and narrow" spaces. The phallus is referred to by a number of technical terms, including *berit* (covenant), *gid* (vein or penis), and Shaddai. According to the Kabbalah, the divine name Shaddai signifies the ninth sefirah of Yesod (Foundation), which functions as the phallus of the sefirotic body. This identification is made for a number of reasons. In the Bible, the phrase "I am El Shaddai," appears twice. First, when God promises Abraham that he will be "the father of a host of nations," and makes a covenant with him, "This is My *berit* . . . that you must keep. You must circumcise every male. You shall circumcise the flesh of your foreskin. This shall be the sign of the *berit* between Me and you" (Gen. 17:1–11). Second, when God blesses Ya'akov with children, declaring "I am El Shaddai, be fruitful and multiply" (Gen. 35:11). In later sources, these passages are interpreted as linking the name Shaddai with the *berit* and the aspect of fatherhood, in other words, the male organ.

R. Nahman links Shaddai to the phallus by means of the linguistic resemblance between Shaddai and a Hebrew word meaning "to shoot"; thus, the phallus (Shaddai) "shoots *(shaday)* whiteness," that is ejaculates semen. The identification of Shaddai as the phallus suggests a potential conceptual difficulty, however. For another interpretation of Shaddai links it to the Hebrew word for "breasts" or *shadaim*, thereby transforming the biblical El Shaddai into "the God with breasts."[22] This tension is overcome in the text by assimilating the image of the lactating breasts to the dominant image of the ejaculating phallus. As Nahman writes: "This is the meaning of 'An infant nurses from the breasts *(sheday)* of his mother.' He nurses and is raised from immaturity by means of the *tiqqun ha-kelali*, which shoots *(shaday)* and fires like an arrow." Nahman's explicit identification of the breasts with the phallus reflects an older kabbalistic tradition, as Elliot Wolfson explains concerning the Zohar, "Breast-feeding too is valorized as a phallic activity (the milk obviously taking the place of the semen) insofar as anything that sustains by overflowing is automatically treated as an aspect of the phallus."[23] The kabbalistic and Bratslaver masculinization of the female activity of breastfeeding contrasts with Christian descriptions of Jesus as a nursing mother, where the opposite symbolic process appears to occur, namely, the feminization of the male figure of Jesus.[24]

While Nahman's discussion focuses on the sefirotic realm, it must be noted that the zaddik, and specifically, Nahman himself, plays a critical role in the process being described. Indeed, kabbalistic tradition identifies the zaddik with the sefirah Yesod, based on the biblical phrase *Zaddik Yesod 'Olam* or "the righteous in the foundation of the world" (Prov. 10:25). The *tiqqun ha-kelali* or "General Remedy" must be undertaken by the Zaddik Ha-Dor (Zaddik of the Generation) through the constant maintainance of sexual purity, that is by guarding his *berit* or "phallus." When this occurs, the zaddik, in this case Nahman, becomes a conduit for the divine effluence, identified in this text as milk or semen. Intriguingly, this biological/theosophical process is at the same time a process of cognition or intellectualization, whereby divine wisdom in the form of mentalities *(mohin)* is aroused, cultivated, and transmitted, both within the sefirotic realm and between the zaddik (Nahman) and his disciples.

This set of associations brings us back to the original descriptions of Nahman as a mother who nurses his disciples with his milk/wisdom. This biologically female activity must now be viewed as symbolically androgenous within the Bratslaver worldview. It comes as no surprise, therefore, that elsewhere in his writings, Nahman describes the same transmission of wisdom from the zaddik to his disciples as equivalent to the ejaculation of semen during sexual intercourse between a husband and his wife.

> To arrive at truth *['emet]*, only by means of getting close to Zaddikim, and following the path of their advice. . . . For the advice which you receive from them, this is the aspect of marriage and intercourse *[hu behinat nisu'in ve-zivvug]*. . . . And why is advice *['etsah]* called by the aspect of marriage? Because (BT Berakhot 61a) the organs excrete *[yo'atsot]*, and the organs are the organs of engenderment, the organs of semen *[zera']*. Thus, when you receive advice from a man, it is as if you receive semen from him . . . And the advice of the Zaddik is entirely the semen of truth.[25]

According to kabbalistic symbolism, the term *'emet* (truth) is another name for the sefirah commonly known as Tiferet, which, like the lower sefirah Yesod, has a phallic connotation. The word for advice *('etsah)* is another name for the masculine sefirah Hesed (mercy), which is identified with the color white in kabbalistic sources, thereby linking it symbolically to semen. Moreover, the very act of speech has phallic connotations, since various kabbalistic sources identify the mouth *(peh)* with the phallus *(milah)*.[26] Theosophically, therefore, the final line in this quotation may be parsed as follows: "And the advice (Hesed) of the zaddik (Yesod) is entirely the semen of truth (Tiferet)." Thus, the zaddik serves as a microcosm or homologue of the divine phallus, inseminating disciples with his advice/divine effluence. This process is functionally and symbolically equivalent to the nursing of the disciples from the milk of the zaddik's breasts. Instead of interpreting the former as a masculine image and the latter as a feminine one, however, both activities may be viewed as androgenous in nature.[27]

This symbolic transformation reveals the degree to which concepts of gender may differ from biologically grounded sexual roles and functions. Indeed, precisely those physiological aspects of the female that are viewed as positive, such as nursing, are appropriated and symbolically androgenized. The male zaddik, therefore, assumes both the positive roles of the biological mother and of the husband, insofar as he nurses/inseminates his disciples with his wisdom.[28]

## R. Nahman as Binah

Given Nahman's description of himself as a nursing mother, it is not surprising that later Bratslaver tradition identifies Nahman with the sefirah Binah (Understanding), that is, the supernal Mother.[29] This identification is interesting for a number of reasons. First of all, it places Nahman in a higher place within the sefirotic hierarchy than any of his spiritual precedessors, including Abraham (Hesed), Moses and Jacob (Tiferet), and Shimon bar Yohai, the hero of the Zohar (Yesod). Moreover, it does not describe Nahman as united with Binah in a kind of *hieros gamos*, as the Zohar sometimes describes both Moses and Jacob,[30] but instead actually identifies him as the embodiment of the sefirah itself. Unlike male figures such as Abraham, Moses, Jacob, and Shimon bar Yohai who are identified with traditionally male sefirot, Nahman is equated with a sefirah that is typically considered female, although as we will see, is actually better described as an androgyne. In this respect, Nahman resembles King David, who is associated with the sefirah Malkhut (i.e., the lower Mother).[31]

At first glance, the identification of Nahman with Binah may appear to conflict with his identification with the sefirah Yesod. Upon reflection, however, a harmony emerges between the two approaches. One way of understanding the two sefirotic designations is through the prism of Bratslaver messianic speculation. Traditionally, the biblical figure Joseph is identified with the sefirah Yesod. Jewish sources, including those that influenced Bratslaver Hasidism, frequently depict two messianic figures. The first is Messiah ben Joseph, who prepares the way for the second figure, Messiah ben David. In so far as he embodies the sefirah Yesod (Joseph), Nahman assumes the role of the Messiah ben Joseph in Bratslaver sources.[32] Yet, Nahman may have also assumed the role of Messiah ben David.[33] The same Bratslaver text that identifies Nahman with Binah also links him to Malkhut, for "all the power of Malkhut and all the structure of Malkhut are from the aspect *[middah]* of Binah."[34] As the embodiment of both Malkhut and Binah, Nahman fulfills and indeed surpasses the sefirotic designation of David, and assumes the status of Messiah ben David. Thus, the later Bratslaver identification of Nahman with Binah (and therefore Malkhut) combined with his earlier identification with Yesod, may be interpreted as confirmation of his dual messianic role.

The association of Nahman with both Yesod and Binah also functions as a sefirotic analogy to Nahman's self-descriptions as an inseminating husband and a nursing mother. It therefore reinforces the essentially androgynous character of Nahman, an androgyne in whom the female has been assimilated to the male. On yet another level, the sefirah Binah, like the image of the nursing mother in Bratslaver sources, is itself androgynous. In so far as Binah receives influx from her male consort Hokhmah (Wisdom), she functions as a female, but when Binah overflows and generates the lower sefirot she becomes male, as the Zohar states, "Even though that supernal world *(Binah)* is feminine, it is called male when it emanates all the goodness and all the light comes out from it."[35] Isaac Luria describes the androgynous character of Binah as follows: "even though she [Binah] is female she ends with the masculine. When she is clothed in the six extremeties [sefirot] of the masculine whose end is Yesod, she is called Binah, *ben yah,* and she is one with the All. Similarly, in the case of Malkhut, by means of the arousal of the lower beings. . . . she becomes male and is called Lord."[36]

As the embodiment of Yesod, R. Nahman signifies the phallic end or completion of Binah, the generative womb of the lower seven sefirot.[37] Just as Nahman assumes the image of the nursing mother, so he assimilates the image of the mother's womb; in the process, both images are androgenized and in fact symbolically equated with the phallus. Thus, Nahman's identification with Binah, although a feminization of Nahman on one level in so far as Binah is female vis-a-vis Hokhmah and Keter, may also be interpreted as an intensification of the masculine aspect already present within Binah according to kabbalistic sources.

### Pregnancy and Androgyny

A final example of how Bratslaver writings androgenize the image of the mother appears in Nahman's theosophical interpretation of the aspect of pregnancy *(be-hinat 'ibbur).* "When a person studies Torah and is unable to understand anything new, this is because the mentalities *[mohin]* and the intellect of this Torah and this study are in the aspect of pregnancy *[bi-behinat 'ibbur].* And this is called by the name Ya'akov, for Ya'akov is the aspect of pregnancy, as in (Hoseah 12:4): 'In the womb, he grabbed his brother by the heal *['akav et ahiv].*'"[38] According to standard kabbalistic symbolism, Yaakov signifies the masculine sefirah Tiferet, which in Nahman's discourse, is the location of the male *in potentia,* that is, in the aspect of pregnancy. When the *mohin* (mentalities) are revealed, this masculine potential is actualized in the form of Israel, as Nahman writes,

> But, "Israel is his special one *(segulato)*" (Ps. 135:4). Israel, the letters are [the words] *li rosh* ("my head"). This is the revelation of the *mohin,* the drawing of the light of the face, the divine effluence, into the inner part [of the mind], . . . And this is the aspect of Israel, as in (Isaiah 49:3) "Israel, in you I am glorified *['etpa'ar].*" Specifically, "in you"—the crown of splendour *['ateret tiferet],* that is, the transcending mentalities *[maqifin]* mentioned above, should be drawn "in you"—internalized.[39]

Just as in the Bible, Ya'akov "becomes" Israel, so in Nahman's text, the embryonic male (Ya'akov) must be transformed into the mature male (Israel); put differently, the intellectual potential or divine influx must be actualized and internalized. On one level, the identification of Israel with the "head" and the "crown of splendor" signifies the emergence of the child's head during birth.[40] On another level, it symbolizes the revelation of the corona of the phallus during circumcision, which was previously concealed. Thus, the aspect of pregnancy may be identified with the enclosure of the corona by the foreskin. The birth of the mature Israelite male, that is the circumcised male, is signified by the transformation of Ya'akov (Tiferet) into Israel *('ateret tiferet)*. This process of maturation also signifies the moment of intellectual revelation, according to Nahman, a view supported by another etymology of Israel as "the one who sees."[41]

The text becomes even more interesting when we recall that the traditional sefirotic designation of Israel is Malkhut/Shekhinah. Thus, following an older kabbalistic tradition that links theosophical revelation with the revelation of the corona (i.e., Malkhut) during circumcision,[42] Nahman identifies the Shekhinah as the exposed corona of the divine phallus, that is the "crown of Tiferet." What this text implies is that the immature or uncircumcised male (Tiferet) can only become mature by incorporating his female aspect (Malkhut), thereby achieving what Isaiah Tishby has described as the "completion of the male image," in the sefirotic realm.[43] In other words, the female sefirah Malkhut is the exposed opening or crown of the phallus belonging to the divine androgyne.

## Circumcision and Androgenization

While the previous passages do not explicitly mention circumcision, it is clearly an underlying theme, one that emerges elsewhere in Bratslaver writings. One of the more enigmatic references to circumcision in this literary corpus appears in R. Nathan of Nemirov's biographical account of Nahman, *Shivhey Ha-RaN* ("Praises of Rabbi Nahman"), first published in 1816. Here, Nahman declares that

> Sexual intercourse is difficult for the true Zaddik. It is not enough that he possesses no desire for it at all, but he actually experiences real pain from it, like the pain of an infant during circumcision. This very real pain is felt by the Zaddik during sexual intercourse and more so. For the infant has no cognition, therefore his pain is not so great, but the Zaddik who has cognition suffers greater pain than the infant.[44]

The key to understanding this passage is that during sexual intercourse and—symbolically—during circumcision, the male comes into contact with the female. This contact is extremely painful but absolutely necessary in order for the male to become complete. For the male only becomes whole by joining with the female during sexual intercourse and circumcision, a process that recalls the verse from Gen. 2:24. "Hence a man leaves his father and mother and clings to his wife, so that they become one flesh." As I will show, for Nahman the result of circumcision is a symbolic androgyne in which the female is contained within the male or, more precisely, within the exposed corona of the circumcised penis.[45]

Nahman is clearly ambivalent about both circumcision and sexual inter-course. Although these acts perfect the male by symbolically restoring him to an Edenic state of androgyny, they also involve a tremendous amount of pain and sacrifice. In his own writings, Nahman explicitly describes this pain as resulting from the encounter with the female which must be transformed.

> And know that by means of the holy *tiqqun berit,* he is saved from the face of the Other Side *[sitra ahra]*. By means of the blood of circumcision *[berit]*, the blood of menstruation—the desire for money—is rectified.[46] As it is written (Zechariah 9:11), "Also the blood of your covenant," by means of circumcision, "I have freed your prisoners from the pit." . . . For *berit* is the aspect of salt, which sweetens the sorrow of earning a living. As is brought in the Zohar (I, 241b): "Were it not for salt, the world *['alma]* could not bear bitterness." And this is the meaning of (Numbers 18:19), "The covenant *[berit]* of salt is eternal *['olam]*." And it is (Leviticus 2:13), "Do not leave out the salt of the covenant of your Lord." Specifically "your Lord" for by means of this your are bound to godliness and separated from idolatry. As it is written (Job 19:26): "From my flesh I behold God." For by means of the *tikkun ha-berit,* he causes the light of the Living King's face to shine on him.[47]

According to Nahman, the blood of circumcision functions like a sacrificial atonement for the blood of menstruation, which results from the separation of the female (Shekhinah) from the male.[48] Elsewhere, Nahman compares the circum-cised phallus to the scapegoat which, during the time of the Temple, was cast off a cliff on Yom Kippur in order to remove the sins of Israel. Symbolic verification of the people's atonement came when, at the same time the goat was killed, a crimson-colored strap *(lashon shel zehorit)* hanging in the Temple became white, according to the verse in Is. 1:18. "Though your sins are like scarlet, they will become as white as snow; though they are red like crimson, the will be like white wool."[49] As Nahman writes, "after the *tiqqun* [circumcision], it [the *berit* or "phallus"] brightens and purifies the firmament like the crimson-colored strap which whitens the sins of the 365 negative commandments, and brings whiteness to the 365 *gidim* [filled with blood]."[50]

In both passages, the male blood of circumcision positively transforms or "whitens" the sinful female blood of menstruation. This is the significance of the link between the *berit* and salt: just as salt absorbs blood from meat, so the circumcised phallus eliminates menstrual blood by symbolically taking it on. Thus, there is a kind of symbolic resonance between the menstruating woman and the circumcised male,[51] though one posesses the polluting blood of the Other Side *(sitra ahra)* while the other possesses the atoning blood of the sefirot.[52]

On one level, therefore, circumcision results in the symbolic feminization of the male, the opening of the circumcised phallus substituting for the vagina. Yet, as a result of circumcision, the female is reintegrated into the original androgyne: the menstrual blood is whitened and the corona of the phallus is exposed. This process also results in the revelation of God to the circumcised male. Thus, circumcision, while painful and bloody, is necessary in order to purify and complete both human and divine bodies and to expose an opening in the male (i.e, the female) where contact can be established between human and divine.

The uncircumcised male is wholly male, but he is not whole from the Bratslaver perspective. Only the circumcised male, that is, the reconstituted androgyne, reflects the ideal form of the male who has integrated the female. This act requires a sacrifice, he must literally offer part of himself and undergo a process of feminization. At the same time, the female is also redeemed, but only in so far as she has become purified by her contact with the male and absorbed into the primarily male androgyne and localized within a small space of this corpus—the corona of the phallus *('ateret berit),*[53] or, in the words of Luce Irigaray, the female is reduced to a *"place separated from its 'own' place,* a place deprived of a place of its own."[54]

Always present in the act of circumcision is the danger of castration, the risk that instead of sacrificing a part of the male (the foreskin) in order to reintegrate the female into a primarily male androgyne, the male will be emasculated and transformed into a neuter or, perhaps, an androgyne that is primarily female. Put differently, there is the risk that rather than the male transforming and absorbing the female, the female will transform and absorb the male.

The symbolic identity between the menstruating female and the circumcised male once again raises the issue of appropriating those aspects of the female that are viewed as powerful and identifying them with the male and masculinity. Although the menstruating woman is characterized as polluting and dangerous, she is also clearly very powerful. Like the nursing or pregnant woman this power challenges the hegemony of masculinity. By characterizing the blood of the circumcised male as a valorized form of menstrual blood, the power of menstruation is symbolically transferred to the male and masculinized, while at the same time, its polluting, negative features remain linked with the female. Thus, the Jewish male, who has already symbolically taken over the biologically female functions of nursing and pregnancy, also performs a kind of rectified menstruation, as well.

My kabbalistic analysis of circumcision in Bratslaver thought may be fruitfully compared and contrasted with Howard Eilberg-Schwartz's anthropological analysis of circumcision in ancient Israelite religion. Eilberg-Schwartz emphasizes that circumcision in the Hebrew Bible fosters symbolic and physical links between generations of men, while at the same time "it also establishes an opposition between men and women. Women cannot bear the symbol of the covenant."[55]

This observation illuminates a critical feature of Israelite circumcision, namely, that it occurs on the eighth day following birth. According to Leviticus, "When a woman at childbirth bears a male, she shall be unclean seven days; she shall be unclean as at the time of her menstrual infirmity. On the eighth day the flesh of his foreskin shall be circumcised. She shall remain in a state of blood purificition for thirty-three days" (Lev. 12:2–4).

Concerning these verses, Eilberg-Schwartz writes, "Circumcision is mentioned here because its timing is coordinated with the diminishing of the mother's impurity. We see that here as in other cultural contexts, circumcision is a postpartum ritual associated with the separation of a male child from the impurity of his mother."[56] Thus one of the chief symbolic valences of Israelite circumcision is the separation of the male (child) from the impure female (mother); indeed this occurs on the first day possible, once the week long period of impurity communicated to the male child by his mother has ended. The goal of separating male and female is even more graphically depicted in certain African traditions, where the "foreskin is compared to a woman's labia and its removal signifies the removal of a boy's feminine attributes."[57]

As I argued above, the primary significance of circumcision in Bratslaver thought is not the separation of male and female but their symbolic *integration*. Indeed, circumcision physically exposes the female aspect of the phallus— according to Nahman, the corona—rather than removing it, as in the African example. If in ancient Israelite and numerous other religious traditions circumcision is effectively a process of sexual differentiation and masculinization, in Bratslaver thought circumcision is a process of sexual integration and androgenization.

Notwithstanding this important contrast, there are several similarities between Bratslaver and ancient Israelite attitudes toward circumcision. In both cases, circumcision is symbolically linked to male sexuality, although in different ways. The Bible accomplishes this in Gen. 17 by connecting the rite of circumcision to the sexual fertility of Abraham and to his male descendants; Nahman explicitly links circumcision and sexual intercourse by describing both acts as excruciatingly painful for the true zaddik. Like Bratslaver writings, the Bible implies that the pure blood of the male child symbolically rectifies the impurity engendered by the blood of the mother, which Leviticus compares to the contaminating blood of the menstruant. As Eilberg- Schwartz writes, "When the child has recovered from the impurity of his mother's blood, he is brought into the covenant when his own male blood is spilled. His blood is clean, unifying, and symbolic of God's covenant. His mother's is filthy, disruptive, and contaminating." Finally, as Eilberg-Schwartz has noted, the Bible establishes a symbolic link between the blood of the circumcised child and the blood of animal sacrifice.[58] Not only is an animal sacrifice required following a new mother's period of purfication (Lev. 12:6–7), but animals, themselves, cannot be sacrificed before the eighth day after birth. "When an ox or a sheep or a goat is born, it shall stay seven days with its mother, and from the eighth day on it shall be acceptable as an offering by fire to the Lord" (Lev. 22:27; cf. Exod. 22:28–29).

## Conclusion

The greatest danger for the kabbalists was the separation of the female Shekhinah from the rest of the sefirot. Yet, the same kabbalists frequently criticized and on occasion even demonized the feminine. How can this apparent tension be explained? It may be that the kabbalists' emphasis on not "cutting the shoots" (separating the Shekhinah), represents a profound case of repressed desire. In other words, some, though certainly not all, kabbalists may have desired a lifestyle and a divinity without a female presence. But biblical and rabbinic sources made both an all-male social existence and an all-male theology impossible. Instead, such kabbalists could only hope to contain the female by, or even, within, the male. Socially, this was achieved by excluding women from kabbalistic circles and limiting their contact with male kabbalists to the domestic sphere; theosophically, the female was localized within the otherwise male divine corpus; physiologically, circumcision resulted in a parallel symbolic containment of the female within the exposed corona of the human phallus.

The profound homology between social, divine, and human bodies recalls the anthropologist Mary Douglas's observation that

> The body is a model which can stand for any bounded system. Its boundaries can represent any boundaries which are threatened and precarious. The body is a complex structure. The functions of its different parts and their relation afford a source of symbols for other complex structures. We cannot possibly interpret rituals concerning excreta, breast milk, saliva and the rest unless we are prepared to see in the body a symbol of society, and to see the powers and dangers credited to social structure reproduced in small on the human body.[59]

Whereas for Douglas the human body encodes social structures, in the kabbalistic worldview, both the human body and human society encode sefirotic structures. Human menstruation, lactation, and ejaculation symbolize processes within the body of God; likewise, the physical containment of women within Jewish society mirrors the theosophical status of the female. Phrased differently, instead of the body being "a symbol of society," both the Jewish body and Jewish society are symbols of the divine corpus. The ultimate sources for this kabbalistic viewpoint are biblical verses such as Gen. 1:26, where the human body is created in the "image and likeness" of the divine and Lev. 20:26, where God requires Israel to observe the Law since "You shall be holy to Me, for I the Lord am holy."

Of all the Hasidic masters, R. Nahman appears to have most inherited and perhaps even intensified the standard kabbalistic approach to gender. Indeed, Nahman was one of the greatest Hasidic interpreters of the Kabbalah; in particular, the theosophical material of the Zohar and Lurianic writings. From Nahman's statements, one sometimes gets the impression that he would have liked to avoid contact with women entirely.[60] Yet the very act that apparently most terrified Nahman—intercourse with a woman—was required of all Jewish men in order to be fruitful and multiply. The result of this act, like the result of circumcision, was the symbolic reconstitution of the original androgyne, but for Nahman and any other "true zaddik," it was also extremely painful. In this regard, Nahman was more radical than other Hasidic masters who explicitly rejected pleasure during sexual intercourse but did not valorize suffering pain during the act.[61] That Nahman took his halakhic responsibilities very seriously is evidenced by the fact that although he described sex as agony, he engendered at least seven children. Only by encountering and even embracing the female, therefore, could the zaddik achieve the ideal state of androgyny.

### Notes

1. As cited in Jerome Mintz, *Hasidic People: A Place in the New World,* (Cambridge, Mass., 1992,) p. 383, n. 1.

2. Arthur Green, *Tormented Master: The Life and Spiritual Quest of Rabbi Nahman of Bratslav,* (Woodstock, Vt. 1992), (rpt. 1979), has argued that although R. Nahman claimed to have eliminated his sexual desires in his youth, he actually continued to be plagued by his sexuality throughout his adulthood.

3. Nahman ben Simhah of Bratslav, *Liqqutey MoHaRan,* (Jerusalem, 1986), 4:8. Green mentions this tradition and the following one of R. Nathan, ibid., p. 155; on the image of the zaddik as mother, see also, Mendel Piekarz, *Hasidut Braslav,* (Jerusalem, 1972), pp. 77; 138ff. On the rabbinic reactions to the case of a man who actually developed breasts and nursed his own child, see BT Shabbat 53b, "The Rabbis taught: It once happened that a man's wife died and left a nursing son and the father didn't possess the means to pay for a wet-nurse. Then a miracle happened to him and he developed breasts like the two breasts of a woman, and he nursed his son. Rav Joseph said: Come and see how great is this man that such a miracle was wrought for him! Said Abaye: On the contrary, how inferior is this man, that natural order was changed for him."

4. Nathan of Nemirov, *Yemey MaHaRNaT,* (Beney Beraq, 1956), p. 12.

5. *Shir Ha-Shirim Rabbah,* trans. Maurice Simon, *Midrash Rabbah* (London and New York, 1983), p. 198.

6. See Thomas of Celano, *St. Francis of Assisi: First and Second Life of St. Francis with Selections from The Treatise on the Miracles of Blessed Francis* (Chicago, 1963), p. 248.

7. *The Letters of St. Bernard of Clairvaux,* trans. Bruno Scott James (London, 1953), pp. 3, 7, as cited by Caroline Walker Bynum, "And Woman His Humanity," in eds. Caroline Walker Bynum, Steven Harrell, and Paula Richman *Gender and Religion: On the Complexity of Symbols,* (Boston, 1986), p. 264; see also, Bynum's discussion of this and other examples in *Jesus as Mother: Studies in the Spirituality of the High Middle Ages* (Berkelely 1982), pp. 113ff.

8. As cited in Valerie Hoffman, "Eating and Fasting for God in the Sufi Tradition," *Journal of the American Academy of Religion,* (1995), 481, with discussion.

9. Najm al Din al Razi, *Mirsad al-'ibad min al-mabda' ila al-ma'ad* [The Path of God's Bondsmen from Origin to Return] trans. Hamid Algar (New York, 1982), as quoted in Margaret Malamud, "Gender and Spiritual Self-Fashioning: The Master-Disciple Relationship in Classdical Sufism," *Journal of the American Academy of Religion,* (1996), 223–224. Malamud also notes that Al Razi was commonly known as *Daya* or "wetnurse."

10. While some of my conclusions concerning Bratslaver conceptions of gender may be applicable to Christian and Moslem traditions as well, such discussion is beyond the scope of the present work.

11. As we will see, this theosophical model provides a critical insight into Bratslaver ideology, namely, that gender categories are remarkably fluid and are not limited to a strictly dichotomous relationship between male and female.

12. *Liqqutey MoHaRan* 29:3. Elsewhere in kabbalistic sources, for example, Moshe Cordovero's *Pardes Rimonim* 23:10, the Shekhinah is referred to as Jerusalem, "thus when the Shekhinah is separated from the other sefirot it is as if Jerusalem were engulfed in bloodshed. The expression *'ir ha-damim* or "city of blood" also involves a linguistic pun, since the word *'ir* recalls the word *'er* that means "awake," rendering the alternate reading of awakening or arousing blood, rather than city of blood.

13. See Isaiah Tishby, *The Wisdom of the Zohar,* trans. David Goldstein, (Oxford, 1989), pp. 373–376, for a list of the zoharic passages that describe the sins which separate the Shekhinah.

14. For a different view, see Moshe Idel, "Sexual Metaphor and Praxis in the Kabbalah," in *The Jewish Family: Metaphor and Memory,* ed. David Kraemer, (Oxford, 1989), p. 211, "The return to the primal androgyne state of humans . . . or the endeavor to transcend the feminine plight by mystic transformations of the

female into a 'male,' . . . is alien to the talmudic and theosophical kabbalistic Weltanschauung."

15. *Liqqutey MoHaRan* 29:3. See also, *Liqqutey MoHaRan* 21:7.

16. As Carol Walker Bynum has noted in *Jesus as Mother Studies in the Spirituality of the High Middle Ages* (Berkeley, 1982), pp. 132–133, according to medieval physiological theory breast milk is processed blood. Thus, she writes, "What writers in the high Middle Ages wished to say about Christ the savior who feeds the individual soul with his own blood was precisely and concisely said in the image of the nursing mother whose milk *is* her blood, offered to the child."

17. *Liqqutey MoHaRan* 29:3.

18. Ibid. Here the similar Hebrew words for "your garments" and "in your blood vessels" are being linked.

19. On the *tiqqun ha-kelali* and its possible relationship with Sabbatianism, see Yehuda Liebes, "R. Nahman of Bratslav's *Ha-Tiqqun Ha-Kelali* and His Attitude Towards Sabbatianism," in *Zion* XLV, 1980, pp. 201–245 (Hebrew).

20. On the messianic background of this lesson and the significance of messianism in Bratslaver thought in general, see Arthur Green, *Tormented Master,* pp. 182–220, esp. 210ff. On messianism and Bratslav Hasidism, cf. also, Liebes, op. cit., and Joseph Weiss, *Studies in Bratslav Hasidism,* pp. 189–214 (Hebrew).

21. *Liqqutey MoHaRan* 29:4.

22. On this interpretation, see David Biale, "The God with Breasts: El Shaddai in the Bible," *History of Religions* 20, (1982), 240–256. On the motherhood of God in the Bible, see Mayer Gruber, *The Motherhood of God and Other Studies* (Atlanta, 1992), pp. 3–15.

23. Elliot Wolfson, "Crossing Gender Boundaries in Kabbalistic Ritual and Myth," in *Circle in the Square: Studies in the Use of Gender in Kabbalistic Symbolism* (Albany, 1995), p. 102. Wolfson adds that "The maturation of the *Shekhinah* from a woman without breasts to one with full-grown breasts in effect symbolizes her gender transformation from a female to a male. Thus the breasts are described in the obvious phallic image of a tower from which all beings are sustained." See also, p. 218 n. 125. Nahman's text appears to draw on Lurianic sources such as the one quoted by Wolfson in this note, MS New York, JTS, Mic. 2155, fol. 69a, which reads, "After birth [Binah] nursed him in the secret of the milk until he grew up and was weaned (cf. Gen. 21:8) and this is [the significance of] *'el 'elyon gomel* [the supernal God bestows goodness] from the expression *wa-yigmol sheqedim* [it bore almonds] (Num. 17:23). During the time of the nursing she is called El Shaddai from the expression of *shadayim*." (Wolfson's translation). Interestingly, this set of associations also underlies Rashi's interpretation of Ya'akov's blessing of Joseph in Gen. 49:25 "and Shaddai will bless you . . . you will have the blessings of *shadaim* (the breasts) and *rachem* (the womb)." Rashi explains *"shadaim varachem"* as the blessings of the father and the mother based on the connection between *shadaim* and the semen that shoots *(shaday)* out of the phallus.

24. A similar observation is made by Wolfson, "Crossing Gender Boundaries in Kabbalistic Ritual and Myth," pp. 217–218 n. 121, concerning kabbalistic literature, "The masculine valorization of nursing that one finds in kabbalistic literature should be contrasted with the application of the maternal imagery of breast-feeding to Jesus and the prelates that one finds in twelfth-century Cistercian texts." On the medieval Christian sources for this image, see Bynum, *Jesus as Mother*, pp. 110–169; and idem., "And Woman His Humanity," in *Gender and Religion: On the Complexity of Symbols*. For example, Guerric of Igny writes that "The Bridegroom [Christ] . . . has breasts, lest he should be lacking any one of all the duties and titles of loving kindness. He is a father in virtue of natural creation . . . and also in virtue of the authority with which he instructs. He is a mother, too, in the mildness of his affection, and a nurse." (as cited in "And Woman His Humanity," p. 264).

25. *Liqqutey MoHaRan* 7:3. Green, *Tormented Master*, p. 155, mentions this passage as a "daring" example of the "dependency and passivity on the part of the disciples," and "the intimacy of that moment between master and disciple." He does not explore the complex gender implications of this and the other passages he cites in this section.

26. On this issue see Wolfson, *Circle in the Square*, pp. 150–151 n. 62.

27. As Wolfson, *Circle in the Square*, p. 109 has argued concerning the Kabbalah, "The point I am making, however, involves the gender signification of this biological fact. When the the physiological issue is viewed from the standpoint of gender it becomes clear that the lactation of the breasts functionally transforms the female into a male. . . . It must be concluded, therefore, that the breast that gives milk is functionally equivalent to a penis that ejaculates."

28. For a similar symbology but radically different social practices, see Gilbert Herdt's work on the Papua New Guinea tribe known as the Sambia, *Guardians of the Flute: Idioms of Masculinity* (New York, 1987).

29. See the third section, "Hokhmah ve-Binah," of the nineteenth century Bratslaver Abraham Hazan's work *Sefer Kokhvey 'Or*, (Jerusalem, 1987) (rpt. of a work originally published in the 1930s by one of Hazan's Bratslaver successors, Samuel Horowitz). The connection between Nahman and Binah is established by a series of numerological equivalences between various versions of Nahman's name (Nahman ben Simhah and Nahman ben Fegeh, including the names of his father and mother, respectively) and a mind-numbing host of Hebrew terms and phrases related to the sefirah Binah. Concerning this work, Green, *Tormented Master*, p. 6, has written, "While such works as *Kokhvey 'Or* ("*Stars of Light*") and *Sippurim Nifla'im* ("*Wondrous Tales*"), first published by Horowitz in the thirties, must be treated with certain reserve, they do contain a surprising measure of old and authentic source material." See also p. 155, where Green notes the identification of R. Nahman with Binah. On this link, see also, Mendel Piekarz, *Hasidut Bratslav*, (Jerusalem, 1972), pp. 77, 138ff. (Hebrew).

30. See Yehuda Liebes, "Myth vs. Symbol in the Zohar and in Lurianic Kabbalah," in *Essential Papers on Kabbalah,* ed. Lawrence Fine (New York, 1995), pp. 214ff.

31. For an example of the identification of David with Malkhut in Nahman's own writings, see *Liqqutey MoHaRan* 21:7.

32. On the figure of Joseph in Bratslaver sources, see Piekarz, *Hasidut Braslav,* p. 125.

33. Green, *Tormented Master,* pp. 188ff., explores this possibility.

34. *Sefer Kokhvey 'Or,* section 3:43, see also 3:25.

35. *Zohar* I:163a, as cited by E. Wolfson in "Woman—The Feminine as Other in Theosophic Kabbalah: Some Philosophical Observations on the Divine Androgyne," in *The Other in Jewish Thought and History: Constructions of Jewish Culture and Identity,* eds. Laurence Silberstein and Robert Cohn, (New York, 1994), p. 188. Wolfson comments that "the third gradation, *Binah,* is identified as the Mother, or the female consort to *Hokhmah,* the Father; yet that very gradation is referred to on any number of occasions as the king *(melekh),* for when she overflows and produces the lower gradations she assumes the posture of a male."

36. *Sha'ar Ma'amere Rashbi* 7b. As cited in Wolfson, "Crossing Gender Boundaries," *Circle in the Square,* p. 105. Commenting on this passage, Wolfson writes, p. 106,

> Through this gender transformation the *Shekhinah* emulates the attribute of *Binah,* which likewise is characterized as a female that becomes male. In the case of *Binah* this transformation occurs as a result of the production of the six emanations from *Hesed* to *Yesod* that collectively represent the male divine anthropos; hence the name *Binah* is decomposes into the form *ben yah,* for the Mother is named *Binah* on account of the male form that she produces, causing herself to be transmuted into the masculine. More specifically, it is on account of the last of those six emanations, *Yesod,* that *Binah* receives its phallic character.

37. On the image of the phallic mother, see Erich Neumann, *The Great Mother: An Analysis of an Archetype,* (Princeton, 1963), pp. 13, 170, 308–10.

38. *Liqqutey MoHaRan* 21:8.

39. Ibid.

40. On the image of the Shekhinah "giving birth" to the *mohin,* see *Liqqutey MoHaRan* 21:7.

41. For example, in Philo, *Quaestiones et Solutiones in Genesin* 3:49; G. Delling, "The 'One Who Sees God' in Philo," in *Nourished with Peace: Studies in Hellenistic Judaism in Memory of Samuel Sandmel,* eds. F. Greenspahn, E. Hilgert, and B. Mack, Chico, Calif., 1984, pp. 27–49.

42. E. Wolfson, "Circumcision, Vision of God, and Textual Interpretation: From Midrashic Trope to Mystical Symbol," in *Circle in the Square,* pp. 29–48, has thoroughly explicated the kabbalistic texts that serve as the sources for Nahman's identification of the Shekhinah with the corona of the divine phallus and the symbolic link between circumcision and revelation. See, esp. p. 149 n. 55, for a list of kabbalistic passages that employ *'atarah* ("crown") as a technical term for the Shekhinah. Wolfson, "Woman—The Feminine as Other in Theosophic Kabbalah," pp. 186, writes, "According to some kabbalists, the corona of the penis corresponds to the Diadem *('Atarah),* i.e. the *Shekhinah* or feminine Presence. The feminine aspect of God, therefore, becomes localized as part of the phallus itself. . . . The act of uncovering the corona is mystically transformed into an occasion for the revelation of the divine Diadem; indeed, the ritual of circumcision is understood in kabbalistic literature as a theophanic moment."

43. Tishby, *Wisdom of the Zohar,* p. 289. Wolfson, *Circle in the Square,* p. 196, n. 4, however, has noted that Tishby "does not appreciate the full extent of the androcentric representation of the female in kabbalistic symbolism," since Tishby also writes of the "harmonious partnership of male and female."

44. Nathan of Nemirov, *Sefer Shivhey Ha-RaN* 17. For a different translation and discussion of this passage, see Green, *Tormented Master,* p. 39. On Nahman's struggle with sexuality, also see David Biale, *Eros and the Jews: From Biblical Israel to Contemporary America* (New York, 1992), pp. 135–136.

45. Wolfson, "Woman—The Feminine as Other in Theosophic Kabbalah," p. 187, writes concerning kabbalistic sources, "within the kabbalistic tradition there is a conception of the feminine that is an integral part of, rather than distinct from, the masculine. To borrow the formulation of Mircea Eliade, it may be said that circumcision from the kabbalistic perspective is a ritual of symbolic androgenization." And see, Mircea Eliade, *The Two and the One* (Chicago, 1965, pp. 111–114).

46. Nathan of Nemirov, *HayyeyMoHaRan* 470 (first published, Lemberg, 1874), writes that according to R. Nahman, in his day, "the desire for money and influence is greater than sexual desire." In *Liqqutey MoHaRan* 29:5, Nahman emphasizes that earning a proper living is dependent on the *tiqqun ha-kelali* that is the *tiqqun ha-berit:*

> And on this *[tiqqun ha-berit]* depends earning a living without struggle, which is the aspect of (Exodus 16:4): "bread from heaven." This is by means of the General Remedy *[tiqqun ha-kelali]* which is the *tiqqun ha-berit,* which corresponds to (Proverbs 30:19) "the way of the eagle is in heaven." This is the meaning of (Numbers 11:7), "The manna was like the seed of coriander *[gad]*": "seed of *gad,*" this is the white drop [semen, based on *gad/ gid*], the aspect of "flowing from Lebanon" which is the aspect of *tiqqun*

*ha-berit,* upon which livelihood without struggle, the aspect of manna, the "bread from heaven," depends.

47. *Liqqutey MoHaRan* 23:2.

48. When Nahman undertook his self-imposed exile *(oprikhtn golus)* to Navritch, he declared, "My hands are dirtied with blood and female issue in order to purify a woman for her husband." From *Hayyey MoHaRan* 6:4–7, based on BT Berakhot 4a. As Green has noted in his discussion, *Tormented Master,* pp. 230–231, the "woman" in the sentence is the Shekhinah, who must be reunited with the other sefirot by means of Nahman's sacrifice, here depicted as his encounter with unclean female blood and issue.

49. See BT Yoma 66a-67a.

50. Ibid., 29:4.

51. During the Middle Ages, it was sometimes claimed that Jewish men menstruated, although I do not know whether their circumcision was ever given as a reason.

52. In terms of the sefirot, the color white signifies the male sefirah Hesed (Mercy), while red signifies the female sefirah Gevurah (Judgment). Thus, circumcision may be viewed as the transformation of divine judgment by divine mercy. Based on the talmudic tradition (BT Niddah 19a) that there are five types of impure blood, Isaac Luria argued that there were ten types of blood, five pure and five unpure. The five pure types were associated with the five *hasadim* found in the sefirah Da'at, while the five impure types were associated with the five *gevurot* in Da'at.

53. This is precisely the point that Elliot Wolfson has made concerning the kabbalistic material. In this case, as with much of the other material covered in this chapter, R. Nahman has taken over and to a certain degree, perhaps, even intensified the kabbalistic model of androgyny that Wolfson has identified and discussed in his work.

54. Luce Irigaray, "Sexual Difference," in *The Irigaray Reader,* Margaret Whitford, ed. (Cambridge, Mass.), 1991, p. 169.

55. Howard Eilberg-Schwartz, *The Savage in Judaism: An Anthropology of Israelite Religion and Ancient Judaism* (Bloomington, 1990), p. 171.

56. Ibid., p. 174.

57. Ibid., p. 173.

58. Ibid., pp. 174–175. See, also, p. 180.

59. Mary Douglas, *Purity and Danger* (London, 1966), p. 116.

60. Unfortunately, we know little about Nahman's relationships with the various women in his life, mother, wives, and daughters. Indeed, Nahman's silence, particularly concerning the death of his first wife and mother of his (at least seven) children, Sosia, may be telling in itself, particularly when this is compared

with his powerful reaction to the death of his infant son. Although Nahman married again almost immediately, when he was no longer required to by Halakhah, Arthur Green, *Tormented Master,* pp. 232–233, offers convincing evidence that this was due to practical reasons (e.g., Nahman may have been aware of his illness and needed a nurse). Moreover, he does not appear to have consummated the marriage. We do know that Nahman's mother was a powerful figure in her own right and must have made a strong impression on Nahman, particularly before he left home as a young teenager following his marriage. Finally, there is an episode concerning one of Nahman's daughters, Sarah, whom Nahman attended during the final period of a pregnancy, thereby exhibiting some paternal concern, unless we assume that he was primarily concerned with the well-being of a potential male grandchild. Adding to this dilemma is the fact that when Sarah became ill after delivering her son, Nahman quickly departed from her town, perhaps out of fear that he was negatively influencing the situation. On these events, see Green, *Tormented Master,* 227–228.

61. On this contrast, see David Biale, *Eros and the Jews,* pp. 136–137.

# 6

## Saying Nihilism
### *A Review of Marc-Alain Ouaknin's* Burnt Book

### *Martin Kavka*

With the recent translation of Marc-Alain Ouaknin's *Burnt Book: Reading the Talmud,*[1] once again the argument appears that Judaism has always been inseparable from the type of hermeneutics embodied by what Edith Wyschogrod has termed *differential postmodernism,* a term that primarily refers to the writings of Emmanuel Levinas, Maurice Blanchot, and Jacques Derrida.[2] Ouaknin's language in Book Two will be overly familiar to readers of these authors. Here, he analyzes two Talmud passages as "openings" upon the themes of the self-effacing nature of the book and the erotic appeal of the transcendent—the former is a central theme in the entire Derridean corpus,[3] and the latter is central in the work of the early Levinas.[4] By choosing a narrow focus—only these two Talmud passages, B. Shabbat 115a–116a and B. Yoma 54a, and no others—Ouaknin's argument achieves a great degree of elegance that minimizes the potentially jarring effect of constantly oscillating between the differing rhetorics of the fourth and the twentieth centuries. I am not trained as a Talmudist, but in my mind there is no question that Ouaknin has successfully argued for a certain family resemblance between Talmud and postmodern philosophy, two modes of thinking that are at first glance wildly disparate. The fact that this is a sustained argument from *within* Talmudic texts makes the achievement all the more impressive. Book Three of Ouaknin's text, on the theory of the book in R. Nahman, serves as a modern model of the lived performance of the hermeneutic approach detailed in Book Two. This goes further in proving Ouaknin's thesis, since the analysis of R. Nahman not only amplifies the previous arguments about the self-effacement of writing in the light of the theory of *shevirat ha-kelim* (the breaking of the vessels) in Lurianic Kabbalah, but can also turn the reader trained in postmodern texts back to Derrida's groundbreaking essays on performative utterances.[5]

This is not to say that Ouaknin's text is without problems, and this chapter will mention three problems briefly before turning to the fourth. First, Ouaknin accuses historians of killing their texts (BB, p. 58): "a thing can be objectively knowable . . . only when it is so dead that it is only of purely historical interest." When this is applied to the Talmud, the historian is by extension accused of being the cause of revelation's inaccessibility to the culture of today. Yet Ouaknin's strident ahistoricism, in which ideas exist in a vacuum, allows bizarre shadings of thought to occur. Ouaknin establishes a strong Athens-versus-Jerusalem tone throughout, especially where the thought of Martin Heidegger is concerned (e.g.,

BB, pp. 96n. 22, 164, and 292–294). Nevertheless, he also interprets the dialogic theory of Heidegger's student Hans-Georg Gadamer to be in the spirit of Talmudic "open-ended discussion," *makhloket,* and indeed goes so far as to link the project of *Being and Time* itself to the questioning spirit of Talmud (BB, pp. 88–89, cf. pp. 97nn. 38, 39, 41). Second, most of Ouaknin's citations from Blanchot and Levinas are given as prooftexts for his arguments, yet he omits any mention of the philosophical conditions for the position of these arguments within the philosophical tradition. In other words, it is one thing to say that Levinas states that the language of the question is a fissure in the Greek rhetoric of absolute knowledge (BB, pp. 160f.); it is another to explain how certain readings of Heidegger, Hegel, and Aristotle lead to this assertion; it is yet another to argue that Levinas's reading constitutes a *prima facie* denial of Greek thought; it is still another to argue that Levinas's interpretation of Greek thought is correct in the first place. Ouaknin only remains at the first of these four levels; to be sure, *The Burnt Book* is about Talmud and Breslav Hasidism, not about twentieth-century phenomenology. Nevertheless, as I shall demonstrate, when such phenomenological questions are broached, the need to reshape Ouaknin's thesis becomes particularly urgent. Third, I wonder whether the rhetoric of openness, questioning, and can really be applied pari passu from philosophy to Judaism. Ouaknin argues for Judaism as a radical "antidogmatism" (BB, p. 159) and leads the reader to believe that every halakhic ruling is caught up in a web of dialogical *makhloket.* To properly argue against this is outside the bounds of this chapter (the following readings of Levinas and R. Nahman may be seen as a propædeutic to such an argument), but one may briefly state the argument as follows: if there are no dogmas in Judaism and if halakkic conclusions do not definitively exist, then there can be no possible way for Jews to keep the covenant.[6]

Fourth, and most importantly, there is a *philosophical risk* embedded deep within *The Burnt Book,* insofar as its general ahistorical approach to textuality risks a certain nihilistic attitude toward the world, and other people therein. Ouaknin's thesis throughout is that the Talmud is an "atopian text" (BB p. 151) that embodies "the refusal of the place without hope of a place." As such, Talmud represents an approach to interpretation that allows the individual to recuperate a mode of existence that escapes and transcends the usual fate of being thematized into a totality that would refuse the irruption of the exterior, and close off the possibility of revelation. This beyond being is stratum what Levinas calls "saying"; the thematized totality he calls "said."[7] For Ouaknin, to be a Jew—"to enter the Book"—is "to hear Speech as it is being revealed" (BB, p. 3) and to call meaning into question so that (BB, p. 220) "the unutterable is revealed in such a way that its manifestation is nonmanifestation"; after all, haggadah is "Saying par excellence" (BB, p. 37). Meaning in Judaism is for Ouaknin always hidden, never fully at-hand or graspable. Thus, what the Jew does is continually seek and offer interpretive *Hidushim* (innovations) that refuse the fossilization of tradition while simultaneously constituting it. In the discussion of R. Nahman in Book Three, Ouaknin argues that the manifestation of the divine as nonmanifestation necessitates that the world never be comprehended as the knowledge of a definite present now. Thus, *Hidush* is only possible in a world in which the "repair" of *tiqqun* is not possible for humans to accomplish (BB, pp. 295, 302). This assertion—"*shevirah* and not *tiqqun*" (BB, p. 295)—has a myriad of consequences. If this is truly and phenomenologically the case, what then is the proper relation between the Jew and the world? If *tiqqun* is impossible for humans, and therefore can only be performed by God, then there can be *no sufficient reason whatsoever* for Jews to involve themselves in the institutions of the thematized world. According to this allegedly postmodern argument, it is one's interior textual desire for messianic arrival that should govern existence, and not one's acts in the world. But are not persons more worthy of our desire than texts, or at least equally worthy? Is not the erotic precedence of persons the very lesson of the fourth section of Levinas's *Totality and Infinity*?[8] But as long as Jews argue that God only reveals himself in the Book, and not also in the created world or also in created persons, Jews must find the world unnecessary and useless for the task of messianic anticipation. They must see the world as *nihil*, worthless, not even as a transcendent No-thing.

Granted, Ouaknin offers a model of nonmastering caressing conduct as a bridge between the desire of the heart and action in the world in his final footnote (BB, pp. 306–307), a summation of R. Nahman's commentary on the texts concerning the woman suspected of adultery (Num. 5:11–31 and B. Sotah 17a). Ouaknin argues that R. Nahman's conclusion—there is no citation given—is "completely positive" insofar as it "reintroduces the necessity of suspicion as the condition of desire and of relationships." Even if one were to put aside the gender hierarchy of this suspicion, and even if one were to question whether the husband's suspicion might be indeed a totalizing view of his wife, the fact still is that in R. Nahman's discussion of the matter the theme of woman is superseded by the theme of the book: the conclusion of the argument is that "by the destruction of holy books good is produced." Insofar as lived conduct is seen here only as instrumental to the theory of the book, this can only lead to further questioning about the place of the world in Ouaknin's brand of postmodern Judaism.

The problems of Ouaknin's argument, and its claim to be philosophically postmodern, call for a reänalysis of the Levinasian distinction between saying and said, specifically the place of the said in thought after the move from the self-sufficiency of the said to the irruption of saying. In addition, it is necessary to examine more closely Ouaknin's charge that there is no place for *tiqqun* in the writings of R. Nahman. Taking a similarly narrow focus as that of Ouaknin, this chapter will argue from the text of *Liqqutei MoHaRaN* 1:11[9] that without a positive theory of *tiqqun* in Breslav Hasidism, R. Nahman's Luria-influenced cosmology and specifically the relation between YHVH and Metatron cannot possibly make any sense whatsoever to the reader of *Liqqutim*. Indeed, *pace* Ouaknin, this Breslav text demonstrates that the state of the world as *shevirah* means that there can *never* be an escape from *our* project of repentance or *tiqqun*. To transpose this into the language of the later Levinas, it is certainly true that the insufficiency of the said calls for a move to the realm of unutterable saying. However, this is only half of the story, since saying can only be thought within the context of a new and necessarily inadequate totality/said. The realm of being and its beyond is therefore marked by ambiguity through and through.

### Emmanuel Levinas and the Ambiguity of Being

In the closing section of Levinas's 1970 essay "No Identity," there is a brief elucidation of his philosophy as a rejection of traditional notions of humanism.[10] Opposed to a thinking that would reduce all singular subjects to a mathematical equivalency, the Levinasian discourse posits a subject for whom inward identification is not possible in the face of the other. This "defense of man understood as a defense of the man other than me"[11] arises out of an excessive responsibility to the other—"I am responsible even for their responsibility"[12]—in which the very definition of the ego is taken hostage by the other who calls the ego and its freedom into question. As a result, one cannot say that the I has any determinable meaning that can be assigned by social or political theories; to determine "ego" in such a manner would exclude the importance of the very contingency of interpersonal responsibility. I am not a general instantiation of a universal, exchangeable among others; as a responsible self, I am singular and always exist within the context of singular relationships. The transcendent and undefinable nature of vulnerable subjectivity is categorically described by Levinas in "No Identity" and in *Otherwise than Being* as "the saying that precedes the said." The firm distinction between the singular and the general self, and Levinas's obvious and infectious preference for the ethical description of the singular self vulnerable to the other, tempts the reader of "No Identity" to make the following analogy: said is morally bad, and saying is morally good. That is, until one reads the following footnote:

> For unless we renounce society and in the unlimited responsibility for the others engulf every possibility for responding *in fact,* one can avoid neither the said, letters, belles lettres, the comprehension of being, nor philosophy. One cannot do without them if one means to manifest to thought, even if one thus deforms it, what is beyond being itself. This manifestation takes place at the price of a betrayal, but it is necessary for justice, which resigns itself to tradition, continuity and institutions, despite their very infidelity. To not care about them is to play with nihilism.[13]

In spite of the ethical necessity of moving away from the realm of the said to the possibility of saying, it is apparent that Levinas thinks that to stay within the realm of saying on a permanent basis is to forego the very possibility of justice that was the intended telos of assuming one's responsibility to others in the first place. Similarly, the reader is forced to adjust the analogy "Totality bad! Infinity good!" that she may be tempted to make when working through *Totality and Infinity* when eros and parenthood are introduced in section 4 of the text as mediating terms between the two "realms." But why does Levinas give such a place of importance to the realms of totality and said? In other words, why does Levinas care about the world? In order to answer this, it is necessary to turn to the argument of *Otherwise than Being*, and to examine in greater detail the relationship between saying and said.

*Otherwise than Being* deals with the same two questions as *Totality and Infinity*. First, how is it possible, through thinking, to combat the thinking that reduces the individual (other than every other individual) to the general? Second, how is it possible to think transcendence as completely beyond the realm of being? In fact, these are two facets of the same question, since for Levinas it is the very refusal to think transcendence that leads to the heterophagy "in which being immediately includes the statement of being's *other*."[14] Yet it is only through a transcendental phenomenology that the transcendent saying can appear. Because of the phenomenological method involved—the technical analysis, in the spirit of Edmund Husserl (the father of the twentieth-century phenomenological movement), of such structures as face, approach, and caress, which reveals the inability of language to exhaust these phenomena—the conclusions of transcendence cannot be reached without those very linguistic tools that lead to them. Conversely stated, since transcendence is the condition of these thematized descriptions that come under the category of "said," we must conclude that the saying cannot exist without the apophantic said. Levinas asserts this in the introduction to *Otherwise than Being* as follows (OB, p. 6): "In language qua said everything is conveyed before us, be it at the price of a betrayal. Language is ancillary and thus indispensable." Even if language (when taken as absolute) potentially denies the possibility of a radically individuated ethics, that very ethics needs language in order to take place. No dichotomy between ethics and ontology can hold.[15]

This ambiguity of being is necessary if the ethics of radical responsibility to the other is to show itself. Without a situation in which the said acts as a vessel for saying, saying could never be *heard* and therefore persons could never be ethical. But simply because the saying can only be heard through the said does not mean that the ethical project is doomed; rather (OB, p. 44), "the saying is both an affirmation and a retraction of the said."[16] In the linguistic relationship with the neighbor, the situation of my speaking to my neighbor in propositions in no way lessens the insight that my neighbor's freedom is always beyond the pale of my own freedom. The other, totally independent of my own thinking, cannot be included in any thinking of the "essence of man," precisely because the possibilities of his or her own freedom are unknowable to me. The very possibility of expression on the part of the other necessitates that I realize that there exists something beyond the limits of the power of my consciousness to conceptualize. In the Levinasian phenomenology of the other person, every other is encountered as always already saying "no to me by his very expression,"[17] not in any inimical sense, but rather insofar as it always presents a *Jemeinigkeit*[18] that is not my own mineness. In the presentation of the other's mineness, the exercise of my power over it is forbidden, because ultimate truth includes the fact that the other is not part of my mineness, my intentional realm, my totality.

Thus only through *and within* the negative experience of another's interior totality is my own experience of infinity possible. Once I realize this, this does not mean that the discursive relationship between the I and the other suddenly becomes false or inadequate. It is true that the thematization of my action as regards the other person is overflowed by the comportment of responsibility. Nevertheless, the thematization of the relationship still takes place. And this *must* be the case if one is to be ethical with more than one person. Indeed, to comprehend phenomenologically the necessity of Levinas's ethics of radical responsibility, and then to idealize one other, whether corporeal or textual, above all others is to stop the phenomenological inquiry halfway.

In the 1954 essay "The Ego and Totality," Levinas contrasts the loving relationship with the social relation.[19] The intimacy of the loving dual relationship makes it possible for the couple "to keep a hand on all the ins and outs of the society."[20] In the case of the dual, the mastery of the ego and the reässertion of the primacy of its own freedom are assured precisely because love does not know to draw a boundary between the just and the unjust. Love conquers all. Since "justice and injustice presuppose a violence exercised on a freedom, a real wound,"[21] and because for Levinas love infringes upon the freedom of the individual (the face of the beloved says yes, and gives up its own *Jemeinigkeit* for the sake of its own contentment), justice is impossible in any relationship between two people. To argue in response that love overflows thematization and is thus a form of saying is incorrect. Love is a form of thematization because nothing escapes it; it never encounters interdiction. In love (so tradition tells us), I know the other completely, and am also fully present to the beloved. As a result, there is no possibility within the love relationship for ever hearing a command, since the beloved gives up his or her own right for self-expression.

Furthermore, the love relationship ignores the fact that there are more than two people in the world. Even though the beloved may absolve me of any guilt by denying me interdiction, for Levinas there is no way that I can be assured that the beloved is the only one whom I have injured through my fault. In the following passage, Levinas is subtly referring to a Christian view of atonement (but not *the* view) in which the relationship with God is foremost and sins are God's alone to forgive. Nevertheless, it is equally applicable to social dynamics. Neither the satisfaction derived from the love relationship, nor the fact that love may have its own dimension of responsibility, recuse me from my universal ethical responsibilities. For the third exists, whether male or female, Jew or Gentile; this is a fact. There is no avoiding another experience of interdiction, even if it is mediated by the beloved.

> A third man essentially disturbs this intimacy: the wrong I did to you I can recognize to have proceeded entirely from my intentions; but this recognition is then found to be objectively falsified by reason of your relations with *him,* which remain hidden from me, since I am in my turn excluded from the unique privilege of your intimacy. If I recognize the wrong I did you, I can, even by my act of repentance, injure the third person.[22]

Thus, to hear saying breaking through the said is not to fall captive to the seductive gaze of the beloved. A Levinasian ethic (or model of reading or of religious experience) cannot remain within the intimate realm of nonthematization and nonmanifestation, in which meaning, *however fissured by the breaking of the vessels it may be,* makes itself fully present to me without any trace of thematization. To revel in a supposed purity of saying is to exclude the third and to repeat the gestures of ontological mastery on another level; such an ecstatic mysticism[23] collapses into the same ontology it tries to avoid. Ironically enough, the strangulating ontology of the said can only be broken by reviewing[24] it in such a way that highlights the veiled or ghostly nature of saying within the said. The existence of the third person marks the necessary *return* from saying to said, but to a said that is not the same as the oracular said against which Levinas is arguing in the opening of *Otherwise than Being* (OB, p. 5). This new said is (OB, p. 158) "the thematization of the same on the basis of the relationship with the other, starting with proximity and the immediacy of saying." Saying and said simultaneously, leading to the quest for justice.

To sum up the four steps of this argument: first, in the relationship with the other, I realize that the other has relations with others besides myself, and thus I indirectly have relations with these third parties who "obsess" me. My state of "hostage"[25] to the other who "assigns me before I designate him" (OB, p. 87) should thus ideally be not only to the other, but also to all his or her others, and their others, and their others ad infinitum. Second, this cannot be possible, since responsibility is limited only to those people with whom I come in contact. Even though a woman whom I briefly see on CNN publicly mourning her lost son and husband for the benefit of American audiences is indirectly my other, I cannot form a relationship with her, especially in this age of academic budgetary restraint (for philosophers above all). The third party "does not come empirically to trouble proximity [saying]" (OB, p. 160) and as a result "is of itself the limit of responsibility" (OB, p. 157) and the limit of intimacy. But I must do something, for I am obsessed. Third, the third is thus the consciousness of the necessity of justice. Only justice can pay heed to the model of an open society that is engendered by the phenomenological fact that, since the world consists of more than two people, everyone is a third party to an other (OB, p. 158): "the other is from the first the brother of all the other men." Fourth, the calculative thinking of universal justice is a necessary result of the radical noncalculative experience of individuality before the other.[26] (Thus, the authentic Levinasian self is not only "hostage" to the other, but also to the very kind of calculus that Heidegger argued against from "Letter on Humanism" onward.) Justice is the entry of the saying into the institutions of the said, into (OB, p. 157) "comparison, coexistence, contemporaneousness, assembling, order, thematization, the visibility of faces, and thus intentionality and the intellect." All these words that at first glance seem to betray the very essentialist type of thinking that marks the strangling hold of the said on the saying. Yet in the Levinasian phenomenology of the said, the saying of the other's precedence to me is revealed to be the very thing that not only engenders the said as an option for action, but *also requires it as the only possible option for ethical action.* Saying (OB, p. 161) "requires the signification of the thematizable, states the idealized said, weighs and judges in justice, which is putting together, assembling, the being of entities." The rooting of justice in its transcendental condition prohibits society from forming a "technique of social equilibrium" (OB, p. 159) in which *community* is only a legal term defined by gender, nationality, and so forth. The experience with the infinite necessitates that justice be nothing less than universal. There can only be one community, no more and certainly no less.[27]

If the saying requires the said, then the faith in that-which-reveals-itself-to-me (God, the other qua trace) must be ineluctably tied to historically situated institutions. There can be no ethics without historical consciousness. I have discussed how Ouaknin dismisses historiography at the outset of his inquiry into Talmudic thinking. But the requirement of the thematizable appears to be precisely what is also lacking in the talmudic readings that form the kernel of *The Burnt Book.* In Ouaknin's first extended commentary, on B. Shabbat 115a–116a (a passage on the rules for saving holy writings from burning buildings), Ouaknin focuses above all on the role that Num. 10:35–36 ("And it came to pass when the Ark set forward that Moses said, 'Advance, O Lord! May your enemies be scattered, and may your foes flee before you!' And when it halted, he would say, 'Return, O Lord, you who are Israel's myriads of thousands!'") plays in the derash. The rabbis see the purpose of the strange orthography of the verse, written with an inverted *nun* (for *nakud,* "dot") at each end to signify its prior writing with a dot above each letter, as "to teach us that this is not its place."[28] Arguing that the function of the dot in Hebrew orthography is to occupy "the space beyond the verse's beyond" (BB, p. 148) and that the effacing of the dots by the two *nunim* marks the transcendence of the journey of the Ark to any thematized account thereof, Ouaknin concludes that the journey of the Ark, as the journey of Law, "is the journey of meaning" (BB, p. 151). The effacing of the dots, which signifies to the rabbis that "this is not its place," has the broader hermeneutical signification that (BB, p. 152) "meaning is never there where it is given. A given meaning is automatically nonsense. Thematized meaning is dead. The 'journey of the Ark' is, actually, the *dynamism of meaning.* . . refusing to enter into the world of words."[29] Yet as the foregoing analysis of the relation between saying and said in the later Levinas shows, to see thematized meaning as dead once and for all is to see the relationship with meaning as only on the level of loving intimacy. As soon as I leave the text, there is no place for me to go *except* to the world of words, even if I can show that these words betray the pre-origin of the other. How can I embody the rhetoric of journey as "nonplace" (BB, p. 152), if the face of the other includes within it evidence of the existence of third parties, the inability to avoid the *Lebenswelt* and all its places, and the necessity of thematization? In line with the foregoing reading of *Otherwise than Being,* the journey of Torah would be rather to a place within the *Lebenswelt* that is conditioned by a nonplace, a journey to a place in which I am enriched by this new transcendental perspective and therefore I'm always able to interpret the world and its events through the lens of creation, as in part sanctified. But in this journey, I have not gone anywhere; only my perspective has changed.

Ouaknin embraces the rhetoric of "nonreason" that this alleged (non)essence of Talmudic logic embodies, and quotes a passage from the end of *Otherwise than Being* (OB, p. 165) on reason as hegemonically ensuring "the agreement of dif-ferent terms without breaking up the present in which the theme is held." Levinas indeed says this about reason, but the reason of which Levinas here speaks is seen by the rationalist as the unconditioned par excellence. Nevertheless, Levinas does not object to the use of reason in a context of always revisable claims and norms, open to skepticism and aware of the necessity of reason in the construction of social and political orders. Indeed, Levinas views reason as always being broken by its own skeptical application, revealing the falsity of claims to absolute and unconditioned authority. "*In totalizing being,* discourse qua discourse thus belies the very claim to totalize. This reversion is like that which the refutation of skepticism brings out. In the writing the saying does indeed become a pure said, a simultaneousness of the saying and of its conditions" (OTB, pp. 170–71, emphasis mine). Even though reason does, when thought by itself, reduce differences into the unity of the theme, reason can still see discourse in the light of its preconditions and reassert itself. Without the possibility of consciousness' knowledge of the pure-said-simultaneous-with-saying *as such,* there is only the isolated relation with the infinite, and no hope for justice. More importantly, to interpret the journey of the Law as existence in a nonplace, outside of the wordly world, is to make the interior revelatory experience the only source of value for one's existence.

Luckily, there is a figure in the Jewish tradition who embodies a nonnihilistic vision of the relation between what one might today call "saying" and "said." This is, *pace* Ouaknin, R. Nahman, who brilliantly manages to unite the two without sacrificing the integrity of either.

### R. Nahman and the Ambiguity of God

Ouaknin's argument about the oeuvre of R. Nahman uses the well-known passage in *Liqqutim* 1.64 on the two types of heresy. The first type of heresy comes "from extraneous wisdom," and argues that God does not exist because God cannot be found in the created world. Against this philosophical argument, R. Nahman offers the Lurianic myth of the shattering of the cosmic vessels *(shevirat ha-kelim)* during the act of creation. According to Lurianic Kabbalah, the objects of the world contain divine sparks that remain from the creative act of divine light emanating from the eyes of *Adam Kadmon* (the primordial man) overpowering the lower six *sefirot*.[30] Since the world is defined from the beginning as the *kelippot* or "scraps of divinity," every philosophical argument from "exterior wisdoms" again belief can be said to contain within it an argument for belief, since this wisdom itself "comes from excesses and the scraps of holiness."[31] The immanence of God is thus proven. The second type of heresy comes not from philosophy but from an existential experience of the empty space *(hallal ha-panui)* that was formed in the divine contraction *(tzimtzum)* necessary for the infinite YHVH to have room for creation. The created world has traces of the beyond due to the breaking of the *kelippot,* but since the world is created from an empty space that does not contain any of the divine light, God is absolutely transcendent to the world and thereby completely foreign to it. This simultaneous presence of God in the *kelippot* and absence of God in the *hallal ha-panui* is the religious paradox. In order to take the absolute transcendence, that is, absence, of God seriously, R. Nahman asserts that this type of heresy is unanswerable by "reason and language"[32] that are alien to the radical void, empty of language, and intellect by definition. Ouaknin concludes that for R. Nahman, "silence is the impossible *tiqqun*" (BB, p. 281) and language, by necessity, falls into the multiplicity of *makhloket.* The construction of a totality ignores the structure of the world as *shevirah* that makes this very act of construction impossible, since YHVH qua the source of truth is alien to the world. The world is necessarily broken and thereby pluralistic; if it were not, all persons would have experiences of the absolutely transcendent God.

Nevertheless, when we turn to R. Nahman's biography, problems with this stylization of Breslav thinking as embracing the impossibility of *tiqqun* arise (those darned historians again!). Contrary to the usual early modern Hasidic aversion to dwelling on personal sin, R. Nahman in 1805 instituted the rite of *tiqqun ha-kelali*, the recitation of certain Psalms as atonement for sexual sin, among his disciples.[33] In 1804, R. Nahman instituted the practice of *tiqqun hazot*, a ritual that through mourning the absence of the *shekhinah*, is (through the individual's mimesis of King David) theurgically aimed at reconfiguring the sefirot into the proper erotic configuration necessary for hastening the messianic era.[34]

Turning to R. Nahman's writings, one can argue that there is a formulation of an extralinguistic and extrarational mode of *tiqqun*. *Liqqutim* 1.8 opens with the image of the sigh that is *shleimut hahresonot*, literally "the fulfillment of wants" or "the completion of lacks."[35] As a human version of the divine breath that creates life in Gen. 2:7, it is a particularly apt metaphor of *tiqqun*. R. Nahman also sees *tiqqun* as potentially engendered through a primal scream (1.21), which breaks through the silence of the *hallal ha-panui* by placing the individual in a mimetic relation to the *shekhinah* ("as if the *shekhinah* is screaming and makes possible the consciousness of faith which can access the divine everflow") and thus making him able to answer nonverbally the second heresy mentioned in *Liqqutim* 1.64.[36] Furthermore, the role of the *tzaddiq* in all of R. Nahman's writings is that of the person who engenders *tiqqun* on the part of the faithful individual.[37] Arthur Green asserts that R. Nahman saw his own calling as engendering a *tiqqun ha-shekhinah*.[38] One can thus argue that what defines Breslav thought is not the impossibility of *tiqqun*, but the very necessity (albeit difficulty) of *tiqqun*. Why is *tiqqun* so difficult that one needs to learn from the *tzaddiq* to accomplish it? As the following partial analysis of *Liqqutim* 1.11 will show, it is the nature of *tiqqun* to accomplish itself through the individual's positioning himself between the realm of self-sufficient humanity and the realm of the self-sufficient Godhead, and each of these extremes is viewed as a necessary construct for the sake of the cleaning of the muddiness of the ineluctable relation between the two in the world. If *tiqqun* were to be a move from absolute said to absolute saying, as Ouaknin argues, it would truly be impossible. But if *tiqqun* is the union of saying and said and the deconstruction of their reputations as absolute, then in the language of Levinas it is nothing less than working for justice in the ontic realm because of the ambiguity of being, or in the language of R. Nahman completing the glory of YHVH because of the ambiguity of God.

But this argument can only be made through seeing how the closing paragraphs of the sermon deconstruct the opening paragraphs in which the religious journey emphasizes the individual's "vertical" relation with transcendence over and above the "horizontal" relation with the world. Let us examine the opening cluster of concepts that establishes such a hierarchy. In the opening sentence of *Liqqutim* 11[39] R. Nahman presents the listener with a teaching from the *Zohar* that presents two different yet equally necessary paths of encountering the divine. There is the upper *yichud* (unification) of saying the *Shema* and affirming the transcendence of God, and the lower *yichud* of saying *Barukh shem kevod malkhuto* ("blessed be the name of his glorious kingdom") which asserts God's constant immanent relation to the world. Only through saying these prayers properly— saying them in their nature as saying—can these unifications, not only of the letters of the divine names, but also between the human and the divine, be effective. R. Nahman continues by asserting that the act of speaking Torah can enlighten the individual and take him through the necessary stages of *teshuvah* necessary for what R. Nahman terms *deep Torah understanding*. R. Nahman thus begins his lesson by creating a map of faith (indeed, each lesson in *Liqqutim* is such a map), in which here the themes of speech, repentance, and *yichud* as *tiqqun* are linked together. No one of these themes can exist without the other two. The prooftexts for the three links in R. Nahman's opening map are as follows. For the link between Torah and saying, R. Nahman refers to B. Eruvin 54a, which rereads Prov. 4:22 "for they [divine words] are life to those who find them *(ki chayyim hem lemotzaʾeyhem)*" as "to those who verbally express them *(lemotziʾeyhem bapeh)*." For the link between saying and Torah understanding/*tiqqun*, R. Nahman quotes B. Berakhot 22a, "open your mouth and your speech will enlighten *(petach pikha veyaʾiru devar-eykha)*." For the link between Torah understanding and repentance, R. Nahman quotes Haggadah from B. Menachot 85a that postulates a conversa- tion between Pharaoh's magicians and Moses. The magicians ask Moses why he, through his magic, is bringing straw into Apharayim (why he is performing magic in Egypt). Moses replies, "To the vegetable market, take vegetables," proposing that if Egypt is the land of sorcery (the vegetable market), using divine magic is only fair play. R. Nahman, as is often the case, rips the Haggadah out of its Talmudic context to make the following verbal links: *teven* (straw) corresponds to *tevunah* (understanding); and *yarka* (vegetables) corresponds to *vayarek* (he called out), which corresponds to repentance in the context of Bereshit Rabbah 43. In this Haggadah on Gen. 14:14, Abraham recites to his servants Deut. 20:8 ("Is there anyone afraid or fainthearted?"), and this fear is linked to having sins for which one has not yet repented.

In the second paragraph, the concept of "divine glory," *kavod*, is added to this map. R. Nahman argues that only when one speaks in such a way that completes *(shleimut)* the divine glory, can one indeed perform effective saying. R. Nahman's prooftext here is the linguistic convergence between Ps. 24:10 *(mi huʾ zeh melekh hakavod*, "who is this king of glory?")* with a passage in the *Tikkuney Zohar* that links the *sefirah* of kingship *(malkhut)* with the organ of the mouth, since both function as channels between the interior realm (of God, when one is speaking of *malkhut;* of man, when one is speaking of the mouth), and the exterior world. Glory is associated with the linguistic root *mem-lamed-kaf,* which in turn is linked to the mouth.

From this link between glory and speech arises an ethical dimension to saying. Haughtiness is characteristic of a closed mouth that is unable to speak of

God and to God; excessive humility is the characteristic of the authentic religious self that can speak Saying. The prooftext here is relatively simple: a reference to Ps. 17:10 "*sagru pimo divru vege'ut* (their mouth closed up, they spoke haughtily)."

At this point in the lesson, Nahman's teaching seems almost Puritan. Since God is *so* terribly transcendent and *so* terribly majestic, prayer must represent this gap through a purification of the worshiper through both study and ethical action. Indeed, in this model there is no higher calling for the individual than self-hatred and turning the self purely into a conduit of the divine, apparently negating the whole purpose of creating humans qua human. R. Nahman's model of humility is based on a strange reading of Ps. 15:4. The phrase *nivzeh be'eynav nim'as* is usually translated to refer to another person, as "a person contemptible in his eyes is to be rejected"; yet R. Nahman takes the niphal form of *bazah* to be reflexive and adds a *shehu'* before the phrase, thereby rendering it as "he [the humble man] is contemptible in his own eyes and is repulsive." In this very image, it is all too tempting to conclude that the path to deep Torah understanding is a path from the haughtiness of the said to a distinctly different type of language (saying) which leaves the world behind, interested only in the holiness of the self. If we stopped here in our reading of *Liqqutim* 1:11, there would be no choice except to read R. Nahman in accordance with Ouaknin's interpretation of the journey of the ark in Judaism.

Nevertheless, when R. Nahman begins to apply the two unifications to the project of keeping the covenant, the situation becomes thankfully more complicated. In 1.11.3, R. Nahman argues that making *kavod* complete is only possible through keeping the covenant, especially the covenant of circumcision and the ancillary laws of sexual purity. Without the *vav*—which as the number six, corresponds to the sixth sefirah *yessod,* which in turn corresponds to *brit,* particularly circumcision as *brit milah*—*kavod* becomes *kevad,* "heavy," and specifically in the context of Exod. 4:10 *kevad peh,* the "heavy tongue of unenlightened speech." Therefore speech becomes almost instantly linked to sexual behavior. In the fourth paragraph of *Liqqutim* 11, R. Nahman begins to draw a simple dichotomy. On one hand is the person who guards the *brit* and thus corresponds to "the thirty-nine lights" encompassed in the *vav* that distinguishes glory from heaviness. On the other hand is the person who defiles the *brit* and thus "draws upon himself the yoke of earning a living *('ol haparnasah)*—i.e. the thirty-nine works." In this century, such a sermonizing equation between suffering and low spirituality resonates most with offensive post-Shoah theodicies, for example, those of R. Elchonon Wassermann and R. Joseph Schneersohn.[40]

Thankfully, R. Nahman does not let this dichotomy stand. There are two issues that come to the fore here: the meaning of *oz* (strength) and the curious relationship between the thirty-nine works and the thirty-nine lights. First, through the narrative of Boaz, who is able to control his sexual impulses for Ruth on the threshing-floor (Ruth 3:11–13) and thus guard the sexual purity of the covenant, R. Nahman reasserts the zoharic word association between *brit* and *bo'oz* "in him there is strength," a lengthening of the root letters of the name Boaz.[41] Thus, the strength of *oz* is here simply the strength to reflect the thirty-nine lights. Nevertheless, only two sentences later, R. Nahman seems to take a contrary stance on the meaning of *oz*. Here, the numerical value of '*oz* as seventy-eight (with a "fudge factor" of one to count the word itself) is interpreted to be the sum of the thirty-nine lights and the thirty-nine works. Thus, strength would reside not in solely orienting oneself toward the lights, but in *a simultaneous orientation toward light and work*. Since this equation "Lights + works = strength" is gematrically true, then the relationship between this world and the beyond is perhaps not a relationship at all. According to this theory, the "here and now" and the "beyond" would not be two different worlds, but rather two dialectically related *views* of one world. This would still avoid the pantheist heresy, and is in line with the revision of the totalized said in the later writings of Levinas.

R. Nahman furthers this dialectical view of the created world by dealing a severe equivocation to the definition of the thirty-nine works in the following sentence. In a midrash on the necessity of repeating the word *mishkan* (tabernacle) in Exod. 38:21, R. Nahman asserts the possibility that "someone who guards his *brit,* even though he engages in the thirty-nine works, [his works] are an aspect of the works of the Tabernacle—i.e. the Tabernacle when built up, corresponding to [*bechinat*] the thirty-nine lights." The punishment of the *pogem brit,* the "defiler of the covenant," is now taken to be the "thirty-nine lashes" mentioned in Deut. 25:3 as the punishment for guilt. So at this point, the works which R. Nahman opposed to the thirty-nine lights earlier in this paragraph in his repetition of the traditional zoharic view of *shomer brit* are now seen as potentially aligned with the cosmic lights in his own commentary on the tradition; the dichotomy between lights and works is now completely shifted to one between lights and lashes. Works are the path to one of these two existential possibilities. And the path is necessary. Neither lights nor lashes can exist without the works that lead to them; there is no experience of the beyond/Saying/lights through faith alone. In this interpretation, one might interpret as literally as possible the word *bechinah,* the technical term of R. Nahman's method of midrash-by-association that establishes a relationship between two concepts. To say that works (through the notion of "works of the Tabernacle") are the *bechinah* of the thirty-nine lights is quite simply to say that one cannot examine *(bachan)* or study the realm of the divine lights without passing through the worldly realm defined by work. How can one understand creation on the divine photo-optic level without experiencing creation in the concrete sense of the everyday? Is not this *union* of here and beyond, of saying and Said, of direct revelation/light and sense-experience/ work, the very ground of the *hidushe Torah* that are the vehicles of redemption, as Ouaknin correctly notes?

The theme of uniting said and saying, or of seeing the saying in the clothing of the said—a theme that R. Nahman has promised from the opening positing

(1.11.1) of an upper and a lower unification both of which every Jew is obligated to engender *(vekhol 'echad miyisra'el tzarikh sheyihyeh na'asah)*—continues throughout the latter half of *Liqqutim* 11. The dialectic of works and light is reflected in the very structure of Jewish time, the distinction between the weekdays and Shabbat. According to the Talmud (B. Ketuvot 61b-62b), rules concerning sexual relations are different for the elite sages and for the rest of Israel. The sage can only have conjugal relations on Shabbat, while the ordinary Jew, depending on his social status, is allowed to engage in sexual activity several times during the week. Yet in R. Nahman's interpretation of these laws (1.11.5), the ordinary person's guarding of the *brit* on the weekdays corresponds to the lower unification, and the sage's guarding of the *brit* on Shabbat corresponds to the upper unification. The prooftext for Shabbat-to-Shabbat marital relations as the upper unification is relatively simple: in B. Chagigah 12a, in which God on Shabbat says "*Dai* [enough]!" and thereby separates "Himself from all works" (1.11.5), reflecting the uniqueness of divine transcendence. The prooftext for weekday marital relations as the lower unification is an extended chain of concepts. The God of the six weekdays is Metatron; the six of the weekdays is linked to the number of orders of the Mishnah (through a reference to *Tikkuney Zohar),* and thus everyday action; and finally, to return to the opening equation between the lower unification and the prayer of *Barukh shem malkhuto,* R. Nahman points out that the name of Metatron is indeed within the divine name. For not only are the gematric values for *Metatron* and *Shaddai* equal,[42] but R. Nahman explicitly cites a fragment of Exod. 23:21, "since my name is in him," as proof that this gematria is divinely intended and not simply coincidental. But underneath these associations lies a fundamental protodeconstructive point. If the opening sentence of R. Nahman's sermon is still to hold true at this point in the lesson, then it is incumbent upon all Jews, sage or otherwise, to obey both the laws of weekday and Shabbat and thereby to displace the sage/nonsage opposition, since both the lower and upper unifications are incumbent upon all Jews.

This displacement of the sage/nonsage opposition is further developed into a displacement of the opposition between YHVH and the angel Metatron. R. Nahman ends both 1.11.5 and 1.11.6 with a repetition of the Talmudic and zoharic assertion that YHVH "clothes himself in Metat during the six days of the week" and ends 1.11.7 by making a parallel between YHVH-clothed-in-Metat and Kabbala-clothed-in-Halakhah. Thus, the immanent world as (garment of) divine immanence serves as a mode of access to divine transcendence. Indeed, the context of Exod. 23:21, which R. Nahman uses to argue for the correspondence between the lower unification and the rule of Metatron at the close of 1.11.5, is telling here. The angel referred to in Exod. 23:20–22 is sent by YHVH to Israel for the explicit purpose of "lead[ing] you to the place that I have prepared *(velahavi'akh el-hamaqom asher hakhinti),*" which deepens the sense of Metatron as engendering the very possibility of *tiqqun*. In all these equivocations, it becomes apparent that what is important to R. Nahman is not simply the end-goal of knowing the transcendent God, but also the path of the immanent world. We can know the transcendent God by examining *(bachan, bechinah)* the domain of Metatron, and inferring its necessary precondition of radical transcendence and its status as unique path to the experience of that transcendence. Even the argument that the realm of Metatron is secondary to the opportunities given on Shabbat, when YHVH is not in the garment of Metatron, must still take account of the teleological force that the realm of Metatron has given the context of Exod. 23:20–22.

At this point it is necessary to respond to the potential objection that the emphasis on the path of immanence is all well and good, but that the goal remains a goal nonetheless. Once one performs the lower and upper unifications (or realizes that this is necessary and knows the proper method involved), who needs the immanent world anymore? Isn't the unification nothing more than a Hegelian *Aufhebung*, leaving the world of experienced space and time in the dust to die of the starvation that comes with finitude? In the penultimate paragraph of *Liqqutim* 1.11, which focuses on the fantastic interpretation by Rabbah Bar bar Chanah of Ps. 50:11 in B. Bava Batra 73b, the nature of the metaphor of *ziz sadai* (the bird of the field) guards against this lapse back into a self-sufficient totality. R. Bar bar Chanah's vision of *ziz sadai* is of a bird

> standing up to its ankles in water, and its head in the firmament. We concluded that there wasn't much water and wanted to go down into it to cool ourselves. A heavenly voice called out to us, "Do not go down into here, A carpenter's axe fell in here seven years ago, and it has not yet reached the ground. Not only because the water is abundant, but because the water runs so rapidly." Rav Ashi said, "This bird was *ziz sadai*, as is written (Ps. 50:11), 'And the *ziz sadai* is with me.'"[43]

For R. Nahman, the bird is a metaphor for enlightened speech, which serves as "a bridge between man [water, which according to kabbalistic myth is the primordial materiel from which man was created] and the heavens." The apparent shallowness of the water demonstrates that man is currently on a low spiritual level, since the water/man only comes up to the ankles of the bird/speech. The remainder of the story is for R. Nahman a lesson on avoiding egotism, even in the guise of a egoistic attitude toward humility in which pride is derived from one's holy demeanor. Interestingly enough, the objects of the criticism of egoistic "morality" here appear to be the sages who see the world as unnecessary for a proper religious life. For the story of the carpenter's ax is for R. Nahman no less than the story of Metatron; even though R. Nahman is not explicit about this, the *bechinot* that have been made throughout this lesson lead to this conclusion. In his commentary on R. Bar bar Chanah's myth, R. Nahman uses Ps. 129:7 to draw a link between the carpenters' *chatzina* (ax) and *chitzno* (garment corner), and a description of God as a carpenter in B. Chullin 60a is also cited.

Thus, the carpenter's ax is code for "YHVH's garment *(levush)*." Yet this same root *lamed-bet-shin* was used earlier, at the close of 1.11.5, to describe the relationship between YHVH and Metatron, since YHVH *malbish atzmo* (clothes himself) as Metatron. Therefore, the ax can be the figure of *none other than Metatron himself.* Thus, according to R. Nahman's rereading of the myth, YHVH has sent Metatron to man/water, but this has not been heeded (by both Israel and the nations). Why is this the case? Through the image of the water running rapidly, R. Nahman concludes that humanity is "running after glory *(rodphim 'achar hakavod)*." The prooftext here is Ps. 29:3, in which the link between glory and water is made clear. "The God of glory thunders, God is upon many waters *('el hakavod hir'im YHVH 'al mayim rabbim)*." The sin (which R. Nahman asserts is the cause of exile) is thus the belief that the transcendent God is *only* in another realm, and cannot be inferred from the experience of this world here and now because of *shevirah.* The figure of *ziz sadai,* bridging between this world and the beyond, between said and saying, says otherwise. If speech descends from the firmament to water, then saying exists in the human world as part and parcel of the said (even though it may take a *tzaddiq* or a philosopher to lead us to thus realization). The water does not need to run, since *ziz sadai* is standing here. The said that is the totality of Metatron/weekdays/halakha/works is, when seen in the light of its origin (when properly hegemonized), a speech that is of the world *(pace* BB, p. 296) and a path "to the place that I have prepared." This stance, one that now must be called "sociopolitical," is what R. Nahman calls "meriting the bird." It is the "deep Torah understanding" that is the ground of the process of *tiqqun* as *yichud.*

## Afterword

It is clear at this point that the emphasis on worldly justice in *Otherwise than Being* and on the angel Metatron in *Liqqutim* 11 necessitates a rethinking of Ouaknin's arguments in *The Burnt Book,* in order to purify the link between Jewish religious existence and postmodern thought of any nihilistic overtones in which the world is seen as unnecessary for life and redemption. But how does Ouaknin come to risk these overtones in his project by emphasizing the saying at the expense of the said-formulated-in-the-light-of-saying? In my opinion, it is a flawed view of *tiqqun,* one which bizarrely uses as its model the Christian myth of incarnation of God in Jesus of Nazareth. For Ouaknin, the interpretive freeplay of the Talmud is the *shevirah* that opposes the *tiqqun* that is the *Aufhebung* of the "Old" Law in the arrival of Jesus (BB, p. 300). "The speech that fissures writing, that breaks the Tables and burns the book, is the speech of interpretation, and this is what is at stake in the whole Judeo-Christian controversy. The event of Jesus Christ lies in the fact that a man arose and said: 'I have come to fulfill Scripture'." According to this model, *tiqqun* is forced into the position of being (BB, p. 302) "a repairing that effaces the fissure." But why should this be the case? Why should anything that is not *shevirah* automatically be a full and complete *tiqqun?* Logically, I can see no justification for such a belief, since mending operates on a continuum; some jobs of mending are better than others. And if *tiqqun* is in part the result of human endeavor, then it should only be natural that *tiqqun* would have many degrees to it. We have within both the philosophical and the nonphilosophical Jewish tradition evidence that the *tiqqun/shevirah* dichotomy is better seen as a continuum. These readings of Levinas and R. Nahman show that one should not dismiss the possibility of a *tiqqun* that is human without being incarnational, one that leaves the stitches visible, open to the critique that the sewing calculations have been performed incorrectly. Simply because humans are finite does not mean they are helpless. That would be the ultimate nihilistic insult to creation.

## Notes

1. Marc-Alain Ouaknin, *Burnt Book: Reading the Talmud* (Princeton, 1995). [Henceforth, BB]

2. Cf. Edith Wyschogrod, *Saints and Postmodernism: Revisioning Moral Philosophy* (Chicago, 1990), p. 223. While the term *differential postmodernism* is Wyschogrod's, she does not argue that Judaism is ineluctably entwined with such a philosophy. The first appearance of such an argument in English is Susan Handelman's landmark "structuralist midrash" in *The Slayers of Moses: The Emergence of Rabbinic Interpretation in Modern Literary Theory* (Albany, 1982).

3. This is perhaps most lucidly argued in Jacques Derrida, *Of Grammatology,* trans. Gayatri Chakravorty Spivak (Baltimore, 1974), pp. 6–26. It is perhaps most rigorously argued in Jacques Derrida, *Edmund Husserl's* Origin of Geometry: *An Introduction,* trans. John P. Leavey Jr. (Lincoln, 1989), esp. pp. 87–93.

4. Cf. Emmanuel Levinas, *Totality and Infinity,* trans. Alphonso Lingis (Pittsburgh, 1969), pp. 251–285; and idem, *Time and the Other,* trans. Richard A. Cohen (Pittsburgh, 1987), pp. 84–94. In addition, Ouaknin has given the title of *Méditations érotiques* to his book on the work of Levinas (Paris, 1992).

5. Cf. Derrida, "Signature Event Context," trans. Alan Bass, in *Margins of Philosophy* (Chicago, 1982), pp. 309–330.

6. One other minor objection to be added, about the English translation itself, which retains the bibliography and the majority of the footnotes in French.

If the reader is expected to follow citations to *Je et tu, ainsi parla Zarathoustra, l'homme de la Halakha,* and *L'entretien infini* with French paginations, then why translate *Le livre brûlé* in the first place?

7. "The saying in being said at every moment breaks the definition of what it says and breaks up the totality it includes." Levinas, "Language and Proximity," in *Collected Philosophical Papers,* trans. Alphonso Lingis (Dordrecht, Netherlands, 1987), pp. 126,

8. For more on the role of eros in Levinas, cf. Martin Kavka, "Saying Kaddish for Gillian Rose," in *Secular Theology,* ed. Clayton Crockett (London, 2001).

9. Further references to *Liqqutei MoHaRan* will henceforth be *Liqqutim.*

10. Emmanuel Levinas, "No Identity," in *Collected Philosophical Papers,* p. 151.

11. Ibid.

12. Ibid., p. 150.

13. Ibid., p. 151.

14. Levinas, *Otherwise than Being,* trans. Alphonso Lingis Dordrecht, Netherlands, 1991), p. 5. [Henceforth OB]

15. This point is also made in the contributions of Adriaan Peperzak ("Presentation") and Jean Greisch ("The Face and Reading: Immediacy and Mediation") to *Re-reading Levinas,* eds. R. Bernasconi and S. Critchley (Bloomington, 1991), pp. 51–66, 67–82.

16. Also cf. OB 47, "The apophansis is still a modality of saying."

17. Levinas, "Freedom and Command," in *Collected Philosophical Papers,* p/ 21.

18. Cf. Heidegger, *Being and Time,* sec. 9.

19. Levinas, "The Ego and Totality," in *Collected Philosophical Papers,* pp. 25–45, esp. pp. 29–35.

20. Ibid., p. 30.

21. Ibid., p. 31.

22. Ibid., p. 30.

23. But not necessarily ecstatic mysticism per se.

24. Cf. my following remarks on R. Nahman's use of *bechinah.*

25. Cf. Levinas, "Language and Proximity," in *Collected Philosophical Papers,* p. 123.

26. Derrida rehearses this Levinasian argument in his "Force of Law: The 'Mystical Foundation of Authority,'" in *Deconstruction and the Possibility of Justice,* Cornell, Rosenfeld, and Carlson, eds. (New York, 1992), esp. p. 28.

27. The necessity of universality proven in the argument of *Otherwise than Being* calls us to interpret Levinas's talmudic readings (so far available in English in *Nine Talmudic Readings, Difficult Freedom, Beyond the Verse,* and *In The Time of the*

*Nations*) as illustrating the mutual preconditionality between and cosaying of Jew and Greek.

28. The translation is Llewellyn Brown's, from Ouaknin's French.

29. Also cf. BB, pp. 204–207, in Ouaknin's interpretation of the passage from B. Yoma.

30. In addition to Ouaknin's summary of the doctrine of *shevirat ha-kelim* (BB, p. 278), there is also a good summary in Gershom Scholem's *Major Trends in Jewish Mysticism* (New York, 1946), pp. 265ff.; the original source of the myth is R. Chayyim Vital's *Etz Hayyim* IX.

31. R. Nahman of Bratslav, *Liqqutim* 1.64.2, quoted in BB, p. 279.

32. Ibid., 1.64.3, quoted in BB, p. 280.

33. Arthur Green, *Tormented Master: The Life and Spiritual Quest of Rabbi Nahman of Bratslav* (Woodstock, Vt., 1992), pp. 169 207.

34. Ibid., 206. Also cf. Shaul Magid, "Conjugal Union, Mourning, and *Talmud Torah,* in R. Isaac Luria's *Tikkun Hazot,*" *Da'at* 36 (1996):52–72.

35. R. Nahman, *Liqqutei MoHaRaN* 1.8.1. It is translated by Moshe Mykoff as "it provides wholeness in place of the lack." The English translation can be found in vol. 2 of the bilingual Breslov edition (Jerusalem, 1993), p. 33.

36. Cf. Shaul Magid, "Through the Void: The Absence of God in R. Nahman of Bratslav's *Likkutei MoHaRan,*" *Harvard Theological Review* 88:4 (1995) 495–519, esp. 504–508.

37. The clearest example of this is R. Nahman's parable of the treasure, possessed by each individual but undiscoverable without the *tzaddiq;* cf. *Rabbi Nachman's Stories,* trans. and ed. Aryeh Kaplan (Jerusalem, 1983), p. 478. As for Nahman's more explicitly philosophical writings, *Liqqutim* 1.8.2 (R. Nahman, op. cit., vol. 2, p. 37) argues that the ability to sigh properly comes from the *tzaddiq.*

38. Green in ibid.

39. R. Nahman, 160–201. Paragraph numbers will be referenced in the body of the text.

40. Cf. Richard Rubinstein, *After Auschwitz: History, Theology, and Contemporary Judaism,* 2nd ed. (Baltimore, 1992), pp. 159–160.

41. R. Nahman, 1.11.4. The reference for the association is *Tikkuney Zohar* 31.

42. Mykoff points this out in his note on the passage in question in ibid., p. 183.

43. B. Bava Batra 73b, Mykoff's translation from R. Nahman, ibid., 1.11.8.

# PART II
# OLD STUDIES

# 7

# Messiah and the Light of the Messiah in Reb Nahman's Thought

## Hillel Zeitlin

### The Transgenerational Zaddik and his Conquests

The statement of Rabbi Nahman ben Simhah of Bratslav "My flame will continue to burn until the Messiah comes," might sound to some ears as a mere Hasidic flourish. They are words that seem to have been uttered in the throes of prayer, or in the midst of a plea for mercy, and stem from a passionate desire to press a stamp of eternity on the teachings of *Likkutei Moharan*. Reb Nathan, R. Nahman's most important disciple, however, saw in these words a real and palpable portend—that this is actually how it will come to be. That is, that R. Nahman, according to his disciple Reb Nathan of Nemirov,[1] was the last among the trailblazers *(mishrei-derekh)* or precursors to precede the King-Messiah. After him, there will be no other precursors until the Redeemer himself arrives in the full splendor of his illumination.

So one is moved to ask: great zaddikim have existed both in the time of R. Nahman as well as after him: so how can one claim that there will be no more holy men until the coming of the Messiah? How is it possible to believe that R. Nahman was, so to speak, the last station in the world's journey to the era of the Messiah? The answer is that there have been and there will yet be zaddikim, and great ones at that. There is, however, a difference—according to Reb Nahman—between a zaddik, even a great one, and *Zaddik ha-Emet,* the Zaddik of Truth or, stated differently, *Zaddik ha-Dorot,* the Transgenerational Zaddik. R. Nahman is, according to R. Nathan the greatest Zaddik of Truth of the last generations and it is his flame that will smolder until the Messiah comes.

What, however, does it mean to be the Transgenerational Zaddik? He is the one who opens the primal, uppermost and untouched celestial chambers, who draws down effluence from distant worlds—emanations and illuminations like no one that preceded him—who reveals the splendors of holiness that were concealed for so many generations; a zaddik who is spoken of like one spoke of *Moshe Robeynu,* Moses Our Teacher: *In every house of mine he is loyal,*[2] a zaddik in whose hand lies the key to all worlds from the highest to the lowest and who, when he unlocks no one can relock, and when he locks no one can unlock.

Let us take the debate even further. We ask Reb Nathan.

If this is so, then what about those zaddikim who are the foundation of the world like R. Yitzchak Berdichever,[3] about whom R. Nahman himself had said, he is the glory of the generation *(pe'ar ha-dor)* the "glory of our entire community"? And what about the Seer of Lublin,[4] Reb Elimelich[5] and Reb Zusia[6] his brother and what of the Rabbi of Lyady,[7] the founder of Chabad? What about the Koznizer Maggid[8] or the Neschitzer Maggid?[9] What of R. Avraham Ha-Malach[10] and so on and so on? Did the Divine Presence not repose on all of these zaddikim, and not only the young R. Nahman (taken from this world when he was still young)? Was he, alone, elected by the Divine Presence to be His redeemer and savior? Did the other zaddikim not open towers in the highest chambers? Did they not draw down the effluence of blessing onto the head of the holy nation? Did they not set Jewish hearts aflame with love for their heavenly father? Did they not hold many men back from sin and did they not endeavor to repair the world in God's kingdom? Are they not among the souls God consulted before He created the world as it states, *Let us make man in* our *image, after* our *likeness:*[11] With whom did He council? Who advised Him? With the souls of the zaddikim, undoubtedly; with the souls of the righteous.

Is it not said of them, "*These were the potters and those that dwelt among Netaim and Gederah; they dwelt there in the king's service*"(Chron. I 4:23) according to the interpretation of our sages? Should we not consider each one of them as an instrument of *God decrees and the zaddik annuls?* Why do you proffer the crown of the Kingdom of Heaven on Nahman alone?

Reb Nathan would answer: In the very first line, it states that we are not pushing away the prophets, or the sages or the *Amoraim,* nor should this be construed as a diminishment of their honor and their wondrous stature.

The very first line of what? Who states this?

The world-redeemers.

Who are they?

Moses our teacher, Rabbi Simeon Bar Yohai,[12] The Ari *z"l* [Rabbi Isaac Luria],[13] Rabbi Israel Baal Shem Tov; and the *Nahal Nove Makor Chochmah*[14] (which, when descrambled, is an acrostic for NaHMaN) and finally the King-Messiah.

If this concept is not stated explicitly in R. Nathan's writings, it can be deduced from his overall teachings, and heard in the words of the *Cheryner Rov*[15] and not just through parable, hint, or symbol, but rather stated clearly, simply and openly as a fundamental truth.

According to the Bratzslaver tradition, it appears that the path is laid out as such: from Moses' Torah *(Torat Moshe),* to the *Zohar,*[16] Etz-ha-Chayim,[17] to *Pri Etz Ha-Hayyim,*[18] and from there to the Baal Shem Tov, to *Likkutei Moharan* and from *Likkutei Moharan* to the Kingdom of the Messiah.

Let us open *Likkutei Moharan,* this wondrous text, a book once mocked by the Maskilim, and let us see what path it sets out for us to the Kingdom of the Messiah. It is an indisputable fact concerning Hasidic texts in general, among adherents of Hasidism as well as among those who simply research these texts for the sake of history, among those who praise Hasidism and those who oppose it, that the most central principle of R. Nahman's teachings is the concept of the zaddik. This understanding was even adhered to by Reb Nathan, himself the *Joshua* to R. Nahman's *Moses* as implied in R. Nahman's use of the verse *Call Joshua and present yourselves at the Tent of Meeting* (Deut. 31:14)[19] in his Tales *(Sippurei Mayses)*, in a tale about a teacher and his student whom he calls his *Lesser Light* who relies on the effulgence of the *Greater Light* and the two of whom are bound tightly together.[20]

I, too, thought the same. However, after plunging deeply into each sermon, each discussion, each teaching of the Bratzslaver I would stake the claim that it is not the zaddik that rests at the core of R. Nahman's world-conception: *it is the Messiah.* Of course the zaddik occupies an important place in the teachings and tales of the Bratzslaver. The zaddik only attains such an elevated status, however, since he is a bridge, or transition, to the King-Messiah. When we speak of the Transgenerational Zaddik or Zaddik of Truth, it is not only as the transition to the Messiah but even a premonitory reflection—premonitory revelation—of the Messiah himself. Moses our Teacher, Rabbi Simeon Bar Yohai, Rabbi Isaac Luria (the *Ari),* Rabbi Israel Baal Shem Tov, and Reb Nahman, are, if you will, according to this system, those who prepare the way for the Messiah. In fact one may also say that, in their own time, they also constituted various manifestations of the soul of the Messiah itself, which appear from epoch to epoch, revealing itself to the world and its inhabitants little by little, and purges and purifies the world until the process of purification is complete.

The first teaching in *Likkutei Morahan* speaks of the divine intellect *(sechel eloki)* which is connected to *ya'akveney, he has has supplanted me* (Gen. 26:36) translated by *Onklos* as *ve-chakhmeni,*[21] *"and he outwitted me"* and endows the People of Israel with its charm, importance, and distinction. This divine intellect is also the sun that alights the wanderings of the Jewish people throughout the world and throughout all the adversities of exile. To the extent that the Jew absorbs within himself this divine intellect, it is like the moon that obtains its light from this sun and approaches—along with the other nations of the world—the redemption. He [Jacob] subjugates the heat of the *kelipah* (extraneous demonic power): *Then the moon shall be ashamed, and the sun shall be abashed* (Isa. 24:23). This means, when the true Kingdom of Heaven will reveal itself, the son will be ashamed by the false knowledge and idolatry.

In this teaching there is no explicit mention of the Messiah but already, in this first lesson, there is discussion of the heavenly sphere of *Malkut,*[22] (Kingship) which becomes subjugated, diminished, and suffers severe dejection. Only through Torah and prayer—not by rote, but rather by deep, clear, and purely honest knowledge—will She *(Malkhut)* rise from her dejection.

The second teaching already speaks to the tenet of the King-Messiah and his conquests. We must keep in mind that for the Bratzslaver, the King-Messiah was a warrior and a conqueror, his weapon being prayer: *be-chervi* ube-kashti, *"with my sword and with my arrow"* (Gen. 48:22) or, alternatively, *with my sword and with my supplications.*[23]

R. Nahman's view is that conquests in materiality come only after spiritual conquests in the highest of places. The lowest conquests occur as ends in themselves or as a means to a higher goal of justice. They might also occur as punishment ( *"and even the wicked for an evil day"* (Prov. 16:4) to repay nations when the measure of evil is great.

Moreover, since the conquests of the Messiah constitute the final reckoning, or the ultimate purification, they are the most severe and most laborious. Against these, are the immense and gruesome forces of the impudent and insolent nations, armed from head to toe, laden with arrogance and among whom exist those who compete to bring about a human redemption in a crooked way through science and technological innovation. What was the purpose of R. Nahman's journey to Eretz Yisrael with all of its tribulations, dangers, and wanderings, with its exceptional measure of self-sacrifice. At the height of Napoleon's campaign in the Orient, without the knowledge of any languages or the world in general, without any means of protection, and with a sum of money that would be just enough to get a man from a tiny village in Podolia to the port of Odessa, in the company only of a man,[24] who, though ready to sacrifice himself at any moment for his rebbe, was not able to help him in his moment of need. What was all this if not the journey of a spiritual, spiritual-messianic, "supplicative," protoconquest of the land?

According to R. Nahman, those nations that occupied Eretz Yisrael had a legitimate grievance with the Master of the Universe. "If one man takes possession of another man's field over a period of three years, he may lay claim to it. In our case we have had Eretz Yisrael in our possession for almost two thousand years." How do we Jews respond to that? Our answer is, "He who possesses another man's field for three years is presumed to have a rightful claim[25] to it only when he who was wronged does not protest against the injustice. However, we have not ceased in our supplications against this theft since we were driven from our land. We have not, even for a moment, given up on our forebearers' inheritance.[26] Other nations occupy our land unjustly, and when the time comes, they will pay the full price for the occupation of the land and for the fruits they tasted in it for over two thousand years.

This protest, however, must be living and concrete, not merely the stuff of words. The justice that the Jews seek in respect to their land is extensive and complicated due to their own sins against their God, their land, and the Kingdom of David and due to many accusations leveled against them by many nations and over so many generations. Prayers, therefore, are not enough to wrest the stolen property from the hands of the thief; only when there is a scream to God and when the protest is constant, mighty, and heaven-splitting—only then can it produce results.

Therefore when great zaddikim appear, especially those Transgenerational Zaddikim, who are of the category of the Messiah, they must not only call out and cry out to God but they must also initiate a concrete act.

Accordingly, R. Nahman acted in the spirit of the education he received and the influences he was under from the Baal Shem Tov's milieu that lived on inside him. He was not able to conduct any other act of conquest but to journey to Eretz Yisrael accompanied by his protest, equipped with his bow and arrow of supplication and his sword of prayer.

And there are indications that visions of other forms of conquest that were more earthly and more politically concrete hovered before his eyes. Let us gather these indications: R. Nahman's admiration for Napoleon whom he saw as a king at the very root of his soul, and a ruler by God's word; the various lines about the king and the hero in the story *The Master of Prayer;* the talk about the heavy significance of "heroism of the heart" *(gevurat halev)* in *Likkutei Morahan;* and if we were to remember Napoleon's promise to return Eretz Yisrael to the Jewish people and keep in mind what is written in *Shivhei Ha-Besht*[27] that the Baal Shem had seen Rabbi Akiva (Bar Kokhba's aide) dressed as a soldier in the cave of King David—if we do not forget R. Nahman's talk in his sermon *"Tisha tikunin etmasru le-dikna," Nine tikkunin I will convey to the beard" (Likkutei Marahan* 1: 20) the zaddik must retrieve from Edom the power of the sword. If we are to penetrate the force of these words and allusions—we would finally get close to the truth. We might say that R. Nahman. in his own time had such thoughts that today we would call "political-Zionist" even "Revisionist"; even though, you understand, he did not say it outright, he conceived of the idea of creating a Kingdom of Israel without a Kingdom of God. Even then, as he entertained such thoughts, he did not cease in believing that the fundamental element of redemption would arrive in the end only through the "sword of prayer" from the King Messiah—and the renewal of Creation that results from a supernatural force.

## Belief, Prayer, Eretz Yisrael

"The greatest weapon of the Messiah, with which he will lead all of the battles and conquests, is prayer," says R. Nahman in his second sermon of *Likkutei Moharan* 1:2. Why, we might ask, only prayer and not with the force of other mitzvot? The answer can be found in other sermons of *Likkutei Moharan.* If we clarify what prayer is, as understood by R. Nahman, and what constitutes the act of prayer, one

comes to the realization—the "Bratslaver realization"—that the essence of prayer
and the essence of the Messiah are knotted together and bound, one to the other,
in a higher, otherworldly bond. Or stated in more mystical terms: "Prayer and
Messiah are the same. Prayer is *Shekhinah,* Queen,[28] speech and kingdom."

"They know," the Bratslaver teaches us,

> that the concept of Diaspora came into being from the dearth of faith and
> faith is the embodiment of prayer, prayer being in the category of miracles.
> Prayer is supernatural because nature dictates the way things must be. But
> prayer comes and changes nature by way of miracles and it is at such a time
> when faith is needed, faith that there exists a Creator and a Renewer that
> can create things anew according to his knowledge and judgment and,
> moreover, the core of faith as it has to do with prayer and miracles, exists
> only in Eretz Yisrael as it is stated: *Abide in the land and remain loyal* (Psalms
> 37:3) as Eretz Yisrael is also the central place of ascension of prayer as it is
> states *And this is the gate of heaven.* (Gen. 28:17)

Therefore, as Abraham was rendered defective with *bemah a'dah,* "With what will I
know?" (Gen. 15:8) and transgressed while in the land of prayer and faith he was
forced into exile and went down to Egypt.

"Through prayer," maintains R. Nahman, "one is favored with general
peace and becomes a continuation of God's mercy towards all other creatures until
one brings into existence *"And the wolf shall dwell with the lamb and the leopard
shall lie down with the kid."*[29] Through prayer one earns peace in every world
*("shalom be-khol ha-olamot"),* and comprehensive peace *(shalom ha-klali)* eliminates the give-and-take of the world that feeds off the world, where there is no
peace among divergent wills *(eyn shalom ben ha-retsonot).*

Prayer possesses all of the messianic qualities. "Israel," we learn further from
R. Nahman, "exists above and beyond nature," and only when Jews sin do they fall
under the (lower) force of nature and fate just like the pagans who live under the
dominion of Nature and Destiny. When God shows them mercy and wants to
redeem them from their oppression he resumes his own supervision over them and
eliminates that of Nature and Fate (which, according to law they needed in order
to live under their own jurisdiction for a time). This very type of supervision is
personified by the zaddik who is the embodiment of Moses Messiah who will
continue supervision from the end of the world since at that time Nature will be
abolished and there will only be a pure singular dominion. Until now we have
established R. Nahman's view of "prayer" as diametrically opposed to "Nature"
and of the same stuff as "miracle" and "Messiah."

Now we approach a more painstaking question: After thousands of years of
people pleading, calling, splitting open the heavens with their cries; generation

after generation, Israel shed its tears for their God—from their lands of wandering and their prison holes. The People of Israel is, as a whole, prayer; it prays from the first watch[30] until late at night. Even in the deepest night, its heart is never calm. It rises before dawn, places ashes on its head and cries with heaven and earth, stars and constellations, cries with the Angels of Peace and, as if it were possible, cries also in concealed worlds.[31] Today if the force of prayer is that powerful, how is it that the Messiah has not yet come? Why has the world not yet been redeemed from slavery and baseness? Why is it that from hour to hour and from day to day adversity intensifies and fratricide, "Cain murder,"[32] and the wars between nations, classes, parties, and individuals continue?

This question had great immediacy for R. Nahman. His answer was: It is a Divine war against Amalek. The lowest war is a resonance of the war that burns in all the other worlds. Strong, bitter, and cunning are the legions of the enemy that abide concealed even under the dominion of God himself, and each generation is engaged in its own battle, which one day will see victory finally achieved. In each era people must renew this struggle with fresh methods and strategies because the enemy itself manages to renew its stock of cunning plots to lay waste to the rule of His Holiness and to obliterate Jerusalem, the holy city.

Therefore, people are in need of a single chief-commander of holiness who will stand at the head of every soldier that does battle with Amalek and all the generals and soldiers must submit themselves to his command. Those generations that lack such a chief-commander go astray. There are generations who do have such a leader among them but not even the lowest-ranking soldiers recognize his authority and therefore scarcely possess enough power to withstand a time of distress.

Nonetheless, no effort is lost, not even one exerted by the weakest generation. Each "Divine War with Amalek" leaves at least an impression, and works to gradually wear down the power of the enemy, strengthening the power of holiness. There is no good that will be destroyed and no prayer that comes from the deep corners of one's heart can ever dissolve in an empty void—everything gets collected somewhere unrevealed, and everything is taken into account.

When the great conqueror, the redeeming zaddik appears, who embodies the figure of Moses the Messiah, he is sustained not only by his own powers and the powers of those of his own generation but also assisted by the power that has been gradually collecting throughout time, over preceding generations.

This idea is put forth by R. Nahman in one of his interpretations of the legends of *Rabba Bar Bar Hana*.[33] He breaks down each word, drawing out an elliptical meaning *(remez)* from each expression. His gloss is given to the following tale: "*Zimna chada havah ka azlinu be-sfinata.* . . . *One day we were travelling on a ship and we saw a fish whose back, protruding out of the surface of the water, was completely covered with sand. At first, we had thought that we had spotted land, and we got out and cooked our dinner. With this, the fish's back became very warm and he turned over. Had it not been for our ship that was docked close by, we all would have surely drowned."*[34]

R. Nahman understands the fish to be a symbol of the Zaddik of Redemption *(Zaddik-Goel)* which is on the level of Moses-Messiah, and understands the cooking that happened on the fish's back to represent the supplications of the souls that are transferred to the zaddik and their request that he induce the prayers' ascension. With this, *"and he turned over,"* the element of justice is *"turned over"* to affect the element of mercy and the souls are saved from drowning in exile.

The Zaddik of Redemption is, according to R. Nahman's reading of this parable, the mythical Leviathan on the sea of *Eyn-Sof* (the infinite dimension of God). All the supplications that did not ascend earlier gather around him and cleave to him, like glowing sand and he triggers the flight of the souls that are stored in these prayers. This sand around the Zaddik of Redemption multiplies by the thousands like the grass of the field and he, the Transgenerational Zaddik repairs both the prayers and the souls achieving the union of God with the *Shekhinah*. The Transgenerational Zaddik brings each prayer and each soul to the right place and in this way reconstructs the full stature of the *Shekhinah* until he establishes the Holy Tabernacle *(mishkan)* in its fullness, which will stir God's compassion for the world, in general, and specifically for Israel that is constantly sunk in sorrows and laments, and the entire reality will be replete with open and revealed grace. Even then, after the Transgenerational Zaddik affects these repairs, we are still in need of special benevolence from God. Sunk in the abysmal depths of vanity, it is upon us to seek refuge aboard the ship of the grace of God.

How do we recognize the Zaddik of Redemption? The souls fly to the Zaddik of Truth and he raises them and clothes these disembodied souls[35] who wander naked and bring to this place their prayers that stray in the void of the worlds. How can we know, however, the difference between the Zaddik of Truth who is the Transgenerational Zaddik (i.e., the zaddik who is the precursor of the Messiah and only appears once among the generations) and other zaddikim hwo are also great in relation to Torah, holiness, and purity? What are the markers that allow us to recognize him? What qualities mark the Zaddik of Redemption? What comprises the core and essence of the elevated soul that occupies the body of the Zaddik of Truth? And what is the towering wisdom that this zaddik possesses with which he casts hearts under his holy sway and draws the mighty near to him? The answer to these questions are located in various places in R. Nahman's writings.

"Know," says the Bratslaver,

> that somewhere there is a field where there grows wondrous trees and grass. The splendor from the field and its plants cannot be described. Happy is the eye that sets its gaze upon it! The trees and the grass are like holy souls that

grow there; as well, there are many naked souls that stray outside its borders and they await their repair in order to resume their positions. Even the greatest soul, upon whom so many other smaller souls are reliant, finds it difficult to return itself to the field when it has departed. And all of them, the souls, call for and await the field-leader, the field-manager to engage himself in *tikun*, of which they are in great need. There are also souls whose *tikun* comes only at the expense of someone else's death or through someone else's *mitzvah* or good work.

And whosoever wants to gird his loins and take on the mantle of the field-manager must be a man steadfast and courageous. He must be great in piety and wisdom. There is one such man who can only complete this task through his own death. Even then he must be exceptional since there are many such great men, whom, even with their deaths, cannot help. When it is truly a great man, this man he can affect that which is necessary, even during his lifetime. There are many afflictions that he must endure, but with his greatness and eminence, he can prevail and will guide himself through the work of the field as it needs to be done.[36]

We are already familiar with the concept of The Zaddik of Truth or the Gardener who, through his absolute submission *(eyn-muchlat)* is like Moses Our Teacher, as it is written: *"But where can wisdom be found," "Ve-ha-chochmah me-*eyn *timzeh."* (Job 28:12). Through this *eyn* one is absorbed into the *Eyn-Sof*. This is the *hitpashtut-hagashmiut*, the stripping-away of materiality, whereby man is capable of abolishing his own selfhood *(yesh)*, becoming part of the will of the *Eyn-Sof*. And this will grants life to all other wills. The Zohar writes that Moses Our Teacher's cleaving *(histaklut)* occurred on the Sabbath at the time of *Minchah-Ma'ariv* (late afternoon) which coincides with the revelation of the highest will *(ra'ava de-eyin)*. At this time he merits the nullification of his complete will and his entire existence, as it is stated: *And who are we? (Likkutei Moharan* 1:4).

The Zaddik of Truth, who is the same man as the Gardener and the Moses-Messiah, exhibits courage of the heart. Courage, says the Bratslaver, resides in the heart, because whomever has a courageous heart has no fear whatsoever. He can, with this power of the heart, perform amazing feats of bravery and can even win wars. And this is of the same sort as *Who is mighty? One who subdues his passions.*[37] This is similar to Samson's bravery, which accordingly it states, *The spirit of the Lord first moved him.*[38] *(Likkutei Moharan* 1:249).

In *Likkutei Moharan* 1:20 we find an elaboration on the behavior and the attributes of the Zaddik of Truth or field manager. Such behavior has nine components—that is, the ancient one, Moses-Messiah, and the faithful shepherd received nine signs. Firstly, *"take your rod,"* (Num. 20:8) which means the staff of power that was given to reward the good deeds that he performed. Secondly, *"and assemble the community"* (ibid.) meaning with this very staff of power you should preside over your congregation bringing near those who are good and subdue those who are angry.

*Three: Order the rock to yield its waters* (ibid.) the wicked must be forced with the staff of strength, but before God, the shepherd must stand as an indigent begging for mercy without relying on his own merit, for that is what is meant in the following: *I pleaded (ve-etchanan) with the Lord at the time saying (lemor).*[39] That is, one must utter supplications *(tachnunin)* when it comes time to speak *(lemor)* before the people. The zaddik, who is on the level of Moses the Messiah, must, before he speaks words of Torah, beg for mercy from the source of mercy.

*Four: le-eyneyhem* (lit. before their eyes) he must bind himself with those souls that congregate to see him.

*Five:* The Zaddik of Truth is a continuation of those words of fire. In the world there is a soul who reveals the right interpretations of the Torah and she [the soul] is filled with sadness as it is stated in Pirkei Avot (Ethics of the Fathers): *A morsel of bread with salt thou must eat.*[40] All of the interpreters of Torah are beneficiaries of this soul. All her utterances are like fiery coals since one can only draw Torah from someone whose speech is like coals as it is stated *"And behold my word is like fire"* (Jer. 23: 29).

*Six:* Moreover, the Zaddik of Truth is a continuation of Torah through prayer and supplication and he is a continuation of the celestial heart *(lev ha-elyon)* in which all Torah interpretations are inscribed.

*Seven: Va-yishlach moshe* **melachim** *mikadesh. From Kadesh Moses sent messengers.*[41] The divine powers, which are created from the letters of the Torah are really like angels. These divine forces, these angels, are related to the novella (hidushim) in the Torah: The innovations [of Torah] will multiply below according to how much holiness *(kedushah)* is produced above. The numbers of angels will multiply accordingly to how many [Torah] innovations are produced. The inverse is also true: at times, holiness becomes so diminished that the angels that are created from the innovative understandings of the Torah *(hiddushei-Torah)* are rendered so weak that they cannot receive their force to punish the wicked with sword and battle. They can only set off a fear in the hearts of the wicked—and even this is sometimes beyond their strength.

*Eight:* To whom did Moses send the angels? To the King of Edom (Num. 20:14).[42] The power to punish the wicked must be sought only from Edom, since their power is of the nature of *"Yet by your sword you shall live"* (Gen. 27:40).[43]

*Nine:* The Zaddik of Truth becomes steadfast and mighty only after he attains the level of *Eretz Israel. Eretz Israel* is one of the three things that can be conquered through adversity. Only then the Zaddik of Truth is called a man of war (Exod. 15:3) after he defeats them. But as long as he is not yet arrived at the level of

*Eretz Israel* we might say of him: *Let him that girds on his armor, not boast himself as he that puts it off* (Kings I 20:11).

We may recognize the Zaddik of Truth that readies the path of the Messiah by another attribute; according to the fullness of his possession of the holy tongue *(Lashon Ha-Kodesh)*. This refers to two things. Firstly, the holy tongue itself and the language of the Torah, the prophets, and the holy books; the language in which, according to our tradition, the world was created and the letters of which animate the entire creation. The letters descend and fall, from the heaven of heavens above to the deepest of depths, to the depths of materiality and vulgarity, according to the secret meaning of the Shekhinah. They then repair themselves and return to their source in the heavenly sphere of Emanation according to the secret of the return of the Divine Presence. Secondly, R. Nahman is also referring to the holy language of the Zaddik of Truth himself, his pure and holy words, which can be achieved firstly by holding back from any talk of slander and tale-telling, as well as from saying anything superfluous at all, including—as outlined in the *Tanya*[44]—speech that is not "for God and for Torah"—not from God and not from his way of Torah and secondly through speech that can be likened to fiery coals. This "wholeness of the holy tongue," such speech, which within it is dressed a lofty spiritual power, has great influence without end.

> One can be such a great man, and know the letters of the holy tongue which animates every object, but nonetheless the pleasure that he derives from eating and drinking derive not from the glittering of the letters, nor from their shine. The Zaddik however, merits all of his pleasure to be the product *only of the letters* of such objects as a man who is deserving of the fullness of the holy tongue and is therefore deserving of the ability to break his lust for sex and to bring within himself the brilliance of the language. Only the Zaddik, who [when reaching for] the first thing [the object] can actually grasp the second thing [the letters], and derives no pleasure from eating, drinking and other pleasures; he is instead renewed [by] the letters within them. Happy is he! *(Likkutei Morahan, 1:19)*

### Thirteen Ways of Drawing Closer

Until now, we have learned what constitutes the essence of the Moses-Messiah Zaddik of Truth and the signs by which he can be recognized and distinguished from other great zaddikim. What, however, are the ways in which the zaddik—or to speak plainly, the Bratslaver—draws man closer to the service of God? How can he purify them? What is the advice and the counsel by which he can rescue them from the collective enemy, from the Serpent of the Garden of Eden and from the *madurah* of the seventy stars,[45] or from the forces of anger? Many and varied are the Bratslaver's instructions that can be laid out, more or less, in thirteen points.

*Emunah peshutah.*[46] *Simple faith.* Many maladies, both physical and spiritual proceed from the deficiency of faith that is a result of sequestering oneself in "false wisdom" *(Hokhmot)*[47] and ceasing to serve God in simplicity (i.e., without intellect)—not just the foolish intellect ("foolish wisdom," *hokhmat shel shtot)* of average men, but even true wisdom. Even one who has a really great intellect, when he approaches worshiping of such simplicity, he must cast away all wisdom and serve God in simplicity. *(Likkutei Moharan* 2:5).

*Boundedness* with the Zaddik of Truth. A person must journey to the zaddik in order to retrieve her divestiture or loss *(avedah).* Before a person is born into this world she is taught and shown all that she will accomplish in this world and everything he must conceive. At the instant of birth she forgets all this. This forgetting is in the category of loss *(avedah)* and that which he loses resides with the zaddik since the zaddik searches for it on his behalf until he finds it. And similarly the zaddik searches and finds the losses of other people until he finds all of the loss in the entire world.

The question, than, of why this action cannot be fulfilled merely with ethical and pietistic *(Mussar)* literature, requiring one to journey to the zaddik, is illustrated in the following lesson. It is written: *And the Lord said unto Moses: Write this for a memorial in the book and rehearse it in the ears of Joshua* (Exod. 17: 14). It is less that Moses must transcribe than that Joshua must hear what Moses says to him: "and rehearse it in the ears of Joshua." He must speak to him mouth to mouth. The crux is that it must be heard from the very mouth of the zaddik.

And there are three aspects to the drawing near to zaddikim. The first is to *see* the Zaddik as it is written: *but your eyes will watch your Guide* (Isa. 30:20). Seeing the zaddik banishes the wicked traits that derive from the two elements of the animate and the inanimate, namely, depression and its offshoots and harmful desires. The second aspect is charity *(zedakah)* which one gives to the sage. Through this one is saved from the bestial traits that derive from the other two elements, the animal kingdom and humanity *(hayye* and *midbar),* which themselves are vanity and pride and their other offsprings. The third aspect is when a person confesses rage to a *talmid-hakham* through which he shows the *talmid hakham* the right path according to the root of his soul (his *shoresh-neshmah,) (Likkutei Moharan* 1:4). Each person must bind his prayer to the zaddik of the Generation since the Zaddik knows already how to reach the celestial towers and to lift each prayer to its apropriate tower *(Likkutei Moharan* 1:9).

*Faith in oneself and constant strengthening.* A great obstacle on the path toward fulfillment is the lack of faith in oneself. It begins with doubts in faith and prayer, which is replaced with sadness and in the end, if such an obstacle is not dealt with, total despair. Good people who are sharp-minded and sensitive are destined to flounder because such people scrutinize themselves and their own conduct and see all of their sins, weaknesses, and faults. They compare the colossal powers of the roaring world around them with the feebleness of the thin voice of silence within them; and they see and feel and understand how numerous these blemishes are that man commits in his thoughts and deeds and how ineffectual it is to correct and purify themselves and render themselves holy and they say to themselves, 'Why do I labor? Either we serve God, or we don't, either we multiply our prayers, or we don't—whether we do or don't we are lost . . . what will come of our exertion? Let us go and take in the pleasures of the world, as do all the children of the land, and if does not content us, if we find no substance in such actions, let us fall without conscience and without account."

It is for this reason that the Bratslaver waged such war against doubts and weakness of mind in all its forms. He immersed himself utterly in the state of mind of the person who aspires to divine fulfillment, and discovered, at the outset, that the conditions of doubt, of descent, or of falling are *unavoidable*. For those few people who are not satisfied with accepted habits and with the reality of their environment, they must experience such states of mind in order to mark their own personal path to God. Moreover they must search the source of their own soul, and illuminate it with the heavenly light that is only connected to their souls according to their distinct derivations.

Therefore Reb Nahman never ceases to counsel that one must "strengthen oneself and believe in oneself, and believe that one has strength to influence everything though prayer and discussion with the Creator." *(Reb Nathan in the name of his rebbe in Likkutei halachot, Choshen mishpat, Laws of Acquiring Property.)*

"At times," said Reb Nathan according to his rebbe's framework, "a man of words undercuts the ideas of a person: our forefathers and our leaders accomplished so much through prayer—but, it could be asked, what can be accomplished through prayer by, so to speak, a trivial man like yourself? In truth, since the Almighty heeds every prayer and every Jew is capable of persuading God if his prayer is an honest one.

*Prayer with one's entire strength, with cleaving, and with truth in one's heart.* People receive the essence of life from prayer, as it is written: *tefilah le-el chay,* therefore one must pray with the whole of one's strength. In that way people channel their strength into the letters of the prayer and renew ther strength according to *They are renewed every morning—Ample is your grace!*[48] (Likkutei Moharan, 1:9)

Each utterance is an entire world, and when a person prays and pronounces the prayer he is as one who promenades through a field and gathers flowers and binds them together. . . . And so he goes, all the while picking flowers and bringing them together in one bouquet . . . and he gathers more and more, from *avot* to *gevurot,* from *gevurot* to *kedushot,* and so on and so on. Likewise, who can imagine the utter splendor of the gathering and unity that a person gathers and unites through the utterance of prayer?

He must make from the entire prayer One—so that all utterances of the prayer are found in each separate utterance. *(Likkutei Moharan* 1:65)

*A cry of a pain and a violent scream.* "A person must cry to God as if he was caught in the middle of the ocean barely hanging on to life. And the storm rages to the corners of the sky and there is barely even time to cry . . . *because the person is in great danger which is known to each and every one of us (Sichot Haran* and *Likkutei Etzot).*

"Once," recounts R. Nathan, "I stood before him and he remained on his bed and from his holy mouth fell a few utterances: the essence *(ikkar)* is *mi-beten shaul shavati.*"[49]

*Hitbodedut. Seclusion.* Occasionally one must spend time in seclusion eye-to-eye with nature. "It is very good and pious to be among them"—that is among the grass and the plants. There is an interpretation of the Bratslaver's that is grammatically unusual but whose poetic content is beautiful. He says that *mashiach* is so called because he is nourished and draws strength *mi-siach ha-sadeh* (Genesis 2:5) from the vegetation of the field (spelled the same as *mashiach hasadeh, Messiah of the field).*[50]

*Joy that does not lock out brokenness.*

A broken heart and sadness are not the same thing, since sadness is caused by the *sitra achra* (the evil inclination) and God despises it; but a broken heart is love for God and therefore He cherishes it. It would be worthwhile to have a broken heart all day, but people like you (that is, good people who are nonetheless not exceptional, not distinct among their generation) are not able to sustain such a thing, since from a broken heart one can come to a sadness which is prohibited entirely. Therefore a person must find only one hour a day when he must cry out to God—and only in his thoughts so that nobody hears—and the rest of the day he must be happy. After a broken heart, comes happiness, and this happiness is the sign that he had a broken heart (not sadness).[51]

*An intimate discussion.* "A person must have a chat with God like he does with his rebbe or friend because it fills his heart with Him—God resides everywhere (Likkutei Moharan 2: 91–100)

It is very good when a man can pour out his heart before God like a son before his father, since His Blessed Name has called us "children" as it is written: *Banim atem ladonai elo he chem* [You are the children of the Lord your God] (Deut. 14:1). It is good for a person to speak freely and despair before Him. When a Jew wants to chat with His Blessed Name, spread his speech before Him and entreat Him about drawing near to good works, the Almighty takes His affairs and all His decrees, that He wants, *God forbid,* to decree and He, so to speak, throws them away and turns instead to those people that wish to speak to Him. (ibid.)

*The binding of Torah and Prayer.* It is good to make a prayer from Torah. Namely, when a person hears a teaching from the Zaddik of Truth, she should make a prayer from it that means that she should entreat God that even though she is still far from understanding the teaching she should draw merit from it—for when the teaching becomes a prayer, there will be great rejoicing above *(Likkutei Moharan* 2: 25).

*Holiness in one's conjugal life.* Absolute holiness in one's sex life is merited only by the Zaddik of Truth, who attains the "fullness of the holy tongue." Only he merits the full and thorough freedom from *ra ha-kolel,* (collective evil) from the bonfire of seventy stars resulting in the greatest lust—sexual appetite. That is not to say, however, that each person who truly wants to serve God is released from the obligation of observing *kedushat ha-brit* to the extent that it is possible. For as much as she sanctifies herself in this way, as much as she strives—he is all the more qualified to receive the illumination from the Zaddik of Truth, and to bring prayers to the Zaddik of Truth delivering to her valuable material toward the building of the tabernacle, resulting in the complete elevation of the Divine Presence.

"This is an overriding principle: that there is no man who is capable of comprehending the words of the Zaddik, if he has not repaired himself according to *brit kodesh.* "The principle trial a person encounters is that of adultery since this desire, found among all the nations, is founded in the secrets of other gods (i.e., idolatry). *(Likkutei Moharan* 1:19).

*The breaking of the lust for money and giving charity.*

"To continue supervision of the world is not possible unless one first breaks the lust for money which can be done through charity."

"This aspect," said R. Nahman, "is an aspect of the revelation of the Messiah, because the coming of the Messiah will abolish the lust for money as it is written: *On that day man will cast away his silver idols, and his gold idols.* "As long as the idolatrous worship of money is in the world, wrath will have dominion. When this idol-worship is annulled, wrath will be annulled with it as it says, *The breath of our nostrils, the anointed of the Lord* (Lamentations 4:20). *Hesed,* unlimited benevolence, will be drawn down into the world as it says, *Great salvation he gives to His King; And showeth mercy to His anointed* (Ps. 18:51). As every dimension of *hesed* is revealed, *da'at,* (knowledge) will continue from which the Temple will be constructed. This is likened to what is written, *But as for me, in the abundance of thy lovingkindness will I come into thy House* (Ps. 5:8) and as it states in the *Zohar* " *Ve-yamina do zamin le-mivnai bi mikdasha"* (and on this day the construction of the Temple will be prepared) since it is in the category of knowledge as it is stated in Berakhot 33: " *Whenever there is in a man knowledge, it is as if the Sanctuary had been built in his days"*—and this is also similar to the concept of the future Torah, *Torah she- le-atid lavoh* as the Zohar states that in the future the Torah of *atikah stima* will be revealed (see *Likkutei Moharan* 1:19).[52]

*Umufherleyche tshuve. Uninterrupted repentance.* Even as a person says, "I have sinned, I have dealt iniquitously, I have transgressed," it is not effective self-reflection *(p'niah).* Without this deep self-reflection she must repent on her repentance—on his "I have sinned; I have dealt iniquitously; I have transgressed." Even if a person knows for certain that she has already returned in complete repentance, she must repent on her first repentance, since earlier she had repented according to her conception *at that time,* the deficient conception, the imperfect one. Now, after she has achieved full repentance, she perceives God more than she did earlier, and from the perspective of her *present* conception, her earlier conception seems to her one of materiality. And this is what *chazal* had meant when they said, *He who conquers his evil inclination and confesses his sin over it, Scripture imputes it to him as though he had honoured the Holy One, blessed be He, in both worlds* (Sanhedrin 43b) He who conquers his evil inclination—meaning, he repents and also confesses on it—or in other words he repents on his first repentance, it is as though he is venerating God in both worlds. Why? Because the first repentance is of this world, and the "complete repentance," immediately following the first, when he is worthy to a higher perception and is eminently aware of the greatness of his/ His divinity and repents on his earlier deficient and imperfect repentance, then his repentance is already worthy of the world to come *(Likkutei Moharan* 1:6).

*The beginning always from new.* A prevailing principle in service to God is *O, if you would but heed His charge this day* (Ps. 95:7). This means, one must have in mind only the fleeting day—both in areas of livelihood and divine worship. One must not ponder what will be tomorrow. Moreover, when worshiping one must not contemplate anything but the present day. When one enters the realm of worship, the burden often seems more than one can bear. When one thinks, however, that one has nothing but that very day, it will no longer seem onerous and one will no longer procrastinate. " *Tomorrow* I will begin, *tomorrow* I will pray with purpose and with power as it is supposed to be done. . . . Man (alone and) for himself does not renew the present day, the morrow is completely another world. *Today if on my voice* (Ps. 5:4).

Every thinking person can understand that time is nothing, since the past no longer exists, the future does not yet exist, and the present is like a wink of the eye, so it seems that the only essential time is the present. On such a path, a person can cleave to the Almighty each minute and from any place, even from the depths of the depths.

These enumerated methods and courses of action are, according to R. Nahman, the steps that bring a person closer to the Zaddik of Truth and that assist the Zaddik of Truth in building for himself and for the entire people the edifice of salvation—in the aspect of Moses-Messiah.

The revealing of the Messiah will come only through the Zaddik of Truth, or the Transgenerational Zaddik who encompasses and illuminates all other souls, in his prayers, advice, and counsels. When is such a thing uttered? When the souls *recognize* him as their spiritual father and guide, their purifier and the one who enables them to become purged and when they heed his words and follow the path that he so indicates.

What about those souls, however, who neither know him nor accept him— not out of evil or wickedness, but out of a lack of discernment and a meager emotional sense? Who will repair these souls? How will the help of the final redemption come to the masses who know nothing, are not even able to distinguish their left hand from their right? The crux of it is: Israel is one thing, but the other nations—what will become of them? How will the *entire world* be redeemed?

The prophets spoke of this in such a clear and unambiguous fashion that they left little room for any perversion of their words. They said that each nation will shine with the light of the Messiah *"And the many peoples shall go and say"* (Isa. 2:3); *"I will also make you a light of nations, That my salvation may reach the ends of the earth"* (49:6); *For then I will make the peoples pure of speech, so that they all invoke the Lord by name and serve Him with one accord* (Zephaniah 3:9); *"For from where the sun rises to where it sets, My Name is honored among the nations, and everywhere incense and pure oblation are offered to My Name"* (Malachi 1:11).

One could ask, How and from where will the Torah of Truth be revealed to the distant and strange nations? Who will drive away the heavy and darkened clouds that conceal the Truth from them? Who will overrun all the fortresses that have been erected around the nations, fortresses that prevent the light of truth from Israel's Torah (except that which has penetrated in a perverted and falsified form)[53] to reach them? Maimonides understands the issue of the Messiah's conquests very simply, according to the plain reading: He, the King-Messiah will conquer nations with his soldiers and will force them to take on the yoke of the Kingdom of Heaven, or at the very least, the Seven Noahite Laws.[54]

The Kabbala treats this issue in great depth. The rabbi of Liady states that in the time of the End all materiality of the body and of the world will be purged, and from the overabundance of light, which will lead to Israel will also spill over and light up the darkness of the other nations.[55]

Nevertheless, one may ask, How will this come about? How will the light of the Messiah—no matter how great it will be for the nation of Israel—approach the nations of the world? Will they not be quick to refuse the light? It seems that they would close their eyes, as not to see the truth.

The King-Messiah will show wonder. But the person, as we know, is an agent of free-will, and God does not deprive her of her freedom to choose except in times of need—and only then for a short span of time—for how could the stone heart be taken from peoples that have *chosen* this wickedness?

There are various ways that may guide us to answer this question. They are all found in the essential Hasidic works, especially in those texts of *Chabad* (see, most importantly, *Sefer ha-chinuch* from the wondrous researcher of Godliness, R. Dov Baer, the son of the rabbi from Lyady).[56] A singular path to take in answering this question—and similar questions—can be found in a profound tract about *klalot ha-nisim* (the principles of miracles) toward the end of the Berditchever's *Kedushat Levi*.[57]

Among all those who search for the Messiah and all those who prepare his path, the Bratslaver is the only one who has demonstrated almost unambiguously the ways in which God will divest the minority of worthy Jews of its *heart of stone* and how, through the Messiah, God will bestow clear language upon the peoples with which they will call His name. The Messiah will impress his light upon those who are so absolutely distant from him and his people—distant from him in descent and place, in knowledge and conduct, and in faith and lifestyle.

The teachings on this theme are scattered throughout the Bratslaver's books. But when one binds them together an exceptional framework emerges concerning the laws of Divine influence, the roots of the souls and their transmigration, how the souls of Israel become open and revealed including those souls of Israel that are captive among the myriad nations of the world—often themselves not conscious of this state. These souls suffer and languish, without knowing why until finally there rises the light of redemption of Israel, especially, the light of the Zaddik of Truth, and later, at the end of the day, the light of *The Last Zaddik of Truth*, the King-Messiah.

In the lesson entitled, *And it came to pass when they emptied their sack* (Gen. 42:35) in *Likkutei Moharan* 1:17 this matter is discussed in depth. The concealed parts of the souls of Israel are active in hiding only until the time comes when they become enlightened and begin to strive for their source. This is what is at work in proselytes.

Whosoever reads these words with the required obedience, lucidity, and depth and shakes themselves free from *Mitnagdish* (anti-Hasidic) or *Maskilic* (Enlightened) prejudices against the creator of Hasidism in general (R. Israel Ba'al

Shem Tov) and the most original and wondrous among them—the Bratslaver, will find in these words an explanation and a heavenly parallel to the movements of conversion to Judaism. These movements have recurred persistently throughout history from the groups that converted at end of the Second Temple period to the movement of the Shabbatniks[58] of Russia, until today, in the remote villages of Volozhin and Podolia.[59] This occurred without any inducement on the part of Jews. In fact the opposite is the case. Even with a *distancing* on the part of Jewish circles who relished in recalling the saying: *lo gilu Israel ela be-kday she-yitvasfu alehem gerim.*

Such movements of conversion that have emerged among various nations and within various historical periods, which are so unlike each other, are self-generating phenomena and spread without the slightest efforts of cultivation on the part of anyone else—and even become detained in their movement because of their enemies who perceive them as a danger to their own political vision. It is not infrequent, however, that in such cases such movements surface from their places of hiding among the nations and gush out with an even greater strength.

There is an internal law at work in the "Good" that has been imprisoned for over generations and is then suddenly released under the influence of the primordial Holiness—both in an open and self-evident way or in a hidden way. . . . (That is, just as there is an instinct toward Good that functions as a force against Evil in the Evil-doer himself, in reaction to the Evil in society there awakes an internal, latent force of Good that is embodied by the proselyte, either actual or potential.)

However this same internal law that is at work in the Good is also at work in the Evil. We see this today in our times: idolatry, which was repressed over generations by a minute impulse toward Good, which stole its way among the nations in the form of a dark "shadow-of-a-shadow of Jewishness," has today revealed itself with great power, and has tore itself away from its hiding-place with the strength of the *omek ha-rah,* with a formidable power of the will, and with the desire to destroy and uproot. On its side, Good is still at work in the deep recesses of the nations and the *dibbur ha-Israel* gradually takes shape, and the Good will now cause the greatest destruction in the Kingdom of idolatry, and the Last Zaddik of Truth, the Last Redeemer of R. Nahman's vision that has not yet arisen, will collect the homeless sparks of holiness and bind them together and produce from them a cosmic power that would be the very holiness of holiness and courage of courage and that will, once and for all vanquish all the impurity from the Land. . . .

Hillel Zeitlin (1871–1942) was born in Korma Belarussia, received the education of a Habad Hasid, and was self-taught in secular studies. Distinctly more religious than the others, Zeitlin was one of a group of twentieth century thinkers like Isaac Leib Peretz and Samuel Horodetsky who initiated a modern rereading of Hasidism. His writings on Nahman reveal a scholarly bent as well as an intense spirituality and a sense of kinship he felt for his subject. Zeitlin was also the first to begin synthesizing the various scattered accounts of Nahman's life. The text that appears in this volume was originally entitled *Oroshel Mashiakh be-torat ha-braslavi* and has been translated according to his son Aaron's abridged version published in *Reb Nahman Bratslaver der zeer fun podolia*. In it Zeitlin draws our attention to the powerful messianic message in many of Nahman's discussions. He also revitalizes his call for prayer and repentance, seeing its heightened relevance in his own day as well as its messianic possibilities. Zeitlin died a martyr's death wrapped in his prayer shawl on the way to Treblinka.

## Notes

1. Nathan Sternhartz of Bratslav (d.1845). He is sometimes refered to as R. Nathan (or Noson) of Nemirov, as he served as a leader in the city of Nemirov before becoming a disciple of R. Nahman. However, he made it clear to his disciples and in his writings that he preferred to be called R. Natan of Bratslav (Breslov). He dies and was buried in Bratslav.

2. Num. 12:7

3. Levi Isaac of Berdichev (d.1809). Levi Isaac of Berdichev, as well as the rebbes that Zeitlin will list in this paragraph, all belong to the third generation of Hasidic leaders.

4. Jacob Isaac, ha-Hozeh mi-Lublin (d.1815).

5. Elimelech of Lyzhansk (d. 1787).

6. Meshullam Zussia of Anapol (d.1800).

7. Shneur Zalman, ba'al ha-Tanya of Lyady, was the founder of "Chabad" or "Lubavitch" Hasidism, (d. 1813).

8. R. Israel Hapstein of Kozienice (d.1814).

9. R. Mordechai of Neskhiz (1752–1800). He was a disciple of R. Yehiel Mikhal of Zloczow (1721–1786), disciple of the Maggid of Mezritch, and one of the early Hasidic masters in Gaicia. R. Mordecai became a leading Hasidic master in the Ukraine.

10. Abraham "the Angel" Ha-Malakh (d. 1776). He was the son of Dov Baer, the Maggid of Mezeritch and the father of R. Israel of Ruzhin. A collection of his teachings was printed in *Hesed l'Avraham* (Chernovitz, 1845).

11. Gen. 1:26.

12. Simeon Bar Yohai. Mid-second century c.e. rabbi and pupil of Rabbi Akiva. Tradition attributes to him the authorship of the Zohar and he hence became a central figure in Kabbalistic lore.

13. Issac Luria (1534–1572) founder of the school of Lurianic Kabbala.

14. Taken from Prov. 18:4, "The words a man speaks are deep waters, a flowing stream, a fountain of wisdom." R. Nahman became known for this acronym. Its earliest appearance is likely *Hayye MoHaRan*, "Journey to Uman" # 189. *Hayye MoHaRan* was written by R. Nathan and posthumously printed in Lemberg in 1874 by R. Nahman Goldstien and R. Nahman of Cheryn. The text was translated into English in its entirety as *Tzaddik*, trans. A. Greenbaum, ed. M. Mykoff (Jerusalem, 1987).

15. R. Nahman of Cheryn, a disciple of R. Nathan and editor of his posthumous writings. He was the author of two important Bratslav works, Parpera'ot l'Hokhma, one of the most widely read commentaries to *Likkutei MoHaRan* and *Zimrat Ha-Atez*, a collection of R. Nahman's sayings regarding the Holy Land.

16. Zohar (*The Book of Splendour*) the central work in the literature of the Kabbala.

17. *Collected Teachings of R. Issac Luria* first published in Karetz, 1788.

18. Lurianic Kabbala on the mitzvat, ed. by R. Meir Poppers, Karetz, 1785.

19. See *Likkutei Moharan* 1:6.

20. These two lights are cosmic categories in Lurianic Kabbala that are used in Hasidism to define the master/disciple relationship.

21. Nahman adopts Onklos' interpretation of *ya'akveney*, the word that Esau employs in bemoaning the loss of his blessing: "*Ya'akveney*. According to Reb Nahman, "Yaacov merited the blessing because he was first in terms of intelligence." *Likkutei Moharan* 11: 1). Before this Jacob and Esau were referred to as *ze le-umat ze* (one juxtaposed to the other) implying that they were equals.

22. *Malkhut* is the lowest *sephirah* of the ten mystical *sephirot*, first appearing in the early Kaballa of Isaac the Blind and later developed in the Zohar. It embodies the final stage of emanation and is depicted as feminine in nature.

23. The word play here is simply that *keshet*, Hebrew for "bow" is read as *bakasha*, Hebrew for "supplication."

24. His disciple Simeon accompanied Nahman on his trip to Eretz Yisrael. See Arthur Green, *Tormented Master* (Woodstock: Jeanshhight Publishers, 1992), 63–93.

25. Zeitlin applies the technical term, *din chazakah*, which is a halakic presumption of what amounts to squatter's rights to a particular piece of land. See Mishnah *BabaBatra* 28a, *Rambam Mishneh Torah "Laws of Ownership" (toen ve nitan)* 11:2; and *Tur and Shulkhan Aruch, hoshen mishpat chapter 140, halakhah 7.*

26. This seems to be a play on Rashi's comment to Gen. 1:1 where he states that the story of creation will be used against the allegations that the Gentiles rightfully inherited the Land of Israel.

27. Shivhei Ha-Besht was a collection of stories about the Baal Shem Tov

published by Israel Yoffe (Kopys 1814). It was published in English as *In Praise of the Baal Shem Tov,* trans. and eds. Dan Ben-Amos and Jerome Mintz (Bloomington, 1970).

28. "Queen," *Matronita,* or *Matrona* is the word used by the *Zohar* in referring to the Divine Presence. Usage originally found in the Talmud.

29. Isa. 11:6.

30. The "watch" or *ashmurah* refers to the Talmud's division of the first part of the day into three *ashmurot* watches. (Berakhot 32a).

31. This Refers to *Tikun Hazot,* a midnight prayer vigil instituted by R. Isaac Luria and his disciples to commemorate the destruction of the Temple. For an explanation and interpretation according to Bratslav traditions see *The Sweetest Hour.*

32. Zeitlin alludes to the first act of violence in the Bible; the murder of Abel by his brother Cain.

33. The fantasy legends are collected in the Talmudic tractate Baba Batra. R. Nahman uses them in *Likkutei Moharan* to expand ideas developed in the lesson in which it is cited. R. Nahman's infatuation with legends and fantasy, culminating in his Thirteen Tales, are apparent in this complex interpretations.

34. Bava Batra 73b. All translations of the Talmud taken from Soncino.

35. According to kabbalistic thought these disembodied souls are those of sinners, which roam the world until they are forgiven. For a detailed analysis of this phenomenon in kabbalistic literature and Bratslav Hasidism see Yakov Travis's chapter in this volume.

36. This is a paraphrase of *Likkutei Moharan* 1:65.

37. Pirkei Avot 4:1.

38. Refers to Samson, Jud. 13:25.

39. The passage refers to Moses begging God for entrance into the Promised Land (Deut. 3:23).

40. *Pirkei Avot* 6:4.

41. Zeitlin is using the words *melachim* and *mekadesh* since the angels are an outcome of the *kedushah* generated above. See Num. 20:14. It also plays with the double meaning of melachim, messengers and angels.

42. "From Kadesh Moses sent messengers to the king of Edom."

43. According to the biblical tradition, the nation of Edom is a descendant of Esau who is commanded by God *by your sword you shall live.* See Gen. 25:30 and Gen. 36:1.

44. *Likkutei Amarim Tanya,* first published in 1796 was written by R. Shneur Zalman of Lyady, founder of Habad Hasidism in White Russia. Zeitlin was educated as a youth in Habad Hasidism and often referred to the Habad tradition in his writings.

45. The *madurah* of the seventy stars is the celestial counterpart of the seventy nations and the seventy tongues.

46. Individual words have been transliterated according to their Hebrew pronunciation. Longer phrases that include Hebrew words have been transliterated according to the Yiddish pronunciation.

47. *Hokhma* is translated as "wisdom" but has the negative connotation of cutting oneself off from the divine source. See the prelude to "The Tale of the Seven Beggars," in *Sippurei Ma'asiot* of R. Nahman.

48. Lam. 3:23.

49. *Sihot Ha-Ran*, (Jerusalem, 1995) # 302, p. 326.

50. This is also a play on *siah* as "informal prayer" as in Gen. 24:63, *And Isaac went out walking [alt. to meditate] (l'suah) in the field toward evening*. The rabbis understand this to mean "praying". Cf. Ps. 143:5, 119:27, and 148. See *Likkutei Moharan* 2:1, 2:11 (par. 11).

51. This is a loose translation from R. Nahman's *Sihot Ha-Ran*, # 41 p. 50. The statement is based on *Likkutei Moharan* 2: 24.

52. The concept of *atika satima* is a complex term in the Zohar representing the concealed Torah of the future, those element of Torah that have not yet been revealed. It is often likened to the *ma'amar satum*, the silent divine utterance of creation. Zeitlin's use of this passage here is interesting. He seems to read R. Nahman to be saying that the desire for money, like sex, is a natural inclination but an exilic one. The only way for this to be broken is through the revelation of the heretofore concealed dimension of Torah, *atika satima*. All we can do is prepare for the that day, but we can never fully overcome these natural desires.

53. 55 This may be a veiled illusion to Christianity.

54. See Maimonides, *Mishneh Torah*, "Laws of Kings," chaps. 11, 12.

55. R. Shneur Zalman of Lyady (d. 1813). This reference may be to his most widely read work *Likkutei Amarim Tanya* but this idea is replete throughout his writings. Zeitlin was trained as a youth in Chabad Hasidism and was well versed in that tradition. See n. 44.

56. This is a reference to R. Dov Baer Schneersohn, the son of R. Shneur Zalman and second rebbe of the Habad dynasty. He is also known as the "Mittler Rebbe."

57. R. Levi Yizhak of Berditchev, a leading Hasidic figure in early nineteenth-century Hasidism. The collection of his writings *Kedushat Levi* was first printed in 1798 containing only essays on Hanukkah and Purim. Subsequent editions, the most well-known being the 1850 Lemberg edition contained teachings on all the Torah portions and comments on talmudic tractates. The sections on Purim and Hanukkah were relegated to the back of these later editions. Zeitlin is apparently referring to the Purim essays on miracles at the end of the later editions of *Kedushat Levi*.

58. The Subatnikes or Somrei Shabbat (possibly refer to the same groups) denote groups of Christians who theologically moved away from strict Christian doctrine toward Judaism. For some subatniks this meant the denial of the trinity;

others believed only in the Old Testament not the New Testament, observed Sabbath on the Saturday instead of the Sunday, observed dietary laws, and even went so far as to identify themselves with Jews rather than Christians. They were persecuted by the Russian government who scattered them throughout the Russian Empire to halt their growth.

59. In his edition of this article, Aaron Zeitlin remarks that such proselytes would travel to Warsaw to visit and talk to his father.

# 8

# Rabbi Nahman, Romanticism, and Rationalism

## *Samuel Abba Horodetzsky*

Even before the struggle of heart against intellect, of feeling against reason, had been aroused in German civilization at large—even before the great German romantics were conscious of a "longing for God" and pined for the mystical experience characteristic of medieval religion in their love of the "nameless" and in their "striving after the unattainable"—a similarly spiritual phenomenon had already arisen in the small Jewish community. Here the heart prevailed, as religious sensibility *(Empfinden)* gained the upper hand over sense-perception *(Wahrnehmung)*. The need for religious mysticism and for the imagination connected with it had already made itself felt. It was from this environment that the Hasidism of the Besht (b. 1698) arose.[1]

As a result of the strict rules that the rabbis drew up for the observance of various laws, thereby overstepping the bounds of their effectiveness, each tender impulse of religious feeling and poetry was nipped in the bud. Monotonous ceremoniality ossified the sensibility of the heart, which was receptive to mysticism in Judaism. Thus, on the one hand the budding Hasidic movement was compelled to lead a terrible struggle against fossilized legalism; but on the other hand, it had to assume little more than a heartfelt and sensitive attitude with the people in order to elicit the longing for the alluring poetic mysteries of Judaism that had been slumbering secretly all along.

Whereas religious romanticism in Germany met with only isolated advocates because the majority of people had no appreciation of it, Jewish romanticism—Hasidism—engendered a great upheaval among the Jewish masses with amazing speed. The Jewish spirit is, it would seem, predestined for emotional intuition *(gefühlsmäßige Anschauen)*. Its spiritual disposition is to become absorbed in the highest truths and in the deepest profundities of its nature. Various happenstance events, of which a more thorough treatment is here unnecessary, caused an overburdening of the people with all sorts of difficult studies and many oppressive laws, which superseded intuition and emotional contemplation in the people during certain periods. Yet it only required a little instigation, a trifling effort, to break through the enormous fence of legal prescriptions and instantly meet with assent and participation from the majority of the people.

The common opinion that "The Israelite religion has and knows no secrets, no mysteries"[2] is an incorrect generalization made by those who deny Judaism any understanding of mysticism. This is true only of official Judaism, of the Judaism of laws, of the intellectual aristocracy *(Geistesaristokratie)* in Judaism. It is there that the principle of "the subjugation of feeling to reason" reigns.[3] The majority of the Jewish people decidedly prefer mystery, full of feeling. The prophets, Aggadah, Kabbala, and Hasidism testify to this fact. The majority of the Jewish people knows only this religion of intuitive sensibility, for which Arthur Schopenhauer's expression "religion is the metaphysics of the people" is appropriate.[4] Hasidism gratified the yearning expectations of the people and attracted them to the movement, so that they withdrew from Rabbanism and its type of study.

The cradle of the movement was situated in the district of Vilna, including Ukraine and Podolia. It was there that the founder of Hasidism, the Besht, lived and had his following. He himself traveled the entire region and planted his teaching there, which shaped the fundamental principles of Hasidism. In other places his students then spread the teachings of the "Master." Hasidism quickly gained a solid position in this area.

After the deaths of the Besht, of his immediate "successor" Rabbi Ber of Mezeritch, and also of his prominent student Rabbi Jacob Joseph (the Apostle of Hasidism), Hasidism began to take on another form in the places just mentioned. This form was essentially different from that of the original founder. Emotion inordinately grew out of hand; Hasidism became excessively popular, the direct opposite of its original form. To be sure, feeling predominated in its original form as well, yet it had no shortage of the depth based in rational understanding *(verständnisinnige Vertiefung)* which increased its appeal and kept interest alive.

A religious movement of this kind cannot possibly endure without the necessary extent of both depth and spiritual content, or else it should not endure at all. Hasidism, just like religious romanticism in Germany, aspired to a union of reason with feeling in which the former is always meant to help the latter.

Religious romanticism in Germany found its champion of religious mysticism in Friedrich Schleiermacher. His knowledge of God was not based on understanding and rational comprehension, or on ethical foundations, as in Kant; rather it searched for its origin in emotion and in the heart, supported by the philosophy of Benedict de Spinoza.[5] His religious feelings were so clearly pronounced, and his yearning after the "infinite" and religious mysticism so greatly suffused him, that it subordinated philosophy to religion and to its accompanying mysticism. This is exemplified in his statement that "every philosophy directs someone, who can see far enough and is willing to go far enough, towards a mysticism."[6] Religious romanticism, Hasidism, discovered all this (even though in another form) in Rabbi Nahman ben Simhah of Bratslav (1772–1810).

"Le roi est mort, vive le roi!"[7] In 1771, one year before the death of Rabbi Ber of Mezeritch (the successor to the Besht), Rabbi Nahman was born in Medzhibozh, in Podolia. His father, Rabbi Simchah, was descended from an eminent family of rab-bis, and his mother Feige was a granddaughter of the Besht. The young Nahman thus found himself between two great extremes: on the one side the Rabbinate, representing Talmud study; on the other side Kabbala (the mystical secret teaching) and Hasidism. Two orientations, which faced each other in an extremely hostile relation and fought each other in different manners, simultaneously attempted to influence the delicate and sentimental nature of the young Nahman, until finally the latter (the mystical) prevailed. Perhaps the powerful attraction of this secret teaching with its allure of knowledge and intuition of the depths—inaccessible to an ignoramus—had won the heart of the young Nahman. Or, as is far more probable, the influence of his mother tipped the balance. His mother assumed a notable position in the circles of Hasidism, in contrast to his father, who did not go beyond the milieu of the simple modest citizen.

Women were often permitted to take part in a popular movement such as this, whereas they had earlier been completely banned from the camp of the rabbis. We even come across women who had leading roles in Hasidism. Thus, one was known by the designation "the Maid of Ludmir," a Hasidic type of "maiden of Orléans."[8] This woman enjoyed so great a reputation that many Hasidim made pilgrimages to her in order to learn the teachings of Hasidism directly from her mouth.[9] With this status, women received equal rights for the first time. They were also permitted at that time to look upon the countenance of the zaddik (the righteous man, as a Hasidic rabbi was called), even to speak with him as a man would. Indeed, they also received the feminine designation Hasidah (pious woman).

Rabbi Nahman's mother belonged to those women who took an active part in the development of Hasidism. All prominent zaddikim of that period knew to value her clear mind and acumen.

Her two brothers, Rabbi Moshe Chaim Ephraim and Rabbi Baruch, may have influenced the upbringing of the young Nahman to an even greater extent than his mother: the former through his self-absorption into Hasidism, the latter through his self-conscious demeanor and through his style of looking beyond (*hinwegsehen*) all other people. In these qualities the disciple later superseded his master.

Rabbi Nahman was brought up in intensely Hasidic surroundings. Legend has it that he had begun to envy the majority of people in his environment when he was already six years old, because they were capable of reciting their prayers with a selfless rapture. At this age, he began to practice excessively ascetic rituals. He would adhere to days of fasting, and only when he was unable to sustain the fast any further did he begin to take food into his system; he would then only swallow it quickly, since through the sense of taste he would have heightened the enjoyment of his worldly existence. He himself relates that, already as a small child, he wanted to be "in fear of God." He wanted to perceive in himself the type of holiness that is meant to endow the reception of the Sabbath with a special blessedness. To this end, he undertook ritual ablutions immediately after midnight on Sabbath eve. Then he put on Sabbath garments and dashed to the house of study. He began to pass from one end of the room to the other in a quick walk, back and forth, in order to grasp this holiness of the Sabbath, in order to partake of the transfiguring disposition of the soul, this "soul-expansion." In general, he wanted to behold *something*, yet all his longing and all his preparations were in vain; he saw nothing.[10]

It is to that strong a degree that he was under the influence of the atmosphere that surrounded him. The six-year-old boy was by nature of a merry and cheerful mind and devoted himself with abandon to wild games, jumping around and delighting in walks. Yet he was so under the influence of Hasidism that he was even then conscious of a longing for the comprehension of God, a deeply rooted love of the holiness of religion, a craving for the intangible.

He was also extremely diligent in study. By his own means, he increased the salary paid by his father to his teacher, thereby enabling his teacher to work with him over and above the hours appointed. According to legend, even in *heder* (Jewish primary school), he continually strove to imagine God, in order to comply with the maxim "I always imagine myself face-to-face with God."[11]

In general, he loved solitude after returning from *heder*. He had chosen a corner of the attic of his father's house, which removed him from others' observation. There, in his innocently naive nature, he conceived quite peculiar prayers, which he sent on high from the depths of his heart. What an abundance of naïveté coupled with an incandescent desire to know with spiritual eyes what is denied to physical eyes! Very often he went to the grave of the Besht, his grandfather; indeed, even at night he was not reluctant to seek out the grave in order to carry on a conversation with his grandfather.[12] We see now how the inventiveness of Hasidism, with its rich imagery, sought to portray the youth of Nahman, surrounding him in a beautiful wreath of fables, and embellishing his childhood years with almost supernatural capabilities and qualities.

At the age of fourteen, he married the daughter of a wealthy man from the village of Usyatin in Russia (the present-day village of Usyatin in Podolia) and moved into the home of his father-in-law. There he made preparations for his future position, which he later occupied as the renewer of Hasidism and the leader of the Hasidim.

It was only with great difficulty that he made up his mind to take this path. Again and again he relapsed from his chosen direction into his original situation, which he was able to leave only with great self-control and after a difficult inner struggle.[13]

Rabbi Nahman assumed his mission neither as a successor to his parents nor as a successor to his teachers. It was from within himself that he began to go along the new path of Hasidism. He derisively countered the assumption of his contemporary zaddikim—that the "exalted soul," conferred from heaven upon the zaddik alone, constituted the zaddik's proper essence,—with his own contention that it was up to the individual to develop a good or a bad soul. Everything has its proper cause in the individual's personal qualities and deeds, and each single person can individually get quite far and climb upward to a spiritually high level.[14]

In Usyatin Rabbi Nahman finally blazed the path that he wanted to follow. There he absorbed himself in the study of Bible and Talmud, of early as well as Lurianic Kabbalah, and ethics. Next he took on the teaching of Rabbi Luria, especially his practical method of bodily mortifications and diminutions of pleasure in life.[15] On occasion, he fasted from Friday to Friday, with the result that he took up this mortification eighteen times during the course of the year. According to legend, he renounced all human desires here in Usyatin, even those connected to marital obligations. The following expression is attributed to him at the moment of the highest level of transfiguration: "I know no difference between man and woman."[16]

## VI.

Schleiermacher based his system of religion—"to behold the infinite in everything finite"—on the Spinozistic principle that everything finite may be included in the infinite.[17] The individual person, who unites both the finite and the infinite within herself, must recognize the infinite within through self-observation and self-intuition. Then the individual has found God, the Infinite, and thus has also reached the heights of religious experience.

Through self-observation, she acquires the union of the finite with the universal.[18]

From this idea, which already has its foundation in Spinoza,[19] it is only a small step to the worship of the great religious person, who has found the infinite in herself and in all of creation, and who therefore surpasses all other persons. Whereas the other German romantics had worshiped the "genius" of art, Schleiermacher is said to have arrived at a worship of the great religious person following his religious struggles.[20]

We find this entire chain of thought also in Rabbi Nahman.

The search for, and the observation of, God in each and every thing in the entire universe is the highest religion. An individual must seek out her God and that of the universe and unite with Him, merge with Him. But the system of Rabbi Nahman differs from Schleiermacher's system as to the means by which union with God can be achieved. Schleiermacher attains intuition and union with the universal, with the infinite, through self-observation. "Time and again (when) I turn myself back into my inner self, I am simultaneously in the realm of eternity."[21] Rabbi Nahman wants to attain union through self-denial, through the annulment *(Aufhebung)* of all desires and evil qualities. After that, the material stuff of the person has been made spiritual. The body must be transformed into the essence of the pure soul, into reason and knowledge. Only on this condition can this person be properly placed in his or her core *(Stamm);* only then does he or she acquire "union with the unity of God."[22] We also find a similar mystical idea in the German mystics Meister Eckhart and Jakob Boehme.[23]

There is a sort of person who is able to transform material into form and to discern God in everything, and thereupon attains the rank of *Übermensch.* This is the zaddik.

The zaddik holds the primary position in all Judaism based in feeling *(Gefühlsjudentum),* the Judaism of spiritual pantheism. In a manner of speaking, he forms the center of all creation. Rabbi Nahman accorded him a particularly high rank. According to his view, the zaddik is in the position to do everything. He can "create a new heaven and a new earth, perform miracles here and there." He influences the world's harmonic cooperation. The Torah is given into his hand to use as he sees fit; his own words are "more meaningful than those of the Torah and the prophets."[24]

The *Übermensch* of Rabbi Nahman is also essentially different from that of the romantics. For them, the *Übermensch* simply stands above all others, and has no point of contact whatsoever with the people. But Rabbi Nahman joins the zaddik to the people as to a body. The zaddik is like the soul of the body politic *(Volkskörpers).* He forms "the essence, the bone and the people, the flesh." They relate to each other as "quill to author." They are therefore continuously, ineluctably connected.[25]

The duty of the zaddik, which grows out of his behavior toward the people, is to be their teacher and guide, to continually lead them along the right path, and to gradually bring them to a higher level of the knowledge that God may be found in everything, stretching "from the elementary steps of thought to a great spiritual grasp of the material world." In the beginning stage, that of the purely corporeal, God may still be "shrouded in many covers." An individual can attain the highest point of divine knowledge by traveling along a path of gradual development, always drawing nearer to the Lord. To be sure, this is a very difficult point. Most importantly, no lone and unguided person is allowed to traverse this path. Not just *any* eye is able to penetrate the many shrouds that surround God. A guide—the zaddik—is absolutely necessary for this. Only he possesses the capability to comprehend God, and there is no other teacher except the zaddik.

Rabbi Nahman explains the ways in which zaddik operates.

A spiritual ability comes into being through his inner yearning. But as he endows this inner yearning with oral expression, an authentic soul comes into being. The expression is the stuttering breath which communicates itself to people in the vibrations of the air *[Luftschwingungen]* and influences them. It is well-known that the tools of speech leap through the air, until they reach the person addressed next, so that this person then perceives a language and in such a manner also receives his [the zaddik's] soul and his inspiration.[26]

In such a manner, the zaddik guides the people and inspires them to penance and good deeds. He sustains their faith in God and lets them share in his spiritual inflow *(einflusse)*. Yet all this is only possible if a person is tightly connected with the zaddik. To put it quite simply, the individual must give all of her trust to the zaddik without posing all sorts of questions and without picking out contradictions that may arise. She must discover in the zaddik a similarity to God. Just as something can seem open to doubt with respect to God, this can likewise happen with respect to the zaddik.

A strong bond must unite individuals with the zaddik. Only under this condition can the latter ensure the welfare of the former—not only in the here and now, but also in the beyond. The true Hasid, who attaches himself closely to the zaddik, should therefore entrust everything to him and trust him completely. He must also confess his transgressions to him, for the zaddik "forgives sins."[27]

The view of Rabbi Nahman on the position of the zaddik is almost that of a representative of God.[28] Yet the institution of confession remained scattered in all of Jewish literature, because it contradicts the Jewish spirit.

The prayer that each Hasid from Breslav performs is interesting:

Let us be worthy in Your great kind-heartedness, to make a true confession before the genuine zaddik and the wise one of the ages, from all our youth to the present day. With this confession, may he, in his wisdom and gentleness, forgive us our sins which we have committed against You. May he lead us along the right path which we follow, and may he guide us to actions which we should do.[29]

In this prayer we discover the zaddik as a kind of helper of God. In another prayer we see exactly the opposite. There the confession concentrates primarily on the zaddik, who stands alongside God in helping (the penitent). The Breslav hasid prays:

May my confession to You be accepted as pleasing, as if I had confessed before the great wise one and the true zaddik. Grant us all good qualities and merits, as well as the casting off of all passions, and grant us all other merits which we may acquire through our true zaddik. Grant us what we request from You, and what we have neglected to mention. Help us to achieve everything, O Eternal one, our God, in your great mercy. You are our Father, and we have no other support than You, O our Father in Heaven.[30]

One of the earlier Hasidim from Breslav writes me that Rabbi Nahman received none of his followers before he or she had made a proper confession.

This introduction of the confession and these prayers naturally comprised the oil for the great fire of uproar against Rabbi Nahman, whereby the conflict and the persecution became even more severe.

## VII.

At the time of the circulation in Berlin of Mendelssohn's teaching that Judaism is a religion of practical action *(Betätigung)* and is not based on dogmas of faith,[31] Rabbi Nahman was teaching exactly the opposite. For him, Judaism is radically a religion of faith "without any sophistry" and only in it can one find both spiritual and material happiness. In Judaism, the oppressed, under the burden of collapse from everyday afflictions, find comfort and refreshment from their worries.[32]

He protested against those Jewish rationalists *(Forscher)*, who "can grasp what is proper only on the ground of philosophy and profane knowledge." Rabbi Nahman—who surrounded the entire community with immense love, who perceived "a part of the highest God" in each Jew, who called everybody "zaddik"—could not endure such an aristocratic point of view. He asked, What should those people, who are not capable of searching for the basic axioms, do? How then are they supposed to understand and grasp their purpose? Aside from the fact that philosophical inquiry in and of itself brings neither intellectual gains (because it is more likely to confuse human understanding) nor practical and principled results, it is by no means so constituted as to have an edifying effect upon the *heart*. "These great rationalists and intellectuals concentrate their entire thought on the construction of a weapon, which is meant to kill thousands of men with one blow," exclaimed Rabbi Nahman at one time, ironically. "Jacob has no share in this system. We believe in God, praised be He, without any musings (on the rationality of our faith), as did our ancestors." When our teacher Moses gave us the Torah, he began it with one principle. "In the beginning God created without any investigation or proofs whatsoever. He charged us to believe in God straightforwardly." We must reflect upon life only in a simple and honest faith, without any investigation or criticism. "Everything is certainly arranged in an orderly fashion; we are merely incapable of understanding the ways of God with our insufficient intellect. Our intellect is not like that of God. Were God to govern the world according to our understanding, then His apprehension would be the same as our own. Yet far from it." In the end, the philosophers are indeed not in the position to explain all the happenings in practical life. This is only possible through faith. And where the ABCs of philosophy come to an end, there begins the wisdom of Kabbala.[33]

Thus Rabbi Nahman inaugurated a struggle against the entire literature of Jewish rationalism. "One must steer clear of it; it is exceedingly harmful for faith." He prohibited his followers from consulting texts such as various commentaries on the Bible, Maimonides' *Guide of the Perplexed, The Book of Knowledge* (in the *Mishneh Torah)* and the *Treatise on Logic,* the section "Gates of Unity" in (Bahya ibn Pakuda's) book *Duties of the Heart,* and the sacrifice of Isaac. In particular he vented his anger on the *Guide;* this book was especially odious to him. "Whoever studies this," he said, "will most certainly lose his similarity to God, the holiness of His countenance." He distinguished between the *Guide,* "based on the teaching of the pagan Aristotle," and books such as the *Zohar* and the works of Rabbi Luria, which are born of the Holy Spirit.[34] In writings not yet published, Rabbi Nahman says, "Many people hold so many rationalists, e.g. Maimonides, to be great men. But thereafter they will be convinced that he was an *apikoros,* a blasphemer."[35]

The zeal of Rabbi Nahman is also found in that of his student Rabbi Nathan, who published a book entitled *The Names of the Zaddikim* under the influence of Rabbi Nahman. In this book all the zaddikim are enumerated, from Adam up to the time of Rabbi Nahman. And though many of Rabbi Nahman's students are mentioned, the names of such great men as Judah Halevi, ibn Gabirol, ibn Ezra, Gersonides, and Rabbi Isaac Arama are missing. Among the rationalists, only the name of Maimonides is to be found, probably because the author feared reprisal *(üble Nachrede).*

In such a manner we find Rabbi Nahman as the guardian spirit of simple faith. Each of his followers had a prayer arranged under his redaction, which ran as follows: "I hope to be worthy of You and to serve You honestly, in perfect simplicity without any sophistry. Protect and guard me in Your great mercy from criticism and heretical teachings. Have mercy upon me and upon all Israel and, in Your great grace, allow me to partake of true piety."[36]

"Honesty without Sophistry" was Nahman's motto, not only regarding one's pure faith, but also in reference to the practical performance of the command-ments. He advocates that one "serve God honestly" and not to investigate "whether everything has really been calculated precisely" by splitting hairs, for this is barely possible for an average mortal and God does not perpetrate such tyranni-cal acts. After all, the Torah is not given to angels. The expression "One should live through it and not die through it"[37] is meant for the exceedingly diligent person and the person who makes everything more difficult for herself. But this cannot be called "life," if one is in constant anxiety as to whether one has indeed precisely observed this or that commandment. In reality, humanity has nothing to fear. It only has to follow the straight path. "A person should be able to walk along a quite narrow bridge and, above all, have no fear." And if he or she is sometimes hindered from strictly carrying out service to God, "then grace is conferred by necessity." "Nothing," says Rabbi Nahman, "is truly prescribed, if it is not possible. And if it is not possible, then it just must not be commanded."

When his student Rabbi Nathan refused to accept an official position as Rabbi Nahman's assistant *(Religionsassessor)* because he sometimes might be tempted to permit something that would actually be forbidden, Rabbi Nahman shouted to him, "There is no anxiety here! A possibility of lightening one's load has barely presented itself, and right away one is allowed to do it. The Torah was revealed to the scholars of the time, so that they might explain it according to their best knowledge." Rabbi Nahman did not only try to ease everything for others but also for himself. He in no way made anything more difficult; he even applied the very strict laws of Passover with special mildness to himself and also to others.[38]

In this view Rabbi Nahman was like his grandfather, the Besht, who had always likewise said, "One should not ponder so much about everything that one does. Living in constant anxiety as to whether one has adhered to everything properly and exactly is an example of the evil inclination."[39] This teaching is a direct antithesis to that of Rabbi Luria, which, it would seem, developed a pedantry in regards to the performance of commandments.[40]

According to the view of Rabbi Nahman, Judaism is founded on faith as its original basis, and in no way on philosophical or even practical inquiry. The Jew must believe honestly and simply. But from this one must not infer that reason is entirely superfluous. It is merely forbidden to use reason for profane knowledge, and this profane reason is not necessary for simple faith. Rabbi Nahman thought highly of reason—he only distinguishes external reason, which acts rather harmfully (because it clogs a person's heart and head), from that reason which is found in the interior region of a person and is holy because it flows from a pure source, the "highest reason of holiness." This reason is the most important in a person's life. This forms his "I," his soul. One must always aspire to rejuvenate and develop it. "Its rejuvenation goes hand in hand with the rejuvenation of the soul." One must search for God and involve oneself deeply in contemplation of Him. "One must search for God everywhere in the deepest depths." Thought itself must be sanctified, as one thinks of God. Through this one merges with Him. "Where reason is active, there is also the entire person." Out of this good thought, out of the "intense yearning for God," the soul emerges and reason is transformed in action. An intellect *in actu (in Wirklichkeit)* comes into being and that is "the immortal in him." What essentially perdures of persons after death is the acquired intellect, the "persisting and active *(wirkende)* intellect." The person who possesses this, knows "no difference between life and death, but is constantly united with God, and therefore lives an eternal life, somewhat as God does." One can only achieve this level of the intellect through "true, honest faith." "Through faith we become wise."[41]

Rabbi Nahman's view essentially occurs already in his detested Maimonides. Maimonides says, "The soul of every person is the form that God has given to him, and the higher knowledge, which resides inside him, shapes the form of the perfect individual." The soul is thus immortal. "The immortal souls are radically different from those in human bodies during their lifetimes. These are simply an aptitude, a potential, whereas the others are actual." And these souls, formed from intellect and knowledge, "partake in the glory of the Shekhinah." It has been gran-ted to them "to indulge in the consciousness of the knowledge of God, as the holy creatures and all sorts of angels understand and recognize the essence of God."[42]

In these words of Maimonides, the words of Rabbi Nahman are clearly included. They essentially differ only in the interpretation of the quiddity of the acquired intellect. A Maimonidean, after sitting in an open field, would place his trust in God *and* science.[43] Yet Rabbi Nahman would let it emerge only from a pure and simple faith and from the knowledge of Torah, because one acquires knowledge of God without sophistry and profane knowledge.

In conformity with his teaching, he prohibited "various speculations in life" for his people. One should trust only in God, who no doubt will help those who honestly appeal to God. Of himself he said, "Even if I were to sit in an open field, I would nonetheless have confidence that God could grant me what I need." For the same reason he prohibited recourse to doctors, to whom he referred as actual killers, who murder people with their own hands. Of them he ironically said, "They ease the workload of the angel of death, which he would be able to carry out only with difficulty, were he alone." A person has only oneself to blame for all privations under which one has to suffer, be it a lack of nourishment or health; nothing bad comes from God. It is only because of one's sins that a person loses her ability to receive the light of God that shines upon her eternally. Hence, one must believe in God, and take delight in His light. But Rabbi Nahman was not able to withstand temptation—when he himself became sick, he sought out medical assistance in Lemberg. His students, though, knew to depict it as a special duty that had been imposed upon him from heaven. It was supposed that he wascon-cerned with medicine for reasons were known only to him.[44]

Thus Rabbi Nahman also dealt with scientific-rational inquiry. According to legend, he himself studied many rationalist books and then bragged about it, stating that the following expression proceeded to be true of him: "And know how to take steps against the *apikoros*."[45] Relying on the wide scope of his reading, he tried to refute the statements of many rationalists. An interesting example is his refutation of the hypothesis that the moon is populated. "The moon," he said, "is like a mirror in which is reflected everything that is located in its view. Therefore we see in the moon only what is on the earth, but not other beings which might be established there."⁴⁶ Now and then he let a stream of criticism shine through, which by all means disclosed the reading of so many books. One of his utterances has a deeply moving effect in the Hasidic world and brought the suspicion of heresy upon him. "The world is subordinate to the understanding of the knowledge of the Torah and of the sciences."⁴⁷ Thus he associates the study of Torah with that of natural science. Coming from his mouth, this is an incredible expression.

—Translated by Martin Kavka

## Notes

1. Besht = Baal Shem Tov, lit., "Master of the Good Name," founder of Hasidism. Cf. S. A. Horodetzky, *Rabbi Israel Bal-Schem* (Berlin, 1909).
2. Ludwig Phillipson, *Israelitische Religionslehre* (Leipzig, Germany, 1861), I:34.
3. Ambrose, *On the Duties of Church Officers* [De officiis], I:119, cited in Chamberlain, *Fundamentals* (Münich, 1903).
4. [No citation given.]
5. William Windelband, *Geschichte der Philosophie* (Leipzig, Germany, 1907), II:303. [*History of Philosophy*, trans. James H. Tufts (New York, 1914), pp. 582ff.] Compare Hermann Siebeck, *Lehrbuch der Religionsphilosophie* (Leipzig, Germany, 1893), p. 226.
6. *Aus Schleiermachers Leben: In Briefen* (1863; Berlin; 1974), IV:73. Cf. M. Isserl, "Torat ha-'olah" (1520), vol. 3, chap. 4, "Philosophy and Kabbalah are one and the same; they only speak in different languages."
7. [In French in the original.]
8. [The reference is to Friedrich Schiller's play about Joan of Arc, *The Maiden of Orléans: A Romantic Tragedy*.]
9. S. A. Horodetzky, "Ludmirskaja diewa," in d. russ. Ztschr. Jewrajskaja Starina II.
10. R. Nathan [Sternharz, of Nemirov], *Hayyey MoHaRaN*, II.
11. R. Nathan, *Shivhey MoHaRaN*, 4. [Nathan (Sternharz) of Nemirov, "The Praise of Rabbi Nahman," in *Rabbi Nahman's Wisdom*, trans. Aryeh Kaplan, ed. Zvi A. Rosenfeld (Jerusalem and New York, 1973), p. 5.]
12. Ibid., p. 20. [*Rabbi Nahman's Wisdom*, p. 21.]
13. Ibid., p. 16. [*Rabbi Nahman's Wisdom*, p. 17.]
14. Ibid., p. 52.
15. Cf. R. Hayyim Vital in his Preface to *'Etz Hayyim* (Sedilkov, 1817).

16. R. Nathan, *Hayyey MoHaRaN*, II:2. [*Rabbi Nahman's Wisdom*, pp. 19–20.]

17. W. Dilthey, *Lebens Schleiermachers* (Berlin, 1870), pp. 3–4. Cf. R. Heym, *Die romantike Schule* (Berlin, 1870), p. 524.

18. Schleiermacher, *On Religion*, 2nd ed. (Berlin, 1870). [*On Religion: Speeches to its Cultured Despisers*, trans. John Oman (New York, 1958).]

19. Spinoza, *Ethics*, IV:28.

20. Cf. Oskar Walzel, *Deutsche Romantik* (Leipzig, Germany, 1908), p. 66. [*German Romanticism*, trans. Alma E. Lussky (New York and London: G. P. Putnam's Sons, 1932), 75.]

21. Schleiermacher, *Monologen* (Stuttgart, Germany, 1835). [Horodezky gives no page reference. The reason may be that this quote as well as the paraphrase of Schleiermacher is taken directly from Walzel's *German Romanticism*, p. 50.]

22. R. Nahman of Bratslav, *Liqqutey MoHaRan*, I:30, 104; R. Nathan of Nemirov, *Liqqutey 'Ezot*, s.v. "Da'at."

23. Cf. Windelband, *Geschichte der neueren Philosophie* (Leipzig, Germany, 1878), I:28–30, 120–21.

24. R. Nahman, *Liqqutey MoHaRaN* 94, 142.

25. Ibid., p. 44, 98; R. Nahman, *Sefer ha-Middot*, s.v. "Gav."

26. Ibid, I:60, 62, 66, II:16.

27. R. Nahman, *Liqqutey MoHaRaN* II:50; *Sichot HaRaN* 46. Also cf. R. Nathan of Nemirov, *Hayyey MoHaRaN* II:38.

28. In other words, Rabbi Nahman almost equates the zaddik with a Catholic priest, someone who also has the power to absolve penitent sinners.

29. R. Nathan, *Liqqutey Tefillot* 4.

30. Ibid.

31. Moses Mendelssohn, *Jerusalem* (Berlin, 1783), II:31. [*Jerusalem, or on Religious Power and Judaism*, trans. Allan Arkush, with commentary and introduction by Alexander Altmann (Hanover and London, 1983), p. 102.]

32. R. Nahman, *Liqqutei MoHaRaN* II:12, *Sihot HaRaN*, 64.

33. R. Nahman, *Liqqutei MoHaRaN* I:98, 146; *Sihot Haran*, 64, 224. R. Nathan, *Liqqutey 'Ezot*, s.v. "Haqirot," *Hayyey MoHaRaN* II:220.

34. R. Nahman, *Liqqutei MoHaRaN* II:94; R. Nathan, *Hayyey MoHaRaN*, II, s.v. "lehitraheq mahqirot."

35. These words were quoted by one of the Breslav Hasidim in his name.

36. R. Nathan, *Liqqutei Tefilot* 10.

37. B. Yoma 85b.

38. R. Nahman, *Liqqutei MoHaRaN*, II:24, 94, 104; *Sihot HaRaN*, 207. R. Nathan, *Hayyey MoHaRaN*, II s.v. "Avodat adonai."

39. In *Zava'at RIVaSH*, ed. Isaiah of Dinovits.

40. R. Hayyim Vital, Introduction to *'Etz Hayyim* (Sedlikov, 1802).

41. R. Nathan, *Liqqutey 'Ezot*, s.v. "'Emunah," "Da'at"; R. Nahman, *Liqqutei MoHaRaN* I:70; *Sefer ha-Middot*, s.v. "'Emunah."

42. Moses Maimonides, *Yesodei ha-Torah* IV:8; *Guide of the Perplexed* I:70, I:40–41; *Commentary to the Mishnah, Sanhedrin Helek.*

43. [There appears to be a printer's error, and perhaps a missing line, in the third sentence of this paragraph in the German edition ("Nach / im offenen Felde sitzen. . . ."); the metaphor of sitting in a field is explained in the next paragraph.]

44. R. Nahman, *Liqqutey MoHaRaN*, I:24, II:144; *Sihot HaRaN*, 100.

45. M. Avot I:2.

46. R. Nathan, *Hayyey Moharan* II; R. Nahman: *Liqqutei Moharan* I:62, 140.

47. R. Nahman, *Sefer ha-Middot*, s.v. "Da'at."

# 9

## Mystical Hasidism and the Hasidism of Faith
### *A Typological Analysis*

### *Joseph Weiss*

To Professor Julius Guttman
A student's gift upon his seventieth birthday

If one examines Hasidism—the most recent religious movement in our history—through the lens of critical scholarship, one sees a uniform image. At first glance, the image seems free of internal contradiction. At most it seems to consist of "different paths for serving the Creator"; but even these different paths spread forth from a place of unity. The unity itself is not subject to doubt. Ultimately, all the paths converge under a single heading: Hasidism. The vast majority of critical scholarship in the field has assumed this essential unity about all decisive points of religious vision within Hasidism; this presumptive unity is disturbed only—perhaps—by subtle variations in atmosphere and tone among the groups.

Perhaps for a study in folklore one could claim a measure of unity for Hasidism, and likewise for certain forms of its religious life. A certain common framework of enthusiastic prayer and dancing, or other customs, does indeed unify all the streams of Hasidism. But this is clearly insufficient to posit a unity of vision: Both at the conceptual level and in terms of religious values one must object to treating Hasidic teachings as if they were a single, uniform entity. Once one seeks to examine Hasidism from a perspective beyond folklore, this idealized unity becomes dubious.

It is precisely in the conceptual, theological realm and in terms of its religious values, that one must highlight fundamental differences within Hasidism. When we pose critical questions about theological visions and of systems of religious ideals, the principal Hasidic streams acquire clear, unambiguous orientations. Behind disagreements among the Hasidic saints—which at first glance seemed to be only personal feuds—an intellectual background emerges. The artificially monochrome, idealized image of unity disappears, ceding its place to a general division into two broad camps. As will become clear, what divides these two camps is greater than what unites them. And if the idealized picture of unity can be refuted precisely on conceptual, religious, and theological questions, then the question of a putative essence of Hasidism—of a supreme concept by virtue of which Hasidism exists—is driven into dialectical retreat; such a question becomes meaningless within a system of ideas. Our brief survey will address typological and characterological problems from a conceptual perspective. It is appropriate to note here that within Hasidic literature itself there are comments—indeed, highly affectionate comments—which distinguish among the different schools, orientations, and streams of Hasidism. These observations are sometimes made with very subtle characterological analyses, and often are right on-target. Within these incidental observations, one discovers a clearly typological vision, running along clear lines of religious understanding and core vision.

Our intention is to investigate the two religious typologies to be found among the streams of Hasidism: that of mystical religiosity, on the one hand, and that of the religiosity of faith, on the other. These typologies do not merely differ from one another; about most critical religious points; they are polar opposites. The application of these two categories from the scientific study of religion— categories that modern theology has used as weapons in its own polemics, thus honing their meaning—may be highly instructive for the understanding of Hasidism in general.

It seems that not only are these two typologies represented in Hasidism by specific examples, but the truth is that all of Hasidism—to the extent that it has any theoretical base at all—is divided into two camps: the mystical camp and the camp of "faith," or *emuna*. This survey is not intended to evaluate the historical development of these typologies within the development of Hasidism. Ceding the historical analysis, we shall employ the typological analysis, illustrating each paradigm by an extreme example. For mystical Hasidism, we will take the teachings of R. Dov Ber, the Great Maggid of Mezritch, and occasionally the teachings of his principal disciple, and the developer of his system, R. Shneur Zalman of Liady, the founder of the Habad school. From the other side, we take R. Nahman to illustrate the Hasidism of faith. Because of the complete crystallization of their thought and because these carried their tendencies to their fullest ripening, these two schools are worthy representatives of the two paradigms. One must note that in R. Dov Ber of Mezritch and Rabbi Nahman ben Simhah (1772–1810) we have chosen two extreme examples; but because of their conceptual profundity, they represent more than themselves alone. One can find traces of mystical Hasidism outside of the Maggid of Mezritch and Habad, in ideas that are very central to the Baal Shem Tov. Thus, as its founder's tradition, mystical Hasidism dominated most areas of the movement, and the Hasidism of faith continually wrestled with it. Nor is Bratslav—which we have chosen as an exemplar of the profound approach to problems of faith—an isolated case. We must mention other examples of this paradigm: R. Abraham of Kalisk, R. Menahem Mendel of Rymanov, R. Menahem Mendel of Kotzk, R. Alexander Zusha HaKohen, R. Zvi Elimelekh of Dinov, and on and on. Our tactic here is not to overflow with source material, but to highlight key tendencies. Restricting this source material to the two representative examples of Mezritch and Bratslav nearly exempts us from the obligatory apology that in historical reality there are no pure paradigms. But we owe another apology: that no typology is ever adequate before the authentic, vivid multiple tints of historical phenomena.

When we investigate the essence of the God-idea of the two paradigms, contrasting the Maggid's vision to that of Bratslav, the difference emerges immediately in all its extreme sharpness. It is the difference between a pantheistic (or nearly pantheistic) theology—an impersonal understanding of God—and a personalist, even voluntarist theology. The scholarly debate over the pantheistic nature of Hasidic thought is well-known. Some seek to soften the pantheism into panentheism. And justly one may ask whether there exists Hasidic teaching on the *actual* presence of God within that which exists, or whether what is claimed here is merely that God's *power* exists within the world. This typological study is not suited to sink into such questions "with the thick end of the beam," or to reach any decisive answers. One cannot resolve such questions except through precise analyses of the various Hasidic systems. Indeed the degree of pantheism and its essential meaning is not the same in all the systems. But one must stress that all such controversies are really about the degree and character of the pantheistic tendency: the existence of such a pantheistic tendency is not subject to debate. Let us leave as a question, then, whether before us in the teachings of the Besht, the Maggid, or in Habad there is a total pantheism or merely panentheism, or even less than this; but the tendency in this direction, common to all these, is not in question. Moreover, in the Habad system pantheism clearly reaches utter acosmism—that is, that the world is utterly enfolded within God. Thus, in the streams of Hasidism, we have all the gradations of the pantheistic tendency before us. These streams constitute different stages in dominance of the strong immanentist tendency.

However, this immanentist theology and the associated questions of pantheism are found only in what we have called the "mystical stream." Not only its pantheistic character, but also its impersonal conception of divinity are clear. Although these two important elements are not necessarily connected in the various forms of mysticism, generally they are combined, and such an integration is characteristic of all rigorously systematic mysticism.

The theology of the mystic R. Dov Ber of Mezritch is not based upon a moment of creation, revelation at Mt. Sinai or a messianic redemption; his experience of God is built upon the hidden divine being that pervades all existence. In other words, the God of R. Dov Ber's religious experience is not the God who creates being from nothingness, who is revealed in a singular historic revelation, who executes a final eschatological redemption. Needless to say, this suggests no heretical rejection of these principles of Judaism. Nonetheless, his mystical-contemplative experience is not of a personal God, but of that divine life force *(hiyut)* that pervades all worlds and all existence. The life force that dwells in them is the Shekhina of Being. This is not the concept of Shekhina, the indwelling presence of God, of the Talmudic-Midrashic tradition, which, for all its immanence, is of the most personalistic, theistic character. In the school of the Maggid, this life force appears with the expansive meaning of dynamic pantheism or panentheism, employing the neo-Platonic teachings of divine emanation. Even if there exist certain moments within this emanation that are not impersonal, the outcome of emanation—that divine life force that arises in the religious experience, and which is the central theological concept in the Maggid's teaching—are utterly impersonal. The impersonal nature of God in the Habad teachings is even clearer. The claim that God and the world are not utterly identical even in the Habad teaching—that is, divinity is not completely garbed within the world, and does not entirely enter immanently into the world—is insufficient to refute this school's general premise that the divinity lacks all personal character.

The mystical theology of the Maggid of Mezritch and of Habad, then, can be articulated in terms of immanence, pantheism, panentheism, and of an impersonal divinity that enters the world through emanation. In contrast, Bratslav theology is articulated through an opposite set of terms: an antirational theism, a divine transcendence, which empties the world of divine presence. Here is a God of will, who directs the world paradoxically, in accord with His absolute will. If R. Dov Ber's mystical experience is founded on God as being, then the foundational experience of Bratslav is of God as will. As a result, there is no mystical blurring of God's personal face, as in the pantheist conception. On the contrary: in the Bratslav school you find the correspondence between God's absolute willful and personal natures.

Indeed, God's entire relation to the world completely changes when He is understood—not as dwelling within the things of this world—but as standing above the world, a sovereign creator who rules without bounds. Here He is limitlessly mighty, the one who decrees life for all the living; the one whose decrees and deeds can never be comprehended, and that elicit only the astonishment and perplexed questions of mortals. It is typical that the motto of Habad was "for the word is very near to you" (Deut. 30:14): in the mystical conception, the boundaries between above and below are blurred. But in the Bratslav school there is no such mystical blurring, and the borders are stark: God is God, the world is the world, and the two realms do not overlap.

These, then, are the different theological conceptions entailed in pantheism, on the one hand, and paradoxical theism on the other. But there is second distinction, no less important, which is entailed by this contrast. By its very nature, pantheistic mysticism is monistic. If all existence is saturated with God, then divine being must penetrate into every corner. And thus the realm of metaphysical evil, of impurity, of the *kelipot,* can have no place in pantheistic mysticism. Therefore it is no accident of historical development, but rather an integral, organic feature of the mystical system, that the powerful monistic tendencies in the teachings of the Maggid—and even more so in Habad teachings—obliterate the dualistic elements in the religious worldview. Such a sharp departure from the Lurianic approach was actualized due to the fact that although Hasidim formally retained the dualistic framework of Lurianic Kabbalah, this system was reinterpreted to exclude some of its most essential features. The concept of *tzimtzum,* the divine self-contraction that preceded creation, is an excellent illustration. The concept that had distinguished this Kabbala from pantheism and transformed it into dualism, now would—with an inversion of its meaning—serve the Maggid's pantheistic/panentheistic tendencies. While the classical Kabbala recognized an independent realm of evil, the Hasidic mystics revolutionized the kabbalistic worldview by nullifying the realm of the *kelipa,* or "shell." Good and evil, sanctity and impurity are no longer polar opposites. With the transformation of the dualistic worldview to one of emanation and divine immanence, they have become only questions of degree. Evil is merely the lowest level of the Good. Sin may become the throne upon which the Good will sit. Thus the monist pantheism precludes any possible dualistic conception.

The situation is otherwise with Bratslav. The dualistic foundations of Kabbala in general, and of Lurianic Kabbala in particular retain all their vitality. And Bratslav teachings acquire a distinctive cast by even adding new dualistic directions. The forces of Evil stake out their own demonic realm. Moreover, alongside abstract demonic forces, Bratslav has the very strong sense of the personal, concrete reality of the forces of Evil. They are not abstractions, but are highly personal figures. One cannot speak of anonymous evil forces, as in Lurianic Kabbala, for these are instruments in the hand of the personality that controls them: the Devil.

Another point in this contrast of the two Hasidic systems emerges by examining the relationship of the human being to God. One may ask both regarding the content on which this relationship operates and regarding its essential character. With respect to the content of the human-divine relationship, the question is, What is the supreme religious value that should determine one's religious conduct? The Hasidic mystics point to contemplation (the Besht) or ecstasy (the Maggid or Habad); Bratslav set faith atop its hierarchy of values. These two categories of religious life—the mystical path of contemplation, ecstasy, and union *(devekut)* on the one hand, and the path of a life of faith on the other—are the two alternative, even contrary poles of religious life in general. These rigorous typologies are not merely complementary, but pose at once both theoretical and experiential contradictions that cannot be dismissed. Only in the ordinary religious life can these two paths intertwine, as if they were complementary. But in cases of a developed religious consciousness there is a stark division between the typologies, and proponents of each path clearly define and distinguish themselves from the alternative.

The path of ecstasy and contemplation posit a unique nearness between human beings and God. It has been stressed that this nearness is extremely evident in the teachings of the Maggid, and even more so in Habad. The act of contemplative union and the ecstasy that attends it constitute an unmediated experience of God. No abyss interposes between divinity and humanity. On the contrary, a bridge of unmediated relation connects them.

But the path of faith is characterized by its circuitousness. The gaping abyss between the believer and the object of his faith is expressed in Bratslav by the paradoxical nature of its faith. The abyss between the human and divine realms is revealed not only by God's ontological transcendence (that He is not "in" the world) but also by His logical transcendence (that He is not rationally comprehensible). This school balances its supreme religious value on a knife's edge. It demands that faith become a paradoxical faith; the believer must be confirmed not by acts of intellectual comprehension, but by a perpetual intellectual crisis and struggle before the one who possesses paradox—the paradoxical God or the paradoxical saint. Thus it is unsurprising that in the Habad teachings—which are a highly consistent development of the Maggid's path—the most prominent elements are subtle tests to authenticate "divine ecstasy." This is most characteristic of mysticism's deep inquiry into itself and its unique problematics; the same weighty problem occupies the medieval Christian mystics. It is no accident, but an integral feature of the system that in place of the authentication of the mystical experience, in Bratslav the problem is authenticating faith, in the face of the subversion and infinite despair that comes when a believer examines his faith and finds that it is baseless, founded upon the void. Here we see a parallel development of questions of verification, flowing in each case from the school's unique problematics.

Beyond questions of the content of the human relationship with God, there is also a fundamental theoretical distinction between the path of contemplative-ecstatic union and the path of faith. In the spiritual exercises of the Maggid, all personal relations are absent; there is no leap of one individual toward another. We have seen that divinity appears in the mystical traditions in impersonal forms; the indwelling divine life force, the ontic-dynamic foundation within things are impersonal categories. Moreover, even the meditative contemplative does not retain his individual identity, for this school's complex meditative techniques all strive for an ecstasy they define as annihilating existence *(bittul ha-yesh)*, that is, annihilating the contemplative's individual identity by annihilating his consciousness. In contrast, faith, as it developed in Bratslav, constitutes the relation of one individual to another. The maintenance of the individual identity—both of the human being and of God—was insisted upon in Bratslav with great rigor. Besides faith in God, in Bratslav there was also a radical development of the concept of "faith in the sages," that is, faith in the Hasidic saint *(zaddik)*, which by definition must be an individual relationship. This faith in the sages reached its apex with the paradoxical faith in "the true saint," that is, in R. Nahman himself. The personal nature of this relationship is evident, and needs no demonstration. Thus, we see that all religious life in Bratslav is built upon the tension-filled relationship between the "I" and the "you." The very absence of this I-You relationship—indeed its rejection—is an essential corollary of the mystical stream.

This distinction between the two streams is further verified when we examine their concepts of prayer, for in prayer one finds the most concentrated essence of religious vision. Again it is no accident that we find in the school of the Maggid, including Habad, that prayer serves primarily as the proper time for contemplation and ecstasy, a sort of special triumph for essence of the contemplative-ecstatic life. In contrast, we discover that the Bratslav prayer-life is crystallized in the new concept of "a conversation between a person and his creator." Prayer as a kind of dialogue between two individuals and not as an ecstatic opportunity for nullifying existence—this is the starkest expression of the unique character of prayer within the Hasidism of faith. It is as if the power of this dialogic prayer-life opened up all the wellsprings of prayer in Bratslav, as the *Sefer Likkutei Tefilot* (the book of R. Nahman's original prayers) attests.

The differences between these two schools are even more profound with respect to the *content* of prayer; thus they reveal a new perspective of the gap between a personal and an impersonal vision of God. Again, these differences revolve around the question of the maintenance of individual consciousness during prayer, in particular with respect to petitionary prayer. According to the mystical teachings of the Maggid, whose source lies in the Baal Shem Tov, it is forbidden to pray for one's physical needs. Thus, the annihilation of the worshiper's individual consciousness occurs not only through the contemplative nature of prayer, which is itself an ecstatic annihilation of all existence; the nullification of the worshiper's individual consciousness is expressed also by abstracting prayer from all the worshiper's physical needs. This demand that the worshiper transcend himself, leave behind his ego and his personal needs, is characteristically mystical. Prayer as a supplication from one caught in crisis in not the mystically ideal prayer. We see, therefore, that the mystical strain of Hasidism teaches the annihilation of individual consciousness in two ways: by extinguishing the worshipper's individual consciousness, and by extinguishing the individual character of his petition. If one must pray only for the sake of "the Shekhina's needs," and if prayer itself is essentially divine, then one faces a closed circuit—not an arch—in which there is no relationship between the speaker of the prayer and one who hears it.

In contrast, the prayer life one finds in Bratslav is always a matter of pleading for mercy, for God to break through the laws of nature, for willful divine intervention in the affairs of the world, for both hidden and manifest miracles.

Thus, prayer always flows from a context of true crisis and agony, and one must not sublimate this personal aspect. Any personal content is permitted, even fitting, in prayer. In the "conversation between a person and his Creator," one's personal requests are not comprehended in a transcendent divine pattern. On the contrary, Bratslav prayer always remains a conversation between two individuals, and the content of this dialogue is the expression of the worshiper's personal crisis, as he comes to beg for mercy upon his soul.

The antagonism of these two diametrically opposite visions is further evident in questions of anthropology—that is, the essence of humanity and its power. One school offers an optimistic evaluation of people and their possibility to discover holiness; the other, a pessimistic reading of people and their metaphysical status. Awareness of peoples' metaphysical alienation from holiness is the obverse of the exaggerated transcendental theology of Bratslav, which stresses God's great distance from the world. The theological and anthropological components are like two sides of one coin. For Bratslav, the human condition is essential alienation from holiness. It is the original sin. There is, then, no greater difference in religious outlook than that between the optimistic atmosphere of the Great Maggid and the Habad teachings—with their vision of the "divine soul" of humanity, and its great potentiality for ecstatic moments of becoming the dwelling place of God—and the pessimistic atmosphere of Bratslav teachings on the fallen state of people. The best thing the Bratslav anthropology can say about humanity is that each soul has some "good points."

The problem of anthropology provides a bridge to the question of the essence of sin. Within its general idealistic framework, the mystical-contemplative stream blurs the definition of sin. As in all mysticism, this strain of Hasidism robs sin of its profound dimensions, by stressing that there is divine life force and sparks of holiness even in sin. It is instructive to compare this mitigation of sin found among the Hasidic mystics, to the rigorous approach of Bratslav. For in Bratslav we find a developed and utterly serious teaching on the essence of sin. Moreover, even a brief examination of the Bratslav concept will demonstrate that sin is not comprehended merely as a practical deed; rather, the content of any sin is always bound up with the essence of sin. Sin is not merely in a person's deeds, but in his very existence as a human being.

The divisions between the schools also can be seen clearly also with respect to their attitudes to the key Hasidic phenomenon: the institution of the "charismatic saint," or zaddik. The teachings of the Maggid and of Habad do not stress the special status of the zaddik and his unique mission as an exceptional person; in contract, in Bratslav we find an extreme theory of the saint and his mission on earth. A close examination of this theory comes to the conclusion that there can be only one zaddik, the most exceptional of all, a human being *sui generis,* the hidden leader of all. This zaddik is the paradoxical messiah; into his hands is given total power, by virtue of his role as the radical counterpart to the paradoxical God. Note that faith in this unique saint is an indirect act between a human being and God, in contrast to the unmediated ecstatic experience of the mystic in the Maggid/Habad school.

The final point in our typological contrast concerns their attitudes to eschatology. Again, the differences are unambigious. The mystical contemplative teaching of the Maggid and Habad nullify the eschatological anxiety surrounding the Messiah and his redemption. And so it must be, for the contemplative-ecstatic experience—which is the key feature of this mode of religiosity—is unrelated to history. Just as the mystical experience fundamentally is not founded on the moment in history known as the "revelation at Mt. Sinai," so too it is fundamentally not related to the moment in history known as "messianic redemption." The well-known mystical indifference to history is completely verified when we examine the Hasidic mystics' teachings on the end-time: the total lack of messianic tension is characteristic of its contemplative religiosity.

In contrast, the eschatological drive in Bratslav is unmistakable. This point is crystallized in two fundamental categories of the Bratslav religious vision: in the eschatological moment, the faith of despair meets the despairing hope for the future. Both of these are oriented toward a messianic redemption, about which— even now, after despair—it is forbidden to despair. Here, too, the two schools consistently fit the typologies. From the Maggid and Habad there is extremely scant teaching on the revolutionary nature of the redemption, and it is difficult to say what turning point their mystical teaching assigns to the messianic era. In contrast, the Bratslav teachings see redemption as a key turning point, which will fulfill the secret hopes of the paradoxical believer. Today, in historical time, the world of faith is a world full of contradictions; religion depends only on paradoxical faith, despite all the contrary evidence. But in the future, this will be a world of clarity, where faith is evident. There could be no greater hope for those believers whose lot in life is paradox.

Thus we may conclude that there is no conceptual unity in Hasidism about the most fundamental religious questions. Indeed, we have seen two contradictory trends, as crystallized in these two profound theoretical systems: a mystical and contemplative orientation, which weaves idealistic inclinations into a unified, coherent pattern of thought; and a religiosity of faith, in which powerful existential elements are at work, giving it a unique character.

# ABOUT THE CONTRIBUTORS

Nathaniel Deutsch is Associate Professor of Religion at Swarthmore College and author of *The Gnostic Imagination: Gnosticism, Mandaeism, and Merkaba Mysticism* (Brill, 1995) and *Guardians of the Gate: Angelic Vice Regency in Late Antiquity* (Brill, 1999)

Aubrey L. Glazer holds a master's degree in Jewish Philosophy as well as ordination from the Jewish Theological Seminary of America. He is a doctoral student at the Center for the Study of Religion at the University of Toronto.

Jeremy Kalmanofsky is Assistant Dean of the Rabbinical School at the Jewish Theological Seminary of America, where he was ordained and is a doctoral student of Jewish Philosophy.

Martin Kavka is Assistant Professor of Religion at Florida State University and specializes in Modern Jewish Thought and Postmodern Critical Theory.

Shaul Magid is Elaine Ravitch Assistant Professor of Jewish Studies and Chair of the Department of Jewish Philosophy at the Jewish Theological Seminary of America. He has published on sixteenth-century Kabbala, Hasidism and Modern Jewish Thought. His book *Hasidism on the Margin: Reconciliation, Antinomianism, and Messianism in Izbica/Radzin Hasidism* is forthcoming with The University of Wisconsin Press.

Alyssa Quint is a doctoral student in Yiddish literature and culture at Harvard University. She is writing her dissertation entitled "Avraham Goldfadn and the Origins of the Yiddish Theatre."

David G. Roskies is Professor of Jewish Literature at the Jewish Theological Seminary of America. His works include *Against the Apocalypse* (Harvard University Press, 1984); *A Bridge of Longing* (Harvard University Press, 1995), and *The Jewish Search for a Usable Past* (University of Indiana Press, 1999).

Yakov Travis is Assistant Professor of Jewish Studies at Cleveland College of Jewish Studies. His areas of research include early thirteenth century Kabbala and Hasidism.

Elliot R. Wolfson is the Abraham Lieberman Professor of Hebrew and Judaic Studies and Director of the Program in Religious Studies at New York University. He is the author of many publications in the history of Jewish mysticism, including *Through the Speculum that Shines: Vision and Imagination in Medieval Jewish Mysticism* (Princeton University Press, 1994), which won the American Academy of Religion's Award for Excellence in the Study of Religion in the Category of Historical Studies, 1995 and the National Jewish Book Award for Excellence in Scholarship, 1995. His most recent book is *Abraham Abulafia—Kabbalist and Prophet: Hermeneutics, Theosophy, and Theurgy* (Cherub Press, 2000). He is currently working on two monographs, *Language, Eros, and the Construction of Gender: Kabbalistic Hermeneutics and the Poetic Imagination* and *Footless on the Path: Law, Ethics, and Asceticism in Kabbalistic Piety.*

# INDEX